Effective GUI Test Automation:

Developing an Automated GUI Testing Tool

Kanglin Li and Mengqi Wu

SYBEX

San Francisco · London

Associate Publisher: Joel Fugazzotto
Acquisitions and Developmental Editor: Tom Cirtin
Production Editor: Erica Yee
Technical Editor: Acey J. Bunch
Copyeditor: Judy Flynn
Compositor: Laurie Stewart, Happenstance Type-O-Rama
Graphic Illustrator: Jeff Wilson, Happenstance Type-O-Rama
Proofreaders: Laurie O'Connell, Amy Rassmussen, Nancy Riddiough
Indexer: Ted Laux
Cover Designer: Ingalls + Associates
Cover Illustrator/Photographer: Rob Atkins, Image Bank

Library of Congress Card Number: 2004108202

ISBN: 0-7821-4351-2

Manufactured in the United States of America

10 9 8 7 6 5 4 3 2 1

To Li Xuanhua and Tang Xunwei

And

In memory of Luo Youai, Luo Xulin,
and Li Congyang

Acknowledgments

To the folks at Sybex, especially Tom Cirtin who made this book available, Acey J. Bunch for his technical expertise, and Erica Yee and Judy Flynn for their contributions to this book. I want to thank Rodnay Zaks, the president of Sybex, who signed the contract. I also extend my thanks to the other people in the Sybex team.

I still need to thank other people, especially the readers who have provided me with their comments and suggestions about my previous works. During the process of writing this book, the test monkey in Chapter 3 frequently reminded me of my early days as a schoolboy. My friends and I spent most of my childhood summer nights listening to the stories of the monkey king told by the old folks in our village. What I learned from both the old folks and my friends makes it possible for me to write this book today.

When I was a small boy, my uncle OuYang Minghong carried me in a bamboo basket to visit my grandma. My uncles Zuomei and Zuodian carried me on their backs or in a wheelbarrow to watch movies and catch fish. Since I was five, my aunt Youai led me to the school and taught me to count with my fingers.

I didn't learn how to swim and fell into a pool when I was eight or nine. Meiqing risked his life and saved me from the water with the help of my uncle Zuohuang, Guicheng, and another whose name I don't know. Meiqing has always been my big brother. Then I learned how to swim at 20 and swam across the Xiangjiang River on a summer day and the Leishui River on a cold fall afternoon. Thank you all for teaching me about water, including Zeng Xilong, Li Wenbing, Kuang Chuanglun, Bai Maoye, Chen Xiaohu, Zeng Yigui, He Hechu, Wen Xiaoping, Long Yongcheng, and Xie Hengbing.

Tang Duzhang, Li Zuojin, Li Zuojun, Luo Xixing, Chen Xinhua, and Kuang Chuangren and I spent our best years in the middle school. At that time we learned food was valuable. Together, we discovered that boys were shy and girls were caring. Thanks to all of the former classmates who form the memory of my childhood.

—Kanglin Li
Leiyang, China
2004

Contents at a Glance

Contents

Introduction

There are many books about software testing management. When they discuss software tes[t] automation, they introduce third-party testing tools. I have used many of the commercia[l] software testing tools. Their developers declare that they have the capability to conduct variou[s] types of software tests and meet the requirements of an organization. But they have limitation[s]. For example, many of GUI testing tools require users to record a series of mouse clicks and keystrokes. Others require users to write test scripts in a specified script language. Furthermore, the test scripts produced by these tools and methods need to be edited and debugged before they can be executed to perform the desired tests.

This book presents ideas for automating graphical user interface (GUI) testing. The sampl[e] code in this book forms a foundation for a fully automated GUI testing tool. Using this too[l], users don't need to record, edit, and debug test scripts. Testers can spend their time creatin[g] testing cases and executing the testing.

Who This Book Is For

Software engineers have long relied on the tools and infrastructures supplied by the curren[t] software testing tool vendors. Some engineers tell successful stories. But more engineers experience frustration. The tools are not automated enough, the tests are not efficient, th[e] tests are not driven by data, and the test script generation and data composition methods need to be improved. One solution to software test automation is to develop testing tools instead of purchasing commercial tools based on the current inadequate infrastructure[.]

This book is written for people who are involved in software engineering and want to auto[-] mate the software testing process for their organizations. With the methods introduced in thi[s] book, software engineers should gain a good understanding of the limited automation provide[d] by the available testing tools and how to improve the current test infrastructure and conduc[t] a fully automated software test.

This book is for software engineers who want more effective ways to perform software tests[.] The automated testing tool introduced in this book can serve as an independent software tes[t] tool as well as an adjunct to the commercial tools.

To get the most out of this book, you should be a moderately experienced software deve[l]oper and a test engineer in the process of conducting software tests for your organization[.] The explanations and examples in this book can be easily understood and followed by an[y] intermediate- to advanced-level programmer interested in expanding their knowledge in both software development and software testing.

This book's content includes programming techniques with examples in C#. Then it gradually progresses to the development of a fully automated GUI testing tool. Although the sample code is in C# using the Microsoft Windows platform, the tool has been evolved from a Visual Basic 6 project. I have also used these methods and developed a Java testing tool for a test project.

This book is also for the managers of organizations where software is developed and used. As economists have reported, software failures result in substantial economic loss to the United States each year. Approximately half of the losses occur within the software manufacturing industry. If you are a senior managerial administrator of a software organization, you are most likely interested in an improved software testing method. The other half of the losses is out of the pockets of the software end users. If your business or institution consists of software end users, you probably maintain teams to support the software purchased from the contract vendors. Being aware of testing methods will assist you with efficient software application in your organization.

How This Book Is Organized

To present ideas well, the first two chapters in this book are an introduction to software testing, the available testing tools, and the expectations of software testers. Chapters 3 through 6 focus on Win32 API programming and .NET fundamentals needed for the development of the GUI test library. Chapters 7 through 14 are devoted to designing and implementing the Automated-GUITest tool until full automation is achieved. The following list includes a short description of each chapter.

Chapter 1, "GUI Testing: An Overview," describes the management of software GUI testing and the techniques built into .NET that can make it possible to test software dynamically.

Chapter 2, "Available GUI Testing Tools vs. the Proposed Tool," presents a brief review of some of the automated GUI testing tools on the market and the main points of the testing methods proposed in this book. The available tools have been proved by studies to be inadequate. The purpose of this chapter is to demonstrate the necessity of an new and improved test method, of adding more testing capabilities to a testing tool, and of creating a fully automated test for new and complex software projects.

Chapter 3, "C# Win32 API Programming and Test Monkeys," deals with how to marshal the Win32 API functions to be used as C# code for developing the tool. It also includes the code for you to develop a C# API Text Viewer to take the place of the old API Text Viewer for Visual Basic 6 programmers. The newly developed C# API Text Viewer will be used in three ways. First, it will generate C# code to marshal the Win32 functions needed for developing a fully automated GUI testing tool. Second, it will serve as an application under test for the GUI testing tool as the testing tool is developed throughout the book. Third, the C# API Text Viewer will test the tool with different degrees of automation as the book progresses. In the end of this chapter, the C# API Text Viewer is used to present you with a test monkey.

Chapter 4, "Developing a GUI Test Library," guides you through the development of a GUI test library with functions for finding GUI objects from an interface and manipulating the mouse actions.

Chapter 5, ".NET Programming and GUI Testing," introduces .NET technologies—including reflection, late binding, serialization, and XML programming—with regard to data store, data presentation, and GUI testing.

Chapter 6, "Testing a Windows Form in General," describes how a GUI test script is created manually. This handcrafted test script forms the base on which a fully automated GUI test will be built.

Chapter 7, "Architecture and Implementation of the Automatic GUI Test Tool," lays out the architecture for a automated GUI testing tool and helps you build the first evolution of the proposed AutomatedGUITest tool.

Chapter 8, "Methods of GUI Test Verification," explains how to effectively verify the test results and add code to the AutomatedGUITest project for automatic verification.

Chapter 9, "Testing Label and Cosmetic GUI Controls," describes the processes of testing Label and other cosmetic GUI controls.

Chapter 10, "Testing a TextBox Control with Input from a Keyboard," discusses the SendKeys class of .NET Framework and updates the AutomatedGUITest for testing TextBox controls.

Chapter 11, "Testing RadioButton and CheckBox Controls," shows you how the RadioButton and CheckBox controls are used in software applications and discusses ways to test them.

Chapter 12, "Menu Clicking for GUI Test Automation," introduces more Win32 API functions for discovering menu items and testing them.

Chapter 13, "User-Defined and COM-Based Controls," introduces methods for developing custom GUI controls in the Microsoft Visual Studio .NET IDE and Microsoft Visual Studio 6 IDE and updates the AutomatedGUITest tool for testing such controls.

Chapter 14, "Testing Issues for Non .NET Applications," presents the methods for testing an unmanaged application. This chapter tests Notepad.exe as an example after new code is added to the tool project.

About the Examples

The examples start with the programming precepts of C# and Win32 API functions. The goal is to use the predefined methods of a programming language to complete an AutomatedGUI-Test tool project and avoid reinventing the wheel. There are four kinds of sample code in the chapters:

- Sample code for developing a C# API Text Viewer

- Simple examples to demonstrate using C# and Win32 API functions

- Example projects to be tested by the AutomatedGUITest tool

- Sample code of the AutomatedGUITest tool project

The code examples in the first category most often appear in Chapters 3 through Chapter 6. Thereafter, Chapters 7 through 14 are totally dedicated to automating the test project. The sample code in these chapters is in the third category. There are only three examples of the second category, simulating real assemblies under test. They are implemented in Chapters 3 and 12 and submitted to testing throughout the book.

Besides the C# API Text Viewer, the code in Chapter 3 also develops a test monkey. Chapter 5 develops an XML document viewer that will be used to present the test results for the Automated-GUITest tool.

In Chapter 4 and thereafter, some code is added to the GUI test library and AutomatedGUI-Test project in each chapter. At the end of each chapter, the sample code can be compiled to produce an executable assembly. The testing tool achieves different degrees of automation until a fully automated test tool is developed by the end of the book.

Where to Find the Source Code

The sample and project code for each chapter can be downloaded from www.sybex.com by performing a search using this book's title, the author's name, or the ISBN (4351). This saves you from having to type in the code. It also includes a complete compiled version of the project, which allows you to put the AutomatedGUITest into immediate practice for your software project.

To execute the AutomatedGUITest.exe file, you can copy the files from the Chapter14\ AutomatedGUITest\bin\Debug folder of the downloaded sample code to a computer system. The minimum requirements for a computer system are as follows:

- Windows 95/98/2000/NT/XP

- Preinstalled .NET Framework

- 20MB of free hard disk space

If you are still using earlier versions of the Microsoft Visual Studio .NET integrated development environment (IDE) at this point (older than Microsoft Visual Studio .NET 2003 IDE), you will not able to open the sample projects directly. The problem is that the C# project files with the extension `.csproj` are incompatible with earlier versions of the Microsoft Visual Studio .NET IDE. To use the code, you can follow the procedures in each chapter to create new projects and include the code files with extensions of `.cs` downloaded into your projects.

Although the sample code in this book is developed under the Microsoft Visual Studio .NET 2003 IDE, there are other open-source .NET IDEs available through free download:

Eclipsing .NET   IBM released the Eclipse .NET to the open-source community. This product works on Windows 95/98/NT/2000/XP. You can download the components for the Eclipse .NET from `www.eclipse.org`. After downloading the `eclipse-SDK-2.1.1-win32` `.zip` file, install it with the combination of the Microsoft .NET SDK, which is also a free download from `msdn.microsoft.com/netframework/technologyinfo/howtoget/default.aspx`. Then get the open-source C# plug-in through the Eclipse .NET IDE. An article at `www.sys-con` `.com/webservices/articleprint.cfm?id=360` introduces the downloading and installation in detail.

#develop   Short for SharpDevelop, this is another open-source IDE for C# and VB.NET on Microsoft's .NET platform. You can download #develop from `www.icsharpcode.net/` `OpenSource/SD/Default.aspx`.

DotGNU Portable .NET   This open-source tool includes a C# compiler, an assembler, and a runtime engineer. The initial platform was GNU/Linux. It also works on Windows, Solaris, NetBSD, FreeBSD, and MacOS X. You can download this product from `www.southern-storm.com.au/portable_net.html`.

Chapter 1

GUI Testing: An Overview

The saturation of software in industry, educational institutions, and other enterprises and organizations is a fact of modern life almost too obvious to mention. Nearly all of the businesses in the United States and in most parts of the world depend upon the software industry for product development, production, marketing, support, and services. Reducing the cost of software development and improving software quality are important for the software industry. Organizations are looking for better ways to conduct software testing before they release their products.

Innovations in the field of software testing have improved the techniques of writing test scripts, generating test cases, and introducing test automation for unit testing, white box testing, black box testing, and other types of testing. Software testing has evolved over the years to incorporate tools for test automation. Mercury Interactive, Rational Software of IBM, and Segue are a few of the main tool vendors. The purpose of these tools is to speed up the software development life cycle, to find as many bugs as possible before releasing the products, to reduce the cost of software development by automating effective regression testing, and to increase application reliability. The apparent goal of the software testing tools is to generate test scripts that simulate users operating the application under development. Usually test engineers are trained by the tool manufacturers to write test scripts by hand or to use a capture/playback procedure to record test scripts. Both writing and recording test scripts is labor intensive and error prone. The potential of the available tools to reduce the manual, repetitive, labor-intensive effort required to test software is severely limited.

Recently, organizations have purchased the commercial testing tools but the test engineers can't use them because of their inadequate test infrastructure. Often these tools don't have the capabilities to handle the complexity of advanced software projects, aren't capable of keeping up with technology advancements, and aren't diverse enough to recognize the varieties of third-party components in today's software development business. Needless to say, profitable organizations have trade secrets the commercial testing tools are not aware of. Because of these inadequacies, the United States loses $59.5 billion each year due to the bugs in the software not detected by the current testing means (Tassey 2003). Test engineers and experts are working to develop more effective testing tools for their organizations. Thus, they can improve the current test infrastructure with regard to the following:

- Enhanced integration and interoperability testing
- Increased efficiency of testing case generation
- Improved test code generation with full automation
- A rigorous method for determining when a product is good enough to release
- Available performance metrics and testing measuring procedures

It is estimated that an improved testing infrastructure should try to reduce the current software bugs by one-third, which can save the United States $22.2 billion. Each year, in order to achieve such a software testing infrastructure, researchers have published their findings. For example, in my previous book, *Effective Software Test Automation: Developing an Automated Software Testing Tool* (Sybex 2004), I discussed the methods to develop a testing tool that can be adapted to various software programming languages and platforms. The outcome of the book was a fully automated testing tool. It automated the entire process of software testing—from data generation and test script generation to bug presentation—and broke a number of bottlenecks of the current testing tools in the following ways:

- *By actively looking for components to test instead of recording test scenarios by capture/playback.* This approach can enable the test script to conduct a thorough testing of an application. It is reported that testing cases are more effective in finding bugs after the test script is developed. Thus, testers don't spend time writing test scripts; instead, they spend their time studying and creating multiple testing cases.

- *By effectively generating one script to test all the members (constructors, properties, and methods) of a DLL or an EXE, including members inherited from base classes.* This test script prepares a real and complete object that can be reused for integration testing and regression testing. Therefore, the number of test scripts for one software project can be reduced, making the management of test scripts easy.

- *By effectively reusing the previously built test scripts of lower-level modules for testing higher-level modules with a bottom-up approach.* This helps you avoid stubbing and using mock objects to conduct integration testing.

- *By automatically writing test scripts in a language used by the developers.* The testers don't have to learn a new script language. The developers can understand the test scripts. This enhances the collaboration between testers and developers.

- *By innovatively integrating automated script generation with a Unified Modeling Language (UML).* The project can generate test scripts early when a detailed design is available. The test script can be executed for regression testing and reused for integration testing throughout the development life cycle. Because the test can be conducted nightly in an unattended mode, it guarantees that all the newly developed code will be tested at least once at any stage.

- *By automatically compiling and executing the generated test scripts without editing or debugging.* If the design of the software architecture is modified in middle of the development process, a new test script can be automatically generated immediately with accuracy.

However, due to the uniqueness of the graphical user interface (GUI) components in software products, techniques and programming methods for developing an effective automated GUI testing tool required a separate book. We will use the same philosophy used for automating the non-GUI testing in the preceding book and develop a fully automated GUI testing tool; that is, the users feed the GUI testing tool with an application and get the defect (bug) reports.

Unique Features of GUI Testing

Early software applications were command-line driven. Users remembered and typed in a command and the system performed some actions. A more effective application could display possible commands on the screen and then prompt the user for the next command. Nowadays, the software industry is in the windowing system era. Virtually all applications are operated through graphical user interfaces (GUIs). GUI components are often referred to as windows, icons, menus, and pointers. Users drag a mouse, click buttons, and apply various combinations of keystrokes. The applications are triggered to perform desired actions by the mouse events and keystroke events. Thus, GUIs have made the software friendlier to users.

Software verification and validation through testing is a major building block of the quality assurance process. GUI tests are vital because they are performed from the view of the end users of the application. Because the functionality of the application is invoked through the graphical user interface, GUI tests can cover the entire application,

To automatically test software before the GUI era, testers relied on test scripts with a collection of line commands. The executions of the programs were independent from the screen status. Testing GUI components is different and more difficult because it requires a script to reassign the input stream, to click buttons, to move the pointer, and to press keys. Then the scripts need to have mechanisms to record the responses and changes of the dynamic states of the software. Comparing the responses and changes with the expected baselines, the scripts are able to reports bugs.

There are some specialist tools available to test GUI-based applications. They often come with a variety of features. Testers expect that these features will enable them to conduct GUI testing with regard to platform differentiation, recognition of GUI components, test script automation, synchronization, result verification, and easy management. The currently available tools are very much influenced by platforms. For example, the 32-bit Microsoft Windows operating system (Win32) is currently the dominant platform for development. Testing tools developed for Win32 can not be used with other platforms, such as the Unix, Linux, and Macintosh operating systems.

The broadly accepted method today of generating GUI test scripts relies on the capture/playback technique. With this technique, testers are required to perform labor-intensive interaction with the GUI via mouse events and keystrokes. The script records these events and later plays them back in the form of an automated test. Test scripts produced by this method are often hard-coded. When different inputs are needed to conduct the test, the test script needs to be re-created. Regression testing using these test scripts is also impractical when the GUI components are under development. It is often hard to generate all the possible test cases for all of the GUI components and conduct a thorough test. Human interaction with the GUI often results in mistakes. Thus, the capture/playback procedure records the redundant and wrong clicks and keystrokes.

Based on the current testing technologies, GUI test automation invariably requires manual script writing, editing, and debugging. On one hand, tool vendors keep on informing testers of the powerful functions their tools are capable of. On the other hand, testers must face a great number of technical challenges getting a tool to work with the application under test (AUT). It is well known that GUI components are modified and redefined throughout the development process. The generated test scripts are unable to keep up with design changes.

Compared with non-GUI software testing, a GUI test infrastructure based on the current testing tools is also expensive with regard to purchasing the tools and the efforts that must be made to maintain the tests. Very often, only a part of the GUI components are tested automatically. The other part still requires manual tests. In the following sections, I'll address the inadequacy of GUI testing by discussing an approach for improving the current test infrastructure.

Developing an Automated GUI Testing Tool

The raw GUI test scripts recorded by the capture/playback technique perform the apparent mouse and key actions if they don't fail to execute. But even when the execution succeeds, the captured results don't verify whether the invocation of the business functions (often, non-GUI modules) caused by the GUI events is correct. Complicated graphic output must be tested. The GUI test scripts don't test the input variation to the GUI components. Without manual editing and debugging, these test scripts are not able to test whether the GUI components are created and drawn as desired.

The purpose of this book is to show how to use more effective programming methods to develop a GUI testing tool. This tool will help you avoid the drawbacks and pitfalls of the current testing methods. The generated test script should be able to capture the event actions and changes performed on the GUI component being tested and the invocation of the related non-GUI components caused by the GUI events. It will also verify the position and the appearance of the GUI components and test the input to the GUI components. The result of the event actions and invocations will be converted from GUI to readable text formats. Then the test result reports will be used by the developers to fix the detected bugs.

To achieve an improved test infrastructure, this book will discuss ways to develop GUI testing tools that can generate flawless test scripts. These scripts will have functions to test various aspects of the GUI components. They will not become obsolete due to changes of the GUI components. If more GUI controls are added or reduced, a new test can be regenerated by feeding the modified application to the tool.

In this book, I'll also discuss methods for developing testing tools that require minimum training. The current testing tools have complicated user interfaces and users must be trained to use them. Almost every GUI testing tool has a script language for writing test scripts. Developers are often isolated from software testing automation by the language differences. In this book you'll learn how to develop a tool to write test scripts in the same language that is used by the developers in an organization. Thus, the testing tool, the application under test, and the automatically generated test scripts are all developed in one language. The test projects become more readable and maintainable and bring testers and developers together.

I'll also discuss methods for generating testing cases so the combination of the testing cases and scripts will be more effective in finding bugs. None of the tools on the market that rely on the capture/playback or reverse-engineering technique is able to locate a GUI component and write a relevant test script for it automatically. Thus, we need a method to conduct an automatic and exhaustive survey of the GUI components and write test scripts and test data with respect to different testing issues of the components.

Finally, using these methods to develop a testing tool will save time and money, deliver accurate products, and make the job interesting for the organization.

Expectation of Automated Testing

Automated tests help to greatly reduce the time and the cost spent on software testing throughout the entire development life cycle. Furthermore, automation ensures that tests are performed regularly and consistently, resulting in early error detection that leads to enhanced quality and shorter time to market.

Current testing techniques are not able to automate the GUI testing process before an executable test script is created. The tester is often required to use a capture/playback method to record scripts. The recording process is in fact a labor-intensive interaction between the tester and the GUI. If there is a bug the process fails to record and one bug is detected during testing, the tester must repeat and continue the script recording process until the bug is fixed. Thus, bugs are detected one by one throughout manual script recording. When the recorded script is ready to be executed, the possibility of finding bugs by replaying it is limited.

Testers expect the testing tools to actively find GUI components, generate the respective testing data, and use the generated data to drive the test script generation and execution. There is not a tool that is capable of conducting an active survey for the existing GUI components of an application. Although vendors often claim their tool is capable of data-driven script generation, testers often need to start a wizard and enter testing data. This wizard-driven data generation is also labor intensive and error prone. The first execution of this data is not effective in detecting bugs. To find bugs, one test script should be able to test against many test data sheets. Testers expect a fully automated method to generate multiple copies of testing data.

Commercially available testing tools are very much platform dependent. They often have their own testing environment. A recorded test script usually runs in the environment in which it has been recorded. Tools also are accompanied by tool-dependent script languages. Thus, software testing is often limited by the tester's system. If developers and other personnel need to be involved in testing, more tool licenses need to be purchased from the tool vendors. This limits the test script portability.

Researchers and tool developers are making an effort to achieve a fully automated testing tool that will recognize the GUI components and generate testing data and test scripts in sequence. It should also be capable of being executed for regression testing unattended. Based on the facts reported in *The Economic Impacts of Inadequate Infrastructure for Software Testing* (Tassey 2003), the current approaches to testing need to be revised or improved, and some even need to be discarded. We will therefore heed the experts' advice to develop a testing tool. A new tool capable of locating bugs more effectively will have the following features:

- *The test script language will be the same one used to develop the application under test.* Users won't be required to manually click mouse buttons, press keys, and record test scripts. Thus, testing can be run on the tester's systems as well as on the developer's systems. The capability of executing the test on user's systems will be helpful for the alpha and beta version release of the application.

- *Management of software testing will become easy.* Because the tool will actively search for GUI components and write test scripts, a maximized test will be achieved and the redundancy of test script generation will be reduced. One test script will be capable of testing against an optimal number of testing cases.

- *The developed tool will have an open architecture that makes it flexible and easily modified for extended testing functionality.* Upgrading of the tool can be accomplished within the resource limits of an organization. Thus the tool will always be compatible with the advancement of technologies and the complexity of the software projects. It will also be able to recognize third-party GUI components, custom controls, and generic objects for test data and script generation.

- *Regression testing will be fully automated.* Test execution has always been a boring, mechanical, repetitive, dreary aspect of testing. With this tool, the regression testing process can be conducted nightly and daily without human attention.

- *Test results will be reported and stored in a widely accepted format (e.g., a popular spreadsheet program, an XML document, or an HTML format).* When a bug is found, the report will pinpoint the problem in the source code. Users don't need to be trained in order to understand and use the report to fix defects. In addition, an Internet bug tracing system can be enabled.

Automated Test Teams

We all agree that with a properly automated testing process, more testing cases can be conducted and more bugs can be found within a short period of time. Charles Schwab & Co., a major U.S. stockbroker, reported that, based on the current testing means, a typical system test required 52 hours of effort manually but only 3 hours after automation. Automated Data Processing (ADP) reports that its elapsed time for testing has been reduced 60% through automation. Studies indicate that the number of defects discovered by tool users increase by 10% to 50%. Many organizations today rely on automated testing tools for the high quality of their products.

On the other hand, a survey in 250 organizations found that only 35% of testers were still using automated tools one year after the tool installation due to the reported testing inadequacy. To avoid turning back to the tedious and time-consuming manual testing method, many organizations train their staff to develop more effective automated tests. Figure 1.1 shows an organizational chart for a test team. An effective test team must involve senior administrators interested in quality products and a high degree of test automation. Developers should be willing to share and convey knowledge with regard to testing issues. Tool developers develop more effective testing tools based on the experience of manual testers and tool users. Alpha testers work independently but share test scripts (automated or manual) with other testers.

FIGURE 1.1

The organizational chart of a test team with the components of senior administrators, supportive developers, testers, and alpha testers

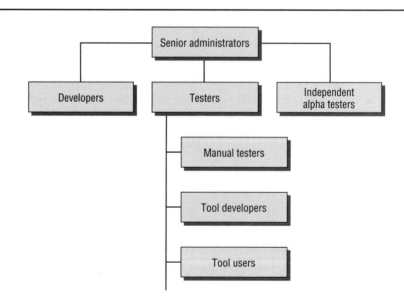

An automated testing process is the result of the evolution and maturity of manual testing efforts. During the tool development life cycle, manual testers continuously make contributions of automation strategies and testing techniques. Thus, before the test of a new component can be automated, manual testing should be conducted and verified. Then the optimal testing method can be implemented and integrated into the automated tool. As the testing methods are accumulated, the tool will become useful for future projects instead of just the current project.

Members of a conventional automated test team are tool users. A new automated test team would ideally include tool developers, tool users, and manual testers. Manual testers analyze project risks, identify project requirements, develop the documentation to design the overall testing scenarios, and specify the test data requirements to achieve the needed test coverage. The manual test engineers also prioritize testing jobs to be integrated into the automated testing tool.

The management strategy for developing a testing tool should resemble the management strategy used in the development of other applications. First, the team will select a development model and environment. The project described in this book will be implemented in the same language as the application under test. This will enhance the collaboration between the testers and the developers. Thus, testers will have the knowledge they need to test the application and make effective testing cases, and developers will make suggestions for improving the tool development and test script generation. The developers can use the tool to complete the unit and integration testing at code time.

Next, requirements need to be collected based on experiences that other testers, developers, and all kinds of end users have had with manual testing. The tool project specification is a cooperative effort between managers of all levels, product learning personnel, testers, and developers. An object-oriented design document is also important for the success of the tool's reusable architecture. This document will not only be used to complete the current implementation, future upgrading will also be based on it. The tool developers should have broad knowledge of software engineering and software testing and automation and programming skills. When it is implemented, the code will need to be tested. Bugs should be found and fixed so that they will not be introduced into the applications under test. Finally, the automated testing team needs to create training materials for the end users. The team can recruit the developers, engineers, and other personnel to test the application. Within a short period of time, maximum testing will be conducted. As many bugs as possible will be detected and fixed, thus assuring high-quality code.

The automated test team benefits the current project as well as future projects because the tool will be maintained. Unlike commercial testing tools, this tool will always keep up with current technology advancements, adapt to project complexity, and be able to test the creative and innovative aspects of an application.

How to Automate GUI Testing

The degree of automation for the tool depends on the testing requirements collected for an organization. With the knowledge of what GUI components to search for, the automated test team can implement drivers to create test scripts in various situations that correspond to the testing scenarios of the manual testing. A team with skillful manual testers can develop a tool with a higher degree of automation. In that case, the tool development will require more investment, but because the technologies of the software industry change quickly, developing a highly automated tool quickly pays off by increasing productivity and quality.

The starting point of testing an application's GUI is to locate the GUI components. Currently available tools depend on mouse events and keyboard actions from users. A fully automated testing tool should recognize these GUIs programmatically. We need to enable the tool to move the pointer automatically to conduct a GUI component survey. If a GUI component is detected at the movement of the pointer, the tool will identify it by its unique properties, check its status, generate testing data, and write code to activate the GUI and catch the consequences. These consequences could be visible (external GUI level) or invisible (internal non-GUI modules) and are stored in the test results.

A GUI component can be recognized by its name, its position in hierarchy, its component class, the title of its parent window, and the programmer-assigned tag or ID. During each session of running an application, the GUI components are located with unique pairs of coordinates on the screen. However, GUI positions are often under modification by programmers, platforms, and screen resolution. A GUI test script should avoid hard-coding the position for tracking the GUI components. The component name is also not useful for writing test scripts. When we write a test script for testing a GUI component, we often find that programmers assign one name to several GUI components. In other cases, the component names are assigned automatically by the integrated development environment (IDE).

Usually, the programmer-assigned properties (label text, button captions, window titles, etc.) are unique and can be effectively used to identify a GUI component. We can develop our automated test tool to use the combination of the title of the parent window, the name of the component class, the caption, and other custom properties to locate the GUI components using test scripts.

After the survey and the identification of the GUI components, test scripts should be created. Current testing tools don't have the capability to generate test scripts automatically. When a tool has a capture/playback or a reverse-engineering processor to generate test scripts, the vendor claims it is a powerful testing tool. Testers in some teams don't trust the test scripts recorded by the capture/playback or reverse-engineering procedure, so they write test scripts from scratch. Because the test script can invoke the application, vendors claim this testing method is automatic. Thus, the testers are often found spending most of their time writing test scripts or playing with the capture/playback tool to edit and debug the generated test scripts. They don't have enough time to manually create testing data, which is time consuming and requires creativity.

However, more and more testers disagree that the capture/playback tools are automated testing tools. We need to develop our own testing tools with full automation. My book *Effective Software Test Automation: Developing an Automated Software Testing Tool* discussed technologies such as reflection, late binding, CodeDom and testing data generation. The result of the book was the creation of a fully automated testing tool for non-GUI components. This book will use an active GUI survey approach to collect GUI test data, and the collected data will drive the test. In order to conduct an automatic GUI survey, this book will also discuss some Win32 applications programming interface (API) techniques. During the GUI survey, some API-implemented functions will simulate a person manipulating the mouse and the keyboard. Reflection techniques can be used to dismantle the component under examination. Late binding can invoke related members of the GUI event. The generation of test data and scripts becomes fast. Furthermore, the survey and script generation will be done automatically without the human tester's attention. Testers will spend most of their time composing effective testing cases. The automatically generated test script will test the component against multiple copies of testing cases and thus maximize the bug finding process.

Based on the preceding discussion, current automated test teams have a lot of manual testing responsibilities because the commercially available automated testing tools are inadequate in data and script generation and the recorded raw scripts lack the capability to verify test results. In addition to a full test automation, the developed tool will have the following advantages:

Less intrusive An intrusive tool requires developers to implement testability hooks in the application. These hooks are not desired by end users. Using an intrusive tool and using extra coding in the application could cause problems in the future. GUI testing methods without capture/playback require less human interaction with the application, making the tool less intrusive.

Platform and language independent Although the sample code in this book will be written in one language within the Windows operating system, the method can be extended to any other environments and coded in different languages. There is also no need to purchase additional hardware to handle the testing overhead.

Flexibility for upgrading Software testing is influenced by continuous evolution and addition of new technology, including advances in computer science, new testing technologies, and new development methods from outside sources. In addition, organizations continuously strive to create profitable new techniques and products. When a technology is implemented in an organization, the testing tool will able to test the new features. If the tool lacks the capability to test new features, developers can upgrade the tool.

Intuitive test automation   Using a fully automated testing tool is natural. You just need to feed the tool an application under test. The tool will take care of the GUI identification, data and test script generation, test execution and save the test results. Because the tool actively looks for GUI components to test, it creates a minimum number of test scripts and tests all of the components. The testers review the results and report the bugs, and the developers fix the bugs. Easy usage and effective testing allow developers to start automated testing right away for software projects.

Test playback   Test scripts are not recorded by the manual capture/playback method, but the scripts can be played back for regression testing. Because the scripts are not dependent on the script language bundled with the tool, they can be generated on one system and played back on other systems. This maximizes the test for multiple testing cases.

GUI Testing and Script Languages

Almost every automation tool on the market has some types of record and playback features for GUI testing. After recording the test scripts, testers will need to edit, add functionality, and input verification points into the recorded scripts. The test script is a collection of readable text commands translated from the mouse and keyboard events manually invoked by a tester. The collections of the text commands can be played back to repeat exactly the events and actions recorded. This technique seems to enable unskilled testers to generate test scripts quickly. Without the additional functionality and verification points, the recorded script is not effective. Thus, capture/playback is not an effective strategy for test automation. Graham and Fewster (2000) have given at least two reasons why this strategy is not effective:

- Users have to manually operate the application under test throughout the capture/playback process.

- The recorded test scripts have been hard-coded with testing data. They also need to be edited and debugged.

Capture/playback tools are easy to use, but using them is still labor intensive and tedious. The recorded scripts are written using unique script languages. A tester without programming knowledge cannot effectively operate the capture/playback tool. A skillful tester must be trained with the testing script language, which is often different from the language used by the developers. This limits the involvement of developers in software testing tasks.

When we start to develop the GUI test tool in this book, we will use a programming language for the implementation. But in the end, the tool will generate test scripts in languages the developers understand instead of in a unique testing script language. Because the test scripts are generated in any preferred programming language, they can be executed in different systems with more testing cases and find more bugs. Using a programming language for test scripts will also have the following advantages:

- A programming language is more popular than a unique test script language. Many people in an organization may already have the knowledge of it. Testers and developers can learn the same language. When necessary, developers can be easily involved in the tool and script development.

- There are numerous learning resources for a programming language, but it is hard to find books on test script languages. For example, *Visual Test 6 Bible* (Arnold 1998) is the only book on Rational Software's Visual Test. *WinRunner 7 in a Hurry! Software Test Automation With WinRunner* (Messerschmidt and Harbin 2001) is the only book on WinRunner by Mercury Interactive. But you can find numerous books and documents on Visual Basic, C++, C#, Java, and so on.

- A programming language has many features that can support the testing process. For example, it has a host of intrinsic functions that can return important information about the test platform and the application under test. Late binding functions can invoke methods of a class. Reflection methods can be used to obtain insight into the application under test. Some functions can run an external application. Other functions can manipulate the graphical user interface of applications.

- The database connection functions of a programming language usually are more powerful than those of a script language. These functions can enable the testing tool and the test scripts to use testing data from various data sources.

These are the basic advantages. A skillful developer can get sophisticated with a programming language and write essentially anything that is needed for testing. Test scripts written in programming languages can also be used to test many behind-the-scenes operations of the GUI. For example, scripts can be written to access external files and the Windows Registry.

However, because a programming language is not specifically designed for software testing, it usually lacks functionality to handle the mouse and keyboard events. It turns out that a programming language can always be customized with many Win32 API functions. The custom functions are very powerful for activating the mouse and the keyboard and manipulating and returning information from the GUI components. Therefore, a programming language will be used in this book to develop the testing tool and write test scripts automatically.

Finally, programming languages can give a higher return on test coverage and automation in key test areas than tool-dependent script language can. In the next section, I'll talk about selecting C# .NET as the programming language for this book's sample code.

Using C# for Automation

Almost any programming language can be used to develop a fully automated tool and generate test scripts. In my everyday work, I don't have a preference for particular languages. Due to the nature of my job, I develop applications using Java, C++, Visual Basic, and C#. I selected C# .NET for the sample code of this book because I have developed a GUI testing tool with code in C#. Reusing code will save time and make the discussion more effective. Although C# .NET is relatively new to the software development community, it has been promoted to the must-have list for software engineers.

C# .NET is a powerful, flexible language that can be used to develop any application. If you have the experience of developing any kind of automation project, then you will find the following points useful:

- *Any experience in programming language helps in undertaking the automation project.* C# .NET is a complete object-oriented programming language. The syntax and structure of C# code are similar to the syntax and structure of C, C++, and Java. It is easy to get used to C# programming. C# uses the .NET Common Language Runtime (CLR). There are a variety of useful data types and functions defined by .NET developers which are ready to invoke GUI events and write test scripts. Using late binding with C# .NET to execute test scripts is more flexible and easier than in many other languages.

- *Interoperability between managed and unmanaged components enhances tool development and test capability.* C# .NET considers the legacy COM assemblies to be unmanaged and the components developed in the .NET environment managed. When an unmanaged COM client accesses a .NET data type, the CLR uses a COM Callable Wrapper (CCW) proxy to negotiate the COM to .NET conversion. Thus, it is easy to reuse some legacy test utilities. Also, the automated tool developed in managed code can be enabled to test the standard COM. The other important aspect of the flexible interoperability of C# .NET is that functions of Win32 API can be programmed. When the base library of the .NET lacks functionalities, developers can implement the Win32 API to accomplish many testing tasks.

- *C# supports XML and XPath. XML has been widely used in various industries to store and retrieve data.* XPath enables you to easily write queries to retrieve specific subsets of the XML data.

- *Flexible database connectivity enables the tool to use testing data stored in different database programs.* Different automated test teams have their own preferred database format due to the configuration of hardware and software in an organization. C# .NET programming provides the full benefit of the ADO.NET (ADO stands for ActiveX Data Objects) for you to access any external testing data using Open Database Connectivity (ODBC), Object Linking and Embedded Database (OLEDB) and SqlClient database connection. After reading the data via ADO.NET, the database connection is broken. Within the .NET type of `DataSet` and `DataTable`, the retrieved data is stored in XML format. At programming time, you can treat the data from different database as XML data.

- *C# .NET is bundled with a few tools that can be used to support testing without doing any coding.* For example, you can use the Visual Database Tools to connect and configure a database. The Object Browser lets you investigate the internal structure of a component under test. Thus, you can obtain a fully automated test tool with a minimum amount of coding.

- *There are a few .NET integrated development environments (IDEs) with support for easy C# programming.* In addition to the Microsoft Visual Studio .NET IDE, there are some open source .NET IDEs available to download, such as Eclipsing .NET from IBM, #develop, and DotGNU Portable .NET. From among these, you can find the best to develop a fully automated GUI testing tool for your organization. The C# sample code in this book will be developed with Microsoft Visual Studio .NET IDE 2003.

The currently available test infrastructures prove to be inadequate to test today's software projects. Inadequately tested applications have caused great economic losses to our society. Developing your own tool will increase the degree of test automation and the effectiveness of fixing bugs. Your organization owns all the code. You can modify and upgrade the tool at any time when new testing requirements appear. Using C#.NET to develop an automated GUI test tool also provides effective management of time and budget. Many .NET libraries are ready to be used for software testing. The tool development life cycle will be shortened, saving time and money for the organization. Developing such a tool will also help the project to meet the experts' expectations for managing automated software testing. These expectations are well documented in *Automated Software Testing: Introduction, Management and Performance* (Elfriede, Rashka, and Paul 1999) and *Software Test Automation: Effective Use of Test Execution Tools* (Graham and Fewster 2000). However, these sources don't provide any programming-level help to automate a test project.

Common Language Runtime (CLR) and COM Callable Wrapper (CCW) Proxy

.NET is a new runtime environment and a common base library. The runtime layer is referred to as the Common Language Runtime, or CLR. The primary role of the CLR is to locate, load, and manage .NET types for the programs. The CLR renders a number of low-level details such as automatic memory management, language integration, and simple deployment of binary code libraries.

In order to enable the communication between the managed and unmanaged components, the CCW in .NET implements a number of COM interfaces. These interfaces automatically ensure the scenario that the CCW proxy is a genuine CoClass in COM. In addition to the set of custom interfaces defined in .NET type, the CCW supports the standard COM behaviors such as IConnectionPointContainer, IConnentionPoint, IEnumVariant, ISupportErrorInfo, IErrorInfo, ITypeInfo, IProvideClassInfo, IUnknown, IDispatch and IDispatchEx. If you need more information about COM, CCW, and CLR, please refer to the bibliography at the end of this book.

Test Scripts

A test script simulates an end user running an application using a prescribed scenario so that a software product can be tested automatically. Traditionally, an automated test script is written by a tester to test the methods of an assembly. When the test engineers write the automated test scripts, they must take time to define and analyze the requirements. As these values change during the software development process, the testers have to revise or rewrite the test scripts. This process will be repeated until the product is stable, and then the scripts can be interactively run to perform unit testing, integration testing, regression testing, and GUI testing. During the whole process, the task of the testing team is to improve and debug the test scripts and to meet the ever-changing testing requirements.

To reduce the tedious and time-consuming manual script-writing process, the automated testing tool is capable of detecting changes to the software definition automatically. If changes are made to the definition of the software, the tool will write a new test script accordingly. If the specification of the software is stable throughout the development life cycle, the test script can be rerun throughout the development life cycle for unit, integration, and regression testing. Testers can spend more time creating more effective testing cases and test the application thoroughly.

The rules for developing a good software application apply to developing a good test script. In order to generate an efficient GUI test script, the tool should be able to conduct a GUI component survey and establish a GUI inventory with detailed information of the application under test. A test script generated by the tool should possess the following features:

Reusability   It requires great efforts to develop a testing tool. Software engineers will be more willing to make these efforts if they can meet the requirements of one project and reuse the tool for future projects. Because this book follows the management of conventional software development to automatically generate reusable test scripts, it uses C# as a highly object-oriented language. The reusable tool and test script explore the GUI components and related non-GUI components. A test script for one testing case can be used for another testing case. Finally, the tool itself can be reused and updated from project to project.

Readability   Standard naming conventions must be used for variables and constants in a generated test script so the tester can review the code. The test script will precisely test the features of a GUI component. If there are some special needs for a software product, you can choose to update the automated test tool or revise the generated scripts. For example, if these special needs happen frequently, it is worthwhile to update the automated test tool. It makes software testing easier for the future projects. If the new requirements are not typical, the test engineer may decide not to update the tool but instead to modify the test script. In this case, a readable test script will be easier to modify.

Maintainability   It is common knowledge that different software organizations use different software engineering practices. Requirements and designs are different from product to product, although they may share many common features. There are enough features in the automated test tool to cover most software products. When new features are expected in future projects, the automated test tool can be updated.

Portability   Test engineers have the motivation to develop tools that can be used by their colleagues or other end users. With a simple installation process, the automated test tool is capable of performing the required testing tasks on different computer systems. Thus, other testers, as well as developers, IT personnel, and technical supports staff can run the testing tool to detect bugs and defects.

As you work through the book, keep in mind that all successful software project rules apply to the development of a GUI testing tool. No engineer writes perfect code. A test engineer is passionate about finding defects in code they write and in code written by others. This testing tool is able to generate an executable test script without debugging, which is a big time-saver. However, one must allow enough time to debug and test the tool during and even after development. Otherwise, it may introduce its own bugs into the software under test or the generated test script may fail to execute and find bugs.

Summary

Recent findings by scientists and economists suggest that the infrastructure of current software testing is inadequate. Experts have long observed that capture/playback test automation is not an effective way to write GUI test scripts. Unfortunately, no one has proposed or invented better ways to increase the degree of test automation. Vendors continue to claim that hand-written test scripts are automated tests. Today, testers are encouraged to develop testing tools for an organization. Continuing on the track of my book *Effective Software Test Automation: Developing an Automated Software Testing Tool*, this book introduces new methods to develop an automated GUI testing tool. The methods and tool development will rectify the deficiencies of current testing tools as follows:

- You can use the methods introduced in this book to develop a testing tool in your preferred language and to develop one that fits the culture and business practices of your organization.

- The discussion of the methods and the tool is general and independent of other testing tools. You can use these methods to develop an independent GUI test tool. Or you can add your own code to make this tool generate test scripts that are compatible and interoperable with your current testing tools and methods.

- You can include this testing method in the source code control. Thus, the development and test team can update and share the testing cases and scripts easily.

- The tool conducts an active GUI survey for the application under test. This GUI testing tool eliminates the need for a capture/playback procedure to write test scripts. An automatically generated data store drives the test script generation. The generated test script can perform a thorough test. Therefore, testers can devote more time to creating multiple copies of effective testing cases and to exploring the high-risk areas of the applications.

- A fully automated testing tool requires less time to learn and solves complex problems effectively. Thus, personnel from different departments can be involved in testing and find as many defects as possible at the early stages of development.

- You can always upgrade this tool with new capabilities to keep up with the testing challenges in your organization.

It is important to observe software development management practices in order to successfully develop a testing tool. Chapter 2 will briefly review the GUI test tools that are currently available on the market. Starting from Chapter 3, the book will include discussions of the technical fundamentals for software test and tool development. When there is enough background knowledge, an AutomatedGUITest project will be created and code will be added in each chapter to gradually increase the degree of GUI test automation.

Chapter 2

Available GUI Testing Tools vs. the Proposed Tool

T esting GUI components is different from testing non-GUI components. To automatically test non-GUI components, engineers usually develop test scripts to invoke members from an application under test and catch the return values of the invocations. Scripts can be developed using late binding and other readily available functions.

Today, almost all software applications are operated through a graphical user interface (GUI). An automated GUI test tool should be able to recognize all the GUI components. Then it needs to generate a test script to perform a set of mouse and keyboard actions to test the functionality of the underlying modules of the GUI. After the desired functions are performed, the tool needs to verify that the visible GUI representations are consistent with the intended functions and make sense to the end users.

Tool manufacturers have studied and developed various kinds of GUI testing tools. These tools have been designed to help test engineers record test scripts. However, none of the commercial tools have the capability of automatically generating GUI test scripts that perform and verify GUI actions and find bugs effectively. Engineers and economists have discovered their inadequacies and reported the economic losses caused by undiscovered bugs in software. This chapter will compare some of the popular tools. The discussion will be brief and aim to introduce the technologies and fundamental features of the current testing tools, which will ultimately help in developing the improved testing infrastructure.

Current GUI Testing Infrastructures

Most of the GUI test tools use the popular capture/playback method as an easy way to record test scripts. The recorded test script then plays back the low-level mouse drags and keystrokes. Some tools can recognize certain GUI components as objects. Others record the coordinates of the mouse pointer actions.

Test engineers have observed that the currently available tools are not able to write robust test scripts to directly complete the software testing. They often spend their time manipulating the tools and later editing the recorded test scripts. If the test scripts fail to execute, they have to debug them. It turns out that tool users don't have enough time to compose effective test cases and execute the test scripts to find bugs.

Capture/Playback Is Not Automatic

Tool vendors have long claimed that the test scripts recorded by capture/playback are automated GUI testing tools. But in reality, there are lots of pitfalls that impair the effectiveness of the test script generation and the test execution. During a test session, a capture/playback tool records all manual user interactions on the test object. In addition to performing operations on the application under test, the tool users are continuously interrupted to insert verification points. Both the capture/playback and the process of inserting verification points are labor intensive and tedious. Then a manual programming process is needed to enter test data and other checkpoints.

After a test script is captured, tests are replayed and thus in principle can be repeated at any time. If the application under test behaves differently during a repeat test or if checkpoints are violated, the test fails. The test script records this as a defect in the application.

It is obvious that the capture/playback relies on trained testers to manually use the application under test. Without editing, the recorded script performs the manual operations in the exact sequence they were entered. In order to complete the desired testing, the recorded scripts need to be edited and debugged. Testers also need to determine and enter the test cases based on the manual testing experience. In many cases, if the system functionality changes, the capture/playback needs to be completely rerun. Otherwise, it requires engineers to edit and maintain the recorded scripts. This only reduces some of the efforts of the completely manual test script development, but it doesn't result in significant savings for an organization, and the automation is minimal.

Another nuisance is that a capture/playback can not be continued when a bug occurs. Re-execution of the capture/playback is needed after the bug is fixed. This scenario happens repeatedly. When the test script is finally captured, the existing bugs have been found during the iterative manual recording processes. The capability of finding bugs by playing back the test script is limited. It only helps with the regression testing.

Many tool vendors tell testers that their tools generate data-driven test scripts, when in fact they use a wizard to prompt the users to enter and store data in an external file. The script is generated by the capture/playback approach rather than by data entry prompted by the wizard. Although re-execution of the test script is driven by the external files, the script generation is independent from the testing data. Thus, during the capture/playback process, the tool users need to operate the application under test, enter verification points, and interact with the data wizard. Less-effective capturing tools even record hard-coded data in the test scripts.

The other often claimed feature by the tool vendors is the capability of comparing bitmaps. However, experts have warned that bitmap comparisons are not reliable. The problem is that even if one pixel changes in the application, the bitmap comparison reports a test failure. Most of the time, this one pixel difference is desirable and is not a bug. Again, if you manually modify the test script, this problem can be avoided.

However, testers have found that the capture/playback functionality can be useful in some ways. When creating small modular scripts, capture/playback provides an easy and fast way to capture the first test. Then testers can go back to shorten and modify the test scripts. Although maintaining the captured test scripts is difficult, some testers have used this method to create quick automated tests. Later, these test scripts are discarded or recaptured. Other testers have used capture/playback to record test scripts by working on a prototype or a mock-up system at design time. Because the real functions of the application are not implemented at this point, there will be no bugs to interrupt the test script capturing. Editing and maintaining are continued thereafter.

Since this book proposes a fully automated method for data creation and script generation, you can use this method independently or adjunct to your existing testing infrastructure and avoid the manually operated capture/playback process. Testers can focus on generating test cases and running the test against as many cases as possible instead of focusing on recording, editing, and debugging test scripts.

Test Monkeys

Software developers and users are all aware that it is inevitable to have bugs in software products, and engineers have used many testing methods to find them. Bugs are found during manual testing based on the test engineers' desire to deliver a high-quality product. Verification is conducted while the testers are operating the applications and comparing the actual results with the results they expect. However, some bugs are still not detected with manual testing. Therefore, it is desirable to automate as many of the manual testing tasks as possible by using test scripts. It is especially true when there are various kinds of computer-assisted tools for generating test scripts. But these scripts lack the common senses of a human being. Manual testers are still needed to test the high-risk areas of the products.

Test monkeys are often used in addition to manual tests and test scripts. Test monkeys are automated tools. Their testing actions are randomly or stochastically performed without a user's bias. They find bugs differently than manual tests do because they have no knowledge of how humans use the application. Test monkeys and automated test scripts can also be used adjunctly because test monkeys randomly assign test cases. These random actions can employ a large range of inputs. Because all the actions and inputs are automated without a human's attention, often all possible combinations could be performed to test the application. Microsoft reported that 10 to 20 percent of the bugs in Microsoft projects are found by test monkeys (Nyman 2000). Some of these bugs might not be found by other means. The following list includes some of the immediate benefits of using a simple and properly programmed test monkey:

- *It can be used to randomly find some nasty bugs that other means could miss.* Because a dumb test monkey doesn't need to know anything about the user interface of the application, it can be used to test different projects. Any change or addition of the GUI components will not affect the performance of the test monkey. It can also be used at any stage of the development cycle. Using this method toward the end of the development life cycle can shake out additional defects.

- *A test monkey will run and find bugs continuously until it crashes the system.* By pushing memory and other resources to the system's limits, it finds memory and resource leaks effectively. The application under test can be complex or simple. Running the test monkey continuously for days without failure increases the tester's confidence in the stability of the application.

- *The test monkey is a useful complementary tool for covering the gaps left by manual testing and automated testing.* When its random action finds a bug or causes the application to fail, it reminds the testers that there is an area that should be addressed by the test plan.

- *A test monkey can be set up to run on a system of any kind (old, slow, and unwanted).* It can be set up to run unattended by the end users. Testers can check its progress every day or so. If the monkey finds a bug, it is the least expensive and most unwanted bug in the product that could crash and hang the system.

On the other hand, test monkeys have trouble recognizing GUI components. They continuously and randomly perform actions—such as mouse movements, right or left mouse button clicks, and random text entries—in any area of the application. Eventually some actions will hit on all the GUI controls, change the application states, and continue to test until the application crashes. The results are unpredictable.

Test Monkeys

Testers use the term *monkey* when referring to a fully automated testing tool. This tool doesn't know how to use any application, so it performs mouse clicks on the screen or keystrokes on the keyboard randomly. The test monkey is technically known to conduct stochastic testing, which is in the category of black-box testing. There are two types of test monkeys: dumb test monkey and smart test monkey.

Dumb monkeys have a low IQ level and have no idea what state the test application is in or what inputs are legal or illegal. They can't recognize a bug when they see one. The important thing is that they are eager to click the mouse buttons and tease the keyboard. These mouse and keyboard inputs are meaningless to the test monkeys, but the applications under test accept and process these random inputs seriously.

Smart monkeys can generate inputs with some knowledge to reflect expected usage. Some smart test monkeys get their product knowledge from a state table or model of the software under test. They traverse the state model and choose from among all the legal options in the current state to move to another state. Illegal actions may also be added to the state table on purpose. However, each input is considered a single event independent of the other inputs.

Although actions of the test monkeys are random and independent, testers have reported finding serious bugs with them. Reports can be found in articles and books listed in the bibliography at the end of this book (Arnold 1998; Nyman 2000).

The other difficulty is that test monkeys can't log much useful information about faults and failures. In that case, the engineers can't review a meaningful test log, so some of the bugs can't be reproduced later. One method for solving this problem is to run the test monkey with a debugger. When the monkey encounters a bug, the debugger halts the monkey and the developers can examine it. Some testers have used video cameras to monitor and record the monkey's actions. Even when a bug occurs, the monkey continues to test until it crashes the system. Later, testers can fast-forward the tape, reproduce the bugs, and learn how to crash an application.

Although test monkeys can find the most destructive bugs, it doesn't always recognize them. Monkey testing is not considered adequate for GUI test automation. What we need is some intelligent measures to complete a fully automated GUI test.

Intelligent Automation

Unlike with test monkeys, with intelligent automation there should be knowledge of the functional interactions between a tool and an application. No time is wasted on useless mouse clicking and key stroking. When an action does not perform as expected, the problem can be identified and reported. An intelligently automated test tool needs an effective state table. It can be used to perform GUI testing, load testing, and stress testing. A test script is generated to perform the desired actions based on a particular application. Since the test script simulates a human operating the system, it should find a significant number of bugs. The development of an intelligent testing tool will require deep knowledge of testing theories, experience in management of software testing resources, and sophisticated programming skills.

When we develop such a tool, we should implement it with the capability to understand basic Windows elements, such as menus, command buttons, check boxes, radio buttons, and text boxes. Then it should be able to apply a set of predefined actions on each GUI component and make sure it's working properly. The tool will not only apply all possible inputs to test the application, it will also find combinations and sequences that human reviewers could never consider.

Test experts have the tendency to execute complex tests and find more bugs than are found with the available commercial tools (Marick 1994). The available tools create scripts that are able to conduct only simple tests. In such a situation, a test script executes a simple test and compares the outcome with a baseline. It then forgets the first execution and start another simple test. Users expect tools to conduct complex test sequences and find bugs.

The next sections will list some of the currently available GUI test tools and point out the areas in which they're inefficient.

Automatic GUI Testing Tools in the Marketplace

This section will introduce some current testing tool vendors and the tools they offer. The list of the tools and companies is incomplete. Also, I don't mean to criticize the listed ones and endorse the others. My purpose in listing these tools is not to criticize or endorse any but to establish a foundation on which we can base the development of a more effective testing infrastructure. In addition to my personal experience, some of the statements will be quoted from the companies' advertisements and web pages. Others are based on the observation of other test engineers. The capture/playback approach will be repeatedly referred to. The reviews are brief; only the major features of each tool mentioned will be covered.

In general, no matter what the tool vendors claim, all the test automation projects in which these tools are used are programming projects. The tools record the mouse and key events operated by human users and translate these events into computer programs instead of hand-writing code directly. Because each GUI component requires verification points and data storage, users need to invoke functionalities from different programs. For example, users need to interact with the application under test in order to record test scripts and with the tools to insert checkpoints and test cases. These interactions are manual and tedious. Let's look at a few of them here.

CompuWare TestPartner

TestPartner provides functions for testing GUI and non-GUI components. Users can use it to test client- or server-side COM objects through scripts written in Microsoft Visual Basic, so testers can use it before the GUI has been created. If a tester is experienced in programming, they can write test script in VB. Testers who don't have programming knowledge can use the TestPartner Visual Navigator to create GUI test scripts and execute them. Test cases and checkpoints must be coded by the tester. If the tester does not have programming knowledge, they must ask for help in order to perform effective tests to find bugs.

For more information on CompuWare testing tools, visit `www.compuware.com`.

IBM Rational Test Tools

Rational Software has become a branch of IBM. It manufactures tools for testing applications at any stage of the software development life cycle. The tools can be used for requirements management, visual modeling, and configuration and source code control as well as testing. Rational software has acquired various vendors' products over the years, such as Visual Test, SQA, PureAtria, and Performance Awareness. For GUI testing, Rational Robot and Visual Test are often used.

Rational Robot

Rational Robot works with Microsoft Visual Studio 6. To conduct a GUI test, this tool depends on the user to activate the capture/playback recorder. The tool translates the user's action into a basic script in a special language, SQABasic. The syntax of SQABasic is similar to Visual Basic. This language supports data types including String, Integer, Long, Variant, Single, Double, Currency, and other User-Defined. It doesn't have enough functions to effectively capture and verify objects.

Rational Visual Test

Rational Visual Test is not a part of the other bundled Rational tools. It was first developed by Microsoft and then acquired by Rational Software. It has a user interface and allows users to develop test programs and manage test suites. Users can write test programs by hand or use the Scenario Recorder to record test sessions with the same capture/playback approach. The script language is called TestBasic. It creates test scripts for testing applications developed with Microsoft Visual Studio 6. The test program recorded by the Scenario Recorder often requires users to insert test data and verification points. It also has many hard-coded GUI coordinates. Although testers have found that this tool performs more effective testing tasks than other tools do, it is reported that this tool is not easy to work with.

For more information for Rational tools, please refer to www.rational.com.

Mercury Interactive Tools

Mercury Interactive provides products to test custom, packaged, and Internet applications. Testers often use WinRunner and LoadRunner for GUI testing.

WinRunner

This is Mercury's capture/playback tool, again, for Windows, Web, and applications accessed through a terminal emulation (e.g., 3270, 5250). Users can choose to record test scripts based on objects or on analogical screen coordinates. They can then specifically add or remove GUI components from an existing GUI Map, interact with wizards to check window and object bitmaps, and insert checkpoints and testing data. The scripts are recorded in a language named Test Script Language (TSL). The tool can use external database to test against the application. But the creation of data is purely manual using a wizard. Some of the features do not work for some applications or under some conditions. The recorder can not be used to create a full GUI Map to test against large applications.

LoadRunner

This tool uses scripts generated by other Mercury Interactive tools to perform actions a real person would do. Mercury Interactive refers to this feature as a virtual user, or vuser. Thus, LoadRunner conducts load or stress testing for both Windows and Unix environments and can be used to measure the responsiveness of the system. This tool can simulate thousands of virtual users to find locations of system bottlenecks. This allows performance issues to be addressed before release.

For more detail on Mercury Interactive tools, visit www.mercuryinteractive.com.

Segue's SilkTest

SilkTest is a GUI testing tool from Segue. This tool runs on the Windows platform and inter-rogates and tests objects and GUI components created with the standard Microsoft Foundation Class (MFC) library. It uses some extensions to deal with non-MFC GUI components. To con-duct a test, SilkTest provides capture/playback and a few wizards to manually interact with the application under test. When users select GUI components to test, the tool can inspect their identifiers, locations, and physical tags. As the users continue to operate the application, the tool interprets their actions into test scripts based on object properties or screen coordinates of the components. The scripts are in a script language called 4Test.

During the recording session, the users need to use the provided wizards to check bitmaps and insert verification statements. The vendor claims that this is a data-driven tool. In fact, the test code, as well as the test data, must be hand-coded. Thus, the manually created data drives only the execution of the already coded scripts.

For other tools from Segue Software, you can go to www.segue.com.

Open Source GUI Test Tools

Most likely, the open source GUI testing tools are for Java developers. Many testers are developing useful tools for the open source community. Here I will list only a few of them with a brief description. For more information on open source GUI testing tools, you can visit www.qfs.de/en/qftestJUI, www.manageability.org, www.testingfaqs.org, and www.opensourcetesting.org.

Abbot

The Abbot framework performs GUI unit testing and functional testing for Java applications. A Java test library has been implemented with methods to reproduce user actions and examine the state of GUI components through test scripts. The user is required to write the tests scripts in Java code. It also provides an interface to use a script to control the event playback in order to enhance the integration and functional testing.

GUITAR

GUITAR is a GUI testing framework that presents a unified solution to the GUI testing problem. Emphasis of this tool has been on developing new event-based tools and techniques for various phases of GUI testing. It contains a test case generator to generate test cases. A replayer plug-in is responsible for executing the test against these test cases. A regression tester plug-in is used to efficiently perform regression testing.

Pounder

Pounder is an open source tool for automating Java GUI tests. It includes separate windows for users to record test scripts and to examine the results of a test. The approaches for loading GUIs to test, generating scripts, and executing the scripts are similar to the approaches used by other tools.

qftestJUI

Java programmers use qftestJUI on Windows and all major Unix systems with Java Developer's Kits (JDKs) from Sun or IBM. It is used for the creation, execution, and management of automated tests to test GUI components with Java/Swing applications. The tool is written in Java. Test scripts are also hand-coded in Java.

Advantages and Disadvantages of the Commercial Testing Tools

After the preceding discussion, you can see that the available tools all have the general functions to recognize GUI components once the test scripts are recorded. Test scripts can be written by interpreting testers' actions into script languages. Later, they can be edited to include more testing and verifying functions. For testing applications, the tools can record the test scripts based on object attributes. Most of them use the combination of GUI and parent GUI components to identify the GUI of interest. The tools can read testing data from external sources and execute multiple test cases to find problems.

However, all the test projects using the available testing tools are totally manual. Only the execution is automatic if the test scripts are properly programmed. The test script is either written by hand or recorded through a capture/playback approach. Recorded test scripts must be edited and debugged for verification and checkpoint insertions. Testing data must be composed by the users. Thus, effectively using the commercial testing tools is a job for programmers, not for the non-programmers. Furthermore, the tools aren't capable of finding defects deep in the non-GUI modules.

Computer-Assisted GUI Testing

I will start with the good points of the available testing tools. They assist test engineers with regard to recording test scripts, inserting verification points, and testing data, as described in the following examples:

- *When capture/playback is turned on, it can record the actions performed by a real person.* It saves testers from writing test scripts by hand, although the scripts only perform the actions and don't include the functions for verifying the tests. Later, testers can revise the recorded test script, remove the undesired actions, add verification functions, and change the coordinate-based statements to object-based statements. This way is quicker than developing a test script from scratch.

- *Testing tools can record quick test scripts at the early stages of the software development life cycle.* For example, when a GUI prototype of an application is available, the capture/playback feature can record a test script more smoothly than at the later stage when more modules with bugs are integrated. The test script can be maintained and edited later with more testing functions.

- *The testing tools also have test harnesses to manage the automated test scripts.* Testers can use the available harnesses to schedule testing executions and manage effective regression testing by reusing the script library.

- *In addition, testers can use these tools as learning assistants.* Testers can use the tool to learn the properties of different GUI components and learn how to operate different GUI components programmatically. During the process of editing the recorded test scripts, the testers will get familiar with syntax of the script language and structures of the test scripts. An experienced tester discards the capture/playback feature but uses the test script manager in a testing tool.

The Common Features of Capture/Playback

The capture/playback approach records test scripts by recognizing GUI elements by their ID or by a combination of attribute values. Any change to the attributes will deteriorate the scripts from running. When this happens, the test scripts need to be rerecorded, edited and debugged, and it's possible that all the testing data created for the previous test scripts would be obsolete. Continually regenerating test scripts is time consuming.

Testing tool vendors all claim their tools include the capability of recognizing object-based GUI components. However, testers often find that a tool might recognize GUI objects created within one development environment and not recognize objects created within other environments. The reusability rate of the test scripts recorded by capture/playback is usually low. Some of the tool vendors may offer add-ins to support different development systems. Otherwise, the testers have to purchase various testing tools to meet different testing requirements of a software project.

On the other hand, the capture/playback approach assumes the GUI under test can already be functional. When the assumption doesn't hold, the tester has to abandon the current session of recording and report the problem. After the developers fix the problem, the tester can restart the capture/playback. This process of reporting and fixing may be repeated again and again. When a complete test script is finally recorded for an application, many bugs have been detected during the recording process. The effectiveness of executing the automated test script is limited, but the test script is useful for regression testing.

Editing the Recorded Test Script

Of the bugs found using the available automated testing effort, most are found during the process of recording the test scripts. The recording process is totally manual. The testers are well aware that recorded test scripts have hard-coded coordinates to locate GUI components. These coordinate values should be removed and changed to recognizable objects. A recorded test script performs actions in exactly the same sequence they were performed during recording. Playing back the raw script will only test whether the actions happen. It doesn't have code to verify the actions performed by GUI components when users trigger them with keystrokes or a mouse.

With GUI testing, you not only need to test whether a GUI component can be manipulated by a mouse click and a keystroke, you must also test whether the desired functions are invoked correctly. The GUI test involves the execution of both GUI and non-GUI components. For example, when a Save button is tested, the test needs to check whether a file is saved and whether the assigned filename is in the correct folder. It also needs to verify whether the contents of the file are consistent. The GUI testing tools normally cannot perform these functions with raw recorded test scripts.

Thus, after each session of manual capture/playback, the tool users need to edit the recorded test script to remove the undesired actions performed during recording, change hard-coded testing values and GUI coordinates, and add functions to catch the state of the module changes behind the GUI invocation. Also, testers need to add code to enable the test scripts to predict the consequences of each GUI action and verify the invocation of the other components. Finally, testers learn from the script editing and debugging process, write test scripts by hand, and discard the capture/playback tool.

Implementing Testability Hooks

One of the reasons the test scripts recorded by the commercial tools fail is that applications are developed with different development environments. There are various types of GUI components. For example, using Microsoft techniques, developers can choose to populate the GUI of an application with .NET, MFC, ActiveX, or third-party GUI components. Java developers can use Java or Java Swing interchangeably. Sometimes the developers assign names or IDs to components. Other times, they just accept the default values assigned by the integrated development environment (IDE). The complexity of the GUI also makes it difficult for the test scripts to work.

In defense, tool vendors claim that programmers should be disciplined and stick to the software design specifications. The tool would be able to test the applications if developers added testability hooks in the applications. The developers should insert code to call a test recorder where meaningful operations are implemented. The code would also pass all the parameters needed to re-create the interaction with the capture/playback process. Thus, the development disciplines should comply with the testing tools.

In the real world, it is impractical to implement testability hooks in applications. Testers want to operate the testing tools independently from operating the application. Developers don't want a bunch of test code mixed in with the application. They want to develop clean code. Extra code complicates the application and introduces unnecessary bugs. Besides, all software products have undiscovered bugs. Testability hooks in an application will increase the possibility of introducing the bugs in the tools into the application under test. The final result is that these testing tools are often left on the shelf.

Reusability for Regression Testing

Once a program passes a test script, it is unlikely to fail that test in the future. The test scripts don't find bugs by testing against one set of testing data. They find bugs by running against different test cases. Testers should spend more time on generating creative testing data and executing the test to cover many branches of the application rather than operating the testing tools to create and debug test scripts. Effective test cases and multiple executions will increase the reusability of the test scripts.

Applications are subject to change throughout the software development life cycle. Whenever new lines of code are modified, removed, or added, the changes could adversely affect the performance of the application, so the test scripts need to be rerun. Thus, the recorded test scripts should be made useful for regression testing.

The Proposed GUI Testing Approach

As you have learned, the available GUI testing tools don't meet the testing requirements to detect as many bugs as possible. Undetected bugs in software can cause economic losses and sometimes what can seem like disasters to the end users. There is a great need for reliable test technology. In this book, I'll present GUI testing methods that will actively look for components, generate testing data based on individual GUIs, drive the script generation with the testing data, and execute the test to report bugs.

Active GUI Test Approach

All the capture/playback-powered testing tools depend on human users to spot GUI components. They then record the actions performed on the GUI components. Today's testing tools don't have the capability to see and apply actions to the GUI components before a test script is created. The script and data generation is all passive. Many of the tools are shipped with a test monkey. A test monkey doesn't understand software applications and performs software testing by applying random mouse and keyboard actions.

The Microsoft Visual Studio 6/.NET packages are bundled with a Microsoft Spy++ tool. This tool can spot a GUI component with a mouse movement. But it is handicapped without the capability of applying mouse or key actions. This book will introduce a method to use a hybrid of a test monkey and the Spy++. A tool with the arms of the test monkey and the eyes of Microsoft Spy++ will be able to operate the mouse actions, press the keys, and see the GUI components on the screen.

Fortunately, almost all the available testing tools have already been implemented with the capability of translating the mouse and key actions into programs. Once the arms and eyes are implanted into the testing tools, they should be able to write test scripts without the passive capture/playback procedure. Thus, an actively automated test tool can be developed.

The approach in this book to developing an active testing tool will be based on the manual testing experiences of an organization. I will begin with testing simple applications to familiarize you with manual and exploratory testing. Then I will use the knowledge gained during the manual and exploratory testing to create test data. Whenever the improved tool encounters a GUI component, it will comprehend the properties of the GUI component and foresee the consequences when a certain action is applied to this GUI component. The properties of the GUI components and the foreseeable consequences will all be stored in a data sheet. This data sheet can be used to drive the execution of the test scripts. Because the test scripts know what the applications are supposed to do, they can be executed to detect bugs when the applications are doing the wrong thing.

As the development cycle progresses in this book, we can add new features to the tool. Test script generation will eventually become unattended by human engineers and can be continued day and night. Thus, testers will be freed from recording, editing, and debugging test scripts. They can devote their time to generating test data and executing the scripts to test the application as thoroughly as possible. If some features can not be tested automatically at that time and are high-risk areas, the tester can have more time to manually test these areas. Later the tester can enable the tool with new testing requirements based on the manual testing experience.

Generating Testing Data First

Each of the available testing tools has its own format for data store. Some less-effective tools can't read external test cases and their test values are hard-coded in their test scripts. The method described in this book is able to conduct an active survey, so the properties of the GUI components will be collected and saved in a popular data format, such as XML or Microsoft Excel document. Data saved in an XML document is easy to handle and review.

Once the GUI information is collected, the tool will be able to understand and predict the GUI behaviors. The tool can use GUI information to generate sequences of testing values and expected outcomes. For example, if the application requires a number as input for a certain state, a random number will be automatically assigned into the data store. If a string is needed, the tool will guess a string of text that makes sense to the testers and the developers. If other types of data are required, this tool can initialize appropriate objects of the data type when writing the test script.

After the data generation, the tool will be able to provide testers with a chance to view the GUI test cases. Testers can choose to accept the automatically generated test cases or modify the data store immediately. They can also make multiple copies of the data store and assign different values to each test case. It is believed that once the test script executes, it will not find bugs by running against the same test cases. Multiple copies of the data store will enable the scripts to test as many branches of the application as possible, thus maximizing the possibility of finding bugs.

Data-Driven Test Scripts

All the available testing tools have at lease two features to brag about: one is their capture/playback capability, the other is their capability for data-driven script generation. However, in real testing projects, the capture/playback feature has often been reported to record less-effective scripts. Many times, the recorded scripts fail to test the application. The data-driven test script is also on the wish list of tool vendors because many testing tools don't know how to generate testing data automatically. When they record scripts, they ask the users to enter testing data via a wizard. The wizard doesn't have the power to automate the process. In other words, data is often generated after test code in the scripts using these tools, and test scripts are not data-driven.

In this book, the approach will be to conduct a GUI survey of the application under test. After the survey, the tool will collect the properties of the GUIs in a data store. It will also generate testing values in the store. It will then provide an interface for the testers to view and modify the data. After the testers confirm their satisfaction with the data, the tool will save the data in a data store that is independent of the test scripts. Thus, the test script generation and execution is a data-driven process.

GUI invocation is different than invoking a member from a non-GUI component. For example, when a GUI button is clicked, a series of subsequent non-GUI actions can be triggered. It can also cause new windows to appear. To save a file, an application may have a Save button. Clicking the Save button causes a save file dialog box to pop up. You assign a filename to a file folder and click the OK button. For a human user, the task is completed. A test script recorded by conventional tools can perform these actions. But for a manual tester, you need to confirm that the save file dialog box appears after the Save button is clicked. Then you need to verify whether a new filename appears in the folder and whether the content of the new file is as expected. All this is done by comparing the actual results with the expected results. To accomplish the GUI actions and subsequent confirmation and verification, this book proposes an automatic test-scripting process that generates code to achieve the following testing tasks:

- The test script initiates a button click.
- It confirms the expected subsequence.
- It verifies the desired outcome.

If any unexpected event happens in one of the three steps, the result reports an error and the test script continues to test the next GUI component. When all the test cases are executed and all three steps are performed, bugs are reported to the developers.

Summary

The requirement for quicker development and testing cycles for software projects has led to the creation of more effective GUI testing tools. This chapter discussed today's popular GUI test infrastructure briefly. Many of the GUI testing tasks are still accomplished by manual tests. Test engineers believe that a test monkey is an effective and automated testing tool, but the random actions of test monkeys cannot effectively find many of the bugs. There remains a lot of room for improvement with the currently available GUI testing tools. For example, they lack the automatic generation of testing data and test scripts.

This chapter included brief descriptions of some of the GUI testing tools. Most of these tools rely on the capture/playback process to record test scripts. Other tools require testers to write and debug test scripts by hand. These methods of script generation are not effective. The generated scripts are not reliable and become obsolete easily, and it's expensive to maintain them.

I also introduced an active method for GUI survey of an application to improve the current GUI test infrastructure. I then proposed to use the survey result to generate testing data automatically and use the generated data to drive the script execution and to achieve a fully automated testing. The ultimate goal is to dramatically shorten the time required to achieve a higher-quality software application.

In my previous book, *Effective Software Test Automation: Developing an Automated Software Testing Tool* (Sybex 2004), I introduced a tool that achieved testing of non-GUI components of an application with full automation. In that book, *full automation* means that users feed the testing tool with an application and the automated testing tool delivers a bug report. Continuing with concepts in the previous book, in the upcoming chapters of this book I will discuss methods and approaches to building a tool and accomplishing GUI testing with full automation.

The methods of testing GUI components are different than the methods for testing non-GUI components. The techniques involve a discussion of the Win32 API and advanced .NET programming. In Chapter 3 we will develop a C# API Text Viewer to help in the development of a GUI test library throughout the book. The C# API Text Viewer is a GUI-rich application and will also be used under various development stages as the application to be tested manually and automatically by the GUI testing tool. Chapter 4 will start laying out the foundation of the GUI test library. In it, you will be introduced to some useful C#. NET technologies, focusing on GUI testing automation. These GUI testing features will be demonstrated on testing the C# API Text Viewer. You'll notice that some of the programming techniques introduced in Chapter 5 have already been used in Chapters 3 and 4. If you have written programs in C#, you should not have problems understanding Chapters 3 and 4. Thereafter, in Chapters 6, 7, and 8 we will enable the tool to conduct the first GUI testing with minimum human interaction. The rest of the book will address some specific GUI testing tasks and present methods to expand this tool for more testing capabilities.

CHAPTER 3

C# Win32 API Programming and Test Monkeys

There are two reasons available testing tools have used a capture/playback facility to record test scripts. One, they don't have built-in functions that enable them to see GUI component on the screen (as human eyes would). Two, they haven't been built with a function to apply actions with the mouse and the keyboard (as human hands would). But the tools can "feel" the mouse movements and keystrokes. With the assistance of human eyes and hands to accurately operate the mouse and keyboard, the tools are able to translate that into script languages. Although the script languages don't have functions that enable them to see GUI components, they have functions that enable them to receive as parameters the objects of the GUI components clicked and the keystrokes pressed and the coordinates of the mouse movement. When a recorded test script is played back, it repeats the actions exactly as seen by human eyes and in the sequence performed by human hands. Thus, one of the differences between programming languages and test script languages is that script languages have built-in functions to move the mouse, click the buttons of the mouse, and press the keys.

This chapter will introduce some applications programming interface (API) programming techniques to provide functions to perform the mouse and key actions. The API programming declares function calls and other data types by accessing functions of the operating system. Usually, an API consists of one or more DLLs that provide some specific functionality. These functions can be used to work with a component, application, or operating system. The API programming usually defines the interface between a high-level language and the lower-level elements of the device drivers of the system. Starting with this chapter, we are going to use C#. NET as the programming language and use the Win32 device drivers of the Microsoft Windows operating system to complete an automated GUI test tool. Based on the requirements of your organization, you can extend the API programming techniques to other languages and platforms. This chapter will also guide you in developing a C#. NET API Text Viewer that will speed up the API programming.

Understanding the Custom DLLs

After the Microsoft .NET Framework was introduced into the software business, code of the software components has been divided into two categories: managed and unmanaged. The code built with a .NET-aware programming language, such as C#, VB.NET, C++. NET, is in the category of managed code. The code compiled with other compilers is in the category of unmanaged code.

Unmanaged code has two types of dynamic link libraries (DLLs). The first is the COM-based DLLs and EXEs. The second is the traditional non-COM-style DLLs and EXEs, or custom DLLs as they are referred to in this chapter.

Custom DLLs are files containing functions that can be called from any application. At runtime, a function in a DLL is dynamically linked into an application that calls it. No matter how many applications call a function in a DLL, that function exists in only a single file on the disk and the DLL is created only once in memory. The custom DLLs are traditionally developed in C language for C and C++ programmers. For example, when programmers who use previous versions of Visual Basic (VB) need to use functions of the custom DLLs, they invoke an API Text Viewer to locate the functions and create VB 6/5 code. The goal of this chapter is to introduce you to the API programming for calling custom functions in C# applications.

The most frequently used APIs are the Win32 APIs, which includes the DLLs of the Windows operating system. The system DLL files usually reside in C:\Windows\System32. By opening this folder, you can find hundreds of them. The functions that are useful for the GUI test automation described in this book will mostly be found in the following custom DLLs:

kernel32.dll The core Windows 32-bit base API library. It contains low-level operating system functions, such as those for memory management and resource handling.

gdi32.dll The Graphics Device Interface (GDI) library. It contains functions for device output, such as those for drawing, display context, and font management.

shell32.dll The Win32 shell API library. It contains functions used to open web pages and documents and to obtain information about file associations.

user32.dll The user interface routine library. It is for Windows management functions, such as those for message handling, timers, menus, and communications.

Calling functions from the preceding DLLs, we will implement the GUI testing tool to interact with Windows directly or indirectly. The Windows APIs ensure that the generated GUI test scripts will behave in a manner consistent with the operating system.

Once you know the DLLs that are useful for GUI test automation, you need to get familiar with a document describing the available functions and how to declare them in a C# program. This document is the Win32API.txt file included in Microsoft Office 2000 Developer and in Microsoft Visual Studio 6. However, the content of the Win32API.txt file has been developed for VB programmers specifically. VB 6 programmers can conveniently start an API Text Viewer from the Microsoft Visual Studio 6.0 Tools folder. The API Text Viewer can help the programmer write function declarations, constants, and types with respect to custom DLLs.

Unfortunately, there is not a similar tool to display the API function declarations included in Microsoft Visual Studio .NET. Thus, we may have to hand-write them for C# or VB.NET programs. Because later chapters of this book include code to call the custom DLL functions, we will develop a utility similar to the API Text Viewer at the end of this chapter.

NOTE   If Microsoft Visual Studio 6 is installed on your system, you can locate the `Win32API.txt` file in a folder similar to `C:\Program Files\Microsoft Visual Studio\Common\Tools\Winapi`. However, the Microsoft Visual Studio .NET framework doesn't contain similar files to support the API programming. To assist you with the API programming in .NET, you can find a copy of `Win32API.txt` in the source code, which can be downloaded from www.sybex.com (perform a search for the title of this book). This file will be used by the C# API Text Viewer to be developed in this chapter and it will have the Windows XP operating system definitions that were most recent at the time this chapter was written.

C# API Programming

Microsoft Visual Studio .NET provides numerous functionalities using the already developed class libraries. Regular software developers seldom use the API programming to call the custom DLL functions. However, the Microsoft Visual Studio .NET libraries lack functions to directly operate the mouse. We can compensate by enabling C# API programming using the PInvoke technique.

The Microsoft Visual Studio .NET Framework has the interoperability to support both the COM-based and the custom DLL components. This is accomplished by the .NET facility *Platform Invocation*, also called *PInvoke*. The majority of this chapter will be related to the PInvoke of the custom DLLs. When there is a need, I will also discuss the .NET support of the COM-based DLLs.

PInvoke Basics

PInvoke is a .NET service that acts as a bridge between the managed and unmanaged code. This service enables managed code to call functions from unmanaged code. The unmanaged functions are contained in dynamic link libraries (DLLs) such as Win32 custom DLLs. The service locates and invokes an exported function and marshals its arguments (integers, strings, arrays, structures, and so on) across the interoperation boundary as needed.

To use the PInvoke service, an application must use the `System.Runtime.InteropServices` namespace. This namespace contains a `Marshal` class and a *DllImport* attribute. They are the key types that make the custom DLLs and the COM components interoperable with .NET. There are various methods and properties present in these classes to help with all interoperability needs.

The PInvoke service relies on metadata to locate exported functions and marshal their arguments at runtime. When it calls an unmanaged function, it performs the following actions in sequence:

1. Finds the custom DLL containing the function.
2. Loads the DLL into memory.

3. Locates the address of the function in memory, pushing its arguments onto the stack and marshaling data as required. These actions occur only on the first call to the function.

4. Transfers control to the unmanaged function.

Since the `System.Runtime.InteropServices` namespace is a part of the `mscorlib.dll` (`mscorlib.dll` is the core of every managed application developed in the .NET environment), you don't need to add an additional reference in any C# projects. After you start a C# project from a .NET IDE, you simply start a program by a `using` statement to access the managed-unmanaged interoperability, as shown here:

```
using System.Runtime.InteropServices;
```

The *Marshal* Class and the *DllImport* Attribute

The packing/unpacking of parameters and return values across the COM apartments is called marshaling. The *Marshal* class in .NET provides a collection of methods to allocate unmanaged memory, copy unmanaged memory blocks, and convert unmanaged types to managed types.

COM Apartment

A COM apartment is a programming entity that enables the logical concept of components and their clients. The term *apartment* is used to refer to housing software entities within walls. The apartment is neither a thread nor a process. It is an execution context in which components exist. Different types of apartments define how a class object can be accessed from different threads in the same process. An apartment can be a single-threaded apartment (STA) or a multithreaded apartment (MTA). Objects in an STA can be accessed by only one thread at a time. If more than one thread tries to access the object in an STA, the requests are queued in a message pump and access is given based on first come, first-served. In the case of an MTA, it is possible for multiple threads to enter the apartment. The programmer has to take the responsibility of protecting the data in an object from concurrent access and possible corruption.

When you want to interact with a custom DLL in your .NET project, you need to use a marshaling method called custom marshaling. The practical use of custom marshaling is to implement the marshal-by-value. There are many functions in the Marshal class, but you need to learn only a few of them for API programming. The next section includes an example to demonstrate custom marshaling. In addition to custom marshaling, PInvoke provides automation marshaling and standard marshaling functionality to enable COM components via their type libraries to work with managed projects. When you start to develop a tool for C# API programming, you will learn how to marshal values, arrays, functions, and user-defined data types of custom DLLs in C# programs.

The *DllImport* attribute combines the functionality of the Win32 `LoadLibrary()` and `GetProcAddress()` APIs into an encapsulated class. If you have programmed in Visual Basic 6 or earlier VB versions, you'll know that the `DllImport` attribute is equivalent to a VB `Declare` statement. The `DllImport` attribute specifies which custom DLL contains the function needed for the declaration, as in the following example:

```
[DllImport("user32.dll", EntryPoint = "GetWindowText")]
private static extern int GetWindowText(int hwnd,
➡StringBuilder lpstring ,int cch);
```

The first parameter is mandatory for this attribute; it is the name of the DLL, `user32.dll`. It is followed by many optional attributes, like `EntryPoint` in this case, which specifies the name of the function of interest. This option must be specified when you want to use a different name in your .NET project. After all the `DllImport` attributes, the example declares the API function, with appropriate names and parameters. In this case, the name of the function is the same as it is in the custom DLL, `GetWindowText()`.

The syntax of calling the declared method is like the syntax of calling another method developed in a C# program, as shown here:

```
int wStatus = GetWindowText(hwnd, lpstring, cch);
```

This call returns the title caption text of a Windows form.

Data Type Presentation

You now have enough information to start interoperating between managed and unmanaged code. Very often, different programming languages use different styles to represent primitive data types. Understanding these presentations will help you continue the discussion of developing an automated GUI testing tool.

The Windows API uses numerous type definitions to represent primitive data types. The custom DLLs were often developed in the C language. For example, a C programmer can define a constant string of Unicode characters:

```
const wchar_t* autoTestString;
```

But in C#. NET, you have to make this definition look like this:

```
string autoTestDotNetStr;
```

Or you have to use a definition such as this:

```
StringBuild autoTestDotNetStr = new StringBuilder();
```

In case you need references when you use the .NET PInvoke services, Table 3.1 lists the equivalent data types for managed and unmanaged code.

TABLE 3.1 Data Type Presentations of Managed and Unmanaged Code

C-Style Custom DLL	Visual Basic 6	.NET System Presentation	C# Representation
bool	Boolean	System.Boolean	bool
unsigned char	Byte	System.Byte	byte
char	Char	System.Char	char
double	Double	System.Double	double
short	Integer	System.Int16	short
long	Long	System.Int32	int
int	Integer	System.Int32	int
float	Double	System.Single	float
const char	Char	System.String	string
char*	String	System.String	string
const wchar_t*	String	System.String or System.StringBuilder	string or System.StringBuilder
ushort	Integer	System.UInt16	ushort
unsigned long	Long	System.UInt32	uint
unsigned int	Integer	System.UInt32	ulong

A Simple C# API Example

The reason we're using API programming for C#. NET is to enable our testing tool to understand the GUI components on the screen. In this section we will write a simple program using the DllImport attribute and call some custom functions to discover some properties of a Windows form. Throughout this book the term, *function* will be used to refer to a respective member of the custom DLLs, and *method* will refer to a member of the managed assemblies.

It is assumed you have installed on your system Microsoft Visual Studio .NET 2003. You can start a C# console project to discover the class name property of the Notepad application by scanning its GUI:

1. Make a new folder under C:\ and name it GUISourceCode. This folder will be used to organize all the sample code of this book based on chapters. Next, create a subfolder, ..\Chapter03, under C:\GUISourceCode.

2. Start the Microsoft Visual Studio .NET IDE from Start ➤ All Programs menu.

3. Choose File ➤ New ➤ Project. Figure 3.1 shows the New Project dialog box.

4. In the Project Types list, select Visual C# Projects. In the Templates list, select Console Application.

FIGURE 3.1
Creating a C# console
application project

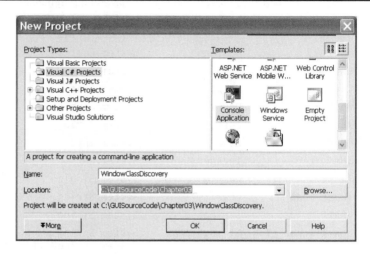

5. Next to the Location field, click the Browse button and locate the `C:\SourceCode\`
   `Chapter03` folder.

6. In the Name field, type **WindowClassDiscovery**.

7. Click the OK button. Your WindowClassDiscovery project is created with some skeleton
   code generated in the code editor.

8. Type the code in Listing 3.1 into the code editor.

Listing 3.1   **The Code of a Simple C# API Example to Find the Class Name of a
Windows Form**

```
using System;
using System.Runtime.InteropServices;
using System.Text;

namespace WindowClassDiscovery
{

  class Win32API
  {
    //Prepare two functions from the user32.dll API
    [DllImport("user32.dll", EntryPoint = "FindWindow")]
    private static extern int FindWindow(string lpClassName,
➡string lpWindowName);

    [DllImport("user32.dll", EntryPoint = "GetClassName")]
    private static extern int GetClassName(int hwnd,
➡StringBuilder lpClassName, int nMaxCount);

    [STAThread]
```

```
static void Main(string[] args)
{
  //Initialize a StringBuilder object, not a string
  //value 100 is the maxmum length of a string
  StringBuilder clsName = new StringBuilder(100);

  //Call the FindWindow to find the Windows handle
  //of an open Notepad application
  int iHandle = FindWindow(null, "Untitled - Notepad");

  //call the GetClassName custom function
  int clsHandle = GetClassName(iHandle, clsName, 100);

  //Print the class name on the screen
  Console.WriteLine(clsName.ToString());

  //Hold the screen for you to view the result
  //You need to hit enter to terminate this session
  string waitToExit = Console.ReadLine();
  }
 }
}
```

The code logic is straightforward. You first add three using statements to refer to the needed namespaces.

```
using System;
using System.Runtime.InteropServices;
using System.Text;
```

The System namespace is required by all .NET projects. The System.Runtime.Interop-Services namespace allows your program to access the PInvoke service. Finally, the System.Text namespace provides a StringBuilder class. This class represents a mutable string of characters, which is more flexible than the primitive string data type.

The program starts with defining a namespace. When you give a name to the project in step 6, the Microsoft Visual Studio .NET IDE automatically assigns this name to the namespace of this project, WindowClassDiscovery. But it names the class Class1 by default. For it to make sense, I recommend that you change this class name. In this case, I renamed it Win32API.

After the class name is defined, you directly use the DllImport attribute to marshal two functions from the custom user32.dll:

```
//Prepare two functions from the user32.dll API
[DllImport("user32.dll", EntryPoint = "FindWindow")]
private static extern int FindWindow(string lpClassName, string lpWindowName);

[DllImport("user32.dll", EntryPoint = "GetClassName")]
private static extern int GetClassName(int hwnd, StringBuilder lpClassName,
➥int nMaxCount);
```

The FindWindow() function takes two string parameters. One is the name of a Windows class. The other is the title caption of the Windows form. It returns an integer, which is the handle of the Windows form. Once a handle number is known, manipulating a Windows form becomes easier. This handle number is created whenever a GUI component is created. The value of the handle is different from session to session, so it can't be hard-coded for GUI test scripts.

The second function is the GetClassName() method. This function takes three parameters. The first is a handle number of the GUI under investigation. The second parameter is a StringBuilder object. This object will be mutated by the GetClassName() function. As is usual with a C# program, you may want to have this string parameter passed by reference. However, for the C# API programming, it passes a StringBuilder object as a regular parameter. The third parameter is an integer that specifies the maximum length of the class name to be retrieved.

To call the declared custom functions, a Main() method is defined. A Main() method is the entry point method for all C# console projects. In this example, the Main() method has only five statements. The first creates a StringBuilder object, clsName:

```
//Initialize a StringBuilder object, not a string
//value 100 is the maxmum length of a string
StringBuilder clsName = new StringBuilder(100);
```

This clsName object is initialized to be able to hold a string with a length of 100 characters. But when a string variable is passed as a parameter and reassigned, a custom function often requires an extra space at the end. For example, when you specify a length of 100 for the clsName object, the GetClassName() function can find the first 99 characters and truncate the rest. Thus, we always generously give an extra space for calling these functions.

The second statement calls the FindWindow() function directly. The syntax is identical to the other C# method calls:

```
//Call the FindWindow to find the Windows handle
//of an open Notepad application
int iHandle = FindWindow(null, "Untitled - Notepad");
```

The FindWindow() function call takes two parameter values: the class name and the Windows caption. But in real life, you don't have to know both of them. You can give the function the literal string of either the class name or the caption text. The other one can be a null value. In this case, since you are going to find the class name of the Notepad application, you give a null value for the first parameter. The second parameter represents the caption, which is visible on a freshly opened Notepad window, such as Untitled - Notepad. The result is a number of the Windows handle.

After the handle number is known, the third statement calls the GetClassName() function and finds the class name by consuming the handle as its first parameter:

```
//call the GetClassName custom function
int clsHandle = GetClassName(iHandle, clsName, 100);
```

Instead of returning the class name as a string, the GetClassName() function takes a StringBuilder object and alters its content. The last parameter is an integer value, 100. As has been discussed, the maximum length of the class name found by this call can be 99 characters.

The last two statements print the class name and hold the console screen open so you have plenty of time to view it when you run this program from the Microsoft Visual Studio .NET IDE by pressing F5:

```
//Print the class name on the screen
Console.WriteLine(clsName.ToString());

//Hold the screen for you to view the result
//You need to hit enter to terminate this session
string waitToExit = Console.ReadLine();
```

The call for the Console.ReadLine() method allows you to press the Enter key to terminate the program. However, the console screen will not disappear if you run this program from a DOS command prompt.

Start a session of Notepad, and run this program by pressing F5. You also can run it from Windows Explorer by double-clicking the executable or you can run it by issuing a command from a DOS command prompt. Figure 3.2 shows the resulting class name of the Notepad application.

The execution of these custom methods finds the class name of the Notepad application to be Notepad. Please press the Enter key to terminate this session.

This section demonstrated how to use the PInvoke service of the .NET Framework. When you coded the examples with the DllImport attribute, you might have wondered how you could manage to remember the names of the custom DLLs, the names of the functions to declare, and the details of the parameter information. Because numerous custom functions will be used in this book, the next section will discuss a way to develop a tool that's similar to the API Text Viewer included in the Microsoft Visual Studio 6 package. As it is named C# API Text Viewer, the developed tool will generate C# code for marshaling custom functions instead of VB code. Although this Text Viewer is not a part of the automated GUI testing tool, it will help in developing the testing tool and will be tested at various development stages by the tool.

FIGURE 3.2
Results of calling the
custom functions

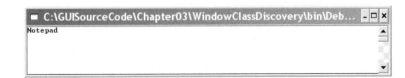

C# API Text Viewer

The Microsoft Visual Studio .NET IDE comes with a variety of tools, but one of the useful tools is missing from the package, the API Text Viewer using a text file with a collection of all possible custom DLLs, functions, constants, and types of the Win32 system. The text file is named as `Win32API.txt` and is usually installed in `C:\Program Files\Microsoft Visual Studio\Common\Tools\WinAPI` by Microsoft Visual Studio 6 Setup. When you need to call a custom function, you use the API Text Viewer to look for it and then you copy and paste the outcome from the API Text Viewer to your program. The outcomes are correct sentences written in Visual Basic 6 language, but they are not usable in C# and in VB.NET programs.

Since Win32 API programming continues to provide extra functions to develop .NET projects, you can call custom functions to extend the functionality of the .NET applications. You have seen in the preceding example two functions of the `user32.dll`. The statements are short and easy to understand. But the Microsoft Visual Studio .NET IDE doesn't provide any clue for you to locate these functions with regard to the names of the DLLs and the parameter information. The example assumes you have all this information in your mind and that the functions can easily be handcrafted. Later, you will be required to solve more complicated problems with regard to GUI test automation with .NET. It will become harder for you to remember the names of the custom functions and DLLs in order to write correct C# code. A tool with the capability of marshaling custom functions into C# code will speed up the development of the automated GUI testing tool. It will also help you understand the .NET PInvoke service. This section is devoted to developing a tool for C# API programming.

We are going to call the tool the C# API Text Viewer. This tool will have a GUI that's similar to the API Text Viewer in the Microsoft Visual Studio 6 package. Instead of reinventing the wheel, the C# API Text Viewer will use the same text file, `Win32API.txt`, but it will translate the Visual Basic 6 code into C# code. For example, when you need to call the `FindWind()` function of the `user32.dll`, the old API Text Viewer writes the Visual Basic code as follows:

```
Public Declare Function FindWindow Lib "user32" Alias _
"FindWindowA" (ByVal lpClassName As String, ByVal _
lpWindowName As String) As Long
```

However, the following code is needed for the C# program in the example:

```
[DllImport("user32.dll", EntryPoint = "FindWindow")]
private static extern int FindWindow(string lpClassName, string lpWindowName);
```

Using the same text file, the new tool will be able to conduct a precise translation from Visual Basic 6 to C# automatically. Besides providing a useful utility to use in developing the GUI testing tool, the C# API Text Viewer will be subject to testing as the GUI testing tool is developed throughout this book with different degrees of automation.

Now, start a C# API Text Viewer project in the folder `C:\GUISourceCode\Chapter03\` by following the steps in the section "A Simple C# API Example" earlier in this chapter. In step 4, select Windows Application from the Templates list. In step 6, name this project CSharp-APITextViewer. Then click the OK button to let the IDE generate a default form and proceed with the next sections. Leave the form as it is for now; we will come back to build it with some GUIs after preparing all the C# marshaling functions.

A Base Class

In the `Win32API.txt` file, there are three categories of Visual Basic code: predefined constants, user-defined data types, and Win32 declared custom functions. A user-defined data type is referred to as a Type in Visual Basic 6 and as a structure in C#. Hereafter, I will refer to it as Type or structure with regard to the context. Constants and structures are not related to DLLs. The function declarations are from respective DLLs and consume the constants and structures by taking parameters.

Programming the C# API Text Viewer will involve the three categories with distinguished classes. A base class is developed here to define the shared behaviors of the three classes. The shared behaviors include the following:

- Preparing a sorted list to store all of the definitions of each category
- Defining a string variable of the filename, such as `Win32API.txt`
- Adding definitions of each category one by one to the sorted list
- Retrieving the name of a definition in need
- Retrieving the C# code of a definition in need
- Retrieving the count of definitions of each category

To begin with the base class, open the CSharpAPITextViewer project in the Microsoft Visual Studio .NET IDE. From the main menu of the IDE, choose Project ➤ Add Class. An Add New Item dialog box appears, such as the one in Figure 3.3.

In the Name field, type **APITextViewer** as the name of the base class. The source code of the base class will be saved as `APITextViewer.cs`. Click the Open button to accept the default choices and go to the source code editor. In the source code editor, a code skeleton is built by the IDE with a `using System` statement, a namespace defined by the project, and an empty class.

After the `using` statement, add another statement to make use of data types in the `System.Collections` namespace:

```
using System.Collections;
```

FIGURE 3.3
The view of the empty
class declaration
dialog box

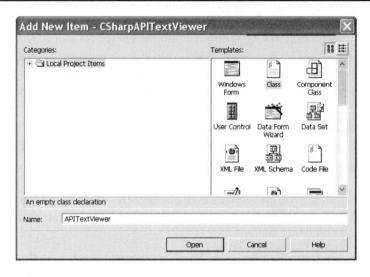

Then, within the empty class, define two fields. In this base class, all the members are defined as public so that they can be accessed by its child classes:

```
public SortedList DefinitionList;
public string filename;
```

The DefinitionList is an object of the SortedList class from the System.Collections namespace. This class has a lot of useful members to manipulate an array of data. The data is automatically sorted in ascending order. Properties and methods include Capacity, Count, Item, Keys, Values, Add(), GetByIndex(), GetKey(), Remove(), and others. This base class will call a few of them. For example, we will use the Key property to store the name of a custom function, a structure or a constant, and the Value property to store the marshaled C# code for the respective definitions.

The filename field receives the path of the text file with the API definitions created when the object was initialized. Whenever an object of this class is initialized, the DefinitionList is created and the filename is assigned within the constructor:

```
public APITextViewer(string m_filename)
{
  DefinitionList = new SortedList();
  filename = m_filename;
}
```

After the constructor prepares the sorted list and the filename, you can add the code for a read-only property, Count. The code for the Count property is as follows:

```
public int Count
```

```
  {
    get
    {
      return DefinitionList.Count;
    }
  }
```

It simply returns the value of the Count property of the sorted list. Then you implement an AddCSharpCode() method to add the title and the C# syntax into the sorted list for each definition (constants, structures, or functions) of the API:

```
public void AddCSharpCode(string key, string data)
{
  if (!DefinitionList.ContainsKey(key))
    DefinitionList.Add(key, data);
}
```

This method invokes the Add() method of the sorted list. The Add() method of the sorted list takes two parameters. The first one is the key on which the list is sorted. The key can be a name of a constant, a structure, or a function. The second parameter is the actual C# code corresponding to the key. In this case, the content is the C# code segment that was used to marshal a custom definition.

After definitions are stored, you need to implement methods to retrieve the specified values so that you can use them. To retrieve the name of a definition stored in the keys property in the list, you add a GetKey() method:

```
public string GetKey(int index)
{
  if (index < DefinitionList.Count)
  {
    return (string)DefinitionList.GetKey(index);
  }
  return "";
}
```

To retrieve the corresponding C# API code, you add another method, GetCSharpSyntax():

```
public string GetCSharpSyntax(int index)
{
  if (index < DefinitionList.Count)
    return (string)DefinitionList.GetByIndex(index);

  return "";
}
```

The GetKey() method of the SortedList class returns the name of the API definition, and the GetByIndex() method returns the C# syntax. These two methods will not be called until you implement the user interface and write C# code.

At last, you need to define a virtual method, `ParseText()`. A virtual method in the base class is an empty method, such as the following.

```
public virtual void ParseText()
{
}
```

This method will be coded in the classes that inherit from the base class to deal with constants, structures, and functions. The purpose of this method is to read `Win32API.txt` and convert the Visual Basic 6 definition into C# code. Therefore, the implementation of the base class is completed. You can press Ctrl+Shift+B to compile the code. In case your code has compiling errors, you can compare your code with Listing 3.2, which contains a full list of the base class.

Listing 3.2   **Code for the Base Class of the C# API Text Viewer Project**

```
using System;
using System.Collections;

namespace CSharpAPITextViewer
{
  public class APITextViewer
  {
    public SortedList DefinitionList;
    public string filename;

    public APITextViewer(string m_filename)
    {
      DefinitionList = new SortedList();
      filename = m_filename;
    }

    public int Count
    {
      get
      {
        return DefinitionList.Count;
      }
    }

    public void AddCSharpCode(string key, string csCode)
    {
      if (!DefinitionList.ContainsKey(key))
        DefinitionList.Add(key, csCode);
    }

    public string GetKey(int index)
    {
      if (index < DefinitionList.Count)
      {
        return (string)DefinitionList.GetKey(index);
      }
```

```
      return "";
    }

    public string GetCSharpSyntax(int index)
    {
      if (index < DefinitionList.Count)
        return (string)DefinitionList.GetByIndex(index);

      return "";
    }

    public virtual void ParseText()
    {
    }
  }
}
```

In this section, the implementations of all the methods in the base class were completed except for the `ParseText()` virtual method, which needs to be coded when the base class is inherited in the code of the next sections. The completed members are readily available for the derived classes. The incomplete virtual method will be coded to produce constants, structures, and functions in C# language.

An API Utility Class

Before we continue the classes for reading the API text file, we are going to build a class to contain a small collection of constants and methods. These constants and methods will be used repeatedly by the other classes.

From the Microsoft Visual Studio .NET IDE main menu, choose Project ➤ Add Class (as you did when you built the base class). But this time, type in **APIUtility** for the class and file name. Click the Open button. When the `APIUtility.cs` appears in the code editor, add the public string constants (as in Listing 3.3) immediately below the class definition.

Listing 3.3   **Predefined String Constants for Converting Visual Basic 6–Style Code into C# Style and for Including Some Methods of the .NET PInvoke Service**

```
public const string CSHP_MARSHAL_EXP_1 =
➡ "[MarshalAs(UnmanagedType.ByValTStr,SizeConst =<<REPLACEABLE>> )]\n   ";
public const string CSHP_MARSHAL_EXP_2 =
➡ "[MarshalAs(UnmanagedType.ByValArray,SizeConst =<<REPLACEABLE>> ]\n   ";
public const string CSHP_MARSHAL_EXP_3 = "[DllImport(<<REPLACEABLE>>)]\n";
public const string CSHP_MARSHAL_EXP_4 = " static extern ";
public const string CSHP_MARSHAL_EXP_5 =
➡ "[MarshalAs(UnmanagedType.Struct)] ref   ";
public const string CSHP_MARSHAL_EXP_6 =
➡ "[StructLayout(LayoutKind.Sequential)]\n";
```

```
public const string CSHP_SCOPE = "CSHARP_SCOPE";
public const string CSHP_CONST_LEADING = "const int";
public const string CSHP_HEX_EXP = "0x";
public const string CSHP_OR = " | ";
public const string CSHP_COMMENT = "; //";
public const string CSHP_END_TYPE = "}\n";

public const string VB_CONST_LEADING = "Const";
public const string VB_HEX_EXP = "&H";
public const string VB_OR = " Or ";
public const string VB_COMMENT = "'";
public const string VB_END_TYPE = "End Type";
public const string VB_AS = " As ";

public const string REPLACEABlE = "<<REPLACEABLE>>";
```

These constants are the conventions of the Visual Basic 6 and C#. NET languages. The purpose is to substitute the Visual Basic 6–style syntax with C# style. For example, in a Visual Basic 6 program, you will use &H to denote a hex number. But in C#, you need to change the leading element to 0x to denote a hex number. Series of the CSHP_MARSHAL_EXP_x constants are strings of the PInvoke marshaling services. Each one marshals a specific case of the custom functions. For example, the CSHP_MARSHAL_EXP_1 will be inserted into the code to marshal a value array for converting a custom Type into a C# struct. The REPLACEABlE constant means this part will be replaced with a correct C# notation. When you understand these examples, you'll find it easy to delineate the other constants in the list. For more information on the marshaling methods, you can refer to the resources listed in the bibliography at the end of the book.

Now, let's code two more methods. These methods are all declared public and static. A public and static method can be directly invoked from outside of the APIUtility class. The first method is named GetRidExtraSpaces(). Its mission is to get rid of the extra spaces between words. The code looks like Listing 3.4.

Listing 3.4 **The Code for a Method to Get Rid of the Extra Spaces of the Visual Basic 6 Code**

```
public static void GetRidExtraSpaces(ref string input)
{
  while (input.IndexOf("  ")>=0)
  {
    input = input.Replace("  ", " ");
  }
  input = input.Trim();
}
```

Compilers read one space between words. It ignores the extra spaces. Very often, the Win32API.TXT file contains extra spaces. So a program can parse a sentence, this method normalizes all the sentences to allow only one space between words. This is especially helpful when the Split() method of the String class is used to separate a sentence into words. The program knows exactly which word to pick up and correctly composes a new line of C# code. The coding uses a while loop to iterate the Replace() method of the String class. When two consecutive spaces are encountered, it replaces these two spaces with one space. The input string is passed to the GetRidExtraSpaces() method by reference. When the iteration is completed, the extra spaces are removed.

In Table 3.1 earlier in this chapter, you saw how C/C++, Visual Basic 6, and C#. NET present primitive data types differently. In order to make flawless C# code from a Visual Basic 6–based text file, you must implement a GetCSharpStyle() method. This method will serve three causes:

- It passes a string of a Visual Basic 6 style data type by reference. After the invocation, the same variable becomes a legal C# type notation.

- It returns a Boolean value to determine whether the Visual Basic 6 style notation is a user-defined data type. If it is a user-defined data type, it needs to be marshaled using the .NET PInvoke service to a structure in C#.

- It overloads once. The overloaded method takes two parameters. The first parameter is the same string variable used in the Visual Basic 6 notation. The second is a Boolean value. A true value tells the marshaling to use a C# System.StringBuilder in place of a Visual Basic 6 String type. Otherwise, it uses a C# string type to replace the Visual Basic 6 String type.

The code of the GetCSharpStyle() method is in Listing 3.5.

Listing 3.5   A Method to Convert Visual Basic 6 Data Types to C# Data Types

```
public static bool GetCSharpStyle(ref string vbStyle)
{
  string returnType = "";
  if (vbStyle.Trim() == "Long") returnType = "int";
  if (vbStyle.Trim() == "Integer") returnType = "int";
  if (vbStyle.Trim() == "String") returnType = "string";
  if (vbStyle.Trim() == "Double") returnType = "float";
  if (vbStyle.Trim() == "Any") returnType = "int";
  if (vbStyle.Trim() == "Boolean") returnType = "bool";

  if (returnType == "")
  {
    returnType = vbStyle;
    return false;
  }

  vbStyle = returnType;
  return true;
}
```

This method passes a Visual Basic 6 type notation, vbStyle, as a reference. The content of the vbStyle variable is a Visual Basic 6 type before the method invocation. It becomes a C# notation after the method invocation.

Its return type is Boolean. Functions in the Win32API.txt file contain language-defined data types and user-defined data types. When this method finds a user-defined data type, it returns a true value. In this case, the content of the vbStyle variable is intact and will be used in the C# code. The user-defined data type needs to be marshaled. The string constant, CSHP_MARSHAL_EXP_5, is for this kind of marshaling. An enumeration value of UnmanagedType.Struct marshals a C-style structure into managed formatted classes and value types. For example, the Visual Basic 6 code to declare the CreateRectRgnIndirect() function of the gdi32.dll is as follows:

```
Public Declare Function CreateRectRgnIndirect Lib "gdi32" _
Alias "CreateRectRgnIndirect" (lpRect As RECT) As Long
```

This method requires a RECT parameter. The RECT is a user-defined data type in the Win32API.TXT file. When this custom function is marshaled in a C# program, the code should look like this:

```
[DllImport("gdi32.dll")]
public static extern int
➡CreateRectRgnIndirect([MarshalAs(UnmanagedType.Struct)] ref RECT lpRect);
```

If the GetCSharpStyle() method returns a false value, i.e., the Visual Basic 6 data type is not a user defined data type, the Visual Basic 6 data types will be converted to their C# notation counterparts.

Finally, the method is overloaded to take two parameters. A true value of the Boolean parameter turns a C# string type to a C# System.StringBuilder type. The code of the overloaded method is in Listing 3.6.

Listing 3.6   Code for the Overloaded *GetCSharpStyle()* Method

```
public static bool GetCSharpStyle(ref string vbStyle, bool forFunction)
{
  GetCSharpStyle(ref vbStyle);
  if (forFunction)
  {
    if (vbStyle.Trim() == "string")
    {
      vbStyle = "StringBuilder";
    }
  }
  return true;
}
```

Many of the custom functions manipulate the string parameters. Because some custom functions don't pass parameters by reference, a C# string type can't be manipulated. But a C# System.StringBuilder type can be manipulated. For example, we called the FindWindow()

and `GetClassName()` functions of the `user32.dll` in the preceding example. The `FindWindow()` method is indifferent as to whether a variable is defined as a C# `string` or `System.StringBuilder` type. But the `GetClassName()` function only works with a variable of a `System.StringBuilder` type. After the necessary conversion from `string` to `StringBuilder`, the method returns a value of `true`.

Now, you are ready to proceed with the three child classes and their methods to read the `WIN32API.TXT` file and obtain the information with respect to constants, structures, and functions.

ConstantViewer Class

The `WIN32API.TXT` file for Windows 95 defines 418 user-defined data types, 1531 functions from various custom DLLs, and 6391 constants. It is reported that Windows XP supports more definitions than these. The Microsoft Visual Studio .NET 2003 documentation includes an article called "Identifying Functions in DLLs." Also, you can find a list of the functions with various releases in MSDN (http://msdn.microsoft.com/library/default.asp?url=/library/en-us/winprog/winprog/windows_nt_3_1.asp). However, there is currently no file similar to the `Win32API.txt` file available for the Windows XP operating system. Thus, the development of this C# API Text Viewer is based on the existing `Win32API.txt` for the older operating systems.

The typical definitions of constants in Visual Basic 6 and in `Win32API.txt` have five possible variations:

```
Const SidTypeUser = 1
Const GMEM_MOVEABLE = &H2
Const PST_SCANNER = &H22&
Const GHND = (GMEM_MOVEABLE Or GMEM_ZEROINIT)
Const ABM_ACTIVATE As Long = &H6
```

The basic formula leads the constant definition with the keyword `Const`. Then the keyword is followed by a name of the constant, an equal sign (=), and a value. The first case assigns an integer decimal value to `SidTypeUser`. The second case assigns an integer hex value to `GMEM_MOVEABLE`. The third case assigns a long hex value to `PST_SCANNER`. The fourth case uses an `Or` operator to assign a combination of two constants to `GHND`. These four cases all omit the `As` keyword and the data type keyword. Possible definitions of constants in the `Win32API.txt` file can also be like the last case with the `As` and data type keywords.

The C# counterparts of the definitions should look like these:

```
public const int SidTypeUser = 1;
public const int GMEM_MOVEABLE = 0x2;
public const int PST_SCANNER = 0x22;
public const int GHND = (GMEM_MOVEABLE | GMEM_ZEROINIT);
public const int ABM_ACTIVATE = 0x6 ;
```

All the constants are declared as integers for C#. The hex number are denoted with an &H prefix in Visual Basic 6 but with 0x in C#. Plus, there are other subtle differences. In order to achieve the correct C# code via a tool, in this section you'll build a ConstantViewer class.

Follow the steps you followed in the preceding sections to add a new class to the CSharp-APITextViewer project. Name this class ConstantViewer. Then with ConstantViewer.cs open in the code editor, add the code in Listing 3.7.

Listing 3.7   **Code for the Completed *ConstantViewer* Class**

```csharp
using System;
using System.Collections;
using System.IO;

namespace CSharpAPITextViewer
{

  public class ConstantViewer : APITextViewer
  {
    public ConstantViewer(string m_Filename) : base(m_Filename)
    {
    }

    public override void ParseText()
    {
      StreamReader sr = new StreamReader(filename);
      string input =sr.ReadLine();

      while (null != input)
      {
        // Ignore comments
        while (input.Trim().StartsWith("'"))
          input=sr.ReadLine();

        APIUtility.GetRidExtraSpaces(ref input);

        if (input.StartsWith("Const "))
        {
          string cKey = input.Split(' ')[1];

          string cshpType = "int";
          if (input.IndexOf(" As ")>0)
          {
            input = input.Replace(" As ", " : ");
            cshpType = input.Split(':')[1].Trim();
            cshpType = cshpType.Substring(0, cshpType.IndexOf(" "));
            input = input.Replace(": " + cshpType, "");
            APIUtility.GetCSharpStyle(ref cshpType);
          }
```

```
          string cSharpCode = APIUtility.CSHP_SCOPE + " " + input + ";\n";
          cSharpCode = cSharpCode.Replace(
➡APIUtility.VB_CONST_LEADING, APIUtility.CSHP_CONST_LEADING);
          cSharpCode = cSharpCode.Replace(
➡APIUtility.VB_HEX_EXP, APIUtility.CSHP_HEX_EXP);
          cSharpCode = cSharpCode.Replace(APIUtility.VB_OR, APIUtility.CSHP_OR);
          cSharpCode = cSharpCode.Replace("&'", "; //");
          cSharpCode = cSharpCode.Replace("'", "; //");
          cSharpCode = cSharpCode.Replace("&;", ";");

          AddCSharpCode(cKey, cSharpCode);
          cSharpCode = "";
        }
        input = sr.ReadLine();
      }
      sr.Close();
    }
  }
}
```

The `ConstantViewer` class is also coded under the `CSharpAPITextViewer` namespace. In order to inherit all the definitions from the `APITextViewer` class, you code the `ConstantViewer` class constructor as follows:

```
public class ConstantViewer : APITextViewer
{
  public ConstantViewer(string m_Filename) : base(m_Filename)
  {
  }
}
```

The `m_Filename` is passed to the base class. The base `APITextViewer` class defines a virtual method, `ParseText()`, which is the only method in need of implementation in this `ConstantViewer` class.

You start to implement a virtual method inherited from a base class by leading the method name with an `override` keyword:

```
public override void ParseText()
{
}
```

Add the code between the curly brackets. This method first uses a `StreamReader` object, `sr`, to open the text file. The following line shows how the initialization of the `sr` object is coded:

```
StreamReader sr = new StreamReader(filename);
```

Then, the `ReadLine()` method is called to retrieve data from the `WIN32API.TXT` file line by line and to assign the content to the `input` variable. The outer `while` loop is used to read the entire file. The inside `while` loop checks whether the line read is a comment by looking for the leading single quotation (') mark. Then it invokes the static `GetRidExtraSpaces()` method from the `APIUtility` class to get rid of any extra spaces the line has. Finally, it looks for the leading `Const` keyword. If the keyword is located, it removes the `As` keyword for the Visual Basic 6 language and changes this line to a C# constant declaration by calling a series of the `Replace()` method of the String class. After this line is converted to correct C# syntax, it is added to the `definitionList` by calling the `AddCSharpCode()` method.

This process will be continued until the last line of the text file is read.

DllImportViewer Class

The following lines show how the custom functions in the `Win32API.txt` file are defined:

```
Public Declare Function FindWindow Lib "user32" Alias _
"FindWindowA" (ByVal lpClassName As String, _
ByVal lpWindowName As String) As Long
```

They can also be defined as follows:

```
Public Declare Sub CopyMemory Lib "kernel32" Alias _
"RtlMoveMemory" (Destination As Any, Source As Any, _
ByVal Length As Long)
```

Here is the C# code for the first example:

```
[DllImport("user32.dll")]
public static extern int FindWindow(StringBuilder lpClassName, StringBuilder
lpWindowName);
```

Here is the C# code for the second example:

```
[DllImport("kernel32.dll")]
public static extern void CopyMemory(int Destination, int Source, int Length);
```

To achieve the C# code, we need to enable this tool to analyze the code word by word. For example, we can divide the preceding C# code into five parts:

1. The C# syntax leads a function declaration with a `DllImport` attribute. The variable part is the name of the custom DLL inside an opening and closing parentheses.

2. A new line begins with the scope keyword, `public` or `private`. The keywords `static` and `extern` are present in all definitions in the same order.

3. The return type follows. It can be extrapolated from the third word of the original Visual Basic 6 text. A `Sub` in Visual Basic 6 denotes a `void` return type in C#. A `Function` in Visual Basic 6 finds the last word to be the return type of C# code.

4. Next is the name of the function, which follows the return type indication.

5. The final elements are the required parameters, which are in a pair of parentheses in the original text.

Now add a new class to the project and name this class DllImportViewer. Before we start to override the ParseText() virtual method, we need to implement five helper methods. The first method, GetDllName(), will help to get the name of the custom DLL from the original text. The code is in Listing 3.8.

Listing 3.8   **Code to Get the Custom DLL Name**

```
private string GetDllName(string dllName)
{
  if (dllName.ToLower().IndexOf(".dll")>0)
    return dllName;

  dllName = dllName.Replace("\"", "").Trim();
  dllName = "\"" + dllName + ".dll" + "\"";
  return dllName;
}
```

The Visual Basic 6 code doesn't have to have the .dll extension to locate the custom DLL, but the C# code must have the .dll extension appended. This helper method checks whether WIN32API.TXT includes the extension in the filename. If the .dll extension is not included, it is added to the name of the DLL to comply with C# grammar.

The second helper method is the GetFunctionReturnType() method to extrapolate the return type for the C# code (Listing 3.9).

Listing 3.9   **Code to Extrapolate the Return Type**

```
private string GetFunctionReturnType(string[] pieces)
{
  if (pieces[1].Trim() == "Sub")
  {
    return "void";
  }
  else
  {
    APIUtility.GetCSharpStyle(ref pieces[pieces.Length-1]);
    return pieces[pieces.Length-1];
  }
}
```

It looks for the keyword Sub. If it finds the word, the return type is void. Otherwise, it goes to the end of the original line to find the return type by calling the static GetCSharpStyle() method from the APIUtility class.

Next you implement a third method, MakeAParameter(), to manufacture a parameter (Listing 3.10).

⊃ **Listing 3.10**   **Code to Coin a C# Parameter**

```
private string MakeAParameter(string paramA)
{
  paramA = paramA.Trim().Replace(" As ", " ");
  string[] pPieces = paramA.Split(' ');
  int pLen = pPieces.Length;

if (pPieces[0].Trim() == "ByRef")
  {
    APIUtility.GetCSharpStyle(ref pPieces[pLen-1], true);
    return "ref " + pPieces[pLen-1] + " " + pPieces[pLen-2];
  }

  if (!APIUtility.GetCSharpStyle(ref pPieces[pLen-1]))
  {
    pPieces[pLen-1] = APIUtility.CSHP_MARSHAL_EXP_5 + pPieces[pLen-1];
  }
  APIUtility.GetCSharpStyle(ref pPieces[pLen-1], true);
  return pPieces[pLen-1] + " " + pPieces[pLen-2];
}
```

The composition of a Visual Basic 6 parameter in WIN32API.TXT usually has four parts, such as in the following two examples:

```
ByVal Length As Long
ByRef Length As Long
```

Here is the corresponding C# code for each example:

```
int Length;
ref int Length;
```

The first statement of this method looks for the keyword As in the Visual Basic 6 code. The word at the left of the keyword is the parameter name, and the word at the right of the keyword is the parameter type. After the Visual Basic 6 parameter composition is split into parts, it checks whether this parameter is passed by reference. If the current parameter is passed by reference, the method invokes the static GetCSharpStyle() method and converts the Visual Basic 6 syntax into C# code. Otherwise, the method determines whether the parameter is a user-defined type by calling the static GetCSharpStyle() method with the last word of the original Visual Basic 6 syntax as the input parameter. Then it calls the overloaded GetCSharpStyle() method to get the System.StringBuilder parameter if the parameter type is string. Finally, it makes a legal C# variable declaration for a parameter not passed by reference.

The MakeAParameter() method makes only one parameter in a function. However, a custom function can take zero to many parameters. Therefore, the next method, ParseParameters(), is implemented to deal with functions taking any number of parameters (Listing 3.11).

Listing 3.11   *ParseParameters*( ) Helper Method to Make Different Kinds of Parameter Compositions in C# Code

```csharp
private string ParseParameters(string input)
{
  int ArrParamCount = 0;
  string tempInput = input;
  foreach (char chr1 in input.ToCharArray())
  {
    if (chr1 == '(')
      ArrParamCount ++;
  }
  if (ArrParamCount > 1)
  {
    input = input.Replace("()", "[]");
  }

  string paramStr = input.Substring(input.IndexOf("("));
  if (!paramStr.EndsWith(")"))
    paramStr = paramStr.Substring(0, paramStr.IndexOf(")")+1);

  if (paramStr == "()")
    return paramStr;

  paramStr = paramStr.Replace("(", "");
  paramStr = paramStr.Replace(")", "");

  string[] paramArr  = paramStr.Split(',');
  paramStr = "";
  for (int i = 0; i < paramArr.Length; i++)
  {
    if (i == paramArr.Length - 1)
      paramStr += MakeAParameter(paramArr[i]);
    else
      paramStr += MakeAParameter(paramArr[i]) + ", ";
  }
  return "(" + paramStr + ")";
}
```

The ParseParameters() method first uses a foreach loop to count the number of opening parentheses. If more than one is found, the custom function has parameters passed by array. A set of opening and closing parentheses declares an array parameter in Visual Basic 6 programs. But C# programs need a set of opening and closing square brackets to declare an array parameter. At this point, if more than one open parenthesis is found, the ParseParameters() method replaces the set of parentheses with a set of opening and closing square brackets.

After the ParseParameters() method handles the parentheses with regard to the array parameter, there is still one pair of open and close parentheses with at least one parameter definition between them. Because the information of all the needed parameters is included in this pair, the ParseParameters() method truncates the text to the left of the open parenthesis. Then, it truncates the text on the right side of the close parentheses by using the SubString() method of the String class. If the remaining text is a pair of parentheses, the custom function takes 0 parameters. The method returns the pair of parentheses and stops here. Finally, it removes the remaining parentheses.

Next, when there is more than one parameter, the method separates the parameters where a comma appears. Finally, it calls the MakeAParameter() help method to complete the parameter declaration one by one within a for loop.

The last helper method is the CompleteDllImportCoding() method (Listing 3.12).

Listing 3.12   Code of the *CompleteDllImportCoding()* Helper Method

```
private string CompleteDllImportCoding(string dllName,
➡string retType, string funcName, string paramStr)
{
  string dllCode = APIUtility.CSHP_MARSHAL_EXP_3.Replace(
➡APIUtility.REPLACEABlE, dllName);
  dllCode += APIUtility.CSHP_SCOPE + APIUtility.CSHP_MARSHAL_EXP_4
➡+ retType + " ";
  dllCode += funcName + paramStr + ";\n";
  return dllCode;
}
```

The CompleteDllImportCoding() helper method simply adds up the code parts found by the first four helper methods. Then it returns the whole declaration as a string with C# syntax. Now you have all the help from the helper methods.

At this point, you are ready to implement the ParseText() virtual method for the DllImportViewer class. Remember, the DllImportViewer class inherits from the APITextViewer base class as the ConstantViewer class does. The base class has prepared a text filename and a sorted list. The goal of implementing the method is to convert the Visual Basic 6 syntax in the text file to C# syntax and push the C# code segments into the sorted lest. The code is in Listing 3.13.

Listing 3.13   Code for Overriding the *ParseText()* Virtual Method in the *DllImportViewer* Class

```
public override void ParseText()
{
  StreamReader sr = new StreamReader(filename);
  string input =sr.ReadLine();

  while (null != input)
```

```
  {
    while (input.Trim().StartsWith("'"))
      input=sr.ReadLine();

    APIUtility.GetRidExtraSpaces(ref input);
    if (input.StartsWith("Declare "))
    {
      string[] pieces = input.Split(' ');

      string returnType = GetFunctionReturnType(pieces);
      string funcName = pieces[2];
      string dllName = GetDllName(pieces[4]);
      string paramStr = ParseParameters(input);
      string cSharpCode =
➡CompleteDllImportCodeing(dllName, returnType, funcName, paramStr);
      AddCSharpCode(funcName, cSharpCode);
    }

    input = sr.ReadLine();
  }
  sr.Close();

}
```

As with the ConstantViewer class, a while loop is used to read the text file line by line to override the ParseText() method. Then it ignores the comment lines and cleans the extra spaces. When it finds a line starting with the keyword Declare, it calls the previously implemented helper methods to get the needed parts and reassemble them in the syntax of the C# language. Finally, it calls the AddCSharpCode() method to add to the definitionList field implemented in the base class the function name and its C# presentation.

Now you can build the project by pressing Ctrl+Shift+B. If your code doesn't compile smoothly, you can examine Listing 3.14, which includes the full code list for the DllImportViewer class.

Listing 3.14   **The Code for the *DllImportViewer* Class**

```
using System;
using System.Collections;
using System.IO;

namespace CSharpAPITextViewer
{

  public class DllImportViewer : APITextViewer
  {
    public DllImportViewer(string filename) : base(filename)
    {
    }
```

```
    public override void ParseText()
    {
      StreamReader sr = new StreamReader(filename);
      string input =sr.ReadLine();

      while (null != input)
      {
        while (input.Trim().StartsWith("'"))
          input=sr.ReadLine();

        APIUtility.GetRidExtraSpaces(ref input);
        if (input.StartsWith("Declare "))
        {
          string[] pieces = input.Split(' ');

          string returnType = GetFunctionReturnType(pieces);
          string funcName = pieces[2];
          string dllName = GetDllName(pieces[4]);
          string paramStr = ParseParameters(input);
          string cSharpCode =
➥CompleteDllImportCoding(dllName, returnType, funcName, paramStr);
          AddCSharpCode(funcName, cSharpCode);
        }

        input = sr.ReadLine();
      }
      sr.Close();

    }

    private string CompleteDllImportCoding(string dllName,
➥string retType, string funcName, string paramStr)
    {
      string dllCode;
      dllCode = APIUtility.CSHP_MARSHAL_EXP_3.Replace(
➥APIUtility.REPLACEABlE, dllName);
      dllCode += APIUtility.CSHP_SCOPE +
➥APIUtility.CSHP_MARSHAL_EXP_4 + retType + " ";
      dllCode += funcName + paramStr + ";\n";
      return dllCode;
    }

    private string ParseParameters(string input)
    {
      int ArrParamCount = 0;
      string tempInput = input;
      foreach (char chr1 in input.ToCharArray())
      {
        if (chr1 == '(')
          ArrParamCount ++;
      }
```

```csharp
    if (ArrParamCount > 1)
    {
      input = input.Replace("()", "[]");
    }

    string paramStr = input.Substring(input.IndexOf("("));
    if (!paramStr.EndsWith(")"))
      paramStr = paramStr.Substring(0, paramStr.IndexOf(")")+1);

    if (paramStr == "()")
      return paramStr;

    paramStr = paramStr.Replace("(", "");
    paramStr = paramStr.Replace(")", "");

    string[] paramArr  = paramStr.Split(',');
    paramStr = "";
    for (int i = 0; i < paramArr.Length; i++)
    {
      if (i == paramArr.Length - 1)
        paramStr += MakeAParameter(paramArr[i]);
      else
        paramStr += MakeAParameter(paramArr[i]) + ", ";

    }
    return "(" + paramStr + ")";

  }

  private string MakeAParameter(string paramA)
  {
    paramA = paramA.Trim().Replace(" As ", " ");
    string[] pPieces = paramA.Split(' ');
    int pLen = pPieces.Length;

    if (pPieces[0].Trim() == "ByRef")
    {
      APIUtility.GetCSharpStyle(ref pPieces[pLen-1], true);
      return "ref " + pPieces[pLen-1] + " " + pPieces[pLen-2];
    }

    if (!APIUtility.GetCSharpStyle(ref pPieces[pLen-1]))
    {
      pPieces[pLen-1] = APIUtility.CSHP_MARSHAL_EXP_5 + pPieces[pLen-1];
    }
      APIUtility.GetCSharpStyle(ref pPieces[pLen-1], true);
      return pPieces[pLen-1] + " " + pPieces[pLen-2];
  }

  private string GetDllName(string dllName)
  {
```

```
    if (dllName.ToLower().IndexOf(".dll")>0)
      return dllName;

    dllName = dllName.Replace("\"", "").Trim();
    dllName = "\"" + dllName + ".dll" + "\"";
    return dllName;
  }

  private string GetFunctionReturnType(string[] pieces)
  {
    if (pieces[1].Trim() == "Sub")
    {
      return "void";
    }
    else
    {
      APIUtility.GetCSharpStyle(ref pieces[pieces.Length-1]);
      return pieces[pieces.Length-1];
    }
  }
 }
}
```

StructViewer Class

Visual Basic 6 uses the keyword Type to start a user-defined data type. The counterpart in C#
is struct. For example, here is how Visual Basic 6 defines a RECT type:

```
Public Type RECT
  Left As Long
  Top As Long
  Right As Long
  Bottom As Long
End Type
```

To translate the Visual Basic 6 RECT type into a C# struct by hand, the code becomes this:

```
[StructLayout(LayoutKind.Sequential)]
public struct RECT
{
    public int Left;
    public int Top;
    public int Right;
    public int Bottom;
}
```

You use the first line to activate the .NET PInvoke service. Then you replace the Type keyword with the struct keyword. You change the Visual Basic 6 grammar to C# grammar. C#
code also requires a pair of curly brackets to start and end the struct definition.

Now, we can start with a simple type such as the RECT to program the StructViewer class. Note that a constant or a function declaration in the WIN32API.TXT file occupies only one line, but a structure definition extends to more than one line. Thus, you first need a helper method to determine whether a type definition is encountered. Listing 3.15 contains the code for an IsStructStart() helper method.

Listing 3.15   Code for the *IsStruct()* Helper Method

```
private bool IsStructStart(string input)
{
  if (input.Trim().StartsWith("Type"))
  {
    return true;
  }
  else
  {
    return false;
  }
}
```

The method simply looks for the keyword Type in the beginning of each line read from WIN32API.TXT. If a leading Type is found, it returns a true value. Otherwise, it returns a false value.

After locating the beginning of a Type definition, you need to implement a DefineCShpStruct() method to create the C# header for a user-defined data type. The code for this method is in Listing 3.16.

Listing 3.16   The Second Helper Method of the *StructViewer()* Class

```
private string DefineCShpStruct(string input, ref string sKey)
{
  string[] structInfo = input.Split(' ');
  string cSharpStruct = APIUtility.CSHP_MARSHAL_EXP_6;
  cSharpStruct += APIUtility.CSHP_SCOPE + " struct " + structInfo[1] + "\n{\n";
  cSharpStruct= cSharpStruct.Replace("'", "//");
  sKey = structInfo[1];
  return cSharpStruct;
}
```

To find the name of the user-defined data type in Visual Basic 6 grammar, the method splits the line into words. Then it creates a string variable with the value of the CSHP_MARSHAL_EXP_6 constant. The CSHP_MARSHAL_EXP_6 constant is a .NET marshaling attribute:

```
[StructLayout(LayoutKind.Sequential)]
```

The next statement combines the scope constant, the struct keywords, and the name of the type in C# syntax. If the line contains a Visual Basic 6 comment notation, the method changes it to two slashes, //, which indicates the C# style comment. Finally, it assigns the type name to a sKey string variable and returns the struct header.

One more helper method is needed to parse the body of the type definition. Listing 3.17 is the helper method of DefineCShpStructBody().

Listing 3.17   **Code for the *DefineCShpStructBody()* Method to Marshal the Type's Body**

```
private string DefineCShpStructBody(string input)
{
  if (input == "")
  {
    return "";
  }

  input = input.Replace(" as ", APIUtility.VB_AS);
  input = input.Replace(APIUtility.VB_AS, " ^ ");
  string[] pieces = input.Split('^');

  string cSharpStruct = "";
  if (input.IndexOf("*") > 0)
  {
    cSharpStruct = APIUtility.CSHP_MARSHAL_EXP_1.Replace(
➥APIUtility.REPLACEABlE, input.Split('*')[1].Trim());
    pieces[1] = pieces[1].Replace("* " + input.Split('*')[1].Trim(), "");
  }

  if (pieces[0].IndexOf("(") > 0)
  {
    string[] arrSeps = pieces[0].Split('(');
    pieces[0] = arrSeps[0];
    cSharpStruct = APIUtility.CSHP_MARSHAL_EXP_2.Replace(
➥APIUtility.REPLACEABlE, arrSeps[1]);
  }

  cSharpStruct += APIUtility.CSHP_SCOPE + " ";
  APIUtility.GetCSharpStyle(ref pieces[1]);
  cSharpStruct += pieces[1] + " ";
  cSharpStruct += pieces[0].Trim() + ";\n";
  cSharpStruct = cSharpStruct.Replace(" '", "; //");
  cSharpStruct = cSharpStruct.Replace("'", "; //");
  return "    " + cSharpStruct;
}
```

The DefineCShpStructBody() method is a little lengthier than the previous methods. But it is not difficult to understand. I intentionally wrote this method into five clusters. The first if statement checks whether the line read is empty and ignores it if it is.

Then it looks for the As keyword to separate the field into name and data type.

The third cluster looks for an asterisk (*) to marshal an array field. In this case, a value of the UnmanagedType.ByValTStr enumeration is used for in-line fixed-length character arrays that appear within a structure.

The fourth cluster looks for an open parenthesis to handle another array situation. In this case, the MarshalAsAttribute value is set to UnmanagedType.ByValArray. A SizeConst is needed to indicate the number of elements in the array. This UnmanagedType can be used only on an array that appears as fields in a structure.

The last cluster rearranges the already defined parts into a field in a C# style structure and returns the rearrangement.

Now you can write the last ParseText() method as shown in Listing 3.18.

Listing 3.18   **Code for the Last *ParseText()* Method**

```csharp
public override void ParseText()
{
  bool structStart = false;
  bool structEnd = false;
  string cSharpCode = "";
  string structKey = "";

  StreamReader sr = new StreamReader(filename);
  string input = sr.ReadLine();

  while (null != input)
  {
    while (input.Trim().StartsWith("'"))
      input = sr.ReadLine();

    APIUtility.GetRidExtraSpaces(ref input);

    if (IsStruct(input))
    {
      structStart = true;
      structEnd = false;
      cSharpCode += DefineCShpStruct(input, ref structKey);
      input = sr.ReadLine();
      continue;
    }

    if (structStart)
    {
      if (input.Trim().StartsWith(APIUtility.VB_END_TYPE))
      {
        structStart = false;
        structEnd = true;
```

```
          cSharpCode +="}\n";
          AddCSharpCode(structKey, cSharpCode);
          structKey = "";
          cSharpCode = "";
          input = sr.ReadLine();
          continue;
        }
        else if (!structEnd)
        {
          cSharpCode += DefineCShpStructBody(input);
          input = sr.ReadLine();
          continue;
        }
      }
      input = sr.ReadLine();
    }
    sr.Close();
  }
```

The major goal of this `ParseText()` method is to set the type name to the `structKey` variable and the C# structure definition to the `cSharpCode` variable. As usual, it uses a `while` loop to read the text file. The nested `while` loop ignores the comment lines. After the text is trimmed to clean out the extra spaces, several `if` statements are used to check and set the Boolean values of the `structStart` and `structEnd` variables. Finally, the `if` statements make the C# structure header, marshal the fields, close the structure definition, and add the C# style structure into the definition list.

You can check the code for the entire `StructViewer` class in Listing 3.19.

Listing 3.19   **The Full List of the *StructViewer* Class**

```
using System;
using System.Collections;
using System.IO;

namespace CSharpAPITextViewer
{
  public class StructViewer : APITextViewer
  {
    public StructViewer(string m_filename) : base(m_filename)
    {
    }

    public override void ParseText()
    {
      bool structStart = false;
      bool structEnd = false;

      string cSharpCode = "";
      string structKey = "";
```

```
    StreamReader sr = new StreamReader(filename);
    string input = sr.ReadLine();


    while (null != input)
    {
      while (input.Trim().StartsWith("'"))
        input = sr.ReadLine();

      APIUtility.GetRidExtraSpaces(ref input);

      if (IsStruct(input))
      {
        structStart = true;
        structEnd = false;
        cSharpCode += DefineCShpStruct(input, ref structKey);
        input = sr.ReadLine();
        continue;
      }
      if (structStart)
      {
        if (input.Trim().StartsWith(APIUtility.VB_END_TYPE))
        {
          structStart = false;
          structEnd = true;

          cSharpCode +="}\n";
          AddCSharpCode(structKey, cSharpCode);
          structKey = "";
          cSharpCode = "";
          input = sr.ReadLine();
          continue;
        }
        else if (!structEnd)
        {
          cSharpCode += DefineCShpStructBody(input);
          input = sr.ReadLine();
          continue;
        }
      }
      input = sr.ReadLine();
    }
    sr.Close();
  }

  private string DefineCShpStructBody(string input)
  {
    if (input == "")
    {
      return "";
    }
    input = input.Replace(" as ", APIUtility.VB_AS);
    input = input.Replace(APIUtility.VB_AS, " ^ ");
```

```
        string[] pieces = input.Split('^');

        string cSharpStruct = "";
        if (input.IndexOf("*") > 0)
        {
            cSharpStruct=APIUtility.CSHP_MARSHAL_EXP_1.Replace(
➡APIUtility.REPLACEABlE, input.Split('*')[1].Trim());
            pieces[1] = pieces[1].Replace("* " + input.Split('*')[1].Trim(), "");
        }
        if (pieces[0].IndexOf("(") > 0)
        {
            string[] arrSeps = pieces[0].Split('(');
            pieces[0] = arrSeps[0];
            cSharpStruct=APIUtility.CSHP_MARSHAL_EXP_2.Replace(
➡APIUtility.REPLACEABlE, arrSeps[1]);

        }

        cSharpStruct += APIUtility.CSHP_SCOPE + " ";
        APIUtility.GetCSharpStyle(ref pieces[1]);
        cSharpStruct += pieces[1] + " ";
        cSharpStruct += pieces[0].Trim() + ";\n";
        cSharpStruct = cSharpStruct.Replace("  ", "; //");
        cSharpStruct = cSharpStruct.Replace("'", "; //");
        return "    " + cSharpStruct;
    }

    private string DefineCShpStruct(string input, ref string sKey)
    {
        string[] structInfo = input.Split(' ');
        string cSharpStruct = APIUtility.CSHP_MARSHAL_EXP_6;
        cSharpStruct += APIUtility.CSHP_SCOPE +
➡" struct " + structInfo[1] + "\n{\n";
        cSharpStruct= cSharpStruct.Replace("'", "//");
        sKey = structInfo[1];
        return cSharpStruct;
    }

    private bool IsStruct(string input)
    {
        if (input.Trim().StartsWith("Type"))
        {
            return true;
        }
        else
        {
            return false;
        }
    }
  }
}
```

Now you have prepared all the pieces for the C# API Text Viewer. The last thing to do is display the converted C# definitions stored in the definition lists. To do this, you will program the Windows form and make a user-friendly GUI.

GUI of the C# API Text Viewer

When you started the CSharpTextViewer project, the Microsoft Visual Studio .NET IDE created a Windows form with a default name, Form1. The code for this form is saved as Form1.cs. Open the Solution Explorer, rename the file CSharpTextViewer.cs, and keep the rest intact. Then add the GUI components onto the form as they are described in the following list (just change the values of the listed properties and accept the default values of the other properties):

Control	Property	Value
MainMenu	Name	mnuMainAPI
OpenFileDialog	Name	opnFileDialog
Label	Text	API Type:
Label	Text	Type the first few letters of the function name you look for:
Label	Text	Available functions:
Label	Text	Selected functions:
ComboBox	Name	cmbAPITypes
TextBox	Name	txtLookfor
	Text	Look for functions
ListBox	Name	lstAvailableFuncs
RichTextBox	Name	txtSelected
	Text	Selected functions
Button	Name	btnAdd
	Text	Add
Button	Name	btnRemove
	Text	Remove
Button	Name	btnClear
	Text	Clear
Button	Name	btnCopy
	Text	Copy

Control	Property	Value
GroupBox	Name	grpScope
RadioButton	Name	rdPublic
	Text	public
RadioButton	Name	rdPrivate
	Text	private

Follow these steps to make a File menu and a Help menu.

1. Select the mnuMainAPI GUI object at the bottom below the form. The menu object on the top of the form displays a gray string Type Here.

2. Type **File** to replace the words *Type Here*. The word *File* appears on the main menu. Select the File menu and its (Name) property. Set its name to mnuFile.

3. Type **Help** as in step 2 to make its (Name) property mnuHelp.

4. Select the File menu. Replace the words *Type Here* with **Open** to create a submenu under the File menu. Set its (Name) property to mnuFileOpen.

5. Type a hyphen (-) below the Open menu. Set its name to mnuFileSep.

6. Type **Exit** below mnuFileSep. Set its name to mnuFileExit.

7. You can repeat step 4 to create a submenu under the Help menu. However, I leave the coding task for the Help clicking event in your hands.

Figure 3.4 shows the populated menu items.

After you finish populating the GUI controls, the Windows form looks like the form in Figure 3.5.

Now, the front end GUI objects are completely done. You need to add code for the buttons and the menu items. Based on the requirements of the API Text Viewer, these menu items and the buttons should perform the following actions when they are clicked:

Exit menu   Terminate the application.

Open menu   Initialize the ConstantViewer, DllImportViewer, and StructViewer classes with Win32API.txt.

FIGURE 3.4
The appearance of the
main menu for the C#
API Text Viewer project

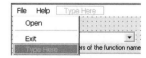

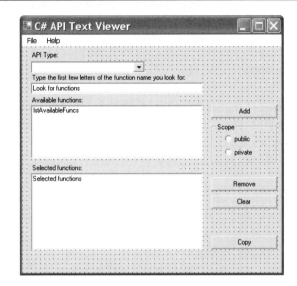

Help menu   Provide users with instructive help. However, this chapter will not include code for this menu. You can add instructional help hints for users later. For reference, the sample source code on www.sybex.com has an example of a Help menu code.

cmbAPITypes ComoBox   Populate items of Constants, Types and Declares. When an item is selected, the corresponding keys of the definition list are loaded into the lstAvailableFuncs object.

txtLookFor TextBox   As the user types in the first few letters, the C# API Text Viewer will select a Win32 custom function which starts with the letters in the lstAvailableFuncs object.

btnAdd Button   Append the C# definition from a definition list according to the selected item in the lstAvailableFuncs object.

btnRemove Button   Remove a line of text located where the cursor is in the txtSelected (RichTextBox) object.

btnClear Button   Clear the text in the txtSelected text box.

btnCopy Button   Set the text in the txtSelected text box to the clipboard. Later, the user can paste the clipboard contents into the code editor in the Microsoft Visual Studio .NET IDE.

To start the implementation for the Exit menu, double-click the Exit menu item from the form editor. The Microsoft Visual Studio .NET IDE brings your cursor to the code editor.

Between the curly brackets of the automated generated code skeleton, type in code like this:

```
private void mnuFileExit_Click(object sender, System.EventArgs e)
{
  Application.Exit();
}
```

Addition of the `Application.Exit()` is self-explanatory. When the Exit menu is clicked, `Application.Exit()` is invoked to terminate this session of the C# API Text Viewer. Then double-click the Open menu and code this `mnuFileOpen_Click()` event as follows:

```
private void mnuFileOpen_Click(object sender, System.EventArgs e)
{
  string filename = "";
  if (opnFileDialog.ShowDialog() == DialogResult.OK)
  {
    filename = opnFileDialog.FileName;
    OpenAPITextFile(filename);
  }
  else
    return;

}
```

The `mnuFileOpen_Click()` event first simply opens a File Open dialog box. After the user selects a text file, it executes an `OpenAPITextFile()` helper method as the following code shows:

```
private ConstantViewer constViewer;
private StructViewer structViewer;
private DllImportViewer dllImportViewer;

private void OpenAPITextFile(string filename)
{
  FillAPITypeCombobox();

  constViewer = new ConstantViewer(filename);
  Thread tConst = new Thread(new ThreadStart(constViewer.ParseText));
  tConst.Start();
  structViewer = new StructViewer(filename);
  Thread tStruct = new Thread(new ThreadStart(structViewer.ParseText));
  tStruct.Start();
  dllImportViewer = new DllImportViewer(filename);
  Thread tDllImport = new Thread(new ThreadStart(dllImportViewer.ParseText));
  tDllImport.Start();

  System.Threading.Thread.Sleep(1000);
  this.cmbAPITypes.Text = this.cmbAPITypes.Items[1].ToString();
}
```

The declarations of the three private fields, constViewer, structViewer, and dllImportViewer, enable other helper methods within the class to have access to them after they are initialized inside the OpenAPITextFile() method. Within the method declaration, the first line invokes another helper method to populate the definition categories into the ComboBox object, cmbAPITypes. The code for the FillAPITypeCombobox() helper method is as follows:

```
private void FillAPITypeCombobox()
{
    cmbAPITypes.Items.Clear();
    cmbAPITypes.Items.Add("Constants");
    cmbAPITypes.Items.Add("Declares");
    cmbAPITypes.Items.Add("Types");
}
```

This FillAPITypeCombobox() helper method calls the Add() method of the ComboBox control and the possible values. The rest of the code in the OpenAPITextFile() method simply initializes objects of the ConstantViewer, DllImportViewer, and StructViewer classes, respectively, and start threads to invoke the ParseText() methods in sequence. When all the objects are initialized, it uses the Sleep() method from the Thread class to let the program pause for a second. This will allow time for the execution to respond to the cmbAPITypes_SelectedIndexChanged() event.

After coding the OpenAPITextFile() method, you double-click the ComboBox object, cmbAPITypes. Add code to the cmbAPITypes_SelectedIndexChanged() event:

```
private void cmbAPITypes_SelectedIndexChanged(object sender, System.EventArgs e)
{
    Thread tConst;

    switch (cmbAPITypes.Text)
    {
        case "Constants":
            tConst = new Thread(new ThreadStart(UpdateConstants));
            tConst.Start();
            break;
        case "Declares":
            tConst = new Thread(new ThreadStart(UpdateDllImports));
            tConst.Start();
            break;
        case "Types":
            tConst = new Thread(new ThreadStart(UpdateStructs));
            tConst.Start();
            break;
    }
}
```

In each case, when the selected index in the `ComboBox` object is changed, the change of selected index starts a thread to invoke one of the three helper methods. The `UpdateConstants()` method is coded as follows:

```
private void UpdateConstants()
{
  int i;
  Monitor.Enter(this);
  this.lstAvailableFuncs.Items.Clear();
  for (i = 0; i < constViewer.Count; i++)
  {
    this.lstAvailableFuncs.Items.Add(constViewer.GetKey(i));
  }
  Monitor.Exit(this);
}
```

The `UpdateConstants()` method calls a pair of static methods, `Monitor.Enter()` and `Monitor.Exit()`, from the Threading namespace. The `Monitor` class controls access to objects by granting a lock for an object to a single thread. Object locks provide the ability to restrict access to a block of code, commonly called a critical section. While a thread owns the lock for an object, no other thread can acquire that lock. You can also use `Monitor` to ensure that no other thread is allowed to access a section of application code being executed by the lock owner unless the other thread is executing the code using a different locked object. Within the monitor method calls, a `for` loop adds all the constant names to the list box by invoking the `GetKey()` method.

The code for the `UpdateDllImports()` and `UpdateStructs()` methods are very similar to the code for the `UpdateConstants()` method. The only difference is that each uses an object of a particular class to update the list box:

```
private void UpdateDllImports()
{
  int i;
  Monitor.Enter(this);
  this.lstAvailableFuncs.Items.Clear();
  for (i = 0; i < dllImportViewer.Count; i++)
  {
    lstAvailableFuncs.Items.Add(dllImportViewer.GetKey(i));
  }
  Monitor.Exit(this);
}

private void UpdateStructs()
{
  int i;
  Monitor.Enter(this);
  lstAvailableFuncs.Items.Clear();
```

```
  for (i = 0; i < structViewer.Count; i++)
  {
    lstAvailableFuncs.Items.Add(structViewer.GetKey(i));
  }
  Monitor.Exit(this);
}
```

Thus, when the text is changed in the combo box, the content in the list box is changed accordingly. Double-click the TextBox object, txtLookFor. Add code to change the selected index in the list box when the txtLookfor_TextChanged() event is triggered:

```
private void txtLookfor_TextChanged(object sender, System.EventArgs e)
{
  lstAvailableFuncs.SelectedIndex =
➥lstAvailableFuncs.FindString(txtLookfor.Text);
}
```

This is also a simple event to code. The list box uses its FindString() method to match the first part of an item with the text in the text box. When an item matches, that item is selected.

Next you are going to code the remaining buttons. To code the Add button, double-click the Add button in the design editor and insert code for the btnAdd_Click() event in the code editor:

```
private void btnAdd_Click(object sender, System.EventArgs e)
{
  string cSharpCode = "";
  switch (this.cmbAPITypes.Text)
  {
    case "Types":
      cSharpCode = structViewer.GetCSharpSyntax(
➥lstAvailableFuncs.SelectedIndex);
      break;
    case "Declares":
      cSharpCode = dllImportViewer.GetCSharpSyntax(
➥lstAvailableFuncs.SelectedIndex);
      break;
    case "Constants":
      cSharpCode = constViewer.GetCSharpSyntax(
➥lstAvailableFuncs.SelectedIndex);
      break;
  }
  if (rdPrivate.Checked)
  {
    cSharpCode = cSharpCode.Replace(
➥APIUtility.CSHP_SCOPE, rdPrivate.Text.ToLower());
  }
  else
  {
```

```
      cSharpCode = cSharpCode.Replace(
➥APIUtility.CSHP_SCOPE, rdPublic.Text.ToLower());
   }

   if (txtSelected.Text.IndexOf(cSharpCode) < 0)
      txtSelected.Text += cSharpCode + "\n";
}
```

The btnAdd_Click() event uses a switch statement to extract C# definitions from the definitionList of the viewer classes based on the selected item in the list box. Then it looks for the radio button that is checked. A checked private radio button makes a private declaration. Otherwise, a public declaration is made. Finally, the retrieved C# definition is added to the rich text box if this definition is not added already.

At this point, the main actions are completed. The following implementation is to make this Text Viewer mimic the old API Text Viewer in the Microsoft Visual Studio 6 package. Because the rich text box is similar to a mini text editor, you can manually perform the tasks that clicking the Clear, Remove, and Copy buttons would perform. However, as the rest of this section continues, you will finish coding these events to provide so these tasks can be performed with the click of a button.

Double click the Remove button. Add code to remove text from the rich text box.

```
private void btnRemove_Click(object sender, System.EventArgs e)
{
   string selectFuncs = txtSelected.Text;
   int currCursorPos = txtSelected.SelectionStart;

   int funcStartAt = currCursorPos - 1;
   int funcEndAt = currCursorPos + 1;
   GetFunctionStartPosition(selectFuncs, ref funcStartAt, true);
   GetFunctionStartPosition(selectFuncs, ref funcEndAt, false);

   string postRmStr = "";
   if (funcStartAt > 0)
      postRmStr = selectFuncs.Substring(0, funcStartAt);
   postRmStr += selectFuncs.Substring(funcEndAt);
   txtSelected.Text = postRmStr;
}
```

The btnRemove_Click() event calls a GetFunctionStartPosition() helper method to find the starting and ending points for the text line to be removed. The GetFunctionStartPosition() method is coded as follows:

```
private int GetFunctionStartPosition(
➥string txt, ref int currCP, bool lookForStart)
{
```

```
    if (currCP < 0)
      return 0;
    if (currCP > txt.Length - 1)
    {
      currCP = txt.Length;
      return 0;
    }
    char[] chr = txt.ToCharArray();
    while (chr[currCP] != '\n')
    {
      if (lookForStart)
      {
        if (currCP > 0)
          currCP -=1;
        else
          break;
      }
      else
      {
        if (currCP < txt.Length-1)
          currCP += 1;
        else
          break;
      }
    }
    return 0;
}
```

Double-click the Clear button. Add code to have the btnClear_Click() event implemented:

```
private void btnClear_Click(object sender, System.EventArgs e)
{
  txtSelected.Text = "";
}
```

The btnClear_Click() event simply resets the rich text box to empty. And finally, double-click the Copy button. The btnCopy_Click() event also executes only one line of code:

```
private void btnCopy_Click(object sender, System.EventArgs e)
{
  Clipboard.SetDataObject(txtSelected.Text, true);
}
```

After the btnCopy_Click() event, the C# code in the rich text box is copied to the clipboard and is ready to be pasted into a C# program.

For users' convenience in the future, you can load WIN32API.TXT automatically when you start the C# API Text Viewer. In order to do this, you double-click on an empty spot of the form and the Microsoft Visual Studio .NET IDE generates a `Form1_Load()` event. Add code between the curly brackets and the completed code look like the following:

```
private void Form1_Load(object sender, System.EventArgs e)
{
  txtLookfor.Clear();
  txtSelected.Clear();

  try
  {
    OpenAPITextFile(@"C:\Program Files\
➥Microsoft Visual Studio\Common\Tools\Winapi\WIN32API.TXT");
  }
  catch (Exception ex)
  {
    MessageBox.Show(ex.Message);
  }
}
```

When the form is loaded, the text boxes are cleared and the method `OpenAPITextFile()` is invoked to open `Win32API.txt` automatically. The path and filename of `Win32API.txt` are hard-coded within a `try-catch` statement. There are two reasons to hard-code this line of code:

• To open an existing copy of the `Win32API.txt` automatically each time when the C# API Text Viewer starts. Thus users can engage in C# API programming immediately. However, if the user's system doesn't have the hard coded path and filename, the C# API Text Viewer will still start without problem. But the user has to open the `Win32API.txt` manually.

• To allow the GUI testing tool developed in the upcoming chapters to test the GUI components of the C# API Text Viewer before the automatic menu handling capability is added. Thus, it is recommended that your hard coded path and filename is consistent with you computer system

If you don't have the old version of `WIN32API.TXT` on your system, you can copy the new version of the file with the same name from the sample code for this book to your preferred directory. You can alter the path name based on the physical location of the `WIN32API.TXT` file. The @-quoted string is called a verbatim string to avoid specifying escape characters.

That is all the code for the C# API Text Viewer. Build and run the project by pressing F5. You will enjoy C# API programming with the assistance of this tool. It will help make your future projects progress more quickly.

NOTE   The source code for this tool is included in the Chapter03/CSharpAPITextViewer folder with the other examples. You can download the updated code from www.sybex.com if you haven't done so yet.

Starting with a Test Monkey

The beginning of this chapter included a discussion about test monkeys. Experts have used various kinds of test monkeys with different degrees of intelligence. These monkeys have found bugs other testing means can't find. They are especially useful for finding out the circumstances under which an application will crash.

This section will guide you in the development of a primitive test monkey and a smarter monkey with some intelligence.

A Dumb Test Monkey

Now you can use the C# API Text Viewer to help with your C# programming. To start the dumb test monkey, follow the same steps you followed in the preceding examples to create a new project. You can save this project in the C:\GUISourceCode\Chapter03\ folder. Make this project a Windows application and name the project TestMonkey. When the automatically generated form appears on the screen, leave it as is for now. I will ask you to come back to this form after you develop a MouseAPI class by calling a few custom functions.

To develop the MouseAPI class, choose Project ≻ Add Class from the main menu in the Microsoft Visual Studio .NET IDE with the newly created project open. When the Add New Item dialog box appears, type the class name, MouseAPI, in the name field. Then click the Open button. The cursor is in the code editor within the MouseAPI.cs file open.

You are now ready to insert some custom functions into the MouseAPI class using the C# API Text Viewer. Start the C# API Text Viewer. If you have a copy of the WIN32API.TXT file installed on your system, the C# API Text Viewer should have loaded it. If you don't have the WIN32API.TXT file, you can download it with the source code from www.sybex.com by searching for this book's title.

Listing 3.20 contains the constants needed for the MouseAPI class coded by the C# API Text Viewer.

Listing 3.20   Constants Needed for the Test Monkey Development

```
private const int MOUSEEVENTF_ABSOLUTE = 0x8000; // absolute move;
private const int MOUSEEVENTF_LEFTDOWN = 0x2; // left button down;
private const int MOUSEEVENTF_LEFTUP = 0x4; // left button up;
private const int MOUSEEVENTF_MOVE = 0x1; // mouse move;
private const int MOUSEEVENTF_RIGHTDOWN = 0x8; // right button down;
private const int MOUSEEVENTF_RIGHTUP = 0x10; // right button up;
private const int MOUSEEVENTF_WHEEL = 0x800; //mouse wheel turns

private const int SM_CXSCREEN = 0;
private const int SM_CYSCREEN = 1;
private const int MOUSE_MICKEYS = 65535;
```

Pixel

Pixel stands for picture element. A pixel is a point in a graphic image. Computer monitors divide the display area into thousands of pixels in rows and columns.

Computers use a number of bits to represent how many colors or shades of gray a pixel can display. An 8-bit color mode uses 8 bits for each pixel and is able to display 2 to the 8th power (256) different colors or shades of gray.

On color monitors, one pixel is composed of three dots: a red, a blue, and a green one. These three dots should all converge at the same point. Some convergence error makes color pixels appear blurry.

A mouse pointer moves in mickey steps. An entire screen has 65,535 mickeys ($2^{16} -1$, or FFFF in hex number) both horizontally and vertically.

When the C# API Text Viewer is running with the Win32API.txt file open, click the API type combo box and select Constants. The names for all the available constants are brought into the list box. You can look for each needed constant by scrolling the list box or by typing in the text field the first few letters of the constant name. After you locate one constant, click the Add button on the right. The definition of the selected constant is appended to the rich text box. Then proceed to the next one. However, if the WIN32API.TXT file on your system could not find the one of the constants, you can type the definition into the program. For example, the MOUSE_MICKEYS = 65535 may not be in your file.

After you finish with the constants, click the API type combo box to select Declares. Declare is the keyword of calling a custom function for Visual Basic 6 programs. Find and add the functions in Listing 3.21 into the rich text box.

Listing 3.21   The Custom Functions Needed for the Test Monkey Development

```
[DllImport("user32.dll")]
public static extern void mouse_event(int dwFlags,
➥int dx, int dy, int cButtons, int dwExtraInfo);

[DllImport("user32.dll")]
public static extern int GetSystemMetrics(int nIndex);
```

The mouse_event function synthesizes mouse motion and mouse button clicks. It requires Windows NT/95 or later. The first required parameter, dwFlags, specifies the desired mouse motion and button click. The elements in this parameter can be any reasonable combination of the first six constants in Listing 3.20. I omitted MOUSEEVENTF_MIDDLEUP and MOUSEEVENTF_ MIDDLEDOWN in the listing. If your test project requires middle button actions in the future, you can add them in Listing 3.20 from the C# API Text Viewer. The second and the third parameters are the absolute positions along the x- and y-axis or the amount of motion since the last mouse event. The movement of the mouse pointer is in mickey steps. A mickey is the minimum amount of distance that a mouse can move per step. A screen has 65,535 mickey steps both horizontally and vertically (or in the x- and y-axis). The fourth parameter can be used to specify how much action the mouse wheel can perform. The last parameter specifies an additional 32-bit value associated with the mouse event.

The GetSystemMetrics() function retrieves the width and height of a display in pixels. It also returns flags indicating whether a mouse is present or whether the meaning of the left and right mouse buttons has been reversed. The required parameter, nIndex, can be the seventh or eighth constant in Listing 3.20. But there are many others in WIN32API.TXT.

After all the constants and functions are added into the rich text box, click the Copy button. Then return to the code editor of the MouseAPI class and paste the contents into the program.

Next, scroll up in the editor to the top of the MouseAPI class. Place the cursor below the TestMonkey namespace. Add a public enumeration declaration, MonkeyButtons. Listing 3.22 has the elements of the enumeration.

Listing 3.22   **A Enumeration of *MonkeyButtons***

```
public enum MonkeyButtons
{
  btcLeft,
  btcRight,
  btcWheel,
}
```

Resolution

The quality of a display system largely depends on its resolution. *Resolution* refers to the sharpness and clarity of an image. It is often used to describe how images appear in the monitors, printers, and bitmapped graphic devices. These devices are often categorized into high, medium, or low resolution. For example, for a dot-matrix or laser printer, the resolution indicates the number of dots per inch (dpi). A 300-dpi printer prints 300 distinct dots in a 1-inch line both horizontally and vertically. For a monitor, the screen resolution signifies the number of pixels. A 640×480-pixel screen displays 640 distinct pixels on each of 480 horizontal lines. Therefore, a 15-inch VGA monitor with the resolution of 640×480 displays about 50 pixels per inch.

The MonkeyButtons enumeration allows the user to decide which button the test monkey should click. To use this enumeration, move the cursor into the code of the MouseAPI class. Place it directly below the GetSystemMetrics() function declaration and add a ClickMouse() method as shown in Listing 3.23.

Listing 3.23   **Implementation of the *ClickMouse()* Method**

```
public static bool ClickMouse(MonkeyButtons mbClick,
                             int pixelX, int pixelY,
                             int wlTurn, int dwExtraInfo)
{
  int mEvent;

  switch (mbClick)
  {
    case MonkeyButtons.btcLeft:
      mEvent = MOUSEEVENTF_LEFTDOWN | MOUSEEVENTF_LEFTUP;
      break;
    case MonkeyButtons.btcRight:
      mEvent = MOUSEEVENTF_RIGHTDOWN | MOUSEEVENTF_RIGHTUP;
      break;
    case MonkeyButtons.btcWheel:
      mEvent = MOUSEEVENTF_WHEEL;
      break;
    default:
      return false;
  }
  mouse_event(mEvent, pixelX, pixelY, wlTurn, dwExtraInfo);
  return true;
}
```

You are ready to use the functions and the constants. First, declare ClickMouse() to be another static method. After the declaration, initialize an mEvent variable as an integer. Then use a switch statement to check what action the user asks for. Finally, invoke the mouse_event() function to perform the action. The Boolean return is used to indicate whether the mouse action is successful.

At this point your monkey has the capability to click a mouse button. Your next task is to move the mouse pointer to a desired spot and perform a click. As we have discussed, the GetSystemMetrics() function finds the width and height of a display resolution in pixels. But the mouse_event function moves the mouse pointer in mickeys. You need a method to convert pixels to mickeys. This method, named PixelXYToMickeyXY(), is shown in Listing 3.24.

Listing 3.24   **Implementation of the *PixelXYToMickeyXY()* Method**

```
private static void PixelXYToMickeyXY(ref int pixelX, ref int pixelY)
{
//pixelX and pixelY have pixel as their units for input parameters
  int resX = 0;
  int resY = 0;
  resX = GetSystemMetrics(SM_CXSCREEN);
  resY =  GetSystemMetrics(SM_CYSCREEN);
  pixelX %= resX+1;
  pixelY %= resY+1;

  int cMickeys = MOUSE_MICKEYS;
//Convert pixelX and pixelY into mickey steps as the output result
  pixelX = (int)(pixelX * (cMickeys / resX));
  pixelY = (int)(pixelY * (cMickeys / resY));
}
```

In Listing 3.20, you copied a constant definition MOUSE_MICKEYS = 65535. The meaning of the MOUSE_MICKEYS constant is that there are 65,535 mickeys in the display both horizontally and vertically. The ratio of the constant value over the total pixels of the screen horizontally or vertically is the number mickey steps per pixel. Based on this ratio, the PixelXYToMickeyXY() static method converts the coordinate position of the x- and y-axis in pixels when they are input parameters into mickey steps when they are output. It first calls the GetSystemMetrics() function twice. One time gets the total pixels of the screen in the horizontal direction (x-axis). The second time gets the total pixels of the screen in the vertical direction (y-axis). Then it uses a modulus operator to ensure that the pixel numbers of pixelX and pixelY are within the display area; that is, pixelX is less than or equal to the total amount of pixels in the x-axis, resX, and pixelY is less than or equal to the total amount of pixels on the y-axis, resY. Finally, the method multiplies the input parameters by the mickey ratios to get the amount of mickeys for the mouse's next location. The mouse doesn't actually move before triggering the mouse_event() function.

The last implementation for the MouseAPI class is the MoveMouse() method. Its code is shown in Listing 3.25.

Listing 3.25   **Implementation of the *MoveMouse()* Method**

```
public static void MoveMouse(int iHndl, int pixelX, int pixelY)
{
  PixelXYToMickeyXY(ref pixelX, ref pixelY);
  mouse_event (MOUSEEVENTF_ABSOLUTE | MOUSEEVENTF_MOVE, pixelX, pixelY, 0, 0);
}
```

This MoveMouse() method tells the mouse_event() function the next mouse location by passing the pixelX and pixelY parameters. Then it calls the method to convert pixels into mickeys. And last, it triggers the mouse_event() function to perform an absolute movement to the desired pixel coordinate indicated by the combination of MOUSEEVENTF_ABSOLUTE and MOUSEEVENTF_MOVE constants. The last two parameters are set to 0s which indicate no mouse wheel movement and no other extra events are specified.

Now you are finished coding the MouseAPI class. It is time to plant some GUI controls for the TestMonkey project Windows form. The MouseAPI class has provided the test monkey with the capabilities to move the mouse and click. The GUI controls will enable the monkey to work by itself. After returning to the TestMonkey's form, add the four controls in the following list:

Control	Property	Value
Timer	Name	tmrMonkey
Button	Name	btnStart
	Text	Start
	TextAlign	MiddleRight
	ImageAlign	MiddleLeft
	Image	Monkey.ico
Label	Text	Interval (sec.)
NumericUpDown	Name	numInterval
	Value	3

For all other properties, accept the default. After the GUI controls are properly populated, the TestMonkey form will look like the form in Figure 3.6.

You may notice that I added a monkey head for the Start button and the form. If you like, you can select the button and the form to change their icon properties. A monkey.ico file is included in the sample code for this project. More important, though, to add code for the mouse actions, double-click the Start button. The Microsoft Visual Studio .NET IDE opens the code editor. You can add the code for the btnStart_Click() event in Listing 3.26.

FIGURE 3.6
The appearance of
your test monkey

Listing 3.26   **Code for the *btnStart_Click()* Event**

```
private void btnStart_Click(object sender, System.EventArgs e)
{
  if (tmrMonkey.Enabled)
  {
    tmrMonkey.Enabled = false;
    btnStart.Text = "Start";
  }
  else
  {
    tmrMonkey.Enabled = true;
    btnStart.Text = "Stop";
  }
}
```

The Start button implementation toggles the tmrMonkey object to be enabled or disabled and the text on the button itself to be Start or Stop. If the tmrMonkey is enabled, the test monkey works continuously. Otherwise, the monkey is idle. Next, double-click the tmrMonkey control. The Microsoft Visual Studio .NET IDE brings you back to the code editor by creating a tmrMonkey_Tick() event declaration. You need to add a few lines of code (shown in Listing 3.27) to complete the event.

Listing 3.27   **Implementation of the *tmrMonkey_Tick()* Event**

```
private void tmrMonkey_Tick(object sender, System.EventArgs)
{
  tmrMonkey.Interval = (int)numInterval.Value * 1000;

  Random rnd = new Random();
  int x = rnd.Next();
  int y = rnd.Next();
  MouseAPI.MoveMouse(this.Handle.ToInt32(), x, y);
  MouseAPI.ClickMouse(MonkeyButtons.btcLeft, 0, 0, 0, 0);
}
```

First, this event reads a value from the numInterval object and resets the clock interval for the tmrMonkey object. Because the tmrMonkey counts time in milliseconds, the value read in seconds is multiplied by 1000. Then the test monkey randomly performs actions on an application. In order to assign a random coordinate position to the monkey, you create a Random object, rnd. Call the Next() method from the rnd object twice, one for a random pixel in the x-axis of the screen, the other for a random pixel in the y-axis. Since you have implemented all the methods in the MouseAPI class to be static, you don't need to create a MouseAPI object to invoke those methods. Therefore, you directly call the `MouseAPI.MoveMouse()` method to move the mouse pointer to a desired position and call the `MouseAPI.ClickMouse()` method to perform a left mouse button click.

Finally, compile and run the TestMonkey project by pressing F5. The monkey is waiting for your orders. Make sure the value in the `numInterval` object is greater than 0. I prefer to click the up arrow and make the value about 3, which is the default value when you place the GUI components on the form. That means the `tmrMonkey` will move and perform a left mouse click every three (3) seconds.

This monkey moves and clicks mouse buttons randomly. After I finished this project, I set it to click randomly on an empty Excel spreadsheet overnight and found the application halted in the morning with the message shown in Figure 3.7.

FIGURE 3.7
An Excel application error message produced by the test monkey overnight

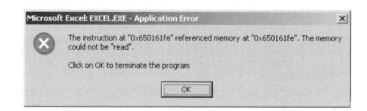

A Smarter Monkey

At this point, you have developed a primitive test monkey. You can continue to give this monkey more capabilities. In this section, you will add a few more custom functions and enable the test monkey to know what it clicks.

To use the developed monkey, copy the entire `TestMonkey` folder and paste it into the same folder. The duplicated folder will be named `Copy of TestMonkey`; rename it `SmartMonkey`. Next, start the Microsoft Visual Studio .NET IDE and open the TestMonkey project from the `SmartMonkey` folder. You need to add the needed custom functions using the C# API Text Viewer again. First, add the `POINTAPI` structure immediately below the `TestMonkey` namespace. The code copied from the C# API Text Viewer looks like the code in Listing 3.28.

Listing 3.28   Code for the Definition of the *POINTAPI* Structure Prepared by the C# API Text Viewer

```
[StructLayout(LayoutKind.Sequential)]
public struct POINTAPI
{
    public int x;
    public int y;
}
```

The POINTAPI structure defines a pair of pixel numbers along the x- and y-axis to form a coordinate point. You need to add the four custom functions in Listing 3.29 into the MouseAPI class.

Listing 3.29   **Code for Marshing the Custom Functions Prepared by the C# API Text Viewer**

```
[DllImport("user32.dll")]
public static extern int GetClassName(int hwnd,
➡StringBuilder lpClassName, int nMaxCount);

[DllImport("user32.dll")]
public static extern int GetCursorPos([MarshalAs(UnmanagedType.Struct)]
➡ref POINTAPI lpPoint);

[DllImport("user32.dll")]
public static extern int WindowFromPoint(int xPoint, int yPoint);

[DllImport("user32.dll")]
public static extern int GetWindowText(int hwnd,
➡StringBuilder lpString, int cch);
```

The GetClassName() function retrieves the name of the class to which the specified GUI component belongs, as with the WindowClassDiscovery example. The GetCursorPos() function finds the cursor's position in pixels of the screen coordinates. The WindowFromPoint() function gets the handle based on the screen coordinates found by the GetCursorPos() function. The last function, GetWindowText(), is similar to GetClassName() but discovers the caption text of the GUI component.

These functions repeatedly pass parameters as StringBuilder objects. StringBuilder is a class from the System.Text namespace. Thus, you need to go to the top of the MouseAPI.cs to add a using statement:

```
using System.Text;
```

After the custom functions are prepared, you have only a GetSmartInfo() method to implement for the MouseAPI class. It is shown in Listing 3.30.

Listing 3.30   **Code for the *GetSmartInfo()* Method**

```
public static void GetSmartInfo(ref int wHdl,
➡ref StringBuilder clsName, ref StringBuilder wndText)
{
  POINTAPI Pnt = new POINTAPI();

  GetCursorPos(ref Pnt);
  wHdl = WindowFromPoint(Pnt.x, Pnt.y);
  GetClassName(wHdl, clsName, 128);
  GetWindowText(wHdl, wndText, 128);
}
```

The GetSmartInfo() method passes three parameters by reference: the window's handle, the class name and the window's text. The values of these parameters will be altered inside this method as it calls various functions. It first initializes a POINTAPI object, Pnt. Then it calls the newly added custom functions one by one. The GetCursorPos() function returns the coordinates in pixels. Actually, it converts the mickeys back into pixels. Subsequently, it calls the WindowFromPoint(), the GetClassName(), and the GetWindowText() functions to assign the handle to the wHdl variable, the class name to the clsName object, and the caption text of the GUI to the wndText object, respectively.

You need to use this method in the TestMonkey form. You built a primitive monkey in the last section. Now, you just need to modify the btnStart click event and the tmrMonkey tick event for the current project. Listing 3.31 is the modified btnStart_Click() event with the new code in bold.

Listing 3.31   Code for the Modified *btnStart_Click()* Event

```
private StringBuilder smtInfo;

private void btnStart_Click(object sender, System.EventArgs e)
{
  if (tmrMonkey.Enabled)
  {
    tmrMonkey.Enabled = false;
    btnStart.Text = "Start";
    SaveSmartMonkeyKnowledge(smtInfo.ToString());
  }
  else
  {
    tmrMonkey.Enabled = true;
    btnStart.Text = "Stop";
    smtInfo = new StringBuilder();
  }
}
```

The first bold line adds a smtInfo field as a StringBuilder object. The bold line in the if statement saves the information of the GUI components tested by the smart test monkey to a physical file. The code in the else statement initializes the smtInfo field, which will be used to store GUI information collected by the test monkey as a string of comma-separated values (CSVs).

Now modify the tmrMonkey_Tick() to be like Listing 3.32, with new lines of code in bold.

Listing 3.32   Code for the Modified *tmrMonkey_Tick()* Event

```
private void tmrMonkey_Tick(object sender, System.EventArgs e)
{
  tmrMonkey.Interval = (int)numInterval.Value * 1000;
  Random rnd = new Random();
  int x = rnd.Next();
  int y = rnd.Next();

  smtInfo.Append(x + ", " + y + ", ");

  MouseAPI.MoveMouse(this.Handle.ToInt32(), x, y);
  MouseAPI.ClickMouse(MonkeyButtons.btcRight, 0, 0, 0, 0);
  MouseAPI.ClickMouse(MonkeyButtons.btcLeft, 0, 0, 0, 0);
  MouseAPI.ClickMouse(MonkeyButtons.btcWheel, 0, 0, x % 2000, 0);

  int wHdl = 0;
  StringBuilder clsName = new StringBuilder(128);
  StringBuilder wndText = new StringBuilder(128);
  MouseAPI.GetSmartInfo(ref wHdl, ref clsName, ref wndText);
  smtInfo.Append(wHdl + ", " + clsName.ToString()
+ ", " + wndText.ToString() + "\n");
}
```

These bold lines are new brain cells and muscles of the monkey. Let's review its evolution. After the random coordinates are created by the Random object, the smtInfo object stores these pixel numbers with the Append() method of the StringBuilder class. When the program proceeds to the code of the mouse click section, it clicks the right button first. Software developers usually program the right button click to pop up a context menu. Then the code for left button click is inherited from the last section. A left button click usually orders the program to perform a desired task. Thus, after the task is completed, the third mouse action turns the mouse wheel to scroll the active screen (I assume you are using a mouse with a wheel between the left and the right button). This is specified by the MonkeyButtons.btcWheel enumeration. The amount of wheel turning is shown in the fourth parameter: the remainder of the mickey steps in the x-axis divided by 2000. The value, 2000, is also an arbitrarily and randomly picked number. Because I used a two-button mouse when writing this book, a middle button click is not implemented for this monkey.

The last cluster of the code in Listing 3.32 simply prepares three objects for the handle, the class name, and the caption text of the window of interest. After the GetSmartInfo() method is executed, the respective information is stored in the prepared objects. The last line of code assigns the information of the mouse actions at this point to the smtInfo object. The test monkey is ready for the next mouse action.

You may have noticed that the btnStart_Click() event in Listing 3.31 calls a SaveSmart-MonkeyKnowledge() helper method. The code for this method is in Listing 3.33.

Listing 3.33   **Code for the *SaveSmartMonkeyKnowledge()* Helper Method**

```
private void SaveSmartMonkeyKnowledge(string textToSave)
{
  string fileToSave = @"C:\Temp\smartMonkeyInfo.csv";
  FileInfo fi = new FileInfo(fileToSave);
  StreamWriter sw = fi.CreateText();
  sw.Write(textToSave);
  sw.Close();
}
```

The SaveSmartMonkeyKnowledge() helper method simply creates an output filename and initializes a StreamWriter object to save a string to a physical file. If you don't have a C:\Temp folder, you need to create one in your system before this program can be executed automatically. The programming method for saving and reading a text file was discussed in my previous book, *Effective Software Test Automation: Developing an Automated Software Testing Tool* by Kanglin Li and Mengqi Wu, (Sybex, 2004). The last thing you need to do is add two more using statements at the beginning of the form if they are not there yet:

```
using System.Text;
using System.IO;
```

These are required by the StringBuilder parameters and the SaveSmartMonkeyKnowledge() method. Now the code is complete. You can build and run the new TestMonkey by pressing F5. This monkey has some more capabilities, such as performing more mouse actions and recognizing GUI properties. But the functions are still very basic. However, the major goal of this book is to develop a GUI testing tool with full automation from data generation and script generation to bug reporting. We will not put too much effort into creating test monkeys. The point of this chapter was to show you how to create and improve a monkey. If your organization requires a more powerful test monkey, you can continue to improve it by adding more custom functions from the C# API Text Viewer.

Before you leave your office, remember to start the monkey on a computer in the corner of your testing lab for a night or two. Come back to check and see what has been done by the royal and diligent test monkey in the morning. I believe it will find some undesirable behaviors of your application under test.

TIP Because the test monkey will click any possible spot on the display, it may be terminated prematurely. To avoid this, you can minimize the monkey and set your desktop to auto-hide the Taskbar by right-clicking Start, choosing Properties, and selecting the Auto-Hide the Taskbar check box on the Taskbar tab. Also, the program moves and clicks the mouse automatically. When you want to stop the test monkey, you may not be fast enough to grab the mouse before it executes the next automatic action. In this case, you can increase the interval value.

NOTE You can download the source code for this book from `www.sybex.com`.

Summary

In this chapter, after the introduction of some test fundamentals, I started to introduce practical GUI testing techniques. Microsoft Visual Studio .NET provides a PInvoke service to marshal the unmanaged code. To marshal the custom Win32 DLLs, we mainly use a few methods of the Marshal class and the `DllImport` attribute.

There are numerous constants, types, and functions predefined by the Win32 API programming method. Many of them need to be used to develop a GUI testing tool. You won't make use all of the functions, but you can use more of them to update your testing tool after you finish reading this book. Older versions of Microsoft Visual Studio came with an API Text Viewer to help programmers, but there is no such tool available for C# programmers. To help you easily locate the useful custom functions, this chapter guided you in the development of a C# API Text Viewer. The C# API Text Viewer is a GUI-rich application. It will be used to provide C# code for marshaling the Win32 custom functions, and it will be tested by the GUI testing tool to be developed in each chapter thereafter.

Using the developed C# API Text Viewer, you developed a test monkey to move the mouse and click the buttons. You then gave the test monkey more capabilities. In the upcoming chapters, you are going to build an intelligent tool to test GUI applications.

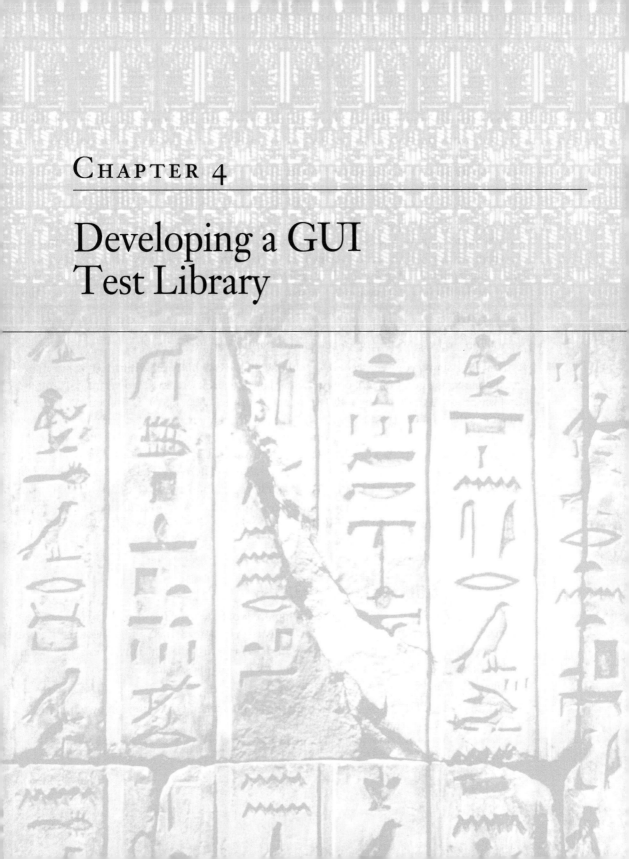

CHAPTER 4

Developing a GUI Test Library

The purpose of developing a test script is to programmatically simulate a person using an application by choosing menu options, clicking buttons, and entering text and numbers. The programming languages provide various GUI controls that developers can include in software applications. Each application has a unique combination of the various GUI controls. On these controls, users can apply one or more of the actions, such as move the mouse pointer or use it to drag and drop an item; left-click, right-click, or click the middle mouse button; single- or double-click; turn the mouse wheel to scroll a page; and press the Tab key, Enter key, Esc key, or other function keys. Users can also enter text, numbers, and other special characters into text box controls. Each of the actions taken on a GUI control invokes a set of internal functions of the application behind the scene. It is easy for the manual testers to see the consequences of each action. But it takes time for the manual tester to verify the actions behind the scene. Automated software test tools provide test script languages and ask testers to write or record test scripts. The goal of the test scripts is to simulate a person performing the mouse and key actions on a selected GUI component and to verify the outcome.

This book shows you how to develop a tool with the capability of writing test scripts in programming languages. Often, a programming language lacks functions to perform the mouse and key actions. Although the .NET Framework has a large collection of functions, there are functions that you can perform by using Win32 API that you cannot perform by using the .NET Framework. When you need capabilities that go beyond the libraries of these languages, you can use the Win32 API to make direct calls to the DLLs. The functions of recognizing the graphical user interface (GUI) reside in the user32.dll. Therefore, the user32.dll will be the DLL most frequently referred to for Win32 API programming. This chapter will briefly introduce you to it and guide you in developing a GUI test library. Occasionally, functions of other Win32 subsystems will also be needed, such as kernel32.dll and gdi32.dll. When this happens, I will explain these functions specifically.

GUI Test and the Custom *User32.dll*

By referring to user32.dll, you can access hundreds of functions that form the backbone of the Microsoft Windows operating system. As discussed in Chapter 3, the .NET PInvoke service can enable applications to link to the functions of the user32.dll dynamically. These applications call the user32.dll functions to display windows and graphics, manage memory, and perform menu, mouse, and other tasks.

Within the .NET Framework, you can call an unmanaged DLL function by telling the Common Language Runtime (CLR) the name of the function, the user32.dll containing the function, and how to marshal the function's parameters (for example, whether to pass a parameter by value or by reference). Usually you need to call several custom functions to perform one desired action. For example, as coded in Chapter 3, in order to move the mouse pointer to a desired position, the test monkey calls the `GetSystemMetrics()` function to know the number of the total pixels of the display horizontally and vertically. Then it converts the pixels into mickeys. Finally, it uses the `mouse_event()` function to move the mouse pointer the appropriate number of the mickey steps.

The internal data of the operating system is kept by the kernel mode components of the Win32 subsystem, which helps protect the internal data from wrecked user mode components. The `user32.dll` is installed in the `C:\Windows\System32` path and publicized with a Registry key:

```
HKEY_LOCAL_MACHINE\Software\Microsoft\
➥Windows NT\CurrentVersion\Windows\AppInit_Dlls
```

This key causes the operating system to load the subsystem DLLs into address space in the system. All the DLLs specified by the value of the Registry key are loaded by each Windows-based application running within the current logon session. The actual loading of these DLLs occurs as a part of user32's initialization. User32 reads the value of the key and calls `LoadLibrary()` for the DLLs in its `DllMain()` entry point. Because every GUI application is implemented to load the user32 subsystem, the following are the advantages to using it to develop a GUI testing tool:

- The user32 initialization saves memory and reduces swapping. Many processes can use functions of the `user32.dll` at the same time by sharing a single copy of it in memory. The operating system doesn't need to load a copy of the library code to memory for each application.

- Disk space is saved by sharing a single copy of the DLL on disk among applications. Otherwise, each application should have the library code linked to the program file image as a separate copy.

- It is observed that calling custom functions to perform functions saves time. The `user32.dll` doesn't need to recompile or relink to the applications that use the functions.

- The `user32.dll` shares functions with other DLLs, and the data is separate for each process.

TIP   The available `Win32API.txt` file is based on Windows 95 header files. It contains 1548 functions, 6407 constants, and 419 structures. More functions have been introduced into the operating system due to the evolution of Windows 98, Windows 2000, Windows ME, and Windows XP. The up-to-date DLL libraries of the current Windows XP header files contain over 6100 functions, 53,000 constants, and 460 structures. You can search the new functions by using the `dumpbin.exe` and the Dependency Walker that are included with Microsoft Visual Studio. These two utilities will be discussed in the next section.

Exploring the *User32.dll*

Continuing our exploration of the user32.dll reveals that the user32 is a memory-mapped DLL, meaning it is shared among all running processes. This is extremely useful for applications calling the API functions because it is visible in all the active address spaces. In fact, we need to develop a GUI testing tool to invoke these functions, thus a GUI test library will ensure that the tool can share these functions to help with writing a test script automatically and performing the testing tasks in the test scripts for various testing projects.

There are hundreds of functions in the user32.dll. We will use only some of these functions in the tool projects. For example, Chapter 3 used a few of them to trigger the mouse functions. The only document we can use to discover the useful functions for GUI testing purposes is Win32API.txt. However, the Windows operating system and Microsoft Visual Studio also provide tools to view the functions and other information. Manual testers have used these tools to troubleshoot system errors related to loading and executing a module. The purpose of discussing these tools is to compare their use with some of the manual efforts to detect application problems such as missing modules, mismatched modules, and circular dependency errors. In the following sections, I will discuss the use of the dumpbin.exe line command and the Dependency Walker in Microsoft Visual Studio. I will also introduce a Spy++ tool to you when we start a GUI testing library project later in this chapter.

Dumpbin.exe

The dumpbin.exe utility is installed in C:\Program Files\Microsoft Visual Studio .NET 2003\ Vc7\bin by the Microsoft Visual Studio .NET IDE 2003 Setup program. It is a command-line tool that gives you the ability to view various details of given managed or unmanaged applications (DLL or EXE). When you open a Visual Studio .NET 2003 command prompt window, from the C:\> prompt, issue the following command:

```
C:\>dumpbin
```

Figure 4.1 displays a list of flags you can use to inform the tool of exactly what part of the application you are interested in viewing.

The following list explains the meaning of five of them:

/all   Display all available information except code disassembly.

/disam   Display disassembly of code sections using symbols if present in the file.

/exports   Display all definitions exported from an executable file or DLL.

/imports   Display the list of DLLs that are imported to an executable file or DLL and all the individual imports from each of these DLLs.

/summary   Display minimal information about sections, including total size. This option is the default if no other option is specified.

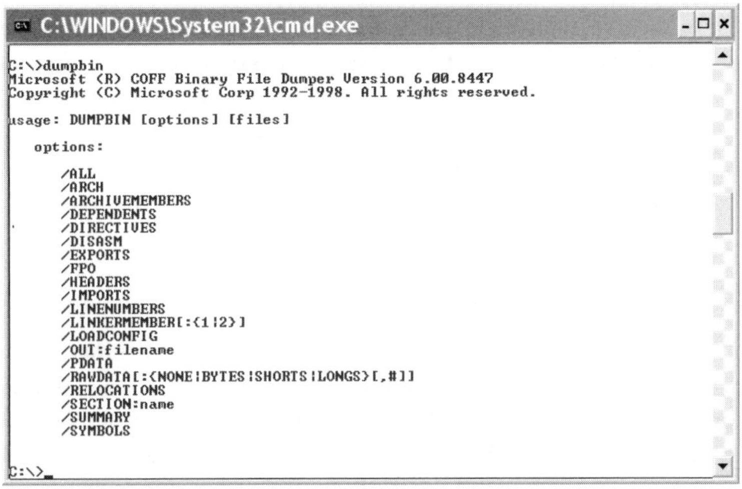

FIGURE 4.1
Options of the
dumpbin.exe
program

Let's check out the *imported* modules of the user32.dll using the dumpbin.exe program. You should have developed programs with the functions to save, copy, and move files. These functions and a lot more are categorized into imported modules within user32.dll. You can change the directory to the C:\Windows\System32 from the DOS command window and issue a command from the C:\> prompt as follows:

```
C:\>dumpbin /imports user32.dll
```

The screen will display a big portion of the imported functions and their dependency summaries. In order to view the entire output information, you can add an option to the command and ask the operating system to save the output to a physical file:

```
C:\>dumpbin /imports user32.dll > c:\temp\user32Imported.txt
```

After the command completes the execution, the imported modules are saved in C:\temp\ user32Imported.txt. You can use a text editor to review the available functions and other information.

The other portion of functions within user32.dll can be viewed with the exports option:

```
C:\>dumpbin /exports user32.dll > c:\temp\user32Exported.txt
```

At the beginning of the output file, there is a brief summary that shows there are 732 exported functions in the user32.dll. As you recall, you used mouse_event(), GetSystemMetrics(), GetWindowText(), WindowFromPoint(), GetCursorPos(), and GetClassName() to build the test monkey in Chapter 3. These functions can be found in the C:\temp\user32Exported.txt file.

Dependency Walker

In the .NET platform arena, the components of an assembly are described in a manifest. A manifest is a block of data that lists the files of the assembly and controls the types and resources that are exposed outside the assembly. For example, some types might be reserved for use only in the assembly. Others might be exported to users of the assembly. The .NET Framework honors the rules that are expressed in the assembly manifest for resolving types and resources to their implementation files in an assembly and for binding to dependent assemblies. This section introduces the Dependency Walker tool, which will help you learn about the content of managed and unmanaged applications (DLL or EXE). The content includes both imported and exported modules and the dependencies of the application.

As you can see, the user32.dll contains numerous functions to develop a GUI testing tool. The user32.dll also depends on other DLLs. You need to know the interdependencies between different DLLs in order to avoid problems when programming with the Win32 API. The Dependency Walker's Depends.exe executable is a tool in the Microsoft Visual Studio 6 package. Unfortunately, it is not found in the Microsoft Visual Studio .NET IDE. You can start the Dependency Walker by choosing Start ≻ Programs ≻ Microsoft Visual Studio 6.0 ≻ Microsoft Visual Studio 6.0 Tools ≻ Depends. When the program is open, choose File ≻ Open to open the C:\Windows\System32\user32.dll. Figure 4.2 shows the interface.

FIGURE 4.2
The GUI of the Dependency Walker with user32.dll loaded

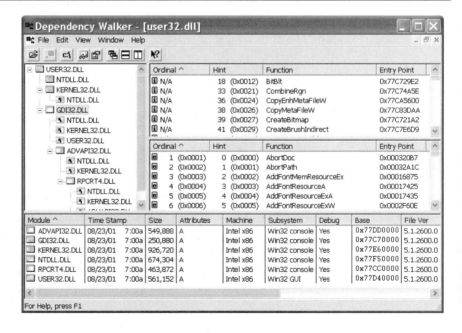

You can see that dependencies of the user32.dll are presented in a hierarchical tree view. User32.dll depends on three other DLLs, ntdll.dll, gdi32.dll and kernel32.dll. These three DLLs depend on other DLLs, such as advapi32.dll, ntdll.dll, and rpcrt4.dll. On some occasions, DLLs can be interdependent between one another and cause problems. The bottom list shows all of the DLLs involved, including user32.dll itself, and other pertinent information, such as version number and debugging information. This information is helpful when debugging an application. It helps to check for problems of version conflicts and detect potential file corruption.

When you select the user32.dll in the tree view, the lower list to the right of the hierarchical tree contains all the available functions of both imported and exported modules. Usually, the upper list tells you the functions that the parent application imports from the current file. The lower list tells you the available functions that the selected application contains. When the user32.dll is selected, the upper list is empty.

TIP

Dependency Walker is a free tool that scans 32-bit or 64-bit Windows modules (EXE, DLL, OCX, and SYS) and builds a hierarchical tree diagram of dependent modules. In case you don't have the Microsoft Visual Studio 6 installation on your system, you can download Dependency Walker from www.dependencywalker.com.

Building a Dynamic Linking Library for GUI Testing

The goal of this book is to build a GUI testing tool with full automation to generate test cases, test scripts, and bug reports. By using a few of the custom functions, you have developed a very primitive test monkey, but it is far from being a fully automated test tool. To achieve the proposed goal, the first and most critical step is to build a reusable GUI testing library. This library will be able to create functions to perform a thorough survey of the GUI components. It will be able to write a test script for each specific component found. The library will be used both for the tool and for the test script to perform the desired human actions. It will also provide a harness to manage the automatically generated test scripts. However, we will use the .NET Framework to develop the testing tool and to enable the tool to write test scripts in C# language. .NET developers have implemented a wide range of functionality for programming. This reusable library will only include the functions that are not supported by the .NET Framework.

The test monkeys you have developed are able to move and click the mouse and turn the mouse wheel. Because they don't have the capability of seeing where the GUI component is, they perform these functions randomly. Although they might click a problematic spot, the test monkeys don't know what it is and what to do with it. To get an idea of how programs perceive

GUIs on the screen, here I introduce one more tool. The Microsoft Visual Studio .NET IDE package comes with Spy++. This tool is capable of telling you the properties of a GUI component when you move the mouse pointer over it. This technique gives a tool the ability to see GUI components.

The Spy++ Tool

You can start Spy++ by choosing Start ➢ Programs ➢ Microsoft Visual Studio .NET 2003 ➢ Visual Studio .NET Tools ➢ Spy++.

The first thing you see in the Spy++ interface is the list of the GUIs of the applications running on your desktop. Figure 4.3 shows the objects I am running at this moment.

To help with GUI testing, Spy++ treats all GUI components as windows, including the main frames of the applications and the buttons, text boxes, and other controls within the main application. The information contains the class names, and the GUI objects are derived from the caption text of all the objects.

You can view the properties of any individual object by selecting a GUI object and choosing View ➢ Properties. Figure 4.4 shows the Properties dialog box.

The General tab tells you about the window as whole. It includes the window's display name, the window's handle, the virtual address, and the size of this window. The other tabs tell you related information. The other useful way to request Spy++ to investigate a particular GUI component is to choose Spy ➢ Find Window in the main window. Figure 4.5 shows the form that appears; notice that the fields are blank.

You can drag and drop the Finder Tool over a GUI component of interest. The information that then appears on the form includes the window's handle, its caption, its class name, its style, and its size as a rectangle.

FIGURE 4.3
View of Spy++ seeing all the objects running on my system at this moment

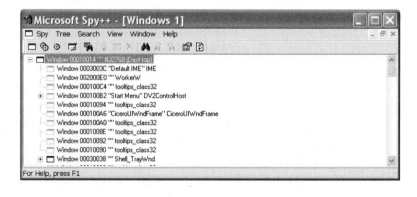

FIGURE 4.4
The Spy++ view of the
Start Menu properties

FIGURE 4.5
The initial form to find
a window with Spy++

Unfortunately, finding information for a GUI component by using Spy++ is a totally manual process; you can not use it directly in the automatic testing tool. But it gives you an idea about what information is needed to test GUIs. Many commercial GUI testing tools have utilities similar to Spy++ for users to manually relocate and probe GUI components. The next sections will explore in more depth how to use the user32.dll to find GUI information automatically.

Functions from the *User32.dll* for GUI Testing

Now, you have enough background to develop a GUI testing library. This library will become the core of a GUI testing tool. You can open the Microsoft Visual Studio .NET IDE to start a new Class Library project, type in **GUITestLibrary** as the project name, and place it in a new C:\GUISourceCode\Chapter04 folder.

When the project shows on the screen, a skeleton code for the project is created. This skeleton has the namespace of GUITestLibrary and a default class name, Class1. You can rename Class1 to GUITestActions to make it easier to identify. The code generated by the Microsoft Visual Studio .NET IDE looks like Listing 4.1.

Listing 4.1   **Auto-Generated Code for the *GUITestActions* Class**

```
using System;

namespace GUITestLibrary
{
  /// <summary>
  /// Summary description for GUITestActions.
  /// </summary>
  public class GUITestActions
  {
    public GUITestActions()
    {
      //
      // TODO: Add constructor logic here
      //
    }
  }
}
```

You are ready to add code for the GUITestActions library. Move the cursor below the first using Sytem; statement and add two more using statements like the following:

```
using System.Runtime.InteropServices;
using System.Text;
```

The System.Runtime.InteropServices namespace is needed to provide the .NET PInvoke service and marshal the custom DLLs. The second namespace, System.Text, prepares the library to use the StringBuilder class to manipulate string parameters of the custom functions.

Some of the code in Chapter 3 for building the test monkeys will be reused. However, you don't have to copy and paste it; you can add it easily by using the C# API Text Viewer.

Adding Structures and Enumerations

The custom functions will pass parameters by the references of some predefined structures in the Win32API.txt file. You need to add these structure definitions at the same hierarchical level as the GUITestActions class under the GUITestLibrary namespace.

First, open your C# API Text Viewer from the C:\GUISourceCode\Chapter03\CSharpAPITextViewer\bin\Debug folder. Use the File menu to open Win32API.txt. Click the ComboBox control below the **API Types** label to display the API options, select Types and add the structures defined in Listing 4.2.

NOTE   Referring to the user defined data type, the term *Type* is used for Visual Basic 6 programming and the term *structure* is used for Microsoft Visual Studio .NET, specifically `struct`
in C# programming.

Listing 4.2   Structures Added from the C# API Text Viewer for the *GUITestActions* Class

```
[StructLayout(LayoutKind.Sequential)]
public struct POINTAPI
{
  public int x;
  public int y;
}

[StructLayout(LayoutKind.Sequential)]
public struct RECT
{
  public int Left;
  public int Top;
  public int Right;
  public int Bottom;
}

[StructLayout(LayoutKind.Sequential)]
public struct MENUITEMINFO
{
  public int cbSize;
  public int fMask;
  public int fType;
  public int fState;
  public int wID;
  public int hSubMenu;
  public int hbmpChecked;
  public int hbmpUnchecked;
  public int dwItemData;
  public string dwTypeData;
  public int cch;
}
```

At the beginning, the POINTAPI structure defines a coordinate point along the x- and y-axis for
a display screen. The points are measured in pixels. You used the POINTAPI in Chapter 3. Thus,
all the visible GUI components will be included in the possible testing tasks of this testing tool.
The RECT structure is prepared to express the edges of a GUI window inside the display area. The
integer numbers for the Left, Top, Right, and Bottom variables are the pixel positions of a specified GUI. Thus the width of a GUI is the difference between the values of Right and Left
expressed in pixels and the height is the difference between Bottom and Top.

The MENUITEMINFO structure contains information about menu items. A menu can display items using text or bitmaps, but not both. This structure is used in the association of the GetMenuItemInfo(), InsertMenuItem(), and SetMenuItemInfo() functions. The following list describes its members:

cbSize   Size of structure, in bytes.

fMask   Members to retrieve or set. This member can be one or more of these values:

- MIIM_BITMAP retrieves or sets the hbmpItem member.
- MIIM_CHECKMARKS retrieves or sets the hbmpChecked and hbmpUnchecked members.
- MIIM_DATA retrieves or sets the dwItemData member.
- MIIM_FTYPE retrieves or sets the fType member.
- MIIM_ID retrieves or sets the wID member.
- MIIM_STATE retrieves or sets the fState member.
- MIIM_STRING retrieves or sets the dwTypeData member.
- MIIM_SUBMENU retrieves or sets the hSubMenu member.
- MIIM_TYPE retrieves or sets the fType and dwTypeData members. In Windows 98/ME and Windows 2000/XP, MIIM_TYPE is replaced by MIIM_BITMAP, MIIM_FTYPE and MIIM_STRING.

fType   Menu item type. This member can be one or more of these values:

- MFT_BITMAP displays the menu item using a bitmap. The low-order word of the dwTypeData member is the bitmap handle, and the cch member is ignored. In Windows 98/ME and Windows 2000/XP, MFT_BITMAP is replaced by MIIM_BITMAP and hbmpItem.
- MFT_MENUBARBREAK places the menu item on a new line (for a menu bar) or in a new column (for a drop-down menu, submenu, or shortcut menu). In a drop-down menu, submenu, or shortcut menu, a vertical line separates the new column from the old.
- MFT_MENUBREAK places the menu item on a new line (for a menu bar) or in a new column (for a drop-down menu, submenu, or shortcut menu). In a drop-down menu, submenu, or shortcut menu, the columns are not separated by a vertical line.
- MFT_OWNERDRAW assigns responsibility for drawing the menu item to the window that owns the menu. The window receives a WM_MEASUREITEM message before the menu is displayed for the first time and a WM_DRAWITEM message whenever the appearance of the menu item must be updated. If this value is specified, the dwTypeData member contains an application-defined value.

- `MFT_RADIOCHECK` displays selected menu items using a radio button mark instead of a check mark if the `hbmpChecked` member is `null`.

- `MFT_RIGHTJUSTIFY` right-justifies the menu item and any subsequent items. This value is valid only if the menu item is in a menu bar.

- `MFT_RIGHTORDER` specifies that menus cascade right to left (the default is left to right). This is used to support languages that are read right to left, such as Arabic and Hebrew.

- `MFT_SEPARATOR` specifies that the menu item is a separator. A menu item separator appears as a horizontal dividing line. The `dwTypeData` and `cch` members are ignored. This value is valid only in a drop-down menu, submenu, or shortcut menu.

- `MFT_STRING` displays the menu item using a text string. The `dwTypeData` member is the pointer to a null-terminated string, and the `cch` member is the length of the string. In Windows 98/ME and Windows 2000/XP, `MFT_STRING` is replaced by `MIIM_STRING`.

fState   Menu item state. This member can be one or more of these values:

- `MFS_CHECKED` checks the menu item. For more information about selected menu items, see the `hbmpChecked` member.

- `MFS_DEFAULT` specifies that the menu item is the default. A menu can contain only one default menu item, which is displayed in bold.

- `MFS_DISABLED` disables the menu item and grays it so that it cannot be selected. This is equivalent to `MFS_GRAYED`.

- `MFS_ENABLED` enables the menu item so that it can be selected. This is the default state.

- `MFS_GRAYED` disables the menu item and grays it so that it cannot be selected. This is equivalent to `MFS_DISABLED`.

- `MFS_HILITE` highlights the menu item.

- `MFS_UNCHECKED` unchecks the menu item. For more information about clearing menu items, see the `hbmpUnchecked` member.

- `MFS_UNHILITE` removes the highlight from the menu item. This is the default state.

wID   Application-defined 16-bit value that identifies the menu item. Set `fMask` to `MIIM_ID` to use `wID`.

hSubMenu   Handle to the drop-down menu or submenu associated with the menu item. If the menu item is not an item that opens a drop-down menu or submenu, this member is `null`. Set `fMask` to `MIIM_SUBMENU` to use `hSubMenu`.

hbmpChecked   Handle to the bitmap to display next to the item if it is selected. If this member is `null`, a default bitmap is used. If the `MFT_RADIOCHECK` type value is specified, the default bitmap is a bullet. Otherwise, it is a check mark. Set fMask to MIIM_CHECKMARKS to use hbmpChecked.

hbmpUnchecked   Handle to the bitmap to display next to the item if it is not selected. If this member is null, no bitmap is used. Set fMask to MIIM_CHECKMARKS to use hbmpUnchecked.

dwItemData   Application-defined value associated with the menu item. Set fMask to MIIM_DATA to use dwItemData.

dwTypeData   Content of the menu item. The meaning of this member depends on the value of fType and is used only if the MIIM_TYPE flag is set in the fMask member. To retrieve a menu item of type MFT_STRING, first find the size of the string by setting the dwTypeData member of MENUITEMINFO to null and then calling GetMenuItemInfo. The value of cch is the size needed. Then allocate a buffer of this size, place the pointer to the buffer in dwTypeData, and call GetMenuItemInfo once again to fill the buffer with the string. If the retrieved menu item is of some other type, then GetMenuItemInfo sets the dwTypeData member to a value whose type is specified by the fType member. When using with the SetMenuItemInfo function, this member should contain a value whose type is specified by the fType member. In Windows 98/ME and Windows 2000/XP, dwTypeData is used only if the MIIM_STRING flag is set in the fMask member.

cch   Length of the menu item text, in TCHARs, when information is received about a menu item of the MFT_STRING type. This member is used only if the MIIM_TYPE flag is set in the fMask member; it's set to zero otherwise. This member is ignored when the content of a menu item is set by calling SetMenuItemInfo. Before calling GetMenuItemInfo, the application must set this member to the length of the buffer pointed to by the dwTypeData member. If the retrieved menu item is of type MFT_STRING (as indicated by the fType member), then GetMenuItemInfo sets cch to the length of the retrieved string. If the retrieved menu item is of some other type, GetMenuItemInfo sets the cch field to zero. In Windows 98/ME and Windows 2000/XP, the cch member is used when the MIIM_STRING flag is set in the fMask member.

hbmpItem   Handle to the bitmap to be displayed, or it can be one of the values in the following list. It is used when the MIIM_BITMAP flag is set in the fMask member.

- HBMMENU_CALLBACK is a bitmap that is drawn by the window that owns the menu. The application must process the WM_MEASUREITEM and WM_DRAWITEM messages.
- HBMMENU_MBAR_CLOSE is the close button for the menu bar.
- HBMMENU_MBAR_CLOSE_D is the disabled close button for the menu bar.
- HBMMENU_MBAR_MINIMIZE is the minimize button for the menu bar.

- `HBMMENU_MBAR_MINIMIZE_D` is the disabled minimize button for the menu bar.

- `HBMMENU_MBAR_RESTORE` is the restore button for the menu bar.

- `HBMMENU_POPUP_CLOSE` is the close button for the submenu.

- `HBMMENU_POPUP_MAXIMIZE` is the maximize button for the submenu.

- `HBMMENU_POPUP_MINIMIZE` is the minimize button for the submenu.

- `HBMMENU_POPUP_RESTORE` is the restore button for the submenu.

- `HBMMENU_SYSTEM` is the Windows icon or the icon of the window specified in `dwItemData`.

If you have not added the structures to the `GUITestLibrary` namespace yet, do so by copying them from the C# API Text Viewer to the GUITestLibrary project. In addition to using the API viewer to add the structures, you need to handcraft three enumerations at the same hierarchical level. Listing 4.3 is the code for these three enumerations.

Listing 4.3	Members of the Three Enumerations: *MonkeyButtons*, *GUIInfoType*, and *RectPosition*

```
public enum MonkeyButtons
{
  btcLeft,
  btcRight,
  btcWheel,
}

public enum GUIInfoType
{
  guiText,
  guiTextClass,
  guiTextParent,
  guiTextClassParent,
}

public enum RectPosition
{
  LeftTop,
  LeftBottom,
  RightTop,
  RightBottom,
  MiddleTop,
  MiddleBottom,
  AnySpot,
}
```

The first enumeration, MonkeyButtons, is used to instruct the tool to click the left or right button or turn the mouse wheel, which has been discussed in Chapter 3. The second enumeration, GUIInfoCombo, instructs the tool to look for a particular GUI component by the combination of the specified caption text, the class name and its parent caption text.

The last enumeration positions a rectangular GUI component by four corner positions, two middle positions, and one any spot position. The corner and middle positions are relative to the middle point of the rectangle. They will be used with the MoveMouseInsideHwnd() and the CenterMouseOn() methods to be developed in the section on adding functions later in this chapter.

Adding Constants

After adding the structures and enumerations, you add the needed constants within the GUITestActions class. While Win32API.txt is still open in the C# API Text Viewer, click the ComboBox control under the API Types label to display and select Constants. Then, add the constants in Listing 4.4 into the text area one by one by clicking the Add button.

| Listing 4.4 | Constants Needed from C# API Text Viewer for the *GUITestActions* Class |

```
public const int WM_GETTEXT = 0xD;
public const int WM_GETTEXTLENGTH = 0xE;
public const int MOUSEEVENTF_ABSOLUTE = 0x8000 ; // absolute move;
public const int MOUSEEVENTF_LEFTDOWN = 0x2 ; // left button down;
public const int MOUSEEVENTF_LEFTUP = 0x4 ; // left button up;
public const int MOUSEEVENTF_MOVE = 0x1 ; // mouse move;
public const int MOUSEEVENTF_RIGHTDOWN = 0x8 ; // right button down;
public const int MOUSEEVENTF_RIGHTUP = 0x10 ; // right button up;
public const int MOUSEEVENTF_WHEEL = 0x800 ; //mouse wheel turns

private const int MOUSE_MICKEYS = 65535;
➥//65535 mickey steps across screen both horizontally and vertically
public const int SM_CXSCREEN = 0;
public const int SM_CYSCREEN = 1;

public const int GWL_ID = (-12);
public const int GW_HWNDNEXT = 2;
public const int GW_CHILD = 5;

public const int IDANI_CAPTION  = 0x3;
public const int IDANI_CLOSE  = 0x2;
public const int IDANI_OPEN  = 0x1;
```

The constants in Listing 4.4 are separated into clusters. Each cluster serves a function with different parameter values. Here, we just present a very brief review of them. For example, the first constant is for an application calling the SendMessage() function to send a WM_GETTEXT message. This message is copied as a string of text that corresponds to a window into a buffer provided by the caller. WM_GETTEXTLENGTH is similar to WM_GETTEXT constant. The difference is that it determines the length (the number of characters) of the text associated with a window.

The second cluster is for the mouse actions. With these constants, you can enable your testing tool and test scripts to automatically click and move the mouse. The MOUSE_MICKEYS constant defines 65,535 mickey steps for a display screen both vertically and horizontally. The SM_CXSCREEN and SM_CYSCREEN constants are used as parameter values of the GetSystemMetrics() function to get the maximum pixels in a display screen along the x- and y-axis, respectively.

The third group has three constants, and they are used as parameter values for the GetWindow() function. For example, the GetWindow() function passes a GW_CHILD value with the retrieved handle to identify the child window at the top of the Z order if the specified window is a parent window. Otherwise, the GetWindow() function passes a GW_CHILD value with a null handle. The function examines only child windows of the specified window. It does not examine descendant windows. The GW_HWNDNEXT value is also used by the GetWindow() function with a specific window handle to identify the window below the specified window in the Z order. If the specified window is a topmost window, the handle identifies the topmost window below the specified window. If the specified window is a top-level window, the handle identifies the top-level window below the specified window. Top-level windows can contain child windows. If the specified window is a child window, the handle identifies the sibling window below the specified window.

Finally, the last three constants specify the type of animation for the DrawAnimatedRects() function. For example, if you specify IDANI_CAPTION, the window caption will animate from the source position to a specified position. The specification of the IDANI_CLOSE and IDANI_OPEN make the animation effect similar to minimizing or maximizing a window.

Z Order

The Microsoft Windows operating system uses the *Z order* to indicate a window's order in a stack of overlapping windows. We have used x- and y- axis to indicate the width and height of a display screen. The window stack is oriented along an imaginary z-axis, which extends from the surface of the screen outward. The window at the top of the Z order overlaps all other windows. This window is called the topmost window. The system maintains the Z order by adding new windows onto the topmost window. A topmost window has the WS_EX_TOPMOST style and overlaps all other non-topmost windows regardless of whether it is the active or foreground window. The non-topmost windows are called top-level and child windows. A child window is grouped with its parent in the Z order.

Windows can become topmost if the BringWindowToTop() function is invoked. They can also be rearranged by the SetWindowPos() and DeferWindowPos() functions. You can use the GetTopWindow() function to search all child windows of a parent window and return a handle to the child window that is highest in Z order. The GetNextWindow() function retrieves a handle to the next or previous window in the Z order.

Adding Functions

You have defined the structures and constants. The structures and constants are used as parameters and values by the custom functions to perform testing actions. The constants and functions are placed in the same hierarchical level as the other methods in this .NET project. You can continue to select functions by using the C# API Text Viewer and clicking the Add and Copy buttons to paste them into the C# project. The additional functions are shown in Listing 4.5.

Listing 4.5   Functions Needed from the C# API Text Viewer for the *GUITestActions* Class

```
[DllImport("user32.dll")]
public static extern int FindWindow(StringBuilder lpClassName,
➥StringBuilder lpWindowName);

DllImport("user32.dll")]
public static extern int SetWindowText(int hwnd, StringBuilder lpString);

[DllImport("user32.dll")]
public static extern int GetFocus();

[DllImport("user32.dll")]
public static extern int GetDlgItem(int hDlg, int nIDDlgItem);

[DllImport("user32.dll")]
public static extern int GetCursorPos([MarshalAs(UnmanagedType.Struct)]
➥ref  POINTAPI lpPoint);

[DllImport("user32.dll")]
public static extern int GetClassName(int hwnd,
➥StringBuilder lpClassName, int nMaxCount);

[DllImport("user32.dll")]
public static extern int WindowFromPoint(int xPoint, int yPoint);

[DllImport("user32.dll")]
public static extern void mouse_event(int dwFlags,
int dx, int dy, int cButtons, int dwExtraInfo);

[DllImport("user32.dll")]
public static extern int GetSystemMetrics(int nIndex);

[DllImport("user32.dll")]
public static extern int GetWindowRect(int hwnd,
➥[MarshalAs(UnmanagedType.Struct)] ref  RECT lpRect);

[DllImport("user32.dll")]
public static extern int SetForegroundWindow(int hwnd);

[DllImport("user32.dll")]
```

```
public static extern int GetWindow(int hwnd, int wCmd);

[DllImport("user32.dll")]
public static extern int GetDesktopWindow();

[DllImport("user32.dll")]
public static extern int GetWindowLong(int hwnd, int nIndex);

[DllImport("user32.dll")]
public static extern int GetParent(int hwnd);

[DllImport("user32.dll")]
public static extern int GetWindowText(int hwnd,
➥StringBuilder lpString, int cch);

[DllImport("user32.dll")]
public static extern int GetWindowTextLength(int hwnd);

[DllImport("user32.dll")]
public static extern int GetDlgCtrlID(int hwnd);

[DllImport("user32.dll")]
public static extern int GetMenu(int hwnd);

[DllImport("user32.dll")]
public static extern int GetMenuItemCount(int hMenu);

[DllImport("user32.dll")]
public static extern int GetMenuItemRect(int hWnd, int hMenu,
➥int uItem, [MarshalAs(UnmanagedType.Struct)] ref RECT lprcItem);

[DllImport("user32.dll")]
public static extern int GetMenuItemInfo(int hMenu, int un, int b,
➥[MarshalAs(UnmanagedType.Struct)] ref  MENUITEMINFO lpMenuItemInfo);

[DllImport("user32.dll")]
public static extern int GetMessageExtraInfo();

[DllImport("user32.dll")]
public static extern int SetRect([MarshalAs(UnmanagedType.Struct)]
➥ref RECT lpRect, int X1, int Y1, int X2, int Y2);

[DllImport("user32.dll")]
public static extern int DrawAnimatedRects(int hwnd, int idAni,
➥[MarshalAs(UnmanagedType.Struct)] ref RECT lprcFrom,
➥[MarshalAs(UnmanagedType.Struct)] ref RECT lprcTo);
```

As we have discussed, to call custom functions from .NET programs, you always place a DllImport attribute in the front of the code. There are 25 functions in Listing 4.5 from the user32.dll. These functions will perform various actions to manipulate windows or GUI components. For example, `FindWindow()` will return the handle of a window based on the class name and the window name. The `SetWindowText()` function changes the caption of the specified window's title bar. The `GetMenu()` function retrieves a handle to the menu assigned to the specified window. With the combination of these functions, you can manage the testing tool and test scripts. I will explain the functions individually as they are used.

At this point, you have experienced writing C# code for marshaling structures, constants, and functions of the custom DLLs. It is easy to copy the accurate C# code from the C# API Text Viewer to a program. The Text Viewer will be more useful in the future when you extend the functionality of your testing tool.

Expanding the Testing Capabilities

When you programmed the test monkeys, you discovered that you need to combine a few custom functions to perform a testing action. In this section, we are going to add some methods by calling the pertinent functions and thus enhance the capabilities of the GUI testing library.

In Chapter 3, you implemented a few methods to enable the test monkeys to move and click the mouse: `ClickMouse()`, `PixelXYToMickeyXY()`, `MoveMouse()`, and `GetSmartInfo()`. The GUI testing library needs these methods too. You can copy the code of these methods from the source code for Chapter 3.

Next, you are going to develop some more useful methods. These methods will enable the tool to know about the GUI components on the desktop, move the mouse pointer to a meaningful area, and click the mouse button to perform a desired action. First, the most frequently used method is the `FindGUILike()` method with its code shown in Listing 4.6.

Listing 4.6   Code for the *FindGUILike()* Method of the *GUITestActions* Class

```
//Chapter 4
private static int level = 0;
public static int FindGUILike(ref int hWndArray, int hWndStart,
➡ref string windowText, ref string className, ref string parentText)
{
  int hwnd=0;
  int r=0;

  StringBuilder sWindowText=new StringBuilder();
  StringBuilder sClassname=new StringBuilder();
  StringBuilder sParentText = new StringBuilder();

  if (level == 0)
  {
    hWndTarget = 0;
    if (hWndStart == 0) hWndStart = GetDesktopWindow();
  }
  level = level + 1;
```

```
    hwnd = GetWindow(hWndStart, GW_CHILD);

    while (hwnd != 0)
    {
      r = FindGUILike(ref hWndArray,hwnd, ref windowText,
  ➥ref className,ref parentText);

      sWindowText.Capacity = 255;
      r = GetWindowText(hwnd, sWindowText, 255);
      sClassname.Capacity= 255;
      r = GetClassName(hwnd, sClassname, 255);
      sParentText.Capacity = 255;
      r = GetWindowText(GetParent(hwnd), sParentText, 225);

      GUIInfoType guiInfoType = GetGUIInfoType(windowText, className, parentText);

      ResetGUIInfo(guiInfoType, hwnd, ref hWndArray, ref windowText,
  ➥ref className, ref parentText, sWindowText, sClassname, sParentText);
      // Get next child window:
      hwnd = GetWindow(hwnd, GW_HWNDNEXT);
    }
    // Decrement recursion counter:
    level = level - 1;
    return 0;
  }
```

In Listing 4.6, before the method declaration, a `private static level` field is defined to progress the GUI finding process. The static declaration of this variable is for consistency with the method, which is going to consume it. Then, `FindGUILike()` is a recursive method used to check all the open GUI components on the desktop along the imaginary z-axis. It takes five parameters:

hWndTarget   An integer variable passed by reference. This is always an unknown variable before the method invocation and becomes known after the invocation. All the other custom functions targeting GUI components are based on the value found by this method.

hWndStart   An integer variable passed by value. When you want to look for a particular GUI, you need to request that this method starts from the zeroth order along the z-axis. Then the method checks windows one by one until it finds it.

windowText   A `string` object passed by reference. Most of the time, the window text (caption) of a GUI is directly seen by the users. For example, when you developed the C# API Text Viewer, you made different buttons read Add, Remove, Clear and Copy. Window text is one of the important properties that help a program find the accurate GUI component. However, if you can't read the text of a window, you can use the values of the other properties to identify a GUI component of interest.

className   Also a `string` object passed by reference. Each GUI object is derived from a class, which has a name. When this variable is known, you can increase the chance of finding a particular GUI. It is especially helpful when some GUI objects carry the same caption. If the class name is passed unknown, this method will assign the text to this variable after invocation.

parentText   Another `string` object passed by reference. Each application has a main window, which doesn't belong to any parent window. But a main window often has multiple child windows. For example, the Add, Remove, Clear and Copy buttons of the C# API Text Viewer are child windows of the application. When the parent text is known, i.e., **C# API Text Viewer** in this case, it narrows the search to find the specified GUI from a particular main window.

After the method declaration, two `int` and three `StringBuilder` objects are declared. The `int` variables are declared to enumerate all the possible windows. The `StringBuilder` objects are declared to hold the window text, class name, and the GUI's parent text. The first `if` statement finds the handle of the desktop. Then it calls the `GetWindow()` function to find the handle of the first child of the desktop by passing a value of the `GW_CHILD` constant. A `while` loop is used to recursively scrutinize every child window. Whenever this method controls the handle of a child window, it derives the window text, the window class name, and its parent text into the `StringBuilder` objects by calling pertinent custom functions.

Remember, when you defined the parameters, your goal was to find the correct GUI handle of this session by matching the known contents of the `string` objects passed by reference. However, you don't have to know the value of all the `string` objects. When at least the window text or the window class name is passed as known, this method should be able to find a matching handle. So that it is aware of which objects are known and unknown, this method calls a helper method, `GetGUIInfoType()`. Listing 4.7 is the code for the `GetGUIInfoType()` method.

Listing 4.7   **Code for the *GetGUIInfoType()* Helper Method**

```
private static GUIInfoType GetGUIInfoType(string winText,
➥string winClass, string winTextParent)
{
  if (winText != "" && winClass != "" & winTextParent == "")
    return GUIInfoType.guiTextClass;
  else if (winText != "" && winClass == "" & winTextParent != "")
    return GUIInfoType.guiTextParent;
  else if (winText != "" && winClass != "" & winTextParent == "")
    return GUIInfoType.guiTextClassParent;
  else if (winText == "" && winClass != "" & winTextParent != "")
    return GUIInfoType.guiClassParent;

  return GUIInfoType.guiText;
}
```

The GetGUIInfoType() helper method returns a value of the GUIInfoType enumeration based on the known combination of the window text, the class name, and the parent window's text. The recognition of such a combination is achieved by a set of if-else statements. As we have discussed, the last return statement assumes the window text is passed if no other variables are known.

Subsequently, it calls one more helper method, ResetGUIInfo(). The ResetGUIInfo() method is coded as in Listing 4.8.

Listing 4.8   **Code for the *ResetGUIInfo()* Helper Method]**

```
private static void ResetGUIInfo(GUIInfoType guiInfoType,
➡int hwnd, ref int hWndTarget,
➡ref string windowText, ref string className,
➡ref string parentText, StringBuilder sWindowText,
➡StringBuilder sClassname, StringBuilder sParentText)
{
  string clsStartedWith = "";
  if (className.IndexOf(".") >= 0)
  {
    clsStartedWith =
➡className.Replace(className.Split('.')[className.Split('.').Length-1], "");
  }
else
{
  clsStartedWith = className;
}
  if (guiInfoType == GUIInfoType.guiText)
  {
    if (sWindowText.ToString() == windowText)
    {
      hWndTarget = hwnd;
      className = sClassname.ToString();
      parentText = sParentText.ToString();

    }
  }
  else if (guiInfoType == GUIInfoType.guiTextClass )
  {
    if (sWindowText.ToString() == windowText &&
        sClassname.ToString().StartsWith(clsStartedWith))
    {
      hWndTarget = hwnd;
      parentText = sParentText.ToString();

    }
  }
  else if (guiInfoType == GUIInfoType.guiTextParent)
  {
    if (sWindowText.ToString() == windowText &&
        sParentText.ToString() == parentText)
```

```
    {
      hWndTarget = hwnd;
      className = sClassname.ToString();

    }
  }
  else if (guiInfoType == GUIInfoType.guiTextClassParent)
  {
    if (sWindowText.ToString() == windowText &&
        sClassname.ToString().StartsWith(clsStartedWith) &&
        sParentText.ToString() == parentText)
    {
      hWndTarget = hwnd;

    }
  }
  else if (guiInfoType == GUIInfoType.guiClassParent)
  {
    if (sClassname.ToString().StartsWith(clsStartedWith) &&
        sParentText.ToString() == parentText)
    {
      hWndTarget = hwnd;
      windowText = sWindowText.ToString();

    }
  }
}
```

The first `if` statement of the `ResetGUIInfo()` truncates the last part of the given class name and assigns the result to a `clsStartedWith` variable when the class name is separated by a few periods (.) into several parts. This is because the Win32 API `GetClassName()` function finds the class names of the GUI controls in applications developed with .NET environment with the last part suffixed with an `.appxx`, in which the xx is a number varying from time to time. The later context will discuss this in more detail. The `else` statement places the given class name into the `clsStartedWith` variable in order that the GUI test library can test applications developed in environments other than .NET.

This helper method assigns the correct values to the unknown window text, the class name, and/or the parent window's text within a few sections of `if-else` statements. These correct values are found through each handle of the child windows. The outside `if-else` statements direct the program to a section of known variable combinations identified by the `guiInfoType` value. If the passed values from the `FindGUILike()` method match all the values found, the GUI object of interest is found and the unknown values of the window text, the class name, and/or its parent text become known. For example, the last `else-if` section deals with a situation in which the class name and the parent text of a GUI are known. When a GUI is found to have the same class name and the same parent text, the `ResetGUIInfo()` method assigns the GUI's handle to the `hWndTarget` and the GUI's text to the `windowText` variable.

The last calling of the GetWindow() function by passing a value of the GW_HWNDNEXT constant continues to obtain each GUI handle until all the child windows are checked. After the while loop, the level value is decremented by 1, which drives the recursive calling of the FindGUILike() method until all the parent windows are checked. This is an exhaustive iteration; eventually all the GUI objects will be checked and the desired GUI object will be found.

Before a person clicks a mouse button, they move the mouse pointer over a GUI object. However, the test monkeys in Chapter 3 simply moved the mouse pointer and clicked randomly. The task of the code in Listing 4.6 is only to find a GUI handle. You want a method to drive the pointer to that GUI object and do something. A CenterMouseOn() method is implemented to pass the found handle as a parameter and move the mouse pointer to the center of the GUI object. Listing 4.9 is the implementation of the CenterMouseOn() method.

Listing 4.9   **Code for the *CenterMouseOn()* Method**

```
public static bool CenterMouseOn(int hwnd)
{
  int x = 0;
  int y = 0;
  int maxX = 0;
  int maxY = 0;
  RECT crect = new RECT();
  int gFound = 0;

  GetDisplayResolution(ref maxX, ref maxY);
  gFound = GetWindowRect(hwnd, ref crect);

  x = crect.Left + ((crect.Right - crect.Left) / 2);
  y = crect.Top + ((crect.Bottom - crect.Top) / 2);
  if ((x >= 0 && x <= maxX) && (y >= 0 && y <= maxY))
  {
    MoveMouse(hwnd, x, y);
    return true;
  }

  return false;
}
```

The goal of the CenterMouseOn() method is to move the mouse pointer to a coordinate point that will be found by executing some custom functions. It first prepares an x- and a y- variable to find the central coordinate of a GUI object. Then it prepares two more variables, maxX and maxY, to make sure the x- and the y-axes of the display screen has as its maximum number of pixels. A RECT object is initialized to hold the pixels to define a rectangle of the GUI object of interest. Finally, a gFound variable makes sure the GUI object of interest is open in the current desktop session. After the preparation, various functions are executed to assign values to the respective variables. The first helper method is GetDisplayResolution() and it is coded in Listing 4.10.

Listing 4.10   **Code for the *GetDisplayResolution()* Helper Method**

```
public static void GetDisplayResolution(ref int pixelX, ref int pixelY)
{
  pixelX = GetSystemMetrics(SM_CXSCREEN);
  pixelY = GetSystemMetrics(SM_CYSCREEN);
}
```

This method simply calls the GetSystemMetrics() function two times to find the width and height of a display screen. These pixel values are the maximum measurements for any windows. Knowing this information ensures that all the testing actions occur within the screen. Then the GetWindowRect() method is called to locate the relative coordinate points of the upper-left and the lower-right corners of the GUI under test within a screen. These two corners determine a rectangle. The coordinates are stored in the RECT object passed by reference.

After the rectangle of the GUI under test is found within the displayable area of the screen, the CenterMouseOn() method starts to count from the left edge toward the right to the halfway across the width of the found rectangle and assigns a value to the x variable for the central point in the x-axis. Then it starts from the top edge downward to the halfway point of the height of the GUI object and assigns a value to the y variable for the central point in the y-axis. The if statement confirms that the central point is inside the display screen and calls the MoveMouse() function to accomplish the movement of the mouse pointer to the center of the GUI under test. After the mouse is moved, a true value is returned. If the calculated x and y values fall beyond the screen, a false value is returned.

You implemented a method to make the mouse perform an absolute movement relative to the screen in Chapter 3 and a CenterMouse() method to move the mouse to the center of a GUI. People also move the mouse pointer to any point inside a GUI rectangle. Listing 4.11 is the code to achieve such a mouse movement.

Listing 4.11   **Code for the *MoveMouseInsideHwnd()* Method**

```
public static void MoveMouseInsideHwnd(int hwnd,
➥int xPos, int yPos, RectPosition rctPos)
{
  int xPixel = xPos;
  int yPixel = yPos;
  if (!rctPos.Equals(RectPosition.AnySpot))
  {
    xPixel = 5;
    yPixel = 5;
  }

  CenterMouseOn(hwnd);
  int width = 0;
```

```
    int height = 0;
    POINTAPI pa = new POINTAPI();


    GetWindowSize(hwnd, ref width, ref height);


    GetCursorPos(ref pa);
    switch (rctPos)
    {
      case RectPosition.LeftTop:
        xPixel = (pa.x - width/2) + xPixel % width ;
        yPixel = (pa.y - height/2) + yPixel % height;
        break;
      case RectPosition.LeftBottom:
        xPixel = (pa.x - width/2) + xPixel % width ;
        yPixel = (pa.y + height/2) - yPixel % height;
        break;
      case RectPosition.RightTop :
        xPixel = (pa.x + width/2) - xPixel % width ;
        yPixel = (pa.y - height/2) + yPixel % height;
        break;
      case RectPosition.RightBottom:
        xPixel = (pa.x + width/2) - xPixel % width ;
        yPixel = (pa.y + height/2) - yPixel % height;
        break;
      case RectPosition.MiddleTop :
        xPixel = (pa.x);
        yPixel = (pa.y - height/2) + yPixel % height;
        break;
      case RectPosition.MiddleBottom:
        xPixel = (pa.x);
        yPixel = (pa.y + height/2) - yPixel % height;
        break;
      case RectPosition.AnySpot:
        xPixel = (pa.x - width/2) + xPixel % width ;
        yPixel = (pa.y - height/2) + yPixel % height;
        break;
    }

    MoveMouse(hwnd, xPixel, yPixel);
}
```

The MoveMouseInsideHwnd() method takes four parameters, the GUI handle, hwnd, the x- and y-coordinates by pixel, and the GUI position, rctPos, you want the mouse pointer to move to. After the method declaration, the initialization of the xPixel and yPixel get the x- and y-coordinates, respectively. If the value of the rectPos parameter is not RectPosition.AnySpot, the MoveMouseInsideHwnd() method requests that the method move the mouse pointer at least 5 pixels inside the boundary of a GUI under test. Then, based on the handle passed as the first parameter, it calls the CenterMouseOn() method to move the mouse to the center of the GUI object of interest. Next, the method continues to initialize three other variables—width, height, and a POINTAPI object, pa—for finding the width and height of the current GUI and the current mouse position by calling GetWindowSize() and GetCursorPos() methods respectively. The GetWindowSize() helper method determines the numbers of pixels of a GUI in both horizontal and vertical directions. Code for the GetWindowSize() method is shown in Listing 4.12.

Listing 4.12   Code for the *GetWindowSize()* Method

```
public static void GetWindowSize(int iHandle, ref int wPixel, ref int hPixel)
{
  int lrC = 0;
  RECT rCC = new RECT();
  lrC = GetWindowRect(iHandle, ref rCC);
  wPixel = rCC.Right - rCC.Left;
  hPixel = rCC.Bottom - rCC.Top;
}
```

This method simply calls the GetWindowRect() method to find the edge of a GUI rectangle in absolute pixel numbers within a screen. These absolute pixel numbers are stored in the rCC object as coordinates of the upper-left and lower-right corners. The difference between the absolute right and absolute left edge is the width of the GUI under test. The difference between the absolute top and bottom edge is the height of the GUI. The pixel values of width and height of the GUI are used to reset the wPixel and hPixel parameters passed by references.

At this point, the MoveMouseInsideHwnd() method knows the size of the GUI of interest and the coordinate pixels of the current mouse pointer, which has been moved to the center of the GUI of interest. Last, a switch statement is used to check the value of the last parameter, that is, where the tester wants to move the mouse pointer for the next step. The mouse pointer can be moved to LeftTop, LeftBottom, RightTop, RightBottom, MiddleTop , MiddleBottom, or AnySpot inside the GUI and the absolute pixels can be calculated with regard to the entire screen area. But it will always be inside the GUI of interest at least 5 pixels toward the closest edges. The last statement invokes the MoveMouse() method and simply moves the mouse pointer from the center to the desired location inside the GUI.

The hard part of GUI test automation is that the tools don't know there are GUI components in an application. The capture/playback facility uses a pure manual process to compensate for this. The automatic GUI testing tool to be developed in this book will use an approach to move the mouse pointer systematically and pixel by pixel inside a GUI under test and determine the presence of a GUI at the current mouse position. In order to achieve this, you need to add a GetWindowFromPoint() method to the GUITestLibrary project. Code for the GetWindowFromPoint() method is in Listing 4.13. Thus, when the tool instructs the mouse to move around the display, it encounters all the GUI components within the application under test and obtains the information for a GUI test.

Listing 4.13   **Code for the *GetWindowFromPoint()* Method**

```
public static void GetWindowFromPoint(ref int hwnd,
➡ref StringBuilder winText, ref StringBuilder clsName,
➡ref StringBuilder pText)
{
  int parentHandle = 0;
  int maxLen = 128;

  POINTAPI pnt = new POINTAPI();
  parentHandle = GetCursorPos(ref pnt);
  hwnd = WindowFromPoint(pnt.x, pnt.y);

  winText = new StringBuilder(maxLen);
  parentHandle = GetWindowText(hwnd, winText, maxLen);

  clsName = new StringBuilder(maxLen);
  parentHandle = GetClassName(hwnd, clsName, maxLen);

  pText = new StringBuilder(maxLen);
  parentHandle = GetParent(hwnd);
  parentHandle = GetWindowText(parentHandle, pText, maxLen);

}
```

The GetWindowFromPoint() method manipulates four reference parameters: the handle, text, class name, and parent text of the GUI the mouse pointer is currently on. When the method is invoked, it first initializes two integer variables; the parentHandle variable is prepared to find the parent window and the maxLen variable is to set the function to make the maximum length of the text to 128 characters for each of the StringBuilder parameters passed as references. Then an initialization of a POINTAPI object, pnt, is used to locate the current position of the mouse pointer by the invocation of the GetCursorPos() function and get the GUI handle by invoking the WindowFromPoint() function. Once the handle of the GUI at the current mouse position is obtained, the code simply invokes the respective functions to assign text, class name, and parent text of the current GUI object to the reference parameters.

To indicate the physical GUI unit from the GUI survey collected by the tool, you have prepared three constants—IDANI_CAPTION, IDANI_CLOSE, and IDANI_OPEN—and a DrawAnimatedRects() custom function for GUI animation. When the DrawAnimatedRects() method is invoked, the corresponding GUI object on the screen will blink a few times when the tester selects a property of a GUI object of a survey list. To handle this feature properly, you can code an Indicate-SelectedGUI() method as shown in Listing 4.14.

Listing 4.14   **Code for GUI animation of the *IndicateSelectedGUI()* Method**

```
public static void IndicateSelectedGUI(int hwnd)
{
  int xSize = 0;
  int ySize = 0;
  RECT rSource = new RECT();
  GetWindowRect(hwnd, ref rSource);
  GetWindowSize(hwnd, ref xSize, ref ySize);

  SetRect(ref rSource, rSource.Left, rSource.Top,
➥rSource.Left + xSize, rSource.Top);

  DrawAnimatedRects(hwnd,
➥IDANI_CLOSE | IDANI_CAPTION | IDANI_OPEN, ref rSource, ref rSource);

}
```

The `IndicateSelectedGUI()` method yanks the handle of a GUI. At execution, it invokes the `GetWindowRect()` function to determine the rectangle position of the GUI by assigning a RECT object to the rSource object. Then it invokes the `GetWindowSize()` method to determine the width and height of the rectangle. After the rectangle of the GUI is known, the `SetRect()` function makes another rectangle to draw the GUI from its original position to the reset position. Then the last line of the code invokes the `DrawAnimatedRects()` method and completes the animation. The animation effect shows the window text of the GUI over a blue bar and blinks a few times.

The already implemented methods are for GUI actions in general. The last part of this section will implement particular methods to handle particular GUI controls, such as how to click a ListBox, a command Button and a TextBox. Listing 4.15 is the code to click the vertical scroll bar and select an item from the list box.

Listing 4.15   **The Code of the *HandleListBox()* Method to Click a Vertical Scroll Bar and Select an Item from a List Box.**

```
public static void HandleListBox(ref int hwnd, ref string winText,
➥ref string clsName, ref string pText)
{
  int r = GUITestActions.FindGUILike(ref hwnd,
➥0, ref winText, ref clsName, ref pText);

  CenterMouseOn(hwnd);
  MoveMouseInsideHwnd(hwnd, RectPosition.RightBottom);
  ClickMouse(MonkeyButtons.btcLeft,0,0,0,0);
  MoveMouseInsideHwnd(hwnd, RectPosition.MiddleBottom);
  ClickMouse(MonkeyButtons.btcLeft,0,0,0,0);
}
```

As discussed in the previous sections, the FindGUILike() method uses various combinations of a window's text, its class name, and its parent window's text to determine a known GUI in the desktop. The HandleListBox() method uses the combination of the class name and its parent window text to locate the handle of a ListBox control in an application under test. Then it calls the respective static methods to move the mouse to the center of the ListBox control. Then, it clicks the mouse button at the lower-right corner to scroll the vertical bar. Last, it clicks at the middle point near the lower edge of the list box to select the bottom item visible from the list box.

Another often-performed GUI action is to click a command button. For example, when testing the C# API Text Viewer, after an item is selected in the list box, you need a method to click the Add button and append the function declaration to the rich text box. Listing 4.16 shows the code for the HandleCommandButton() method.

Listing 4.16   The Code of the *HandleCommandButton()* Method

```
public void HandleCommandButton(ref int hwnd,
➥ref string winText, ref string clsName, ref string pText)
{
  int r = GUITestActions.FindGUILike(ref hwnd,
➥0, ref winText, ref clsName, ref pText);

  CenterMouseOn(hwnd);
  ClickMouse(MonkeyButtons.btcLeft, 0,0,0,0);
}
```

Similar to how a ListBox control is handled, the HandleCommandButton() method also uses the combination of the window's text and its parent window's text to locate a button handle of an application under test. The functions employed to click a button and click a list box are the same. But the invocation of the CenterMouseOn() and ClickMouse() methods occurs only once when a command button is clicked. The ClickMouse() method needs to be invoked twice for a ListBox control.

The next method is to handle a click inside a TextBox control as well as a RichTextBox control. As the book progress, more methods will be needed to handle various GUI controls. Listing 4.17 shows the code for the HandleTextBox() method.

Listing 4.17   The Code of the *HandleTextBox()* Method

```
public static void HandleTextBox(ref int hwnd,
➥ref string winText, ref string clsName, ref string pText)
{

  int r = FindGUILike(ref hwnd, 0, ref winText, ref clsName, ref pText);
```

```
    CenterMouseOn(hwnd);
    MoveMouseInsideHwnd(hwnd, 20, 10, RectPosition.AnySpot);
    ClickMouse(MonkeyButtons.btcLeft,0,0,0,0);
}
```

As you can see, this method requires the same set of parameters and employs the same methods as the ListBox and Button control handling methods do. The difference is the position in which the mouse button needs to be clicked. The HandleTextBox() method is implemented to click at the upper-left corner inside a TextBox. After the click, the TextBox gets the focus and the cursor is at the first line of the text.

A method to handle synchronization for GUI testing is also implemented in this section. When we perform non-GUI testing, the execution of one line of code in the test script can be completed instantly and in sequence. But GUI testing actions often trigger new GUI components to show on the screen, and the next action is to interact with the new GUI components. Usually, there is some time elapsed before the required GUIs are completely drawn. This is the synchronization issue. If the execution of the next action is not synchronized with the appearance of the new window on the screen, the action can not be performed as desired. Thus, you need to implement a SynchronizeWindow() method such as in Listing 4.18.

Listing 4.18   Code for the *SynchronizeWindow()* Method

```
public static void SynchronizeWindow(ref int hwnd,
➥ref string winText, ref string clsName, ref string pText)
{
    int startSyn = DateTime.Now.Second;
    while (hwnd <=0)
    {
        FindGUILike(ref hwnd, 0, ref winText, ref clsName, ref pText);
        if (5 < DateTime.Now.Second - startSyn)
        {
            break;
        }
    }
}
```

First, it marks an integer startSyn variable with the time, in seconds, that the action starts. Then it uses a while loop to execute the FindGUILike() method iteratively until the handle of the GUI control is found. In order to prevent an infinite loop (if, for example, a GUI of interest never shows on the screen), an if statement checks the time elapsing. The maximum time to loop is arbitrarily set to 5 seconds. You can choose a suitable elapsing time for your own testing requirements.

After typing in all the code, you can choose Build ➢ Build Solution from the Microsoft Visual Studio .NET IDE to build the project. This will result in a class library DLL assembly that can be reused to write GUI test scripts. You will refer to this assembly to create a GUI script in the next section.

NOTE   If you need to compare your code with the source code to correct errors, you can visit `www.sybex.com` to download the sample code. You can find the code by searching for this book's title, author, or ISBN (4351).

A GUI Test Application

People have become used to moving the mouse and clicking the mouse buttons (plus some keystrokes) to operate software applications. You have implemented a GUI testing library to move the pointer freely on your monitor and perform clicks. As planned in Chapter 3, the C# API Text Viewer will be used to provide precise C# code for marshaling custom function to build the tool, and it will be subjected to testing manually and automatically throughout this book. This section includes an example to illustrate how to handcraft a script and call the implemented methods to operate the C# API Text Viewer. The script will simulate a person performing the following actions:

- Starting the C# API Text Viewer application
- Clicking the vertical scroll bar of the list box at its lower-right corner to scroll the list downward
- Selecting a function from the list by highlighting it
- Clicking the Add button to add the selected definition into the rich text box in sequence
- Repeat the four preceding actions until all of the functions are added into the rich text box

To accomplish this, you can start a new project by opening the Microsoft Visual Studio .NET IDE. Then choose File ➢ New Project. When the new project dialog box appears, complete the following steps to create a new project:

1. Select Visual C# Projects from the Project Types pane and Windows Application from the Templates pane.

2. Type **GUIScriptSample** as the project name in the Name field.

3. Click the browse button to navigate to the `C:\GUISourceCode\Chapter04` folder for the Location field.

4. Click the OK button. An empty Windows form appears.

5. Place three GUI controls on the form. The control classes and their properties are described in the following list. You can accept the default values of the properties that are not listed:

Control	Property	Value
Timer	Name	tmrAddDefinition
	Interval	3000
	Enable	false
Button	Name	btnStartAUT
	Text	Start AUT
Button	Name	btnStartStop
	Text	Start

After you place the Timer and Button controls on the form—see Figure 4.6 (b) for the final look—double-click each one to add code for their respective tasks. First, double-click the Start AUT button on the form. The Microsoft Visual Studio .NET IDE activates the code editor with a Windows Application template. You can accept this template as it is, but add two more `using` directives at the beginning of it:

```
using System.Diagnostics;
using GUITestLibrary;
```

The `System.Diagnostics` allows the program to initialize a Process object to start the C# API Text Viewer. However, this is a temporary solution at this point. The next chapter will introduce methods to start an application dynamically and return an object of the application for the purpose of test verification. Then, the second `using GUITestLibrary` statement allows the script to use methods from the GUITestLibrary project easily. Last, navigate the cursor into the `btnStartApp_Click()` event and make the code of this event look like the code in Listing 4.19.

Listing 4.19   **The Code of the *btnStartApp_Click()* Event**

```
private void btnStartApp_Click(object sender, System.EventArgs e)
{
  string AUT = @"C:\GUISourceCode\Chapter03\
➥CSharpAPITextViewer\bin\Debug\CSharpAPITextViewer.exe";
  Process p = new Process();
  p.StartInfo.FileName = AUT;

  p.Start();

}
```

When the event is triggered, it first starts a string variable to hold the path and filename of the C# API Text Viewer. Then it initializes a Process object, p. The last two lines of code assign the application path and filename to a `StartInfo.FileName` property of the Process object and invoke the application.

After the code that starts the application, you add code to trigger the `btnStartStop_Click()` event. The code of this event is shown in Listing 4.20.

Listing 4.20   The Code of the *btnStartStop_Click()* Event

```
private void btnStartStop_Click(object sender, System.EventArgs e)
{
  if (!tmrAddDefinition.Enabled)
  {
    tmrAddDefinition.Enabled = true;
    btnStartStop.Text = "Stop";
  }
  else
  {
    tmrAddDefinition.Enabled = false;
    btnStartStop.Text = "Start";
  }
}
```

The `btnStartStop` button is designed to be a toggle button. When the program is running automatically, clicking this button will stop functions from being added to the C# API Text Viewer. When the program is idle, clicking this button will make the program click the list box and the Add button continuously. To achieve this, the event alternatively disables and enables the Timer control, `tmrAddDefinition`, and changes the text of the `btnStartStop` caption from Start to Stop and vice versa. The purpose of changing the caption is to help users know whether the program is busy or idle.

At this point, the program has code to open the application and prepare a timer to continuously and automatically click on the right spots of the list box and the Add button. To add code to the timer, you double-click the `tmrAddDefinition` control in the GUI design editor. The Microsoft Visual Studio .NET IDE generates a `tmrAddDefinition_tick()` event and places the cursor between a pair of curly brackets in the code editor. Type in the code to handle the list box and the Add button clicks as shown in Listing 4.21.

Listing 4.21   The Code of the *tmrAddDefinition_tick()* Event

```
private void tmrAddDefinition_Tick(object sender, System.EventArgs e)
{
  int hwnd = 0;
  string winText = "";
```

```
    string clsName = "WindowsForms10.LISTBOX.app3";
    string pText = "C# API Text Viewer";
    GUITestActions.HandleListBox(ref hwnd, ref winText, ref clsName, ref pText);

    winText = "Add";
    clsName = "";
    pText = "C# API Text Viewer";
    GUITestActions.HandleCommandButton(ref hwnd,
➥ref winText, ref clsName, ref pText);
    }
```

Four variables—hwnd, winText, clsName, and pText—are declared inside the event; they are required by the GUI handling methods of the GUITestLibrary. In order to locate the correct GUI, the values of these four variables will be reset before each of the GUI handling methods is invoked. For the purpose of finding the ListBox control, the clsName variable is assigned with a string value as WindowsForms10.LISTBOX.app3. The class name of a GUI control with the managed application found by the custom functions has a general form of WindowsForms10.<control type>.app<#>. The pound sign indicates a number, which might change from session to session. However, this is different from the class name you can view from the Microsoft Visual Studio .NET IDE at development time. For example, the class names seen by the custom functions of a ListBox and a TextBox are WindowsForms10.LISTBOX.app3 and WindowsForms10.RichEdit20W. app3, but you recognize them in the .NET Framework as System.Windows.Forms.ListBox and System.Windows.Forms.RichTextBox, respectively.

You set the timer interval to 3000 milliseconds when you populated the GUI controls. Therefore, after the tmrAddDefinition control object is enabled, it will invoke the HandleListBox() and the HandleAddButton() methods from the GUITestActions class to click the proper spots inside the list box and the Add button every 3 seconds. Thus, we have handcrafted the first GUI test script of this book.

After all the code is in place, close other applications on your desktop that are open. Then, from the Microsoft Visual Studio .NET IDE, press F5 to build and run the GUIScript-Sample program. You also can start this program by double-clicking the executable from the C:\GUISourceCode\Chapter04\GUIScriptSample\bin\Debug folder. After the GUIScript-Sample program starts, minimize the Microsoft Visual Studio .NET IDE. The desktop now displays only the GUIScriptSample program. I recommend that you drag this window to the lower-right portion of the screen so the automatically invoked application won't cover it. Now, click the Start AUT button to launch the C# API Text Viewer. Click the Start button. Its caption changes to Stop. The mouse starts to move and click on the desired pixels by itself and adds function declarations one by one into the rich text box every 3 seconds. Figure 4.6 shows what the programs look like when they are running.

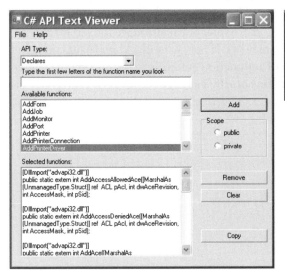

FIGURE 4.6
The automated C# API
Text Viewer (a) and the
GUIScriptSample
program (b) at work

After you observe the automatic operation of a GUI, you can stop the GUIScriptSample program at any time. The purpose of this example is to demonstrate a simple way to write a test script. This GUIScriptSample program accomplishes the job of traditional capture/playback GUI testing tools. There is no verification code in the example script at this point. Also, you need to hand-write the code. The ultimate purpose of the upcoming chapters is to enable the GUITestLibrary project to automatically generate fully functional GUI test scripts that include code for result verification, validation, and presentation.

Summary

This chapter discussed the user32.dll library with respect to GUI test functions. Then we used the dumpbin.exe program and the Dependency Walker to investigate the user32.dll. Based on the knowledge gained from building the test monkeys in Chapter 3 and the concept of the Spy++ program, the rest of this chapter involved using the C# API Text Viewer and building a GUI test library. This library provides functions to perform mouse actions.

Finally, we used the GUI test library to handcraft a script that automatically clicks buttons to operate the C# API Text Viewer. This script is similar to scripts created by using capture/playback testing tools. The difference is that the structured programming is used to record the capture/playback scripts and the object-oriented programming (OOP) method is used to create the hand-written script.

The ultimate goal of this book is to develop an AutomatedGUITest tool to automatically generate fully functional test scripts and complete the GUI test of an application with minimum human interaction. Chapter 5 will introduce the serialization, reflection and late binding within the .NET Framework. Then, we will add more functions to the GUI test library and increase the degree of automation gradually in the upcoming chapters. The automatically generated test scripts will eventually include code for verification, validation, and test presentation.

CHAPTER 5

.NET Programming and GUI Testing

The previous two chapters have included a review of Win32 custom DLLs and their functions. Software developers have a long history of using an API Text Viewer to help with the Win32 API programming before the release of Microsoft Visual Studio .NET. You will also find a way of reusing the C# API Text Viewer for many purposes other than for marshaling custom functions with regard to GUI testing. However, Win32 API programming thrives on the backbone of a programming language. In Chapters 3 and 4, I assumed that you have some basic knowledge about C#. NET programming. Chapter 3 guided you through the development of a C# API Text Viewer. Then you laid a foundation for the GUI testing library in Chapter 4. In order to proceed to the next chapters, you'll begin here to promote your .NET programming skill to the next level. Some of the material in this chapter—an introduction of the .NET namespaces and classes—may be just a review for you.

In this chapter, I will first show you how to use the .NET `System.Xml` namespace to create, read, and navigate XML documents. Then I will discuss a few serialization methods of the .NET Framework for object persistence. Persisting objects by serialization and deserialization will help the GUI testing tool create and save the testing cases and present and save the test results. These data objects and results will all be stored in collections. Thus, the .NET `System.Collections` namespace will be introduced next.

Modern programming languages have functions to reflect software components. The reflection techniques dissect software components into data types, members, and parameters as a prism reflects the sunlight into a spectrum. The .NET `System.Type` class lends a helpful hand to accomplish the reflection tasks. Following the reflection discussion, you will have enough background to dynamically invoke methods of an application at runtime, also called late binding. Late binding will save you from having to write a lot of code for the automatic GUI testing tool.

Starting from Chapter 3, you have worked with some methods from the `System.Threading` `.Thread` class of the .NET Framework in a simple way. The last section of this chapter will introduce more advanced uses of a thread.

XML Programming

This book focuses on techniques that are useful for developing an automatic GUI testing tool. Because testers prefer a data-driven testing tool, it makes sense to employ Extensible Markup Language (XML) programming first. XML is a broad and important topic in today's software industry. This section will not discuss it in a great detail. However, you will learn about writing, reading, and navigating XML documents using C# programming.

XML is based on the Standard Generalized Markup Language (SGML). The flexibility of XML has made it a necessity for exchanging data in a multitude of forms. The organization of the information in XML documents is similar to the organization of material in Hypertext

Markup Language (HTML). But the elements and attributes are flexible in XML and can be customized to suit almost all situations. The following are the testing-tool-related definitions of the parts of XML needed to form a well-structured XML document:

Attribute   A property of an XML element. An attribute has a name and a value to provide additional data about an element, independent of element content.

Element   The basic unit of an XML document. A start and an end tag with associated content define each element.

Nesting   The hierarchical structure of XML. The relationship between the elements of an XML document is a parent-child relationship or a sibling relationship. Child elements start and end within parent elements.

Schema   A data model consisting of rules to represent an XML document. The schema defines elements, attributes, and the relationships between different elements.

Syntax   The rules that govern the construction of intelligible markup fragments of XML documents.

Tag   The markup used to enclose an element's content inside XML documents. Each element has an opening and a closing tag. Well-formed tags adhere to the syntax rules for XML documents, which make the documents easy for a computer to interpret.

The .NET Framework has predefined many ways to present an XML document. I will introduce only a few of them in this chapter.

Writing XML Files

When you use XML, you can use a text editor to write any data following the XML syntax. You also can use other applications to create XML documents more easily, such as the XML file options of the Microsoft Visual Studio .NET IDE, XML Notepad, or xmlspy. But the purpose of this section is to show you how to write XML documents programmatically.

TIP   You can download a trial version of the XML Notepad from `www.snapfiles.com/get/` `xmlnotepad.html`. The use of this tool is intuitive. To use the Microsoft Visual Studio .NET IDE for creating an XML document, you can start by choosing File ➢ New ➢ File. When the New File dialog box appears, select the General category in the left pane and select XML Template in the right pane. xmlspy is commercial software from Altova, Inc. If you are interested in more information, you can search at `www.altova.com`. If you have installed Microsoft Excel XP, you can open an XML document in a spreadsheet or save one to a spreadsheet. Plus, the current Microsoft Office Suite has a new application, Microsoft Office InfoPath 2003, which gathers information by integrating with XML documents and letting teams and organizations create and work with customer-defined XML schema.

One of the respective .NET classes for creating an XML document is `System.XML`
`.XmlTextWriter`. The following example will show you how to use this class to write a
`GUITestActionLib.xml` file. This file uses the names of the GUI control classes for the
names of the XML elements and the names of the corresponding handling methods in
the developed GUITestLibrary for the value of these elements. For example, the full
class name of the ListBox control is `System.Windows.Forms.ListBox`. You implemented
a `HandleListBox()` method in Chapter 4 to click this GUI control. The corresponding
XML element for this GUI control will be written as follows:

```
<System.Windows.Forms.ListBox>HandleListBox</System.Windows.Forms.ListBox>
```

After you finish this example, you will use the resulting XML document as an action library
of the GUI testing tool in the upcoming chapters. You can follow these steps to create a C#
program to obtain the `GUITestActionLib.xml` file.

1. Start the Microsoft Visual Studio .NET IDE. Choose File ➤ New ➤ Project.

2. When the New Project dialog box appears, select Visual C# Project from the right pane
   and Console Application from the left pane. In the Name field, type **XMLCreator**. In the
   Location field, type **C:\GUISourceCode\Chapter05**. Then click the OK button.

3. When the Microsoft Visual Studio .NET IDE brings you to the code editor, an XMLCreator
   namespace with a Class1 skeleton is created. Let's rename Class1 to XMLGuiTestActions
   and code the program as shown in Listing 5.1.

Listing 5.1   Code to Create an XML Document

```
using System;
using System.Xml;

namespace XMLCreator
{

  class XMLGuiTestActions
  {
    [STAThread]
    static void Main(string[] args)
    {
      //create an XmlTextWriter instance
      XmlTextWriter xmlW = new
➡XmlTextWriter("GUITestActionLib.xml", System.Text.Encoding.UTF8);

      //Format the XML document
      xmlW.Formatting = Formatting.Indented;
      xmlW.Indentation = 2;
```

```
        //Start a root element
        xmlW.WriteStartElement("GUIActions");

        //add child elements by calling the helper method
        WriteChildElement(xmlW, "System.Windows.Forms.ListBox", "HandleListBox");
        WriteChildElement(xmlW,
➡"System.Windows.Forms.RichTextBox", "HandleTextBox");
        WriteChildElement(xmlW,
➡"System.Windows.Forms.Button", "HandleCommandButton");
        WriteChildElement(xmlW, "Field", "VerifyField");
        WriteChildElement(xmlW, "Property", "VerifyProperty");
        WriteChildElement(xmlW, "Synchronization", "SynchronizeWindow");

        //close the root element and the XML document
        xmlW.WriteEndElement();
        xmlW.Close();
    }


    private static void WriteChildElement(XmlTextWriter xmlW,
➡string GUIType, string GUILibMethod)
    {
        //Write each GUI action as a child element
        xmlW.WriteStartElement(GUIType);
        xmlW.WriteString(GUILibMethod);
        xmlW.WriteEndElement();
    }
  }
}
```

Writing an XML file by programming in C# is easy. First, you need to add a using System.Xml statement at the beginning of the program. In the Main() method of the XMLGuiTestActions class, you simply create an XmlTextWriter instance. When you create the instance, you give a filename for the XML document and the desired character encoding as parameters of the constructor. The example specifies UTF8, corresponding to what most of us know as 8-bit ASCII characters. If your testing project involves other characters, you can choose other character encoding, such as UTF7 or Unicode. Then you specify the format properties. Setting up values for formatting the XML document is optional, but it makes it easier for those working with the file to recognize the relationship between elements. The name of the root element of the GUITestActionLib.xml file is <GUIActions>. You call the WriteStartElement() method to make a starting tag of it. This tag will be closed at the end of the program by calling the WriteEndElement() method after all the child elements are nested.

To write the child elements and reduce the lines of the statements for WriteStartElement(), WriteString(), and WriteEndElement() invocation, a helper method, WriteChildElement(), is created. This helper method takes the XmlTextWriter instance, the name of the GUI class, and the name of the GUI testing method as parameters. The three lines of code inside the helper method simply invoke the three methods to create a start tag for each GUI class name, assign a string value of the method name to the element, and close the tag, respectively. The `WriteChildElement()` method is invoked six times in the `Main()` method and creates six nodes to properly use the methods of the GUI test library. The GUI test library will grow as the testing tool created , you will have more chances to revisit this example and add more element tags and method names.

Finally, the `WriteEndElement()` method closes the root element. The XML file is completed. After all the code is added to the program, you can press F5 to build and run the XMLCreator project. A `GUITestActionLib.xml` document is saved. If you have implemented this program using the preceding steps, you will find the XML document in the `C:\GUISourceCode\ Chapter05\XMLCreator\bin\Debug` folder.

Reading XML Files

The easiest way to view an XML document is to open it in a text editor such as Notepad. Listing 5.2 shows the raw content of the `GUITestActionLib.xml` document in plain text.

Listing 5.2   **The Raw Content of the *GUITestActionLib.xml* Document**

```
<GUIActions>
  <System.Windows.Forms.ListBox>HandleListBox</System.Windows.Forms.ListBox>
  <System.Windows.Forms.RichTextBox>
➥HandleTextBox</System.Windows.Forms.RichTextBox>
  <System.Windows.Forms.Button>HandleCommandButton</System.Windows.Forms.Button>
  <Field>VerifyField</Field>
  <Property>VerifyProperty</Property>
  <Synchronization>SynchronizeWindow</Synchronization>
</GUIActions>
```

Each XML element starts with a name enclosed in a pair of <> and ends with the identical text of the name enclosed in </>. Besides viewing XML documents in text editors, you can also open an XML document in Internet Explorer or any of the XML tools mentioned in the preceding section. Microsoft Excel XP can be used to create and open an XML document too. These specialized programs display the XML elements in more readable forms. But the purpose of reading an XML document in this chapter is to use the information to conduct software testing. You need a way to read it programmatically and .NET developers have prepared some classes to achieve this. The next sections discuss three ways. The first is by creating an `XmlTextReader` instance and using its `Read()` method to extract the XML elements one by one.

You can use the same steps you used in the preceding example to create another console application. In step 2, name this project XMLExtractor. Accept the rest of the template as it is generated by the Microsoft Visual Studio .NET IDE. The final code of this project is shown in Listing 5.3.

Listing 5.3 **Code to Programmatically Read an XML Document with the** *XmlTextReader* **Class**

```
using System;
using System.Xml;

namespace XMLExtractor
{
  class Class1
  {

    [STAThread]
    static void Main(string[] args)
    {
      string xmlFile =
➥@"C:\GUISourceCode\Chapter05\XMLCreator\bin\Debug\GUITestActionLib.xml";
      XmlTextReader xmlR = new XmlTextReader(xmlFile);

      while (xmlR.Read())
      {
        if (xmlR.Value.Trim().Length > 0)
          Console.WriteLine(xmlR.Value);
      }

      //hold the screen
      Console.ReadLine();
    }
  }
}
```

This code is even simpler. After you add the using System.Xml namespace at the beginning, you move the cursor to the Main() method and create an XmlTextReader instance. Then code the Main() method to invoke the Read() method from this instance to enumerate through the child elements with a while loop. The elements are referred to as nodes in this case. Some of the nodes may not contain a GUI test method in the XML document; for example, the root element contains all child elements. Within the while loop, I use an if statement to print on a console window the value of a node that has a GUI test method. The last line of the Console.ReadLine() method is for stopping the console from disappearing too fast after the execution. With this line in the program, you need to press the Enter key to terminate the program. After you complete the code, you can press F5 to build and run it. Figure 5.1 shows the extracted GUI test methods in a console window.

FIGURE 5.1
The extracted GUI
test methods from
the created XML
document.

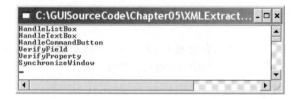

Press the Enter key to exit, and continue to the next example.

XPathNavigator Class

The second way to read an XML document is by using the XPathDocument class. This method loads the entire document into memory and then uses a random access navigator to move around it. In contrast, the XmlTextReader class works in a forward direction.

As you have done for the previous examples, you can start the Microsoft Visual Studio .NET IDE for a new console application project and name this project XmlNavigator. When the code editor appears, accept the template and add code. The code of the completed program is in Listing 5.4.

Listing 5.4   **Code to Programmatically Read an XML Document by using an *XPathDocument* and an *XPathNavigator* Instance**

```
using System;
using System.Xml.XPath;

namespace XmlNavigator
{
  class Class1
  {
    [STAThread]
    static void Main(string[] args)
    {

      string xmlFile =
➥@"C:\GUISourceCode\Chapter05\XMLCreator\bin\Debug\GUITestActionLib.xml";
      XPathDocument xmlDoc = new XPathDocument(xmlFile);
      XPathNavigator xmlNavy = xmlDoc.CreateNavigator();

      xmlNavy.MoveToRoot();
      NavigateXMLDoc(xmlNavy);

      //hold the screen
      Console.ReadLine();
    }
```

```
      //Recursive method
      private static void NavigateXMLDoc(XPathNavigator xmlNavy)
      {
        //Print the value of the current element
        if (xmlNavy.NodeType == XPathNodeType.Text)
          Console.WriteLine(xmlNavy.Value);

        if (xmlNavy.HasChildren)
        {
          xmlNavy.MoveToFirstChild();
          NavigateXMLDoc(xmlNavy);

          while (xmlNavy.MoveToNext())
            NavigateXMLDoc(xmlNavy);

          xmlNavy.MoveToParent();
        }
      }
    }
  }
}
```

Using XmlPathNavigator requires the System.Xml.XPath namespace to be added as a using directive. Then, inside the Main() method, the code first initializes a string object to hold an XML document filename. Similar to how the XmlTextReader class works, the XPathDocument class uses the filename to build an xmlDoc object. The XPathDocument class provides a fast read-only cache for XML document processing. This class is optimized for the XPath data model. It does not maintain node identity, nor does it do the rule checking required XML validation. After the next statement, which calls the CreateNavigator() method to create an XPath-Navigator() object, xmlNavy, the xmlDoc hands the rest of the tasks to the xmlNavy object. Thereafter, each line of the remaining code uses the xmlNavy object.

The xmlNavy object immediately moves to the root element of the XML document by calling its MoveToRoot() method. An XML document is a house of elements with parent-child and sibling relationships. The last working line of code inside the Main() method calls a NavigateXMLDoc() helper method. The NavigateXMLDoc() method is implemented as a recursive method. A recursive method starts to track a family tree from the oldest ancestor to the youngest grandchild until all the branches are visited. The code of the recursive method is in the second part of Listing 5.4. It first calls the Console.WriteLine() method to print the value of the current element on the screen if the element has a text value. The second if statement checks whether the current element has child elements. If it does, it goes to the first child and starts the first NavigateXMLDoc() recursive call. After all the children of the first child are recursively conscripted, it immediately moves to the family of the next child and recursively conscripts all of the children. After all the cousins are enlisted, the xmlNavy object returns to the parent and concludes coding the method. But the completion of the recursion depends on how many generations the XML document houses.

Now, build and run this program by pressing F5. The content printed on the console screen is identical to the content shown in Figure 5.1. Thus, you learned a more flexible way to look for a value from an XML document.

XmlDocument Class

The third method to navigate through an XML document is via the XmlDocument class of the .NET System.Xml namespace. To demonstrate the use of the XmlDocument class, this section will guide you in creating a Windows application with a tree view. The tree view will clearly show the nested structure of an XML document.

1. Start a new session of the Microsoft Visual Studio .NET IDE.

2. Create a new project by choosing File ➤ New ➤ Project. When the New Project dialog box appears, select Visual C# Project and Windows Application in the left and right panes, respectively. Then type in the project name as **XmlTreeViewer** and save the project in the C:\GUISourceCode\Chapter05\ folder.

3. After you click the OK button in the New Project dialog box, the Microsoft Visual Studio .NET IDE generates a Windows form, Form1 as the class name, and the skeleton code. You need to place a TreeView, a Button, and an OpenFileDialog control on the form as shown in the following list:

Control	Property	Value
Form	Name	Form1
	Text	XML Document Viewer
TreeView	Name	tvXml
Button	Name	btnView
	Text	View XML
OpenFileDialog	Name	opnXMLFile

4. Add code by double-clicking the View XML button. When the Microsoft Visual Studio .NET IDE brings the cursor to the btnView_Click() event, you first need to add a using System.Xml statement at the beginning of the code page. Then you start to code the btnView_Click() event between the curly brackets. The code is shown in Listing 5.5.

Listing 5.5   Code to Open an XML Document of the *btnView_Click()* Event

```
private void btnView_Click(object sender, System.EventArgs e)
{
  opnXMLFile.Filter = "XML files (*.xml)|*.xml|All Files (*.*)|*.*";
  if (opnXMLFile.ShowDialog() == DialogResult.OK)
  {

    string xmlFile = opnXMLFile.FileName;
    OpenXmlDoc(xmlFile);
  }
}
```

The btnView_Click() event is straightforward. It first assigns a filter to show files with an
.xml extension in the open file dialog box. Then it invokes the open file dialog box by using the
ShowDialog() method. An open file dialog is a modal window. Users have to finish interacting
with a modal window before proceeding to the execution of the next line of code. Thus, the if
statement directs the program to populate the tree view control after the OK button on the open
file dialog is clicked. If the OK button is not clicked, it will exit this event without doing anything.
After the OK button is clicked, it invokes an OpenXmlDoc() helper method as coded in Listing 5.6.

**Listing 5.6   Code of the *OpenXmlDoc()* Helper Method to View an XML Document within
                       a TreeView Control**

```
public void OpenXmlDoc(string xmlFile)
{
  tvXml.Nodes.Clear();

    //Initailize XML objects
  XmlTextReader xmlR = new XmlTextReader(xmlFile);
  XmlDocument xmlDoc = new XmlDocument();
  xmlDoc.Load(xmlR);
  xmlR.Close();


  //navigate inside the XLM document & populate th
  tree view with recursion
  TreeNode tnXML = new TreeNode("GUI Test XML");
  tvXml.Nodes.Add(tnXML);
  XmlNode xnGuiNode = xmlDoc.DocumentElement;

  XMLRecursion(xnGuiNode, tnXML);

  tvXml.ExpandAll();

}
```

To populate the tree view, declaration of the OpenXmlDoc() helper method passes a filename selected by navigating the file system via the open file dialog. This method is declared to have a public modifier so that it can be invoked programmatically. The project, then, can be reused for later chapters to display test results. The first line of the code clears the tree view if the tree view contains XML elements from the previous event triggering. Then it initializes both an XmlTextReader instance (to open the specified XML document) and an XmlDocument instance. By invoking the Load() method of the XmlDocument instance, it loads the XML document into memory. The XmlTextReader instance can be closed. Closing this instance allows other processes to access the XML document while this program is working on it as well.

After the XML document is loaded into memory, the program can navigate inside it freely. Here, I use a TreeNode instance to walk through every element and every generation of the nested XML structure. This TreeNode instance will get all the elements from the XML document and add them to the tree view by implementing an XMLRecursion() helper method. The last line of the code expands all the nodes of the tree trunk and the branches so they can be viewed readily. The code for the XMLRecursion() method is in Listing 5.7.

Listing 5.7   **Code for the *XMLRecursion()* Method to Go between the XML Document and TreeView Control**

```
private void XMLRecursion(XmlNode xnGuiNode, TreeNode tnXML)
{
  TreeNode tmpTN = new TreeNode(xnGuiNode.Name + " " + xnGuiNode.Value);

  if (xnGuiNode.Value == "false")
  {
    tmpTN.ForeColor = System.Drawing.Color.Red;
  }

  tnXML.Nodes.Add(tmpTN);

  //preparing recursive call
  if (xnGuiNode.HasChildNodes)
  {
    XmlNode tmpXN = xnGuiNode.FirstChild;
    while (tmpXN != null)
    {
      XMLRecursion(tmpXN, tmpTN);
      tmpXN = tmpXN.NextSibling;
    }
  }
}
```

A TreeNode instance and an XMLNode instance have been created in the first part of the btnView_ Click() event. The XMLRecursion() method takes these two instances as parameters and adds the information to the TreeView control. It first creates a temporary TreeNode instance to hold the current XML node information. An if statement is used here to inspect the value of this node. If the value is literally a string of false, the code turns the foreground of this node into the color red. Testers usually use the value false to indicate that an error is found in a software test result report. Later, when you use this project to view a test report, it will highlight the testing steps that find bugs. Then it adds the temporary node to the TreeNode instance as a child node. The if statement inspects whether the current XML node has child elements. If it does, a temporary XmlNode instance is created to hold the first child element. Then the use of a while loop walks through the entire list of the children by recursively calling the XMLRecursion() method and enumerating the siblings. It concludes the recursion until all the XML elements are added to the TreeView control.

After you add all the code into the project, you can press F5 from the Microsoft Visual Studio .NET IDE to build and run the project. If you have compiling errors and need to double-check the code, you can download the sample source code from www.sybex.com (where you'll find the code of this project and all the other sample projects). When the program is running and the tree view is empty, do the following to view an XML document:

1. Click the XML View button to bring up the open file dialog box.

2. Select the GUITestActionLib.xml file by navigating to the C:\GUISourceCode\Chapter05\ XMLCreator\bin\Debug folder, where you created an XMLCreator project in a previous section.

3. Click the Open button from the open file dialog box. At this moment, the TreeView control in the form contains an XML document with the branches and nodes fully expanded. You can collapse or expand a node by clicking on the -/+ sign. The expanded GUITestActionLib.xml document is shown in the TreeView control in Figure 5.2.

FIGURE 5.2
Viewing the GUITest-
ActionLib.xml docu-
ment by navigating
with an XmlDocument
instance and a
TreeView control

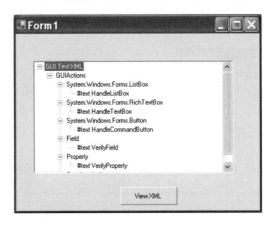

This XML document view is more like a professional application. XML documents have elements, attributes, and string values. The previous examples have simplified the use of the XML document classes. They show the elements and the values but don't show the other information of the elements. However, this illustration is enough to serve the purpose of this book and build a foundation for the automatic GUI testing tool. For more complicated examples of ways to navigate XML documents, I list some references in the bibliography at the end of the book. You can upgrade the GUI testing tool by implementing more powerful methods to enhance software test automation for your organization.

Object Serialization

Today, software applications tend to treat data as objects. We want the GUI testing tool to recognize the testing cases and the GUI components under test as objects too. The object *serialization* of the .NET Framework suits this purpose well. Later, the serialized objects can be *deserialized*, reconstructed and used for verification and regression testing.

Modern programming languages have built-in functions that can easily make objects persistent and store them in a physical file or memory by serialization. You can program in languages supported by the .NET Framework with a few kinds of serializations, such as binary serialization, SOAP serialization, and XML serialization. Developers using the .NET Framework implement data types marked by the attribute [Serializable] or [NonSerialized]. Public properties and fields of a [Serializable] attributed object can all be serialized. With regard to developing a fully automated GUI testing tool, you may use one of the serializations. However, I will discuss each of the three kinds in this section and you can choose one to suit your testing needs.

Binary Serialization

Once an object is serializable, you decide which file format you want to use to save the object data. The .NET Framework has a predefined System.Runtime.Serialization.Formatters.Binary namespace. This namespace offers binary serialization by a BinaryFormatter class. The object data are saved as a stream using compact binary format. The following list describes the core methods of the BinaryFormatter class:

Deserialize()   Deserializes a file stream to reconstruct an object

Serialize()   Serializes an object to a file stream

Now I'll use an example to help you learn the serialization techniques. As usual, start by opening a new session of Microsoft Visual Studio .NET IDE. Open the New Project dialog box by choosing File ➢ New ➢ Project. Select the Visual C# Project and the Windows Application template from the left and right panes, respectively. Name the project ControlSerializer and save it in the C:\GUISourceCode\Chapter05 folder. Click the OK button to accept the project definitions. When the form design editor is open, place the following GUI controls on it:

Control	Property	Value
Label	Name	lblName
	Text	Control Name
Label	Name	lblText
	Text	Control Text
Label	Name	lblType
	Text	Control Text
TextBox	Name	txtName
TextBox	Name	txtText
TextBox	Name	txtType
Button	Name	btnSerialize
	Text	Serialize
Button	Name	btnDeserialize
	Text	Deserialize
Button	Name	btnReset
	Text	Reset
OpenFileDialog	Name	ofdDeserialize
SaveFileDialog	Name	sfdSerialize

Then you need to implement a [Serializable] attributed class by choosing Project ➢ Add Class. When the Add New Item dialog box appears, type **GUIControlProperties** in the Name field. Clicking the Open button brings the cursor to the GUIControlProperties class in the code editor. Code this class as shown in Listing 5.8.

Listing 5.8   **Code for a Serializable *GUIControlProperties* Class**

```
using System;

namespace ControlSerializer
{

  [Serializable]public class GUIControlProperties
  {
    public string GUIName;
    public string GUIText;
    public string GUIType;

    public GUIControlProperties()
    {
    }
  }
}
```

This class contains three members as public fields of an arbitrary GUI control object for simplification. The [Serializable] attribute is placed immediately before the class declaration.

After you type in the code, go back to the form design editor by clicking the Form1.cs tab. Then double-click the Serialize button. When the code editor is active, add two using statements at the beginning of the Form1.cs file.

```
using System.Runtime.Serialization.Formatters.Binary;
using System.IO;
```

The first using statement enables the project to implement the BinaryFormatter class easily. The second is for the project to save and open files. Add the code in Listing 5.9 between the curly brackets of the btnSerialize_Click() event.

Listing 5.9   **Code to Serialize a *GUIControlProperties* Object into a Physical File**

```
private void btnSerialize_Click(object sender, System.EventArgs e)
{
  //initialize a GUIControlProperties object
  GUIControlProperties GuiCtrlProp;
  GuiCtrlProp = new GUIControlProperties();
  GuiCtrlProp.GUIName = txtName.Text;
  GuiCtrlProp.GUIText = txtText.Text;
  GuiCtrlProp.GUIType = txtType.Text;

  //make a filename to serialize the object
  string filename = "";
  sfdSerialize.Filter = "Serializing Files (*.bin; *.soap;
```

```
➥*.xml)|*.bin;*.soap;*.xml|All Files|*.*";
  if (sfdSerialize.ShowDialog() == DialogResult.OK)
  {
    filename = sfdSerialize.FileName;
  }
  else
  {
    return;
  }

  //Start serialization
  FileInfo fi = new FileInfo(filename);
  switch (fi.Extension)
  {
    case ".bin":
      BinarySerialization(filename, GuiCtrlProp);
      break;
  }
}
```

I divided the code in the btnSerialize_Click() event into three clusters. The first cluster initializes a GUIControlProperties object and assigns the values from the text boxes of the form to the fields of the object. The second cluster opens a SaveFileDialog box. The user specifies a filename to serialize the arbitrary object. The last cluster uses the file extension of the specified filename inside a switch statement to choose a serialization formatter and accomplishes the serialization by calling the corresponding helper method for different formatting cases. The first case is the BinarySerialization() method. Listing 5.10 shows the code for the BinarySerialization() method.

Listing 5.10   **Code of the *BinarySerialization()* Helper Method**

```
private void BinarySerialization(string filename, GUIControlProperties obj)
{
  //Create a file stream object
  FileStream serializeStream = File.Create(filename);

  //Start Serialization
  BinaryFormatter binFmt = new BinaryFormatter();
  binFmt.Serialize(serializeStream, obj);
  serializeStream.Close();
}
```

There are two steps in the helper method to complete the serialization. First, the method initializes a FileStream object with the specified filename. Second, it initializes a BinaryFormatter object, serializes the specified object into a physical file, and closes the FileStream object.

The purpose of serializing an object is to reuse it by deserialization. Now, go back to the form design editor and double-click the Deserialize button. The code editor opens with the cursor in it. You can code the btnDeserialize_Click() event as in Listing 5.11.

Listing 5.11   **Listing 5.11 : Code to Deserialize a *GUIControlProperties* Object from a Physical File**

```
private void btnDeserialize_Click(object sender, System.EventArgs e)
{
  //Get the serilized file name
  string filename = "";
  ofdDeserialize.Filter = "Serializing Files (*.bin; *.soap;
➥*.xml)|*.bin;*.soap;*.xml|All Files|*.*";
  if (ofdDeserialize.ShowDialog() == DialogResult.OK)
  {
    filename = ofdDeserialize.FileName;
  }
  else
  {
    return;
  }

  //reconstruct the object from a file
  GUIControlProperties GuiCtrlProp = null;
  FileInfo fi = new FileInfo(filename);
  switch (fi.Extension)
  {
    case ".bin":
      GuiCtrlProp = BinaryDeSerialization(filename);
      break;
  }

  //populate the text of the GUI controls on the form
  txtName.Text = GuiCtrlProp.GUIName;
  txtText.Text = GuiCtrlProp.GUIText;
  txtType.Text = GuiCtrlProp.GUIType;
}
```

I also divide the code for the btnDeserialize_Click() event into three clusters. The process of a deserialization is just the reverse of that of a serialization. After btnDeserialize_Click() event obtains a filename from the Open File dialog box, it also uses the file extension to invoke the respective helper method, BinaryDeSerialization(), and reconstruct the object. The last cluster returns the content of the object to the Text properties of the text boxes on the form. The code for the BinaryDeSerialization() helper method is in Listing 5.12.

Listing 5.12   **Listing 5.12 : Code of the *BinaryDeSerialization()* Helper Method**

```
private GUIControlProperties BinaryDeSerialization(string filename)
{
  GUIControlProperties GuiCtrlProp;

  //Create a file stream object
  FileStream serializeStream = File.OpenRead(filename);

  //Start Serialization
  BinaryFormatter binFmt = new BinaryFormatter();
  GuiCtrlProp = (GUIControlProperties)binFmt.Deserialize(serializeStream);
  serializeStream.Close();
  return GuiCtrlProp;
}
```

The `BinaryDeSerialization()` helper method looks similar to the `BinarySerialization()` helper method. But this method returns an object that needs to be reconstructed by invoking the `Deserialize()` method.

When a GUI has areas for the users to enter text, they like to click a button to clear the obsolete contents and start new entries. You can double-click the Reset button in the form design editor and code the `btnReset_Click()` event as shown in Listing 5.13.

Listing 5.13   **Listing 5.13 : Code of the *btnReset_Click()* Event to Clear the Form**

```
private void btnReset_Click(object sender, System.EventArgs e)
{
  txtName.Clear();
  txtText.Clear();
  txtType.Clear();
}
```

You can conclude the binary serialization and deserialization by pressing F5 to build and test-run the project. If there are compiling errors, you can compare the code with the downloaded sample code from www.sybex.com.

When the ControlSerializer is running, enter text into the three text boxes as shown in Figure 5.3 and click the Serialize button. When the Save File dialog box appears, you can type in a filename such as C:\Temp\objSerialized.bin. Finally, click the Save button and you will find the serialized object in the specified filename and path.

FIGURE 5.3
The ControlSerializer
project running with
text entered into the
three text boxes

At this point, you can delete the contents in the three text boxes by clicking the Reset button. Then click the Deserialize button. An Open File dialog box appears. You can navigate to and select the C:\Temp\objSerialized.bin file. The object is reconstructed and the properties of a virtual GUI object are shown in the text boxes again.

The code in this section has two switch statements to recognize file extensions and conduct serialization and deserialization, respectively. In the next two sections, you will enable this project to serialize and deserialize objects with two more serialization methods, one for the SOAP format and one for the XML format.

SOAP Serialization

The SOAP formatter represents an object as a Simple Object Access Protocol (SOAP) document, which is a type of XML document. The SoapFomatter class is defined in the System.Runtime .Serialization.Formatters.Soap namespace. Continuing with the preceding example, the first thing you need to do is to add a reference to the System.Runtime.Serialization.Formatters .Soap.dll assembly by clicking Project ➢ Add Reference. Then add a using directive at the beginning of the Form1.cs file of the ControlSerializer project:

```
using System.Runtime.Serialization.Formatters.Soap;
```

Now, you are ready to code a SoapSerialization() and a SoapDeSerialization() helper method. The code of these two methods is in Listing 5.14.

Listing 5.14   Code of the *SoapSerialization()* and *SoapDeSerialization()* Helper Methods

```
private void SoapSerialization(string filename, GUIControlProperties obj)
{
  //Create a file stream object
  FileStream serializeStream = File.Create(filename);

  //Start Serialization
```

```
    SoapFormatter soapFmt = new SoapFormatter();
    soapFmt.Serialize(serializeStream, obj);
    serializeStream.Close();

}

private GUIControlProperties SoapDeSerialization(string filename)
{
    GUIControlProperties GuiCtrlProp;

    //Create a file stream object
    FileStream serializeStream = File.OpenRead(filename);

    //Start Serialization
    SoapFormatter soapFmt = new SoapFormatter();
    GuiCtrlProp = (GUIControlProperties)soapFmt.Deserialize(serializeStream);
    serializeStream.Close();
    return GuiCtrlProp;
}
```

The code for the SoapSerialization() and SoapDeSerialization() helper methods is similar to the code for the BinarySerialization() and BinaryDeSerialization() methods. The only difference is that this section uses a SoapFormatter class to initialize a formatter instance and deals with SOAP documents. To invoke these two methods, you need to add a SOAP extension case in the switch statement of the btnSerialize_Click() event and in the btnDeserialize_Click() event, respectively, as shown in Listing 5.15; some of the code before the switch statements is omitted and the new code is in bold.

Listing 5.15   **New Addition to the *btnSerialize_Click()* Event and the *btnDeserialize_Click()* Event**

```
private void btnSerialize_Click(object sender, System.EventArgs e)
{
    //initialize a GUIControlProperties object
    ...
    //make a filename to serialize the object
    ...

    //Start serialization
    FileInfo fi = new FileInfo(filename);
    switch (fi.Extension)
    {
        case ".bin":
            BinarySerialization(filename, GuiCtrlProp);
            break;
        case ".soap":
            SoapSerialization(filename, GuiCtrlProp);
            break;
```

```
    }
  )

  private void btnDeserialize_Click(object sender, System.EventArgs e)
  {
    //Get the serilized file name
    ...

    //reconstruct the object from a file
    GUIControlProperties GuiCtrlProp = null;
    FileInfo fi = new FileInfo(filename);
    switch (fi.Extension)
    {
      case ".bin":
        GuiCtrlProp = BinaryDeSerialization(filename);
        break;
      case ".soap":
        GuiCtrlProp = SoapDeSerialization(filename);
        break;
    }

    //populate the text of the GUI controls on the form
    ...
  }
```

The discussion in the previous section for the binary serialization also explains the SOAP serialization in this section. You can test-run the ControlSerializer project and specify a filename with the .soap extension to save the serialized object. I tested and saved it as an objSerialized.soap file in the C:\Temp folder with the text values shown in the text fields in Figure 5.3. When I opened this file in a text editor (such as Notepad), it looks like Figure 5.4.

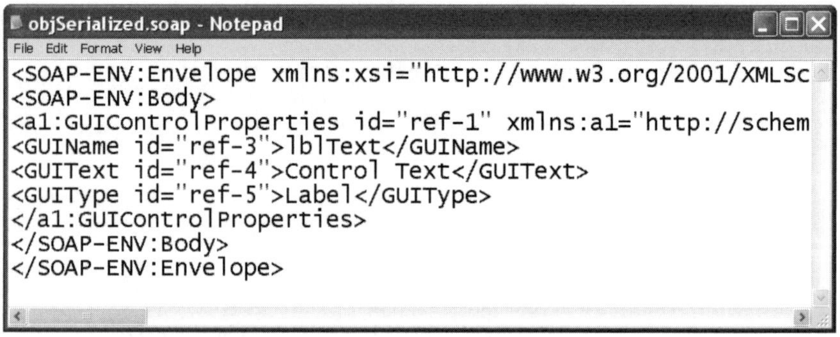

FIGURE 5.4
GUIControlProperties
serialized with a
SoapFormatter

```
objSerialized.soap - Notepad
File  Edit  Format  View  Help
<SOAP-ENV:Envelope xmlns:xsi="http://www.w3.org/2001/XMLSc
<SOAP-ENV:Body>
<a1:GUIControlProperties id="ref-1" xmlns:a1="http://schem
<GUIName id="ref-3">lblText</GUIName>
<GUIText id="ref-4">Control Text</GUIText>
<GUIType id="ref-5">Label</GUIType>
</a1:GUIControlProperties>
</SOAP-ENV:Body>
</SOAP-ENV:Envelope>
```

You most likely recognize the XML tags that mark the field values of a GUIControlProperties object. However, in the previous section, the serialized binary file is a machine-readable file. The next section will use an XmlSerializer to make the outcome more familiar and user friendly.

XML Serialization

As we saw in the code in the previous sections, the differences between serialization formatters start with the using directives and end with the file formats. The programming for XML serialization follows the same pattern. It uses a System.Xml.Serialization directive at the beginning and outputs a regular XML document. The code for the XmlSerialization() and XmlDeSerialization() helper methods is in Listing 5.16.

Listing 5.16   Code for the *XmlSerialization()* and *XmlDeSerialization()* Helper Methods

```
private void XmlSerialization(string filename, GUIControlProperties obj)
{
  //Create a file stream object
  FileStream serializeStream = File.Create(filename);

  //Start Serialization
  XmlSerializer xmlFmt = new XmlSerializer(obj.GetType());
  xmlFmt.Serialize(serializeStream, obj);
  serializeStream.Close();

}

private GUIControlProperties XmlDeSerialization(string filename)
{
  GUIControlProperties GuiCtrlProp = new GUIControlProperties();

  //Create a file stream object
  FileStream serializeStream = File.OpenRead(filename);

  //Start Serialization
  XmlSerializer xmlFmt = new XmlSerializer(GuiCtrlProp.GetType());
  GuiCtrlProp = (GUIControlProperties)xmlFmt.Deserialize(serializeStream);
  serializeStream.Close();
  return GuiCtrlProp;
}
```

I used the same pattern to code different formatters of object serialization and deserialization methods. To invoke the XML serialization helper methods, you simply add another case statement for the btnSerialize_Click() event and the btnDeserialize_Click() event; some of the code before the switch statements is omitted and the new code is in bold in Listing 5.17.

```
private void btnSerialize_Click(object sender, System.EventArgs e)
{
  //initialize a GUIControlProperties object
  ...
  //make a filename to serialize the object
  ...

  //Start serialization
  FileInfo fi = new FileInfo(filename);
  switch (fi.Extension)
  {
    case ".bin":
      BinarySerialization(filename, GuiCtrlProp);
      break;
    case ".xml":
      XmlSerialization(filename, GuiCtrlProp);
      break;
    case ".xml":
      XmlSerialization(filename, GuiCtrlProp);
      break;

  }
)

private void btnDeserialize_Click(object sender, System.EventArgs e)
{
  //Get the serilized file name
  ...

  //reconstruct the object from a file
  GUIControlProperties GuiCtrlProp = null;
  FileInfo fi = new FileInfo(filename);
  switch (fi.Extension)
  {
    case ".bin":
      GuiCtrlProp = BinaryDeSerialization(filename);
      break;
    case ".soap":
      GuiCtrlProp = SoapDeSerialization(filename);
      break;
    case ".xml":
      GuiCtrlProp = XmlDeSerialization(filename);
      break;
  }

  //populate the text of the GUI controls on the form
  ...
}
```

Now that you have accomplished the different serialization methods, you can check the results. The upcoming chapters will use these methods to develop the tools and verify the test results.

.NET *System.Collections* Namespace

When you are developing software applications, you might use an array to present a set of data. The primitive data type of the C# collection is the System.Array class. The System.Array class of the .NET Framework provides quite a few methods, such as reversing, sorting, and enumerating. In addition to using the popular array data type, the GUI testing tool will use other data types of the .NET System.Collections namespace to store and enumerate the testing data and the serialized objects automatically.

You may use the Collections namespace and define a number of standard interfaces when you are involved in other software development projects. The System.Collections namespace has defined the classes listed in Table 5.1.

TABLE 5.1 Classes of the System.Collections Namespace

Class Name	Description
ArrayList	An array whose size is dynamically increased as required
HashTable	A collection of key-and-value pairs that are organized based on the hash code of the key
Queue	A first-in, first-out collection of objects
SortedList	A collection of key-and-value pairs that are sorted by the keys and are accessible by key and by index
Stack	A last-in-first-out collection of objects

The classes in the System.Collections namespace implement interfaces to access their contents. Table 5.2 lists these popular interfaces and their functionality.

In Chapter 3, we used the SortedList objects to represent the custom functions, structures, and constants. We will use these collection classes throughout this book for the tool development and the script automation. More examples of collection classes will be in upcoming chapters. Hereafter, the rest of the chapter will discuss the use of late binding.

TABLE 5.2 Interfaces Implemented by the Classes of the `System.Collections` Namespace

Interface Name	Description
Icollection	Defines size, enumerators, and synchronization methods for all collection classes
Icompare	Defines a method to compares two objects
Idictionary	Defines a collection of key-and-value pairs
IdictionaryEnumerator	Enumerates the contents of a collection with implementation of `IDictionary`
Ienumerable	Defines the `IEnumerator` interface, which supports iteration over a collection
Ienumerator	Supports iteration over a collection, such as using a `foreach` loop.
IhashCodeProvider	Gets a hash code of an object and uses a custom hash function
Ilist	Defines a collection of objects that can be individually accessed by index

Type Class

You used the `GetType()` method in the preceding sections to return the object type for seri-alization. Many of the items defined within the `System.Reflection` namespace make use of the abstract `System.Type` class. The `System.Type` class defines a number of methods used to discover the details of any data type. The list of the complete set of members is quite long. However, this section presents some of the most frequently used properties and methods of the `System.Type` class.

The following are properties of the `System.Type` class used to discover information about basic properties of the data type of interest (e.g., each of following returns a Boolean value based on whether the type is an abstract class, an array, a class, and so forth):

IsAbstract

IsArray

IsClass

IsCOMObject

IsEnum

IsInterface

IsPrimitive

IsNestedPublic

IsNestedPrivate

The following are methods to obtain a collection representing the members (interfaces, methods, properties, and so forth) of a data type:

```
GetConstructors()
```

```
GetEvents()
```

```
GetFields()
```

```
GetInterfaces()
```

```
GetMethods()
```

```
GetMembers()
```

```
GetNestedTypes()
```

```
GetProperties()
```

Each of these method returns a corresponding collection (e.g., `GetFields()` returns a `FieldInfo` array, `GetMethods()` returns a `MethodInfo` array, and so on). And each of these methods also has a singular form (e.g., `GetField()`, `GetMethod()`, `GetProperty()`, and so on) that retrieves a specific member by name rather than a collection of members.

Finally, there are these methods:

FindMembers()   Returns an array of filtered `MemberInfo` types based on search criteria

GetType()   Returns a type instance for a given string name

InvokeMember()   Allows late binding to a given item

The combination of these properties and members can help a tester find all the details of a component under test. The automatic GUI testing tool and its generated test scripts will make use of them to execute test functions and verify test results. For example, to dynamically find the `HandleListBox()` method of the `GUITestAction` class in the `GUITestLibrary` developed in Chapter 4 by using the Type class, you can write a few lines of code like this:

```
GUITestActions guiAction = new GUITestActions();
Type type = guiAction.GetType();
MethodInfo mi = type.GetMethod("HandleListBox");
```

The first line of code initializes a `GUITestActions` instance, `guiAction`. Then, a `Type` variable, `type`, is declared and the `GetType()` method of the `guiAction` instance assigns its `Type` value to the `type` variable. The `MethodInfo` is a class of the `System.Reflection` namespace and it stores the `MethodInfo` of the `HandleListBox()` method in the `mi` object by calling the `GetMethod()` method from the Type class. At this point, you can code the `type` variable to invoke the methods and get the properties as introduced in the preceding paragraphs. More examples will be presented later in this chapter.

Based on the `Type` class, the next section discusses how to use the `System.Refelection` namespace to assist with late binding of the GUI testing tool development.

.NET *System.Reflection* Namespace

If you happen to be a VB 6 programmer, you may have referenced `TypeLib.dll` in your projects to discover information about a dynamic link library (DLL). Now you are in the .NET arena. You use the Reflection namespace for the runtime type discovery. Like a prism reflecting the sunlight into a wavelength spectrum, the Reflection namespace has classes and methods to differentiate a given assembly into its types and members. Therefore, it sees through the software assemblies and knows how to trigger their functions, fields, and properties. This is the most important feature for developing a highly automated GUI testing tool.

The `System.Reflection` namespace provides a method to load an assembly at runtime. Then it obtains a list of all data types and their members contained within a given assembly, including classes, structures, enumerations, methods, fields, properties, and other defined events. It can also programmatically discover the set of interfaces supported by a given class (or structure) and the parameters of a method as well as other related details (base class, namespace information, and so forth). This is the very information a tester must know accurately in detail, and it requires a lot of consideration at the beginning of a testing task for the manual testers and commercial tool users.

To obtain information from a given assembly, the `System.Reflection` namespace is often used together with the `System.Type` class. As you have seen, the `System.Type` class contains a number of methods that are able to extract valuable information about the current `Type` instance. The `System.Reflection` namespace also contains numerous related types to facilitate late binding and dynamic loading of assemblies.

To help you understand the use of the `System.Reflection` namespace, let's build a project to discover how many GUI testing actions have been implemented in the `GUITestLibrary` after Chapter 4.

After starting the Microsoft Visual Studio .NET IDE, choose File ➤ New ➤ Project. In the left and right panes, select Visual C# Project and Console Application template again. In the Name field, type **GUITestDiscovery**, and in the Location field, type **C:\GUISourceCode\Chapter05** to save the new project in this folder. Then click the OK button and the Microsoft Visual Studio .NET IDE generates a Console Application template with a default class name, `Class1`. For simplification, I accept the default values but remove the comments. Now you need to add the code shown in Listing 5.18 to this template.

Listing 5.18   **Use of the *System.Reflection* Namespace and *Type* Class to Explore the Types and Members of a Given Application**

```
using System;
using System.Reflection;

namespace GUITestDiscovery
{
```

```
class Class1
{
  private static Assembly asm;

  [STAThread]
  static void Main(string[] args)
  {
    string programName =
➥@"C:\GUISourceCode\Chapter04\GUITestLibrary\bin\Debug\GUITestLibrary.dll";
    if (args.Length > 0)
    {
      programName = args[0];
    }

    asm = Assembly.LoadFrom(programName);

    DiscoverAllTypes();

    //Hold the screen
    Console.ReadLine();

  }

  private static void DiscoverAllTypes()
  {
    Console.WriteLine(asm.FullName + " has the following types:");
    foreach (Type type in asm.GetTypes())
    {
      Console.WriteLine(type.Name + " has the following members:");

      //discover all the
      foreach (MemberInfo mi in type.GetMembers())
      {
        Console.WriteLine("    " + mi.Name);
      }
    }
  }
}
}
```

As usual, to program a C# project, the first thing you need to do is check whether there are enough using directives at the beginning of the source code. The Microsoft Visual Studio .NET IDE template always remembers to add a using System statement to a new project. You are going to add a using System.Reflection statement beneath it.

After you accept Class1 as the class name for this project, you can define a private static field to prepare an Assembly object, asm. You declare the asm object as a private static field for the purpose of reusing this sample code in the later section discussing the System.Threading namespace. Thus, you know a method can be invoked in .NET by a simple invocation statement, by late binding, and by a thread delegate, all of which will have been discussed by the end of this chapter. A GUI test script will use these invocations for different situations.

A `Main()` method is the entry point of a console application. In this case, the `Main()` method first declares a string variable, `programName`, to get the path and filename of the application under investigation. The example attempts to investigate the `GUITestLibrary.dll` assembly. The path and filename is specified as `@"C:\GUISourceCode\Chapter04\GUITestLibrary\bin\Debug\GUITestLibrary.dll"`. The @ sign leads a verbatim string. Since this `Main()` method accepts a string array as a parameter, users of this project can investigate other assemblies by starting `GUITestDiscovery.exe` from a DOS command prompt and specifying the path and filename of the application as an argument. Thus, an `if` statement is used to reassign the specified application to the `programName` variable.

TIP   Chapter 4 of *Effective Software Test Automation: Developing an Automated Software Testing Tool* (Li and Wu 2004) has a discussion on verbatim strings. It also discussed Reflection relating to non-GUI automatic software testing in detail.

`Assembly` is one of the class types of the `System.Reflection` namespace. By initializing the instance asm of the `Assembly` class, the static method `LoadFrom()` of the `Assembly` class loads the application into the asm instance. Finally, the method calls a `DiscoverAllTypes()` helper method.

The `DiscoverAllTypes()` method uses the initialized, private, and static Assembly instance. It calls two methods of the instance, `GetTypes()` and `GetMembers()`, to return collections of all the types and members within a type iteratively. Types refer to classes, structures, and enumerations within an application and members refer to fields, properties, and methods within a type. The iterations are accomplished by two `foreach` loops. The first `foreach` loop finds all the types by invoking the `GetTypes()` method. The second `foreach` loop is nested inside the first loop and invokes the `GetMembers()` method. The `Console.WriteLine()` methods are called to print the type names and member names onto the screen.

The last line of code in the `Main()` method again uses a `Console.ReadLine()` method to hold the screen before the Enter key is pressed. Thus, it concludes this project with regard to coding as well as to execution. Press F5 to build and run this project. A DOS command prompt windows like the one in Figure 5.5 pops up.

If you want to investigate other applications by running the `GUITestDiscovery.exe` program, you can issue a command from a DOS command prompt with an argument from the folder the program is compiled in, such as in this case:

```
C:\GUISourceCode\Chapter05\GUITestDiscovery\bin\Debug>GUITestDiscovery.exe
➥C:\GUISourceCode\Chapter03\CSharpAPITextViewer\bin\Debug\
➥CSharpAPITextViewer.exe | more
```

This command must be entered on one line; then press the Enter key. The types and members of the C# API Text Viewer created in Chapter 3 are displayed.

In this project, you have learned how to manipulate collections by foreach loops, methods of the Type class and Reflection namespace. You are ready for using late binding and accomplishing more advanced tasks.

NOTE   The Microsoft Visual Studio .NET IDE comes with an ILDasm.exe utility (ILD stands for Intermediate Language Disassembler). This utility uses a GUI front end to enable you to load up any .NET assembly (EXE or DLL) and investigate the associated manifest, Intermediate Language (IL) instruction set, and type metadata. You can start the ILDasm by opening a Visual Studio .NET command prompt and typing the ILDasm.exe command. Then choose File ➢ Open to navigate to the application you wish to explore. You can find the same information the example project in this section reveals.

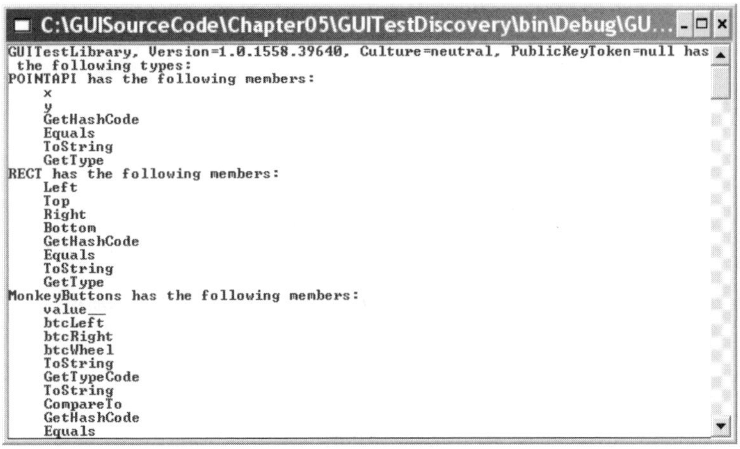

FIGURE 5.5
The first part of the types and members of the GUITestLibrary discovered by reflection

Late Binding

With the assistance of the System.Type class and the System.Reflection namespace, using the late binding technique can enable a program to resolve the existence of the functionality at runtime (rather than at compile time). With regard to a given application, once the presence of a type has been determined, you can code a program to dynamically invoke any of the methods, access properties, and manipulate the fields. Thus, at runtime, the System.Reflection namespace discovers functions in the GUI test library and in the applications under test. Late binding triggers these functions to achieve a fully automated GUI testing tool.

Let's create a new project to dynamically invoke the HandleCommandButton() method in the GUITestLibrary to click the Add button of the C# API Text Viewer. Start a console application project as you did in the preceding section, but name this project LateBindingGUIAction and place it in the folder, C:\GUISourceCode\Chapter05. When the Console Application template opens, you can still accept the default settings and values. After the implementation, the source code of LateBindingGUIAction namespace and Class1 class is similar to Listing 5.19.

Listing 5.19   Late Binding to Invoke the *HandleCommandButton()* Method of the GUITestLibrary and to Click the Add Button on the C# API Text Viewer

```
using System;
using System.Reflection;

namespace LateBindingGUIAction
{

  class Class1
  {

    [STAThread]
    static void Main(string[] args)
    {
      string programName =
@"C:\GUISourceCode\Chapter04\GUITestLibrary\bin\Debug\GUITestLibrary.dll";

      Assembly asm = Assembly.LoadFrom(programName);
      Type type = asm.GetType("GUITestLibrary.GUITestActions");

      object obj = Activator.CreateInstance(type);
      MethodInfo mi = type.GetMethod("HandleCommandButton");
      object[] paramArr = new object[4];
      paramArr[0] = 0;       //initialize a handle integer
      paramArr[1] = "Add"; //GUI window Text
      paramArr[2] = "WindowsForms10.BUTTON.app3"; //GUI class name
      paramArr[3] = "C# API Text Viewer"; //Parent window text

      mi.Invoke(obj, paramArr);

      for (int i = 0; i < paramArr.Length; i++)
      {
        Console.WriteLine(paramArr[i].ToString());
      }

      //Hold the screen
      Console.ReadLine();
    }
  }
}
```

This example has only an entry point `Main()` method. The method assigns the path and file-name of the `GUITestLibrary.dll` to a string variable, `programName`. Then the `Assembly` class uses its `LoadFrom()` method to load the DLL up to an `Assembly` object. The creation of a `Type` object helps hold an instance of the `GUITestLibrary.GUITestActions`, which is obtained by the `GetType()` method of the `asm` instance.

After the Assembly and Type objects are initialized, the `Activator.CreateInstance()` static method from the System namespace is invoked; it uses the Type object to create a real instance of the `GUITestLibrary.GUITestActions` class represented by an object, `obj`. In order to locate the `HandleCommandButton()` method literally, a `MethodInfo` object, `mi`, is declared. The type object is used again to trigger its `GetType()` method, taking the literal name of the method for late binding as its parameter and assigning its outcome to initialize the `mi` object.

As you coded the GUI test library in Chapter 4, the `HandleCommandButton()` method takes four parameters, which are Windows handle, Windows text, Windows class name, and the parent Windows text, in that order. Late binding requires these parameters to be included in an `object` array. Thus, the code first initializes an `object` array with the length of four items. Then the code assigns values to each item of the `object` array. Because, the Add button will be clicked by the execution of this program on the GUI front end of the C# API Text Viewer, its handle is initialized to 0 and will be found during the program execution. The Add button has been labeled with the text Add, which is the Windows text for this GUI object. A string value, `WindowsForms10.BUTTON.app3`, is assigned to the GUI class name. You may have noticed that the conventional GUI control class name of the .NET Framework is different from that found by the custom function, the `GetClassName()` of the custom `user32.dll`. In this case, the Add button is derived from the `System.Windows.Forms.Button` class with Microsoft Visual Studio .NET IDE. The custom `GetClassName()` function finds this button with a class name of `WindowsForms10.BUTTON.app3`. In upcoming chapters, I will discuss this kind of difference for other GUI controls. The last parameter is used to check whether the Add button is related to a parent window. In this case, its parent window has the text C# API Text Viewer.

After the parameter array is initialized, everything is ready for invoking the `HandleCommand-Button()` method dynamically. The `MethodInfo` object, `mi`, just happens to own an `Invoke()` method. This method takes the initialized `obj` object and the parameter array to complete the late binding. If the program is running, the Add button is clicked at this point.

The rest of the code is to print the contents of the parameter array on the screen for confirmation purposes. If a software test is conducted, this screen provides results for verification. Finally, a `Console.WriteLine()` method is used to hold the screen for your review before the Enter key is pressed. After you copy all the code, I recommend you build this project by choosing Build ➢ Build Solution. The executable `LateBindingGUIAction.exe` is compiled into the `C:\GUISourceCode\Chapter05\LateBindingGUIAction\bin\Debug` folder by default.

Follow these steps to test the late binding project:

1. Close the project and all the other applications on the desktop.

2. Start the `CSharpAPITextViewer.exe` from the
   `C:\GUISourceCode\Chapter03\CSharpAPITextViewer\bin\Debug` folder.

3. Manually click the list box to select a custom function.

4. Drag the C# API Text Viewer window to the lower-right with a portion of the window
   disappearing outside of the screen, but make sure the Add button is visible.

5. Start a DOS command prompt and navigate to `C:\GUISourceCode\Chapter05\`
   `LateBindingGUIAction\bin\Debug`.

6. Issue a `LateBindingGUIAction.exe` command. Notice that the mouse pointer moves to the
   center of the Add button and a custom function is marshaled into C# code and appears in
   the rich text box. The DOS command prompt window lists the property values of the Add
   button, as shown in Figure 5.6.

FIGURE 5.6
Late binding to click
the Add button of the
C# API Text Viewer

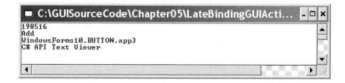

> **NOTE**   The number 198516 in the first line of the window shown in Figure 5.6 is the handle of the
> C# API Text Viewer for this session. After you close this session and start a new session, this
> number will be different. This is why a GUI test script can't be hard-coded with the handle to
> look for a particular GUI component. But the related custom functions must have this number
> in order to get the correct GUI.

The `HandleCommandButton()` method is successfully invoked by late binding.

> **NOTE**   For more information about late binding, you can refer to Chapter 4 of *Effective Software Test*
> *Automation: Developing an Automated Software Testing Tool* (Li and Wu 2004).

.NET *System.Threading* Namespace

The `System.Threading` namespace provide a number of types to enable multithreaded programming. In addition to the Thread class, the `System.Threading` namespace has classes to manage a
collection of threads, such as the `ThreadPool`. You have used the `Timer` class to automate the GUI

actions in the previous chapters for some sample script and test monkey implementations. The Timer class is a simple thread class; it is non-GUI based, although you can implement a Timer object as you drag and drop other GUI controls. Some other classes or types of the System .Threading namespace include functions for synchronized access to shared data. This section will focus on the Thread class, which will be used more often to execute testing functions.

The Thread class is the most common type in the Sytem.Threading namespace. It represents an object-oriented wrapper around a given path of an application. You can use the methods of this class to create a new thread as well as suspend, stop, and destroy a given thread. Table 5.3 lists some of the public properties and methods of the Thread class.

TABLE 5.3 Some Properties and Methods of the Thread Class

Method Name	Description
CurrentThread	Extracts the currently running thread.
IsAlive	Indicates the execution status of the current thread in Boolean values.
IsBackground	Gets or sets a value indicating whether or not a thread is a background thread.
Name	Allows access and mutation of the name of the thread.
Priority	Gets or sets a value indicating the scheduling priority of a thread.
ThreadState	Retrieves a value containing the states of the current thread.
GetData()	Retrieves the value from the specified slot on the current thread and within the current thread's current domain.
SetData()	Retrieves the domain in which the current thread is running.
Interrupt()	Interrupts a thread that is in the WaitSleepJoin thread state.
Join()	Halts the calling thread until a thread terminates.
Resume()	Resumes a thread that has been suspended.
Sleep()	Stops the current thread for the specified number of milliseconds.
Start()	Begins execution of a newly created thread that is specified by the ThreadStart delegate.
Suspend()	Suspends the thread. If the thread is already suspended, the invocation of this method has no effect.

You have learned other techniques by examples; the next paragraphs use an example to initialize a thread to start a Type discovery session by reusing the sample code in Listing 5.18.

Let's create a new console application by starting a new session of the Microsoft Visual Studio .NET IDE. After you choose File ➤ New ➤ Project, select Visual C# Project in the left pane and Console Application in the right pane. Then, in the Name field, type **DiscoveryByThread** as the project name, and in the Location field, navigate to the C:\GUISourceCode\Chapter05 folder by clicking the Browse button. Finally, click the OK button to create a code template with a namespace of DiscoveryByThread and class name of Class1. You can accept the generated template for this example.

Whenever a new namespace is introduced to a project, you will need to add a using directive pointing to it. Navigate to the beginning of the template and add the following using statement below the using System line:

```
using System.Reflection;
using System.Threading;
```

Now, you can copy the code of the private static asm field, the Main() method, and the DiscoverAllTypes() method from Listing 5.18 and paste it appropriately inside this template. After pasting, remove the DiscoverAllTypes() method invocation from the Main() method. Replace it with the following code snippet to call this method:

```
Thread TypeDiscThread = new Thread(new ThreadStart(DiscoverAllTypes));
TypeDiscThread.Start();
```

The code has no secrets. The first statement initializes a Thread object, TypeDiscThread. The initialization invokes a ThreadStart delegate. The second statement calls the Start() method of the TypeDiscThread object to begin the thread. Therefore, you can discover data types of an application by running a thread.

So that you can compare the code to Listing 5.18, the code for the thread sample is in Listing 5.20.

Listing 5.20   **Using a *Thread* Object to Start the Discovery of Data Types in an Application**

```
using System;
using System.Reflection;
using System.Threading;

namespace DiscoveryByThread
{

  class Class1
  {
    private static Assembly asm;

    [STAThread]
    static void Main(string[] args)
    {
      string programName =
➥@"C:\GUISourceCode\Chapter04\GUITestLibrary\bin\Debug\GUITestLibrary.dll";
```

```
      if (args.Length > 0)
      {
        programName = args[0];
      }

      asm = Assembly.LoadFrom(programName);

      Thread TypeDiscThread = new Thread(new ThreadStart(DiscoverAllTypes));
      TypeDiscThread.Start();

      //Hold the screen
      Console.ReadLine();
    }

    private static void DiscoverAllTypes()
    {
      Console.WriteLine(asm.FullName + " has the following types:");
      foreach (Type type in asm.GetTypes())
      {
        Console.WriteLine(type.Name + " has the following members:");
        foreach (MemberInfo mi in type.GetMembers())
        {
          Console.WriteLine("     " + mi.Name);
        }
      }
    }
  }
}
```

Running this project will obtain the identical results as shown in Figure 5.5. You have implemented the Timer class and the Sleep() method earlier.

In the upcoming chapters, you will use the techniques you've learned to develop the GUI test library and the automatic testing tool.

Summary

The .NET Framework owns a number of sophisticated namespaces and classes useful for software testing. This chapter showed you how to use some of them, such as XML programming, collection, reflection, and late binding. The examples demonstrated how to use methods to save and access data in XML documents, how to use collection classes for loading the data in the memory, and how to invoke an application or a method dynamically from a specified assembly with the help of the Type class and the Reflection namespace.

Chapter 6 will discuss the architecture of a general test script. You'll use what you learned in this chapter to enhance the testing capability of the GUI test library. I will also show you how to build a general-purpose GUI test script. Then, in Chapter 7 we will build the proposed automatic testing tool, which conducts an active survey of the GUI components in the application under test, generates specific testing data for testing a GUI unit, and uses the data to write a test script based on the script architecture introduced in Chapter 6.

CHAPTER 6

Testing a Windows Form in General

n Chapter 4 we started building a GUI test library and accomplished mouse clicks on GUI objects similar to the raw capture/playback recorded test scripts. To make a tool that is analogous to the commercially available testing tools, you can manually add some verification and checking points to complete an automated test script by combining the GUI test library and other functions. However, the ultimate goal of this book is to enable a tool to automatically generate code both to operate the application and verify the test results.

This chapter will present the fundamentals of software testing and testing tool architecture. Computer science has evolved through many trends and alternatives for software development. Currently, the majority of software organizations are practicing object-oriented programming. With technology advancements, developers are using Java and Microsoft Visual Studio .NET and moving toward *component-oriented programming*. Test engineers have the motivation to challenge the developed applications and find bugs in them. An effective testing tool must be able to communicate these development paradigms along with the technology advancement. The discussion in this chapter will start with basic software architecture and explore effective methods for testing software and verifying the outcome.

After a brief introduction to software architecture in general and a discussion of the GUI components of the presentation layer, this chapter will show you how to expand the `GUITestLibrary` namespace. In the last part of the chapter, we will reuse the methods of the `GUITestLibrary` and handcraft a fully functional script to test the C# API Text Viewer application and verify the test results manually and semi-manually.

Overview of Software Architecture

Before the GUI era, a software test script was just a collection of the command lines that are executed in sequence as a batch file. However, today's systems require high complexity and high scalability in order to address changes in the needs of businesses and organizations. Software engineers have gone from procedural programming to object-oriented programming to component-oriented programming. Object-oriented programming has evolved from single-tier to two-tier to three-tier applications. When Internet accessibility is integrated into an application, some software architectures implement four tiers. The goal of object- and component-oriented techniques is to reduce the complexity as much as possible.

Before we get into the business of GUI testing, we need to review a few basic concepts of software architecture and get ideas for how to test GUI-rich applications and how to verify the consequences caused by the corresponding GUI actions.

When starting to implement a software application, the software architecture allows the developers to understand what the system does and how the system works. It also define the ways how the developers will collaborate to complete the project, extend and reuse the components to build

OOP and COP

Object-oriented programming (OOP) consists of four main features: polymorphism, late binding, encapsulation, and single- and multiple-inheritance. Component-oriented programming (COP) supports polymorphism and only single inheritance to increase the maintainability of developed applications. Late binding and encapsulation are better structured in COP than they are in OOP. A new feature of COP is data type safety. Data type safety supports both static type checking and dynamic type checking. More about OOP and COP with regard to GUI testing will be discussed in the following sections.

other systems. It is crucial for testers to know the architecture in order to test the object-oriented and component-oriented products. This knowledge gives the testers a good idea of the application outline, the infrastructure components, the procedures used to build the application, and how to test every part of the application.

From a software engineering point of view, applications are composed of fundamental disciplines. These disciplines require software developers to design and implement databases; use Structured Query Language (SQL) in addition to ADO or ADO.NET to manipulate the database; code the application in Java, C++, C# .NET, or other object-oriented languages; employ different packages for the GUI, such as Microsoft Foundation Class (MFC), Java Swing, and .NET Windows forms; and adopt various formats for data storage and presentation. Each of these technologies needs to be tested by specialists just as there are software development specialists. With regard to developing the automated GUI testing tool, we need to use the current technologies, methods, and programming languages to solve the testing problems of the ever complex architecture. We need a testing tool with full automation that will simulate a human user to manipulate the application from the visible GUI frond end and inspect the back scene behaviors of the business functions. We are also in the position of evolving the testing means and tools by increasing the degree of test automation to correspond to the level of complexity in software.

Dividing a system into objects enables rapid system implementation and saves labor through software reuse. Java, C++, and the languages in the .NET family are object-oriented programming (OOP) languages. These languages support *encapsulation* of data by defining abstract data types, such as classes and structures. Therefore, everything in these programs is an object and the behavior of an object contains some of the data of the system. In order to access the data, we need to access the immediate object that encapsulates the data. Objects communicate with each other through messages. For example, you implemented a method in the GUI test library in Chapter 4 to click the Add button in the C# API Text Viewer. To verify whether the data was added to the rich text box, you need to compare the contents in the text box before clicking with the contents after clicking.

The second feature of OOP is *polymorphism*, which is a form of reuse of component specifications. Component specifications are local or global standards that are widely reused throughout an application, an organization, or an industry.

Another feature of OOP is *inheritance*. Writing encapsulated classes usually requires careful design and extra work in the initial stage. But, it requires less time to integrate the robust and encapsulated classes into the final products. These classes can also be easily reused later in circumstances identical to, similar to, or even a little different from the circumstances in which they were designed. For example, you implemented a base class, `APITextViewer`, for the C# API Text Viewer in Chapter 3. Then, the `ConstantViewer`, `DllImportViewer`, and `StructViewer` classes inherited all the members from the base class. The only difference between the three derived classes was the implementation of the virtual `ParseText()` method defined in the base class, which is an example of polymorphism. It is obvious that inheriting tested classes reduces the testing burden.

OOP can also enable applications to dynamically invoke the business functions of the objects. The dynamic interoperation between objects is also called *late binding*. Because you have implemented the testing tool with the capability to click a specific GUI object in the front end of an application, you need the late binding property to call the application under test and verify the state of an object behind the scene.

Since Java and .NET entered the software industry, developers are developing applications using component-oriented technology. Although multiple inheritance is not supported in the component orientation, a child class can inherit members from at most one base class. Thus, component-oriented programming avoids multiple inheritances and interdependence among objects. When reusing a component, the developers don't have to be familiar with the details of the base implementation, but can achieve the optimal economy of scale in large organizations for easy adoption of third-party frameworks. Components reuse functionality by invoking other objects and components using the terminology of *delegations* instead of inheriting from them. However, COP overlaps with OOP on encapsulation, polymorphism, and late binding. Plus, it has *data type safety*. As society becomes increasingly dependent upon software technology, the safety property of the component-oriented languages has become a serious legal concern and one of the most important areas of software development and testing. For example, when the execution of programs written with Java- and .NET-aware languages use garbage collection for memory management, testers don't need to worry about memory leakage, but this is not the case when testing applications written in C++ and other programming languages.

In order to enable independence among programming languages, Microsoft has introduced the Component Object Model (COM) into object-oriented programming. COM formalized a specific process for building reusable, binary software components. When developers abide by the rules of the COM, testers can take the advantage of these rules to test the COM. In contrast to the .NET environment, COMs are unmanaged components. Managed binaries built by .NET-aware compilers also have the DLL and EXE extensions just as COM components do. However, the managed binaries do not contain platform-specific instructions, but rather platform-agnostic intermediate language (IL). They also contain full and complete metadata that describes every .NET type referenced within the binary. The other difference is that the .NET compiler emits binaries containing a manifest describing the binary shell. Finally, an unmanaged COM can be converted to a managed binary. Thus, a test tool should be able to test the legacy COM and the .NET-developed assemblies.

Presentation Layer

An automated GUI testing tool should be able to simulate human users moving mice, clicking buttons, and pressing keys on the keyboard. With regard to GUI testing, these actions are applied to the presentation layer, which is responsible for the user interface.

Ever since the use of object-oriented programming, presentation layers for n-tiered systems have undergone evolutions. Before OOP, developers created applications tightly coupled with their corresponding systems. Developers were able to deliver document-based applications to users. Without an effective presentation layer, the applications succeeded in delivering document-based data, but it was unsuitable for creating applications with instructive real-time feedback for users. To address this shortcoming, developers created front-end GUIs by placing prefabricated GUI controls such as menus, text boxes, list boxes, and buttons. End users operate the applications by interacting with these GUI controls through mice and keyboards. This has been proved to be intuitive, effective, and user friendly.

With regard to software testing, the available tools have required engineers to interact with these controls as end users would and record these interactions in a test script. Later, the script can be executed to perform the exact actions in the same sequence. But this script lacks the functionality of verifying the consequences of the mouse and keyboard events. Unless testers manually enter data, the script can't verify the consistent and common appearance of colors, fonts, images, alignments, and opacity. We need a tool capable of automatically programming the test script and testing the presentation layer for reliability, consistency, and efficiency.

Business Layer

Business layer components are responsible for supporting business rules and combining into the business layer all the data components necessary to map business activities. Any COM-based applications, such as spreadsheet and word processing programs and programs in C++, Java, .NET, and other languages, can be used to present to the users the business objects mapped on the business layer. In particular, developers implement helper classes to return to the user the functionality required in form of a GUI. Users trigger these functions with mouse and keyboard events. This has provided a powerful medium to present end users with data from various data sources that are hidden from them. An automatic testing tool should be implemented to track the status and be aware of the changes of the business layer when the application is running. Thus, GUI test verification is run in the background.

Data Layer

The data layer is the physical data storage layer that includes the database and external data sources. Data can be accessed via Open Database Connectivity (ODBC), database management systems (DBMSs), object linking and embedding (OLE), or file input/output (I/O) systems. Developers can choose one of these methods to increase the efficiency of database connection. Automatic software testing should be able to verify the data status caused by the method invocation from the business layer and the mouse and keyboard events from the presentation layer.

GUI Components on the Presentation Layer

The discussion of GUI testing in this book has focused on the presentation layer of the software architecture by applying actions on individual GUI components via automatic mouse API programming. Using the API programming techniques for marshaling the custom functions, you have considered all the GUI components as Windows forms. Windows forms on a desktop are related as parents, children and siblings. Parent windows contain child windows. However, in the Microsoft Visual Studio software development environment, a Windows application usually has a startup form as the ancestor. The other individual GUI components are called controls at development time. There are numerous prefabricated controls with different appearances and purposes. Users can only apply limited mouse actions to a control, such as moving the mouse pointer, clicking the right button, clicking and double-clicking the left button, and turning the mouse wheel. Each control responds to these mouse actions differently. Throughout the years, a set of standards has been developed to implement the combination of mouse actions on a certain control. These standards are considered intuitive and they make sense to users. For example, clicking a text box control passes the focus to or activates it. Left-clicking a command button invokes the application to perform the desired tasks. Double-clicking a command button usually doesn't make sense to the end users. Test engineers are interested in finding out whether a control responds to a mouse action correctly. This section introduces some fundamentals of these controls.

Buttons

Button controls are useful and obvious to end users. Developers can implement a button click to perform one function or a set of functions. An automated test script can find the handle of a button by using the `FindowWindow()` custom function. Testers would be interested in testing the following most often seen properties of a button:

Text   Indicates the caption of a button. Users and testers can use this property to recognize the button.

Enabled   Some events of the application will enable or disable a button. When a button is enabled, it can be clicked to perform functions. Otherwise, it turns gray and becomes unusable.

Visible   Indicates whether the button is visible under certain conditions. If a button becomes invisible due to an event, it must become visible after other events occur.

The most important events of a Button object could be these:

Click   Occurs when a Button control is clicked

DoubleClick   Occurs when the Button control is clicked two times consecutively.

TextChanged   Occurs when the `Text` property value changes.

A `Button` object could have numerous other events and properties. Very often most of these events will not be implemented and need not be tested. A tester could be interested in testing a certain event or property depending on the test requirements of the application.

ComboBoxes

ComboBox controls allow users to enter or select a value from a drop-down list and set the value for the `Text` property. They are composed of two parts: a text editing box and a drop-down list that is accessed by clicking an arrow button. Testing tasks performed on such controls need to check the accuracy of the text in the text editing area and verify that clicking the arrow button activates the drop-down list and that the items are correct. Testers are interested in testing the following properties of a ComboBox control:

Text   Almost all of the controls in the Microsoft Visual Studio .NET environment have a `Text` property. It is important to test the accuracy of the value of the `Text` property.

Items   Everything in a component-oriented program is an object. The `Items` property is an object representing a collection of a value list contained in a ComboBox. To test this property, testers can capture the listed values from the visible display screen as well as extract the value list. Then, they can compare the captured and extracted values against an expected value list to complete the testing task.

Sorted   When a list is presented in the ComboBox, users tend to have the list sorted in an ascending alphabetical order for convenience. Because the controls are reused, most of the properties are already tested by the IDE vendors. The importance of our testing task is to verify whether the `Sorted` property is enabled or not.

The often seen events of a `ComboBox` need to be tested are as follows:

`Click`   A ComboBox control has two clicking points. When the text editing area is clicked, the control has the focus and is ready to accept text entries via keystrokes. When the arrow button is clicked, the value list is activated and pops up. Clicking inside the value list selects an item and enters it into the text editing box.

`SelectedIndexChanged`   Developers often create an event handler for this event to determine when the selected index in the ComboBox has been changed. This is useful when users need to display information in other controls based on the current selection in the ComboBox. Developers use this event handler to load the information in the other controls. Testers should observe the correct data flow by checking the respective controls.

`TextChanged`   A ComboBox control has some interesting aspects for users and testers. For example, developers may implement this event to insert some new items from the text editing box to the value list. Therefore, the value list can be updated dynamically and provide convenience to the users. Testers should verify when such an event is implemented.

DialogBoxes

In the Microsoft Visual Studio .NET IDE environment, DialogBox controls include OpenFile-Dialog, SaveFileDialog, FolderBrowserDialog, FontDialog, ColorDialog, PrintDialog, and others. Different dialog boxes serve different purposes. For example, an `OpenFileDialog` control has properties of `CheckPathExists`, `CheckFileExists`, `FileName`, `FileNames`, `Filter`, and others. The names of these properties are self-explanatory. The difference between the dialog boxes and the other controls is that the dialog boxes are not directly populated on the presentation layer of the application. Their appearance is usually caused by menu or button events.

The events of dialog boxes are not as complicated as the events of the other controls. The `OpenFileDialog` control has only three events, such as `Disposed`, `HelpRequest`, and `FileOk`. The `Disposed` event occurs when the dialog box accomplishes its mission. The `HelpRequest` event occurs when the user clicks the Help button on a common dialog box. The `FileOk` event is triggered when the user clicks on the Open or Save button on dialog box.

Labels

Labels are common controls for instructive purposes. Developers often use labels to explain other GUI controls such as text boxes and to give feedback to end users. The captions of the Label control help the user operate the application properly. Thus, testing a Label control focuses on whether it exists, whether the caption text is accurate, and whether the label is large enough to display all of the text. Among all the control varieties, Label controls could be the simplest to test.

Menus

Menus are among the most important and complicated GUI controls and differ from the other controls with regard to testing. The handles of the other controls can be found through the custom `FindWindow()` function. Menus can be found only by a `GetMenu()` function. Fortunately, once a menu is found, the most meaningful mouse action to end users is left-clicking, which either opens a submenu list, serves as a checklist or performs a function. A clicking event can also be triggered by a shortcut key or access key defined for the menu item. Sometimes the developers implement a menu clicking to bring out a dialog box and invoke a series of methods. Testing a menu item should verify these consequences.

In addition to clicking, there are a few other events developers could implement for a menu item based on the current Microsoft Visual Studio .NET IDE:

DrawItem   Occurs when the `OwnerDraw` property of a menu item is set to true and a request is made to draw the menu item.

MeasureItem   Occurs when the menu needs to know the size of a menu item before drawing it.

Popup   Displays a list of menu items.

Select   Occurs when the user places the cursor over a menu item

Testing events of a menu item requires verification of some member invocation of an application. Testers may need to verify only a few of the events. A menu item also has numerous properties. The following are the properties of a menu item testers are most interested in:

Checked   Some menu items are implemented as a check box. When they are clicked, no methods may be invoked except that the check box is checked or unchecked.

Enabled   Some events of the application will enable or disable a menu item. When a menu item is enabled, it can be clicked to perform functions. Otherwise, it turns gray and becomes unclickable.

Text   This property indicates the caption of a menu item. An automated test script uses this property to identify a certain menu item.

Visible   Indicates whether the menu item is visible. If an item becomes invisible due to an event, it must become visible after other events occur.

There are many other menu properties. Some applications may only require testers to test one or a few of these properties.

TextBoxes

In Microsoft Visual Studio .NET IDE, there are two kind of TextBox controls. The first is the regular TextBox inherited from Visual Basic 6. The second is the RichTextBox control. The RichTextBox control allows users to create formatted text, such as bulleted, bold, and colored text in Rich Text format (RTF). This file format can then be read by other programs like Word-Pad and MS Word. Therefore, this kind of control works as a word processor. The following properties and events can assist with testing TextBox and RichTextBox:

Font   Indicates the font of the text displayed by a TextBox..

SelectedText   Indicates the selected text within a TextBox.

Text   Indicates the current text in a TextBox. A test script should be implemented to get the text from the TextBox and compare it with the expected text.

TextLength   Counts the number of characters in a TextBox. This could be a useful property to test whether the text in a TextBox is updated when an event occurs.

Some events of the TextBox that would interest testers include the following:

Click   A clicking event usually will not be coded to perform complicated tasks. Users trigger this event to activate a TextBox control. When testing a clicking event, you verify whether the TextBox is active.

KeyDown, KeyUp, and KeyPress   The TextBox controls are developed to accept text when a keystroke is triggered. However, a developer may implement some special uses of the key events when a TextBox has the focus; for example, in many cases, users can move the arrow key to highlight text while holding the Shift key.

TextChanged   This event is used in word processor for many intelligent tasks. For example when a word is completely entered, a word processor should be able to conduct a spelling check. When a sentence is completed, it should check the grammar. When a typo is encountered, it should use some mechanism to mark it. Depending on the requirements of an application under test, you can develop your testing tool with all the desired testing capabilities.

This section covered only a few of the numerous properties and events of TextBox controls. You can find references to more information on these topics in the bibliography at the end of the book.

Other Controls

At this point, you understand how GUI controls differ from one another with respect to testing their properties and events. There are many other GUI controls of interest to testers. Although we haven't included an exhaustive list of them, they all inherit properties and events from a base class; for example, the base class for the controls of the Microsoft Visual Studio .NET is the `System.Windows.Forms.Control` class, which establishes the common behaviors required by all the GUI components. Developers could use these common members to configure the size and position of a control, extract the underlying handle, and capture keyboard and mouse input and output. Testers might be interested in testing some of them based on the requirements of the application under test. From the preceding discussion, you have seen that they all have a `Click` mouse event and a `Text` property. The following list includes some other common properties:

`Top`, `Left`, `Bottom`, `Right`, `Height`, and `Width`   These represent the dimensions of the current derived GUI control classes.

`Enabled`, `Focused`, and `Visible`   These are the states expressed with Boolean values of the GUI controls.

`Handle`   This is a numerical representation of a GUI control, which differs from session to session. A test script can not hard-code this number in order to find the window to test. But this number must be determined in order to use the other custom functions to verify the keyboard and mouse events of a control under test.

`Parent`   This returns a Control object that represents the parent of the current control.

`TabIndex`, and `TabStop`   These two properties are used to configure the tab order of the control under test.

The Control base class also defines some common events. As a test engineer, you may observe that any one of the events might be triggered either by a mouse action or by a keystroke. For example, the events of `Click`, `DoubleClick`, `MouseEnter`, `MouseLeave`, `MouseDown`, `MouseUp`, `MouseMove`, `MouseHover`, and `MouseWheel` are triggered in response to mouse input. And the events of `KeyDown`, `KeyUp`, and `KeyPress` are triggered in response to keyboard input.

Expanding the GUI Test Library

In Chapter 5, you added the code to enable the GUI test library to perform various kinds of actions and trigger GUI control events of the application under test from its front-end interface (simulating a person). These actions are coded with C# code, but the original functions come from the custom `user32.dll`.

The previous chapters introduced the serialization, reflection, and late binding features of the .NET Framework with regard to GUI testing. You also have used these techniques to build a C# API Text Viewer and the first part of the GUI test library. In this section, you will use advanced .NET technology to add more GUI test functions to the GUI test library. The main purpose of the GUI test library is to invoke the functions to perform front-end actions on an application under test as well as to verify the actions performed in the background.

To develop the GUI test library in parallel with the progress made in the chapters of this book, you need to make a new folder, C:\GUISourceCode\Chapter06. Then copy the GUITestLibrary project folder from C:\GUISourceCode\Chapter04 to C:\GUISourceCode\Chapter06. Start the Microsoft Visual Studio .NET IDE to open the GUITestLibrary project from the new folder. When the project is open, you can implement a new class to separate the new functions from the functions developed in Chapter 4. Thus, you can organize the functions that are for marshaling custom functions and DLLs in the GUITestActions class. The GUITestActions class is responsible for triggering the front-end GUI events of an application, and the new class is for monitoring the status changes in the background caused by the front-end GUI events.

To create a new class for the GUITestLibrary namespace, choose Project ➢ Add Class to open an Add New Item dialog box. In the Name field, type in **GUITestUtility** to be the class name. Clicking the Open button generates a GUITestUtility class template. Accept the template and start to add code.

First, add the following .NET namespace using directives:

```
using System;
using System.IO;
using System.Xml.Serialization;
using System.Xml;
using System.Text;
using System.Collections;
using System.Reflection;
```

An explanation of each directive follows:

- The System namespace is needed for all .NET projects and is added when the template is generated.

- The System.IO namespace is responsible for synchronous and asynchronous reading and writing on data streams and files. This namespace will be needed for object serialization.

- The System.Xml.Serialization and System.Xml are for XML serialization.

- The System.Text namespace provides the UTF8 character encoding for XML serialization.

- The System.Collections namespace supplies the ArrayList class for the GUITestLibrary to collect test data.

- Finally, the System.Reflection namespace is needed for late binding in order to start an application under test (AUT) and verify the test results of method invocation and field and property evaluations.

Methods for XML Accessibility and XML Serialization

In Chapter 5, you learned to implement three methods to access any XML document. The third method used an XmlDocument object and built a tree viewer to display a family tree for an XML document. The GetAGUIAction() method in Listing 6.1 also uses such an object. But it will not build a tree view. Instead, it will find a specified GUI handling action based on a GUI type from the resulting GUITestActionLib.xml document of the XMLCreator sample project in Chapter 5 (Listing 5.1).

Listing 6.1   ***GetAGUIAction()* Method Using an *XmlDocument* Object to Find a GUI Handling Method Based on the GUI Type**

```
public static string GetAGUIAction(string xmlFile, string actionOnType)
{
  XmlReader reader = new XmlTextReader(File.OpenRead(xmlFile));
  XmlDocument doc = new XmlDocument();
  doc.Load(reader);
  reader.Close();

  XmlNodeList rootList = doc.GetElementsByTagName("GUIActions");
  XmlNode rootNode = rootList[0];

  XmlNodeList actionList = rootNode.ChildNodes;
  foreach (XmlNode action in actionList)
  {
    if (action.Name == actionOnType)
    {
      return action.InnerText;
    }
  }
  return "";
}
```

The GUI type and the filename of the XML document storing the GUI handling method are coded as parameters of the GetAGUIAction(), where the XML document is created by running the XMLCreator project. The initialization of the XmlTextReader and XmlDocument objects are similar to the code in Listing 5.5. Since we used a simple structure to create the XML document storing the GUI actions, a recursive call is not needed to simplify this method for this book. However, you can code a more powerful method for your testing purposes.

After the XML document is loaded into the doc object and the reader object is closed, an XmlNodeList object, rootList, is initialized to gather the children under the GUIActions element literally. Then, the next statement assigns the first node, indicated by an index 0, of the rootList to a new XmlNode object, rootNode. All the GUI actions in the created XML document are siblings of this node. A new XmlNodeList object, actionList, extracts all the ChildNodes from the rootNode object. At last, the foreach loop enumerates each of the GUI actions. If the value of the GUI type parameter matches an element name, it returns the corresponding GUI actions and terminates the invocation.

The next chapter will implement an AutomatedGUITest tool to conduct a GUI survey and allow the tester to decide the sequence of performing the GUI actions. After a GUI action order is confirmed, the tool needs a method to remember it. .NET serialization can accomplish this task well. Listing 6.2 show the code of a SerilizeInfo() method for the GUITestUtility class.

Listing 6.2   **Code for the *SerilizeInfo()* Method of the *GUITestUtility* Class**

```
public static void SerilizeInfo(string FileName, object obj)
{
  try
  {
    XmlSerializer serializer = new XmlSerializer(obj.GetType());
    StreamWriter sw = new StreamWriter(FileName, false, Encoding.UTF8);
    serializer.Serialize(sw, obj);
    sw.Close();
  }
  catch(Exception ex)
  {
    Console.WriteLine(ex.Message);
  }
}
```

The code of this method is similar to that in Listing 5.14. But it uses a StreamWriter object instead of a FileStream object to save the serialization. A StreamWrite object allows the serialized file to specify a character encoding format. In this case, the UTF8 is assigned because some browser can not display the content with other formats, such as UTF16. A try-catch statement is used here to inform the tester of potential problems.

A capture/playback test tool replays recorded scripts. The AutomatedGUITest tool will read the serialized GUI actions to simulate a person to complete the test. Listing 6.3 implements a deserialization method, DeSerializeInfo().

Listing 6.3   **Code for the *DeSerilizeInfo()* Method of the *GUITestUtility* Class**

```
public static void DeSerializeInfo(string FileName, ref object obj)
{
  try
  {
    XmlSerializer serializer = new XmlSerializer(obj.GetType());
    TextReader reader1 = new StreamReader(FileName);
    obj = serializer.Deserialize(reader1);
    reader1.Close();
  }
  catch(Exception ex)
  {
    Console.WriteLine(ex.Message);
  }
}
```

The code of the DeSerilizeInfo() method is also similar to the second half of Listing 5.14. But, it uses a StreamReader object instead of an OpenRead() from a FileStream object to read the XML document. Thus, the automatic serialization and deserialization will take the place of the traditional capture/playback to achieve a maximally automated GUI testing tool.

Methods for Late Binding

The late binding method will be used to invoke the front-end GUI actions from the GUITest-Actions class and verify the status of the fields and properties of the application under test. The StartAUT() method is implemented as shown in Listing 6.4.

Listing 6.4   **Code for the *allFlags* field and the *StartAUT()* Method**

```
private static BindingFlags allFlags = BindingFlags.Public |
➥BindingFlags.NonPublic | BindingFlags.Static | BindingFlags.Instance;

public static object StartAUT(string applicationPath, string typeName)
{
  Assembly asm = Assembly.LoadFrom(applicationPath);
  Type typeUT = asm.GetType(typeName);
  object obj = Activator.CreateInstance(typeUT);
  MethodInfo mi = typeUT.GetMethod("Show", allFlags);
  mi.Invoke(obj, null);
  return obj;
}
```

Sometimes the fields and properties of an application might be private, public, or protected. By law of programming, private methods can't be accessed by applications outside of the class. However, a tester could be interested in value changes of the fields and properties with any kind of modifications. In order to access the private members for verification, you first define an allFlags field before declaring the StartAUT() method. This field is a filter required by the last remaining methods to start the application under test and verify all fields and properties, private or public.

The purpose of the StartAUT() method is to initialize an instance and bring the GUI interface of the application under test onto the screen by invoking a Show() method of the application dynamically and returning the initialized instance as a System.Windows.Forms.Form object. The parameters include the full path and filename of the AUT and the class name, which contains the entry point method, the Show() method, in order to invoke the GUI application. The invocation sequence starts by loading the application, extracting the data type, and initializing an instance for this data type derived from the System.Windows.Forms.Form base class. Then it initializes a MethodInfo instance, mi, to locate the Show() method. The Show() method is a publicly modified method. Executing the Invoke() method from the MethodInfo instance starts and displays the application under test. Finally, it returns the instance of the application under test as an object. The purpose of returning such an object under test is to enable the test script generated in the upcoming chapters to extract values of the fields and properties and verify the GUI testing results.

Very often a GUI event invokes one or more methods of the application class. The invocation causes the values of the fields and properties to change. Testers want to verify whether the expected changes happen and whether the final values of the changes are desirable. To achieve such testing missions, you need to implement a VerifyField() method as shown in Listing 6.5.

Listing 6.5   Code of the *VerifyField()* Method

```
public static object VerifyField(object typeUnderTest, string fieldName)
{
  Type t = typeUnderTest.GetType();
  FieldInfo fiUT = t.GetField(fieldName, allFlags);
  return fiUT.GetValue(typeUnderTest);
}
```

The declaration of the VerifyField() method takes the instance of the application under test and the name of the field of interest as parameters. The body of the method has only three statements to return the field as an object:

- Initializing a Type object, t, to represent the application under test.

- Initializing a FieldInfo object, fiUT, by getting the name of the field of interest in the application under test. The allFlags value tells the GetField() method to scrutinize every possible field in the application until the desired field is located.

- Returning the current status of the field of the application under test.

The code of the `VerifyProperty()` method in Listing 6.6 is similar to the `VerifyField()` method (see Listing 6.5).

Listing 6.6   Code for the *VerifyProperty()* Method

```
public static object VerifyProperty(object typeUnderTest, string propertyName)
{
  Type t = typeUnderTest.GetType();
  PropertyInfo piUT = t.GetProperty(propertyName, allFlags);
  return piUT.GetValue(typeUnderTest, new object[0]);
}
```

The only difference between the `VerifyField()` and `VerifyProperty()` methods is that the former invokes a `GetField()` method from the `Type` object to get a field of the application under test and the later invokes a `GetProperty()` method to specify the property of interest in the application under test. The field and property are returned to the tool as objects.

If you are interested in implementing a method to verify the execution of other members, such as methods and events, you can use the same code pattern to achieve it. However, the methods and events of an application under test are usually invoked through GUI actions. The `GUITestActions` class has implemented functions to simulate a human tester performing mouse and key events. Testers are more interested in verifying the status changes of the fields and properties caused by the method and event invocations than in triggering the methods and events programmatically. Thus, we will not implement more methods in this chapter.

Two Helper Classes

In the preceding sections, the serialization and deserialization methods are implemented. The last section will implement a serializable helper structure and a serializable helper class for the GUI test library. The first is a `GUIInfo` structure. A GUI component refers to is a visible unit that may reside in the container of a parent, have children, or just be a widow. However, all GUI components have some properties in common, which can be used to help the GUI testing tool find them. These common properties are represented by the `GUIInfo` structure as string and integer variables (Listing 6.7).

Listing 6.7   Code for the *GUIInfo* Helper Structure

```
[Serializable]public struct GUIInfo
{
  public int GUIHandle;
  public string GUIText;
  public string GUIClassName;
  public string GUIParentText;
  public string GUIControlName;
```

```
public string GUIControlType;
public string GUIMemberType;



}
```

A structure in C# is coded as `struct` and it is a light-weight class type. In C#, you are not allowed to define a default structure, but you are free to define additional parameterized constructors. Another difference between a class and a structure is that a class definition is always a reference-based object with regard to memory allocation in the .NET Framework and a structure definition is a value-based object. Thus, to make a new copy of a structure object by using an equivalent assignment, modification of one object is independent of the other. This feature will be used in the future when parts of a `GUIInfo` object need to be modified and saved.

The code for the `GUIInfo` structure is simple and straightforward. It is declared with a `[Serializable]` attribute as discussed previously. When the tool runs, the `GUIHandle` field value of a GUI component is visible to both the custom functions and the .NET methods. But this handle is not a constant from one session to another. The values of `GUIText`, `GUIClassName`, and `GUIParentText` will be obtained through calling the custom functions, and the rest will be obtained through some .NET methods.

Last, a test is a collection of GUI actions. You need to add the initialized `GUIInfo` instances into a collection list. Thus, you can derive one more helper class, `GUIInfoSerializable`. Listing 6.8 shows the code for the last helper class.

Listing 6.8   **Code for the *GUIInfoSerializable* Helper Class**

```
[Serializable]public class GUIInfoSerializable
{
  public string AUTPath;
  public string AUTStartupForm;

  [XmlArray("GUIInfoSerializable")]
  [XmlArrayItem("GUIInfo",typeof(GUIInfo))]
  public ArrayList GUIList = new ArrayList();
}
```

The first field, `AUTPath`, represent the pathname and filename of the application (EXE or DLL) under test. The second string field, `AUTStartupForm`, represents the startup form of the application under test.

The rest of the code has two lines of code for attributes of the last field, `GUIList`, as an `ArrayList` collection. When a custom object is added to an `ArrayList`, it becomes non-serializable. The two attributes play a trick to complete the serialization. The first attribute tells the serialization function that the `ArrayList` field is a member of the `GUIInfoSerializable` class, and the second tells that this `ArrayList` will collect items as `GUIInfo` objects.

Thus, this section completes the `GUITestUtility` class for the GUITestLibrary so far. You can build the GUITestLibrary by choosing Build ➤ Build Solution. Later, when you have more testing requirements, you can expand the classes in the GUITestLibrary project.

Building a General Basis of a GUI Test Script

You developed a C# API Text Viewer in Chapter 3 and implemented a script to click some of the GUI controls in Chapter 4. The C# API Text Viewer is a relatively GUI-rich application that has a main menu, text boxes, list boxes, combo boxes, labels, and command buttons. To help you develop a fully automated testing tool, this section describes a test script using the traditional manual approach. The upcoming chapters will build a test script to test complex GUI interfaces based on the structure of the GUI test library created in this section.

Normally, when the C# API Text Viewer starts, it loads the `Win32API.txt` file by default. The API type in the combo box has been set to Declares. Based on the raw script recorded by testing tools with capture/playback utilities, this application can be tested by starting from the following scenario:

1. Select the name of a custom function directly from the list box.

2. Click the Add button to add the C# definition of the selected function into the rich text box.

3. Click the Copy button to set the function definitions in the rich text box to the clipboard. At this point, the contents of the clipboard can be pasted into other applications, such as the code editor in the Microsoft Visual Studio .NET IDE.

4. Click inside the rich text box and place the cursor in a line of text.

5. Click the Remove button to remove one line of C# code from the rich text box.

6. Click the Clear button. After the selected definitions are pasted, you can clear the contents in the rich text box and select other functions, structures, or constants.

Starting the Test Script Project

Now, let's manually implement a test script with code to trigger the controls' events. Some code of the methods might look similar to the sample script in Chapter 4. However, this section shows how to operate an application as a whole.

Start the Microsoft Visual Studio .NET IDE from the Start menu. From the main screen of the IDE, choose File ➤ New ➤ Project. From the Project Types pane in the New Project dialog box, select Visual C# Project. From the Templates pane, select Windows Application.

Then, in the Name field, type **HandCraftedGUITest** as the project name. In the Location field, type `C:\GUISourceCode\Chapter06` to save the project source code and click the OK button. A new project is created.

To reuse the GUI test library, add a reference by choosing Project ➤ Add Reference in the main screen. Then, in the Add Reference dialog box, click the Browse button, navigate to `C:\GUISourceCode\Chapter06\GUITestLibrary\bin\Debug`, and select the `GUITestLibrary` `.dll` assembly.

Now you are ready to add some GUI controls on the generated Windows form. On this form, you need three Button controls to start the application under test, to start the GUI events, and to verify the consequences of the events. You also need two Timer controls, one for triggering the control events one by one in sequence, the other for turning on/off the first Timer control to allow it to execute only one action each enabled session. One GUI action of each enabled Timer ticking event allows the verification to obtain the consequences of this GUI event. The property values of the Button and Timer controls are listed here:

Control	Property	Value
Button	Name	btnStartApp
	Text	Start Application to Test
Button	Name	btnStartSctipt
	Text	Start Script
Button	Name	btnVerifySctipt
	Text	Verify Script
Timer	Name	timer1
	Enabled	false
	Interval	100
Timer	Name	timer2
	Enabled	false
	Interval	100

Implementing the Command Buttons

After the GUI controls are placed, you are ready to code this project by adding statements to the automatically generated template. To start coding, double-click the button labeled Start Application to Test. The Microsoft Visual Studio .NET IDE brings you to its generated template. The template has the minimum code for building a Windows form, including the related using directives, a `HandCraftedGUITest` namespace, a `Form1` class, a default constructor, an `InitializeComponent()` method, a `Dispose()` method, and a `Main()` method. When you double-clicked the Start Application to Test button, it also produced a skeleton for the Button control click event. Before you insert code between the curly brackets, move the cursor to the beginning of the code page and add two using directives, such as the following:

```
using System.Text;
using GUITestLibrary;
```

The `System.Text` namespace of the Visual Studio .NET provides the `StringBuilder` class for the custom function to manipulate strings. The implementation of `GUITestLibrary` namespace already has the capability to make the scripts trigger various kinds of GUI control events. The combination of the Microsoft Visual Studio .NET IDE generated using directives and the added namespaces will be able to develop a fully automated GUI test script by behaving like a person using an application and verifying test results.

By moving the cursor back to the `btnStartApp_Click()` event definition, you can insert the code in Listing 6.9.

Listing 6.9   **Code for the *btnStartApp_Click()* Event**

```
private object AUTobj;
private int clickNum;
private ArrayList statusCollection;

private void btnStartApp_Click(object sender, System.EventArgs e)
{
   string AppUT = @"C:\GUISourceCode\Chapter03\CSharpAPITextViewer
➥\bin\Debug\CSharpAPITextViewer.exe";
   string TypeUT = "CSharpAPITextViewer.Form1";

   AUTobj = GUITestUtility.StartAUT(AppUT, TypeUT);
}
```

Before the declaration of the `btnStartApp_Click()` event, the three fields, `AUTobj`, `clickNum`, and `statusCollection`, are declared to hold the started application as an object, keep tracking which GUI has been clicked, and collect the status of a GUI event after it has occurred, respectively.

The sole mission of the `btnStartApp_Click()` event is to start the application under test. In this case, we are still interested in the C# API Text Viewer developed in Chapter 3, and its startup form is named `CSharpAPITextViewer.Form1`. The path and filename and the startup form are required by a `GUITestUtility.StartAUT()` implemented in the preceding section. This method uses late binding to start an application and returns an instance of the application as an object.

Now, go to the form design editor again by clicking the Form1.cs tab on the IDE. Double-click the btnStartScript GUI control. When the cursor is in the code editor, you can code the btnStartScript_Click() event as in Listing 6.10.

Listing 6.10   The *btnStartScript_Click()* Event to Run the GUI Test Script

```
private void btnStartScript_Click(object sender, System.EventArgs e)
{
   timer2.Enabled = true;
   statusCollection = new ArrayList();
   clickNum = 0;
}
```

When you placed the GUI controls, you set false values to the Enabled properties of the Timer controls. The btnStartScript_Click() event has a line of code to enable the timer2 control, and the second line of code initializes the statusCollection object of an ArrayList class. The third one sets the clickNum variable to zero.

As you have the previous two Button controls in the Windows form, you need to double-click the Verify Script button to code one more click event. The code for the verification event is in Listing 6.11.

Listing 6.11   The Verification Code for the *btnVerifyScript_Click()* Event

```
private void btnVerifyScript_Click(object sender, System.EventArgs e)
{
   object obj1 = statusCollection[0];
   int clickNum1 = 0;
   foreach (object obj2 in statusCollection)
   {
      clickNum1++;
      string verification = "After click # " + clickNum1 +
      " the text is:\n" + obj2.ToString() + "\n"  +
      "Before click # " + clickNum1 +
      " the text is:\n" + obj1.ToString();

      if (obj1.Equals(obj2))
      {
      MessageBox.Show("Text not Changed by the current event\n\n" + verification);
      }
      else
      {
         MessageBox.Show("Text Changed by the current event\n\n" + verification);
      }
      obj1 = obj2;
   }
}
```

The code first declares an object, obj1, to hold the contents of the first item (index 0) in the ArrayList object, statusCollection, which should be empty. Then it initializes an integer variable, clickNum1, to pass a count to an item of the ArrayList when a foreach loop is enumerating the list. The variable name clickNum1 is to differentiate it from the previously defined clickNum. Both are defined to track the number of clicks by this script. One of them tracks the physical clicks and the other tracks a particular click collected in the list. Last, the foreach loop uses an obj2 object to enumerate the list. Each increment of the loop iteration assigns an item from the list to represent the status after a newer click. It also logically uses the obj1 object to represent the previous click. Then it assigns the content of obj1 and obj2 to a string variable. An if statement inside the foreach loop inspects whether the newer click changes the status of a GUI component and uses a MessageBox object to show the status after each GUI action. The last line of code assigns the current status of obj2 to obj1 and continues to the next item in the list. Thus, the content in obj2 is always newer than that in obj1 until all the statuses are checked.

Coding the Timer Controls to Trigger GUI Events

After the three button events are coded, your next job is to complete the two timer events. A timer event can be started by double-clicking the respective Timer control from the form design editor as well. This will generate a Timer tick event declaration similar to a button event. The final code for the timer1_Tick() event is shown in Listing 6.12.

Listing 6.12   **The Sequetial Actions Performed in the *timer1_Tick()* Event**

```
private void timer1_Tick(object sender, System.EventArgs e)
{
  if (clickNum < 7)
  {
    clickNum++;
    timer1.Enabled = false;
    timer2.Enabled = true;
  }

  int hwnd = 0;
  string winText = "";
  string clsName = "";
  string pText = "";

  switch (clickNum)
  {
    case 1:
      //1. click the list box
      hwnd = 0;
      winText = "";
      clsName = "WindowsForms10.LISTBOX.app3";
      pText = "C# API Text Viewer";
```

```
        GUITestActions.HandleListBox(ref hwnd,
➥ref winText, ref clsName, ref pText);
        break;

    case 2:
        //2. click the Add button
        winText = "Add";
        clsName = "";
        GUITestActions.HandleCommandButton(ref hwnd,
➥ref winText, ref clsName, ref pText);
        break;

    case 3:
        //3. Click the Copy button
        winText = "Copy";
        clsName = "";
        GUITestActions.HandleCommandButton(ref hwnd,
➥ref winText, ref clsName, ref pText);
        break;

    case 4:
        //4. Click the text box
        Control ctrlTested;
        StringBuilder sb = new StringBuilder(1000);

        ctrlTested = (Control)GUITestUtility.VerifyField(AUTobj, "txtSelected");
        GUITestActions.GetWindowText((int) ctrlTested.Handle, sb, 1000);
        winText = sb.ToString();

        clsName = "WindowsForms10.RichEdit20W.app3";
        GUITestActions.HandleTextBox(ref hwnd,
➥ref winText, ref clsName, ref pText);
        break;

    case 5:
        //5. Click the Remove button to remove one line of code
        winText = "Remove";
        clsName = "";
        GUITestActions.HandleCommandButton(ref hwnd,
➥ref winText, ref clsName, ref pText);
        break;

    case 6:
        //6. Click the Clear button to clear the text box
        winText = "Clear";
        clsName = "";
        pText = "C# API Text Viewer";
        GUITestActions.HandleCommandButton(ref hwnd,
➥ref winText, ref clsName, ref pText);
        break;

    default:
```

```
        //Complet this clicking sequence
        timer1.Enabled = false;
        timer2.Enabled = false;
        break;

    }
}
```

The script performs six mouse actions. After the declaration of the `timer1_Tick()` event, an `if` statement inspects whether the six mouse actions are performed in order to increment the value of the `clickNum` variable by one. Then it turns off `timer1` and turns on `timer2`. In general, all the mouse actions occur in the `timer1_Tick()` event. But the actions are not triggered within one `timer1_Tick()` event. In order to be able to verify a GUI event, each triggering of the `timer1_Tick()` event invokes only one GUI action as a human does. Thus, the consequence of this GUI event can be collected. After the `timer1` control turns itself off by setting its `Enabled` property to `false`, it activates `timer2` by setting the respective property to `true`. The `timer2_Tick()` event collects verification data. In returning the favor, the `timer2_Tick()` event will turn on `timer1` again to trigger the next event guided by a `switch` statement and the incremental `clickNum` variable.

Then, four variables, `hwnd`, `winText`, `clsName` and `pText`, are declared to be a zero and three empty strings to represent the GUI handle, the window text, the class name, and the parent window text values of a GUI control. They will be reinitialized in each `case` clause inside the `switch` statement in order to find the correct GUI control. Finally, these four values are combined as parameters needed to invoke a respective GUI handling method from the GUI test library before a `break` statement is executed.

The six clusters of the code within the `switch` statement perform the operations exactly as described in the previously discussed scenarios. It performs mouse clicks on the list box, the Add button, the Copy button, the rich text box, then the Remove and Copy buttons in sequence. After the designed sequence is completed, the default `switch` statement turns both `timer1` and `timer2` off.

When the custom functions use a combination to locate a GUI control, the values of the handle differ from one running session to another. The values of the class names are usually constants. However, the values of the `Text` properties of GUI controls could fall in the following three situations:

- Values of the Text properties are constant from their design time throughout their lifetime, such as the Text properties for Label and Button controls.

- Some controls have empty values for Text, such as ListBox controls.

- The `TextBox` and `RichTextBox` controls are placed for accepting text entries from users. The values of the Text properties are supposed to be under constant change.

Therefore, assigning constant values for the first two kinds of GUI controls could be reasonable for the custom functions to find the GUI of interest. But to look for a GUI control with a text value that changes, you need to get the current text of the GUI. Case 3 in Listing 6.12 is coded for finding and clicking inside the RichTextBox control of the C# API Text Viewer. In order to have the current value of the window text of the RichTextBox as an identifier for the custom functions, the code snippet is extracted from Listing 6.12:

```
Control ctrlTested;
StringBuilder sb = new StringBuilder(1000);

ctrlTested = (Control)GUITestUtility.VerifyField(AUTobj, "txtSelected");
GUITestActions.GetWindowText((int) ctrlTested.Handle, sb, 1000);
winText = sb.ToString();
```

The code snippet first declares a Control object, ctrlTested, and a StringBuilder object, sb. Then it calls the VerifyField() method of the GUI test library to find the current handle of a control named txtSelected as an object instance and converts the instance back to a control using the *unboxing* technique. When the corresponding GUI control is found, the GetWindowText() method of the GUI test library uses the control handle and assign the control's text to the sb object. Last, the content of the sb object is assigned to the winText variable. Thus, the GUI object of interest can always be located programmatically and the combination is prepared for invoking the GUI handling methods of the GUI test library, in this case, the HandleTextBox() method.

NOTE   Boxing and unboxing are explained in my previous book, *Effective Software Test Automation: Developing an Automated Software Testing Tool* (Sybex, 2004).

The last coding task of this project is for the timer2_tick() event. After you double-click the timer2 control in the form design editor, you implement the event and the code as shown in Listing 6.13.

Listing 6.13   **The Code to Collect GUI Event Consequences and Turn On the *timer1* Control of the *timer2_Tick()* Event**

```
private void timer2_Tick(object sender, System.EventArgs e)
{
  if (clickNum > 0)
  {
    Control ctrlTested;
    ctrlTested = (Control)GUITestUtility.VerifyField(AUTobj, "txtSelected");
    statusCollection.Add(ctrlTested.Text);
  }
  timer1.Enabled = true;
  timer2.Enabled = false;
}
```

The `timer2_Tick()` event starts with an `if` statement to make sure the first click has occurred. Within the `if` statement, it invokes the `VerifyField()` method from the GUI test library to get the current status of the `RichTextBox`, which is named `txtSelected` in Chapter 3, and convert the returned object type into a Control type. Then the value of the `Text` property of the current status of the `RichTextBox` is added into the declared `ArrayList` object, `statusCollection`. When the C# API Text Viewer is running, most of the GUI events cause the text change inside the `RichTextBox`. For simplification and easy explanation, this script only collects the status of the `RichTextBox` control after each of the GUI events. In a real-world testing project, a GUI event could cause status changes of several objects. The upcoming chapters will discuss automatic verification in more detail.

The last two lines of code, in contrast to the `timer1_Tick()` event, simply turn `timer1` on and `timer2` off to complete the `timer2_Tick()` event and enable `timer1` for the next action.

WARNING   If the incrementing of the `clickNum` variable and the `Enabled` properties of the `timer1` and `timer2` controls are not coded properly the first time, the `timer1_Tick()` and `timer2_Tick()` events may not cooperate properly and never stop by themselves. Because the script allows only 100 milliseconds for the `Interval` values of these two Timer controls, it might be hard for you to keep the mouse under control. This becomes annoying. When this happens, you can stop this execution by pressing the Delete key while holding down the Ctrl and Alt keys. The Windows Task Manager pops up. Use the arrow keys to select the `Form1` process, and press the Delete key again to end the script. Correct the error and test again. Or, you may increase the `Interval` values of the Timer controls to be above 2 seconds until all errors are corrected.

Visualizing the GUI Event Outcomes

The code of the script project is completed now. You can press F5 to build and run the script. When the project starts, a Windows form like the one in Figure 6.1a appears. Click the button labeled Start Application to Test, and the C# API Text Viewer starts (Figure 6.1b). Then click the Start Script button on the Windows form to execute the mouse actions. You can visually follow the positions of the mouse movement. After the scripted actions are completed, you can visually verify the button clicks by observing the following phenomena:

1. The first GUI handling method clicks the `ListBox` control. The content in the `ListBox` control advances one step and one of the custom functions at the bottom of the visible area is selected. This indicates that the `ListBox` clicking event triggers the desired functionality.

2. In the second step, the Add button is clicked. You may or may not see the change of the text addition into the `RichTextBox`, depending on the speed of your processor.

3. In the third step, the HandleCommandButton() method is invoked again to click the Copy button. The result of the Add button click cannot be viewed without the help of a third-party application. At this point, in order to verify visually whether clicking the Add and the Copy button accomplished the software requirements, you can start a ClipBook Viewer application by choosing Start ➤ Run. Then, in the Open field of the Run dialog box, type **clipbrd.exe** and click the OK button. The ClipBook Viewer appears on the screen (Figure 6.1c). If you see that the C# definition of the custom function in the ClipBook Viewer is for the selected function in the ListBox, the events triggered by clicking the Add and Copy button have been implemented correctly.

4. Next, the invocation of the HandleTextBox() method clicks on the first line inside the RichTextBox. The fifth step clicks the Remove button and attempts to remove the first line of text inside the RichTextBox. It may be too fast to see these two steps.

5. The last action clicks the Clear button, and the mouse pointer stops at the center of the Clear button. The RichTextBox becomes empty now. It is obvious that the Clear button click event accomplished the task as designed.

However, a tester can not visually verify all testing cases. This is tiresome and, under many circumstances, impossible. An automated test script must have a mechanism to save the status of the GUI controls after each operation action. In the preceding script, the implementation of an ArrayList object, statusCollection, is for such a purpose. At this point, don't stop the script session, the next section will walk you through the objects collected in this ArrayList and see the consequence of each GUI event. This walk-through is still a manual process. The upcoming chapters will implement an automatic method in the GUI testing tool for the presentation of the test results.

TIP   The ClipBook Viewer (Figure 6.1c) is a Windows accessory that is not listed in the Start menu at installation. The Windows operating system installs it in the System32 folder as a clipbrd.exe. If the current security settings permit it, the ClipBook Viewer can be connected to all machines in a network and users can view remote instances of Windows and spy into the Clipboard on other machines. The ClipBook Viewer only displays the contents of the Clipboard and lets users delete it, but users can't enter new text to the clipboard. The ClipBook Viewer is sometimes referred to as Clipboard Viewer. The clipbrd.exe file appears with a title of ClipBook Viewer on the Windows XP system I am using to write this chapter.

FIGURE 6.1
(a) The test script
project at run, (b) the
application under test,
and (c) the ClipBook
Viewer for manual
verification

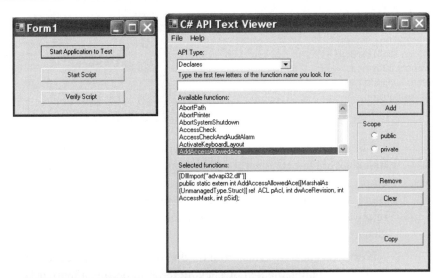

A Semi-Automatic Way of Verifying the Test Script

The preceding script implemented a Verify Script button to start an investigation of the
statusCollection object, which has a collection of the status of the RichTextBox after each
GUI action. After you view the collection as discussed, you can click this button. A message box
such as the one in Figure 6.2 appears.

FIGURE 6.2
The contents of a
message box shows
that the RichTextBox
is empty after and
before a click on the
ListBox control.

The first line of the message box reports that the mouse events of the ListBox caused by the first click did not change the content in the RichTextBox. The text inside the RichTextBox is empty after and before the action occurred. This is expected and the mouse events of the List-Box passed the test. However, in a real-life test, we should also have inspected the status change of the ListBox to verify whether the content was advanced and whether the selected index was changed.

Next, you click the OK button on the message box to view the change caused by the next mouse event implemented by clicking the Add button (Figure 6.3).

The Add button was designed in Chapter 3 to add C# code to marshal a selected custom function in the ListBox into the RichTextBox. The message box reports that the content changed inside the text box and prints the text after the Add button click. For easy comparison, it also prints the text before this mouse action, which is an empty string. Thus, the Add button is verified to perform correct functions.

The purpose of the C# API Text Viewer is for writing C# marshalling code of Win32 custom functions and transferring the code to a C# project by copying and pasting. The next mouse action of the script clicks the Copy button. Figure 6.4 displays the text inside the text box after and before the clicking.

FIGURE 6.3
Clicking the Add button
to marshal a selected
custom function from
the ListBox control into
the RichTextBox in C#
syntax.

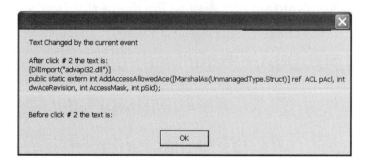

FIGURE 6.4
Clicking the Copy button did not change the text inside the text box.

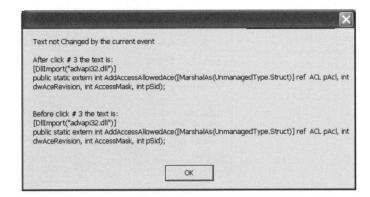

The Copy button causes the text inside the text box to be imported into the clipboard. You can see the copied content by open the ClipBook Viewer as discussed in the preceding section. However, you can verify this action automatically by coding the script to inspect the Clipboard programmatically.

After the desired C# marshalling code is copied, users may want to remove some of the functions from the text box. The script made a click inside the RichTextBox and placed the cursor at the first line of its content, which was meant to remove the first line by clicking the Remove button. However, the text remained the same, as shown in Figure 6.5.

We expect the first line to be removed after clicking the Remove button. Figure 6.6 reports the content of the text box changed and displays the desired outcome. The Remove button click event is verified with correct functionality.

FIGURE 6.5
Clicking inside the RichTextBox did not change its contents.

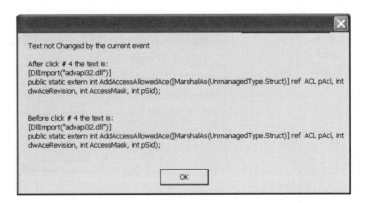

FIGURE 6.6
The first line inside the
text box is removed by
clicking the Remove
button.

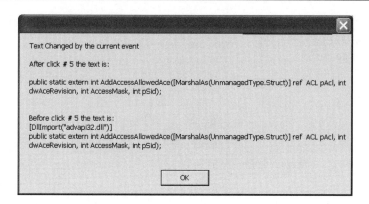

Text Changed by the current event

After click # 5 the text is:

public static extern int AddAccessAllowedAce([MarshalAs(UnmanagedType.Struct)] ref ACL pAcl, int
dwAceRevision, int AccessMask, int pSid);

Before click # 5 the text is:
[DllImport("advapi32.dll")]
public static extern int AddAccessAllowedAce([MarshalAs(UnmanagedType.Struct)] ref ACL pAcl, int
dwAceRevision, int AccessMask, int pSid);

OK

When you finish marshalling custom functions for one project, you may need to marshal other custom functions for another project. To do this, you need to clear the content in the text box first. The last step of the script is to click the Clear button. Clicking the OK button on the message box again, you will see that the content inside the text box is empty after the click and the first line is missing before the click, as shown in Figure 6.7.

Clicking the OK button from the message box the last time concludes the verification. So far, we have used two ways to verify a test script. The first is a purely manual process and depends on the eyes of the tester. Its verification capability is limited and error prone. The second is more desirable and can be fully automated with a GUI testing tool. However, the tool should broaden the verification scope by collecting status changes of more GUI components of the application under test. The following chapters will focus on the tool development for test script generation and result verification.

FIGURE 6.7
The contents of the
text box is cleared
by clicking the Clear
button.

Text Changed by the current event

After click # 6 the text is:

Before click # 6 the text is:

public static extern int AddAccessAllowedAce([MarshalAs(UnmanagedType.Struct)] ref ACL pAcl, int
dwAceRevision, int AccessMask, int pSid);

OK

Summary

This chapter introduced the basics of modern software architectures. In a multitier structure, the data layer processes the data and the business layer controls the data flow logic. The GUI components of an application are all gathered within the presentation layer. Available testing tools have functions to record test scripts from the tester's manual inputs. But the verification of the changes in the data layer and business layer caused by the GUI events of the presentation layer has long challenged the testing capabilities of these tools. Because these tools can't automatically write test scripts with functions to trigger the GUI events and functions to verify the consequence, testers seldom consider them as automatic software testing tools.

I listed a few of the common GUI controls in order to giver you a clear insight into the GUI components and how to figure out a way to test them programmatically. Because this book is primarily concerned with creating a general test script, the list was limited, so I recommend that you refer to programming introduction books for a full list of the GUI controls when they are needed for your specific testing project. For the purpose of this book, however, the list was adequate.

After you had a good understanding of how the presentation and business layers work in multitier architecture, you added a GUITestUtility class into the GUITestLibrary project. A significant contribution from the GUITestUtility class is that it returned the application under test as an object. The test script is able to use this object to navigate inside the application for each component, including GUI and non-GUI components, lower-level modules in the hierarchical architecture, fields, properties, and other members. Thus, it provides a mechanism to verify the status of the back-end components during the runtime of the application.

In the last part of this chapter, you manually developed a test script for the C# API Text Viewer. By using the GUI test library developed in the preceding chapters, you found that it is easy to enable a script to manipulate the mouse actions. Later, the GUI test library will also be extended to operate the keyboard as a test engineer would.

You have developed the GUITestLibrary namespace with two classes, GUITestActions and GUITestUtilities. The members implemented in the GUITestActions class are responsible for GUI exercises of the presentation layer, and the members of the GUITestUtilies hold the application object and verify the consequence in the data layer and business layer caused by the GUI events in the presentation layer.

In the next chapter, I will discuss the basic architecture of an automatic GUI testing tool and walk through the steps of building such a tool. This tool will be able to generate a GUI test script based on the architecture of the manually created script discussed in this chapter. In Chapter 8, we will continue to implement the tool with automatic functions for test verification and presentation. The rest of the book will be devoted to examples of how to test a few of the common GUI controls. You can extrapolate the concepts to develop your tools to include capabilities for testing other controls.

CHAPTER 7

Architecture and Implementation of the Automatic GUI Test Tool

Computer scientists and economists alike have commented on the inadequacy of the current software test infrastructure. None of the available testing tools are capable of generating a simple test script automatically. Manual test scripts, including handcrafted and recorded test scripts, overlook some testing aspects easily and leave potential bugs in the software.

Starting with this chapter, this book will present the life cycle of developing an automatic GUI testing tool. The ultimate goal of this tool is to fully automate the GUI testing process from discovering all the GUI components and generating test scripts to test each of them and presenting the test results.

Meeting Current and Future GUI Test Requirements

As mentioned, the current commercial testing tools can't generate test scripts automatically. Tools with the capture/playback facilities record all the manual actions from user's inputs and play back exactly the same actions. There are no verification statements in the raw script. Tool users are required to understand the specific script language in order to insert and debug the recorded test script. To improve the current testing infrastructure, we will develop a tool to address the following testing issues:

- *Capture/playback is not needed.* The tool under development will be able to look for all the GUI components of the application and know the actions to perform in order to trigger the respective GUI events.

- *Verification will be conducted with minimum manual interaction.* Post editing and debugging of the test script is not necessary after the tool collects the verification data. The verification will compare the consequences of the triggered GUI events and confirm the consistency between the visual changes caused by the events and the internal values of the application at that moment.

- *Verification results will be saved so they can be reviewed for fixing bugs and regression testing.* Testers and developers can view the results and report bugs at any time. The test reports can be presented with different types of file formats, such as XML, HTML, or other spreadsheet programs.

- *There will be no hard-coded testing cases in the test script.* This tool will generate a set of testing cases and let users verify and validate the data. The data is stored separately and used to drive the test script execution. Later, the data store can be modified and copied. One script can be executed against multiple testing cases. Thus, the users spend a small amount of time generating test scripts and a majority of their time making testing cases in order to increase the efficiency of the GUI testing.

When new technologies are employed in a software project, testers often wait for the vendors to upgrade the testing tools. Otherwise, they have to manually test the project. Tool vendors often handle well the existing technologies and lag behind in advanced technologies. This creates a tight testing schedule for an organization using commercial testing tools with regard to releasing quality products. On the other hand, because each tool requires its own script language, and many of the script languages have only limited functions to conduct the testing tasks, the sequential nature of the script technique in these languages make them incapable of testing today's complex software projects and technologies. In order to keep abreast of the most recent advancement, the testing tool will be developed to meet the following requirements:

- *The GUI test scripts will be generated in a high-level programming language.* The tool project is implemented in C#.NET language. The tool will also generate test script in C#.NET. Since C#.NET is a high-level language, the generated test script will possess the power to effectively test complex products. Furthermore, a test script written in a high-level programming language can be executed on machines that don't have a test environment.

- *Testers and other personnel can share test scripts.* Using unique test script languages separates testers from developers. It also limits the use of the test scripts to only systems on which a testing environment is installed. Using a programming language for the tool development and the generated test scripts will be the solution to this limitation. It will increase the collaboration between developers and testers and also encourage cooperation between the test teams and alpha and beta testers.

- *The test script will use the divide-and-conquer approach to test products developed with object-oriented programming or component-oriented programming techniques.* The divide-and-conquer approach creates simple methods for testing each aspect of a GUI component. The simple methods will then be combined in sequence to solve complex testing problems. Combining many simple testing tasks to form a complex test script is the key to increasing the testing efficiency to find bugs.

- *The testing cases can be reused for regression testing and system testing.* If the application has a structure of lower-level GUI controls nested in higher-level ones, the test scripts and data for testing lower-level controls can be reused to test the higher-level GUI modules.

- *The testing tool generates easily maintainable test scripts.* Using late binding programming, a test script will be implemented inside the tool. This script will use the GUI testing input information stored in XML documents. The task of software testing becomes a job of creating effective testing cases. Maintenance of the test script will be needed only when new test requirements are encountered. Once a new testing capability is implemented for the test script, the tool exercises this testing power to test applications under all appropriate circumstances. On the other hand, the test script can be separated from the tool and be executed independently across different machines.

- *New testing features can be upgraded as needed.* Computer science has enjoyed the most rapid advancement among all industries. This rapid advancement is still continuing. With an automated software testing tool, your organization has the flexibility to upgrade it in a timely manner.

In addition to the improved test infrastructure, we will build this tool with high maintainability, reliability, reusability, flexibility, and high efficiency in finding bugs. However, this book aims to introduce methods for general GUI testing and establish a foundation for a fully automated testing tool. More ramifications will be illustrated during the process of adding the code to the tool project. You will have other testing requirements and can extend the methods introduced in this book to accommodate specific situations in your organization.

The General Architecture of the Improved GUI Testing Tool

Software testers have experienced tedious, boring, and time-consuming manual testing for a decade. They spend more time to achieve an automated test script than they conduct a manual test and the test scripts are expensive to maintain. Many organizations put these tools aside and look for other approaches for quality assurance.

With minimum human interaction, the fully automated GUI testing tool developed in this book will actively collect data and execute the test. Testers and developers can then trace and fix bugs by reviewing the test reports.

In the next section, you will start a Windows application project in C# language using the Microsoft Visual Studio .NET IDE. The Windows application provides users with a GUI interface from which they can specify an application for testing. It also displays the testable GUI components and the data for verification purpose in a table format. In this book, we will use an XML document to display and store the data. Users can rearrange the order of GUI events and then review and modify the data. After the data is confirmed and saved, the tool is able to use it to test the application. The execution of the test script performs predefined mouse actions and keystrokes, and saves the state of the application after each operation. Figure 7.1 shows the automatic testing process.

The purpose of developing a software testing tool is to solve specific problems within a software test project and an organization, which the commercial testing tools are often not capable of. The simplified architecture of the GUI testing tool in this section provides a foundation and methods for the tool development. The tool development life cycle fits an incremental waterfall model. You can upgrade this tool on a timely manner in order to broaden the testing capabilities and increase the degree of automation and the efficiency of finding bugs.

You can also preferentially use other IDEs and platforms for the tool development. A short discussion of other open-source .NET IDEs and platforms is in the book's introduction.

FIGURE 7.1
A GUI testing process
and data flow with
minimum human
interaction for the
automatic GUI
testing tool

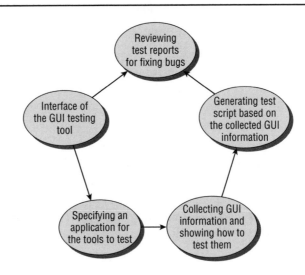

Starting the AutomatedGUITest Project

In Chapters 4 and 5, you developed a functional GUI test library. In Chapter 6, you reused only a few of the methods of the GUI test library and obtained a fully automated test script with limited verification functions. Until now, there is still no evidence that a workable test script has been generated by any tool automatically. From here, you can follow the steps to start a new project. There will be five subsections representing five classes to be developed in this chapter for the new project.

The Startup Form of the AutomatedGUITest Tool

In Chapter 6, you simply used the GUI test library and the HandCraftedGUITest project referenced to the GUITestLibrary.dll assembly. Since the development of the GUITestLibrary will be parallel to the development of your tool, I recommend that you make a new folder, \Chapter07, under the C:\GUISourceCode folder. Then copy the GUITestLibrary project folder from C:\GUISourceCode\Chapter05 to the new C:\GUISourceCode\Chapter07 folder.

NOTE   If you are using version control software to complete the tool project, you can easily check in, check out the source code and go back to the older version. That way, you don't have to copy the GUITestLibrary project from chapter to chapter.

Start the Microsoft Visual Studio .NET IDE and complete these steps:

1. From the main window of the IDE, choose File ➢ New ➢ Project to bring up the New Project dialog box.

2. Select Visual C# Projects from the left pane, and select Windows Application from the right pane. In the Name field, type **AutomatedGUITest**, and for the Location field, click the Browse button to invoke a project location navigator and select the C:\GUISourceCode\ Chapter07 folder. Click the Open button and then the OK button.

3. When the automatically generated Windows form appears, you can resize it by choosing View ➢ Properties Window and changing the Size property with a pair of values such as 552 and 400, indicating the pixel numbers of the width and height of the form (or you can resize it by dragging the lower-right corner of the form). You can also change the value of the Text property of this form by typing in **Automated GUI Test Form** to replace the IDE-generated value Form1.

4. Choose File ➢ Add Project ➢ Existing Project in the main window. Navigate to C:\GUISource-Code\Chapter07\GUITestLibrary. You'll see the GUITestLibrary.csproj file. Select it and click the Open button to add this project to the current solution, AutomatedGUITest.

5. Activate the AutomatedGUITest project in the Solution Explorer. Choose Project ➢ Add Reference. When the Add Reference dialog box appears, click the Projects tab. Select GUITestLibrary in the list box, click the Select button and then the OK button to complete the reference addition.

6. Add GUI controls of five Buttons, one Label, one DataGrid, one SaveFileDialog and one OpenFileDialog onto the form. Assign new values to the selected properties of the controls as in the following list:

Control	Property	Value
Button	Name	btnStartGUITest
	Text	Start GUI Test
Button	Name	btnGUISurvey
	Text	GUI Survey
Button	Name	btnRunTest
	Text	Run Test
Button	Name	btnRerun
	Text	Rerun Test
Button	Name	btnExit
	Text	Exit

Control	Property	Value
Label	Name	lblAvailabelGUI
	Text	Available GUI components:
DataGrid	Name	dgAvailableGUIs
OpenFileDialog	Name	opnAUT
SaveFileDialog	Name	sveDataStore

This is the start form of the AutomatedGUITest project. This form has a class name Form1 at this moment. After you complete the GUI control plantation, the AutomatedGUITest startup form looks similar to Figure 7.2.

FIGURE 7.2
The startup form of
the AutomatedGUI-
Test tool

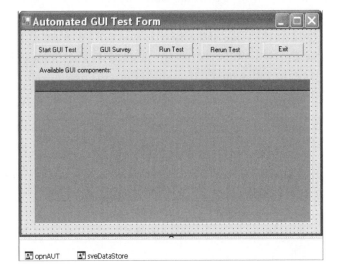

A startup form is the highest level of this architecture. It requires the instances and methods of the other four helper classes. For now, I suggest you leave this form and come back to it when the other classes are implemented.

An Interface to Specify the Form of the Application under Test

Just as the AutomatedGUITest tool has a startup form, all the other Windows applications have their own startup form. When an application starts, the startup form is the first functional graphical user interface for the users to work with. We have designed a Start GUI Test button and an OpenFileDialog control on the AutomatedGUITest form. When the Start GUI Test button is clicked, the open file dialog box appears. The tester can specify the path and filename of an application that needs to be tested. But an application could have more than one form, class, and other data types. The tester needs to tell the tool which form in the application to test. To help the tester identify the form of interest, the AutomatedGUITest form is able to extract all of the classes with and without GUI implementation from the application under test. Then it lists them in a checklist from which the tester choose with a simple mouse click.

To create this form, follow these steps:

1. From the Solution Explorer, right-click on the AutomatedGUITest project name and choose Add ➤ Add Windows Form to make a new Windows dialog form. The Add New Item dialog box appears.

2. In the Name field, type **TypeUnderTest** as a new class name. TypeUnderTest is also the filename for the source code of the new class by default. Because the class name and the file-name do not have to be the same, you can rename them if you want. Click the Open button. An empty form appears in the design area.

3. Change the value of the Text property of this form to Types under Test. This text appears on the title bar. Accept all the other IDE-generated code.

4. Add the following GUI controls onto the new form:

Control	Property	Value
Label	Name	lblTypeAvailable
	Text	Select data types to test from the available list:
	Modifier	public
CheckedListBox	Name	chckListType
Button	Name	btnOK
	Text	OK
Button	Name	btnCancel
	Text	Cancel

After you populate these GUI controls, the TypeUnderTest form should look like Figure 7.3.

This form will use the CheckedListBox to list the available classes within the application under test. The tester can choose the selected startup form from the list to request the tool to perform a GUI survey. Virtually, you don't need to add any more properties or methods for this form, and you need to add only two lines of code responsible for the OK and Cancel button click events in the generated InitializeComponent() method.

Before adding these two lines of code, I will briefly introduce a DialogResult enumeration of the .NET platform. The definition of the DialogResult is directly related to the OK and Cancel button clicks from a custom dialog box. When a button has been assigned to `DialogResult.OK` or `DialogResult.Cancel`, the custom dialog box automatically closes. In the client program, you can query this property to see which button the user clicks by invoking a `ShowDialog()` method of the form within an `if` statement. You should have experienced this when you programmed an OpenFileDialog box. If your OK or Cancel button event needs to accomplish more than closing a form, you can double-click it to create a delegate and add the needed code. But at this point, you don't need to do anything else except close the form.

In order to successfully add the `DialogResult.OK` and the `DialogResult.Cancel` to the appropriate spots, you can perform the following steps:

1. Right click the populated TypeUnderTest form. When the code editor appears, some code is buried inside a `#region Windows Form Designer generated code` directive.

2. Click the + sign to expand this region. The `InitializeComponent()` method appears.

3. Locate the code section for the `btnOK` object initialization. Insert a line of code for the OK button click like this:

   ```
   this.btnOK.DialogResult = System.Windows.Forms.DialogResult.OK;
   ```

4. Locate the code section for the `btnCancel` object initialization. Insert a line of code for the Cancel button similarly:

   ```
   this.btnCancel.DialogResult = System.Windows.Forms.DialogResult.Cancel;
   ```

Make sure the values of `DialogResult.OK` and `DialogResult.Cancel` are specified with their full qualifiers as they are listed in this section. If the partial qualifiers are used, they will disappear from the code page after any changes are made on the form. After these steps are performed, leave the rest of the code intact. The snippets for the `btnOK` and `btnCancel` initialization in the `InitializeComponent()` method of the `TypeUnderTest.cs` file is in Listing 7.1; the added two lines are bold and the other IDE-generated code is omitted.

FIGURE 7.3
A TypeUnderTest form for listing the available forms of an application under test, one of which is the startup form

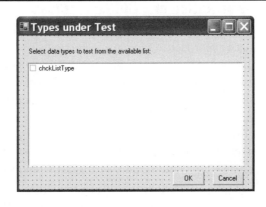

Listing 7.1	Code Snippets for the *btnOK and btnCancel* Initialization in the *InitializeComponent()* Method

```
...
//
// btnOK
//
this.btnOK.DialogResult = System.Windows.Forms.DialogResult.OK;
this.btnOK.Location = new System.Drawing.Point(280, 242);
this.btnOK.Name = "btnOK";
this.btnOK.Size = new System.Drawing.Size(56, 24);
this.btnOK.TabIndex = 2;
this.btnOK.Text = "OK";
//
// btnCancel
//
this.btnCancel.DialogResult = System.Windows.Forms.DialogResult.Cancel;
this.btnCancel.Location = new System.Drawing.Point(352, 242);
this.btnCancel.Name = "btnCancel";
this.btnCancel.Size = new System.Drawing.Size(56, 24);
this.btnCancel.TabIndex = 3;
this.btnCancel.Text = "Cancel";
//
// TypeUnderTest
//
...
```

This concludes the implementation of the TypeUnderTest form. The startup class of the AutomatedGUITest tool will initialize it. Some code in the AutomatedGUITest startup class will also populate the TypeUnderTest form with custom types of the application under test. Users can specify the startup form to test the application.

The Implementation of a *GUISurveyClass*

GUISurveyClass is the class that replaces the capture/playback approach of the commercial tools. It uses an active approach to spontaneously conduct a GUI survey within a Windows form under test. The process of the survey begins with object initialization of the GUISurveyClass. The initialization accepts the handle of a Windows form under test. Passing the handle to a custom function, GetWindowSize(), it finds the size of the form. Any GUI component is regarded as a rectangle by the AutomatedGUITest tool. The size of the rectangle is limited by the size of the display screen. In order to find all child GUI components within an application, a StartGUISurvey() method of the GUISurveyClass divides the entire screen into a grid system. The size of the cells in the grid system is arbitrarily decided by the testing tool developer. This method also assumes that each of the child GUI components must be visible in at least one of the cells and it drives the mouse pointer to visit each cell systematically. The pointer starts from the cell in upper-left corner and moves downward to the cell in the lower-left corner; then it moves back to the top of the grid and one cell toward right until all the cells in the entire grid are visited. The last cell is in the lower-right corner. Throughout the process, when a GUI child is recognized, it is recruited into a list. Thus, an exhaustive search for child GUI components is accomplished in order for the tool to conduct a thorough GUI testing. Such a systematic approach is an analogy of a Monte Carlo simulation mathematically.

Now, you are aware of the automatic survey approach. You can create the GUISurveyClass using the Microsoft Visual Studio .NET IDE with the AutomatedGUITest activated. From the main window, choose Project ➢ Add Class to open an Add New Item dialog box. In the Name field, type **GUISurveyClass** and click the Open button. A GUISurveyClass template is created with the namespace AutomatedGUITest and the class name GUISurveyClass. To code this class, you can accept all the generated code, add some using directives, overload a constructor, and declare two fields and one method, as discussed in the following paragraphs.

The first code addition is a few needed using directives as shown in Listing 7.2.

Listing 7.2   **The Needed *using* Directives for the *GUISurveyClass***

```
using System;
using System.Collections;
using System.Text;
using GUITestLibrary;
```

In fact, the first line, using System, is already generated by the IDE. The second using statement allows this class to use collection types for collecting GUI testing information. The System.Text namespace is required by some Win32 custom functions in the GUITestLibrary project to investigate the GUI components of an application. The GUITestLibrary namespace allows the GUISurveyClass to take advantages of your implementation in Chapters 4 and 5.

Second, the generated class template has already coded a default constructor. You can leave it intact but overload another constructor by passing a GUI handle to initialize an object of the GUISurveyClass as a parameter. Listing 7.3 shows the code of the needed fields and the overloaded constructor.

Listing 7.3   **The Code to Overload a Constructor for the *GUISurveyClass***

```
private int HandleUnderSurvey;
public SortedList GUISortedList;

public GUISurveyClass(int _hndlUnderSurvey)
{
  HandleUnderSurvey = _hndlUnderSurvey;
}
```

The first field declares an integer to grab the handle of the form under survey. The survey will find all the children and grandchildren with regard to GUI controls descended from the current form that is the ancestor of the child and grandchild GUI objects. The second field is a SortedList object, GUISortedList, which holds the whole family of the GUI components and populates them in the DataGrid object of the AutomatedGUITest form.

Then the constructor simply accepts a Windows form handle of the application under test and uses it to initialize the first field, HandleUnderSurvey.

Finally, only one public method, StartGUISurvey(), is needed for this class, as coded in Listing 7.4.

Listing 7.4   Code of the *StartGUISurvey()* Method

```
public void StartGUISurvey()
{
  GUISortedList = new SortedList();

  int width = 0;
  int height = 0;
  int surveyStep = 18;
  int maxLen = 128;

  GUITestActions.GetWindowSize(HandleUnderSurvey, ref width, ref height);

  for (int xPos = 0; xPos < width; xPos += surveyStep)
  {
    for (int yPos = 0; yPos < width; yPos += surveyStep)
    {
      GUITestActions.MoveMouseInsideHwnd(HandleUnderSurvey,
➥xPos, yPos, RectPosition.AnySpot);

      GUITestUtility.GUIInfo GUISurvey = new GUITestUtility.GUIInfo();
      StringBuilder winText = new StringBuilder(GUISurvey.GUIText, maxLen);
      StringBuilder clsName =  new
➥StringBuilder(GUISurvey.GUIClassName, maxLen);
      StringBuilder pText =  new StringBuilder(GUISurvey.GUIParentText, maxLen);

      GUITestActions.GetWindowFromPoint(ref GUISurvey.GUIHandle,
➥ref winText, ref clsName, ref pText);

      GUISurvey.GUIText = winText.ToString();
      GUISurvey.GUIClassName = clsName.ToString();
      GUISurvey.GUIParentText = pText.ToString();
      try
      {
        GUISortedList.Add(GUISurvey.GUIHandle, GUISurvey);
      }
```

```
        catch
        {
        }
      }
    }

    return;
}
```

The StartGUISurvey() method first initializes the GUISortedList object. Then it declares two integer variables to remember the width and height of the form under test. The third integer variable declaration is the size of the grid cell, or the number of pixels the mouse pointer moves in one step to complete the GUI survey. The number of 18 pixels here is an arbitrarily chosen number to allow the mouse to move 18 pixels each step. The four-integer variable declaration is also arbitrarily chosen to extract the GUI properties.

After the variables are declared and assigned, the GetWindowSize() method grabs the passed handle to find the width and height of the rectangle form. Then the StartGUISurvey() method uses two for loops to visit the grid. The outer for loop assigns coordinate position for the mouse pointer in the x-axis, and the inner for loop assigns the position in the y-axis. The increments of the x- and y-axis are bound by the width and height of the form.

Within the inner for loop, the StartGUISurvey() method first invokes the MoveMouseInside-Hwnd() method to move the mouse pointer inside the form. Then the StartGUISurvey() method initializes a GUITestUtility.GUIInfo object and three StringBuilder objects to hold the respective GUI information to the GUITestUtility.GUIInfo object. After the invocation of the Get-WindowFromPoint() method, the GUISurveyClass assures that a child GUI component is found with the current move of the mouse pointer. Last, it assigns values of the GUI properties to the GUITestUtility.GUIInfo object and adds the object as a value item into the GUISortedList object. The handle is also added to the GUISortedList as a key. The handle added as a key and the GUITestUtility.GUIInfo object will be used to help the tester confirm the testing case generation.

Many times the arbitrary surveyStep is defined small enough to guarantee that each of the child GUI components in the form will be visited by the mouse pointer at least once. Otherwise, some of the child GUI components will be skipped. If the step is too small, one of the side effects is that it needs a longer time to move to all the cells. Another one is that one GUI component will occupy many small cells and be visited many times. However, the SortedList class is developed in the .NET Framework as a unique key list. If the mouse pointer visited the same child GUI component more than one time, adding the GUI component with the same handle as a key to the SortedList object will produce an error message such as this:

```
An unhandled exception of type 'System.ArgumentException'
➥occurred in mscorlib.dll
```

To continue the survey without adding the already recruited child GUI component, the `GUISortedList.Add()` invocation occurs within a `try-catch` statement. Therefore, a survey is completed. The code for the `GUISurveyClass` seems so easy because it reuses the method implemented in the GUITestLibrary project. Thanks to the GUI Test Library, the upcoming sections will continue to reuse its methods, and the code of the tool project becomes simplified by reusing these methods.

Adding an Interface for Testing Data Confirmation

The third class to be implemented is also a GUI-rich Windows form, the `GUITestDataCollector` class. Starting from main window of the Microsoft Visual Studio .NET IDE, choose Project ➤ Add Windows Form. In the name field, type **GUITestDataCollector**, and click the Open button to create an empty GUITestDataCollector form. As usual, when you add a Windows form to a project, you need to populate it with some GUI controls. First, change the Text property of this form to **GUI Test Data Collector** for instruction and appearance. Next, you can use the following list to add some Label, ComboBox, TextBox, and Button controls, modify the mentioned property values, and accept the automatically assigned values that are not mentioned:

Control	Property	Value
Label	Name	lblControlName
	Text	Control Name
Label	Name	lblControlType
	Text	Control Type
Label	Name	lblWindowText
	Text	Window Text
Label	Name	lblClassName
	Text	Class Name
Label	Name	lablParentText
	Text	Parent Text
ComboBox	Name	cmbControlName
ComboBox	Name	cmbControlType
TextBox	Name	txtWindowText
TextBox	Name	txtClassName
TextBox	Name	txtParentText

Control	Property	Value
Button	Name	btnOK
	Text	OK
Button	Name	btnCancel
	Text	Cancel

After the GUI control population, the GUITestDataCollector form looks similar to Figure 7.4.

The coding task of this form includes the addition of two using directives, four private or public fields, one public method, and two private events. Right-click the form, and choose View Code to go to the code editor of this class. Move the cursor to the beginning of the GUITestDataCollector.cs file editor and add the following below the exiting using statement:

```
using System.Text;
using GUITestLibrary;
```

Then, navigate the cursor to the spot immediately below the GUITestDataCollector class declaration. Add the following field declaration statements before the IDE-generated fields, which are the GUI controls you just placed:

```
public GUITestUtility.GUIInfo guiInfo;
public ArrayList ControlNameList;
public ArrayList controlTypeList;
```

These are public fields and will be used by other classes to execute testing tasks later. The guiInfo object holds the properties of individual GUI components, the ControlNameList traces the names of the GUI components, and controlTypeList collects the data types of the GUI components.

FIGURE 7.4
Final appearance
of the GUITestData-
Collector form

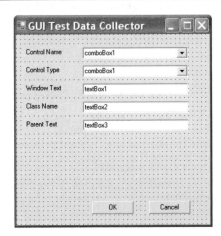

The proposed public method is named `PopulateGUIInfo()`. Its mission is to accept the assigned `guiInfo` field and populate the property values of a selected GUI to the ComboBox and the TextBox controls. It also connects the assigned `ControlNameList` and the `ControlTypeList` to the picking lists of the two `ComboBox` objects. The code of the `PopulateGUIInfo()` method is in Listing 7.5.

Listing 7.5   Code for the *PopulateGUIInfo()* Method

```
public void PopulateGUIInfo()
{
  cmbControlName.DataSource = ControlNameList;
  cmbControlType.DataSource = controlTypeList;

  cmbControlName.Text = guiInfo.GUIControlName;
  cmbControlType.Text = guiInfo.GUIControlType;
  txtWindowText.Text = guiInfo.GUIText.ToString();
  txtClassName.Text = guiInfo.GUIClassName.ToString();
  txtParentText.Text = guiInfo.GUIParentText.ToString();
}
```

Because you can be confident that the GUI text, GUI class, and its parent text found by the custom functions will be assigned correctly after a GUI component is selected to test by the user, TextBox objects are created to display these properties. The control type and name are detected by methods of .NET Reflection namespace or Win32 API methods. The outcome could be inconsistent with the findings of the custom functions in some cases. However, such a chance will be very rare. In case this happens, the ComboBox controls provide lists for the users to correct the confusion with ease.

After you completely code the property and the method, you are going to use the easy double-click approach to code the remaining events from the form design editor. First, click the form design tab from the Microsoft Visual Studio .NET IDE, and then, double-click the OK button. Your cursor is back to the code editor between a pair of curly brackets of the `btnOK_Click()` event. Insert code as shown in Listing 7.6.

Listing 7.6   Code for the *btnOK_Click()* Event

```
private void btnOK_Click(object sender, System.EventArgs e)
{
  guiInfo.GUIControlName = cmbControlName.Text;
  guiInfo.GUIControlType = cmbControlType.Text;
  guiInfo.GUIText = txtWindowText.Text;
  guiInfo.GUIClassName = txtClassName.Text;
  guiInfo.GUIParentText = txtParentText.Text;
}
```

When this OK button is clicked, it looks for the contents in the ComboBox and TextBox controls and assigns them to the `guiInfo` field. The `guiInfo` field bears the information to inform the tool to look for a GUI component with the specified property values and test it. This cluster of code is similar to the `PopulateGUIInfo()` method. But the direction of the data flow is reversed.

In order to indicate that the OK button is clicked from the GUITestDataCollector which is a custom dialog box, you need to perform one more step to complete the OK button click event. Go to the IDE-generated `#region Windows Form Designer generated code` section of the `GUITestDataCollector.cs` editor. If this section is hidden, click the + sign to expand it and reveal the `InitializeComponent()` method. From this method, locate the code snippet for the `btnOK` object initialization by looking for the `//btnOK` comment. Then insert a line of code:

```
this.btnOK.DialogResult = System.Windows.Forms.DialogResult.OK;
```

After the insertion, this section of code looks similar to Listing 7.7 with the inserted code bold.

TIP   Microsoft Visual Studio .NET IDE allows developers to use a `#region` directive to hide a portion of the code in a code file. You can press the Ctrl+M+L combination to expand/collapse these regions.

Listing 7.7   **Inserting a Line of Code to Catch the OK Button Click** *DialogResult*

```
//
// btnOK
//
this.btnOK.DialogResult = System.Windows.Forms.DialogResult.OK;
this.btnOK.Location = new System.Drawing.Point(136, 296);
this.btnOK.Name = "btnOK";
this.btnOK.TabIndex = 10;
this.btnOK.Text = "OK";
this.btnOK.Click += new System.EventHandler(this.btnOK_Click);
```

Since clicking a Cancel button often means doing nothing, you need no code for a Cancel button event. However, you need a line of code to catch that the Cancel button is clicked. To accomplish this, you insert a line of code in the `InitializeComponent()` method by locating the code section for the `btnCancel` object initialization as you did for the `tbnOK` object. Then, add a line of code like this:

```
this.btnCancel.DialogResult = DialogResult.Cancel;
```

The entire section of the `btnCancel` initialization should look similar to Listing 7.8 (the inserted code is bold).

Listing 7.8   Code to Catch the Cancel Button Click *DialogResult*

```
//
// btnCancel
//
this.btnCancel.DialogResult = System.Windows.Forms.DialogResult.Cancel;
this.btnCancel.Location = new System.Drawing.Point(240, 296);
this.btnCancel.Name = "btnCancel";
this.btnCancel.TabIndex = 9;
this.btnCancel.Text = "Cancel";
```

This event simply informs the tool that the Cancel button was clicked. Then it disposes of the GUITestDataCollector form. Thus nothing else happens after clicking the Cancel button.

You can compile the project to check whether there are coding errors for the newly added class. Listing 7.9 is the full list of the GUITestDataCollector class with the IDE-generated code omitted.

Listing 7.9   The Complete List of Code for the *GUITestDataCollector* Class with IDE-Generated Code Omitted

```
using System;
using System.Drawing;
using System.Collections;
using System.ComponentModel;
using System.Windows.Forms;
using System.Text;
using GUITestLibrary;

namespace AutomatedGUITest
{
  /// <summary>
  /// Summary description for GUITestDataCollector.
  /// </summary>
  public class GUITestDataCollector : System.Windows.Forms.Form
  {
    public GUITestUtility.GUIInfo guiInfo;
    public ArrayList ControlNameList;
    public ArrayList controlTypeList;

    ...
    //Microsoft Visual Studio .NET IDE generated code

    private void InitializeComponent()
    {
```

```
...
//Microsoft Visual Studio .NET IDE generated code

//
// btnCancel
//
this.btnCancel.Location = new System.Drawing.Point(240, 296);
this.btnCancel.Name = "btnCancel";
this.btnCancel.TabIndex = 9;
this.btnCancel.Text = "Cancel";
this.btnCancel.DialogResult = DialogResult.Cancel;
//
// btnOK
//
this.btnOK.Location = new System.Drawing.Point(136, 296);
this.btnOK.Name = "btnOK";
this.btnOK.TabIndex = 10;
this.btnOK.Text = "OK";
this.btnOK.DialogResult = DialogResult.OK;
this.btnOK.Click += new System.EventHandler(this.btnOK_Click);

...
//Microsoft Visual Studio .NET IDE generated code

}
...


public void PopulateGUIInfo()
{
  cmbControlName.DataSource = ControlNameList;
  cmbControlType.DataSource = controlTypeList;

  cmbControlName.Text = guiInfo.GUIControlName;
  cmbControlType.Text = guiInfo.GUIControlType;
  txtWindowText.Text = guiInfo.GUIText.ToString();
  txtClassName.Text = guiInfo.GUIClassName.ToString();
  txtParentText.Text = guiInfo.GUIParentText.ToString();
}

private void btnOK_Click(object sender, System.EventArgs e)
{
  guiInfo.GUIControlName = cmbControlName.Text;
  guiInfo.GUIControlType = cmbControlType.Text;
  guiInfo.GUIText = txtWindowText.Text;
  guiInfo.GUIClassName = txtClassName.Text;
  guiInfo.GUIParentText = txtParentText.Text;
}
  }
}
```

At this point, the data is collected for testing one GUI component. Restarting the GUI-TestDataCollector form will allow the users to specify other GUI components to test.

Developing a General-Purpose GUI Test Script

GUI test automation has faced two challenges technically in the past years. The first one is how to locate the correct GUI components for testing. Different approaches have used hard-coded x- and y-coordinates and object-based and keyword-based techniques to increase the GUI search efficiency. From the experiences of exercising the sample project in Chapter 6, the tool in this book uses a certain pattern of the GUI text, the GUI class name, and its parent text to correctly locate a GUI component to test. Thus, a general test script will be the idea solution to a fully automated GUI testing tool. When you develop your own tool based on the ideas in this book, you can alter the GUI search pattern to make it suit your testing projects and your organization.

The other challenge is automatic verification. It seems easy to use the capture/playback method to record a test script. But it is not easy for testers to insert verification points. Some available tools allow the testers to insert verification code during the script recording process, perhaps because they might forget to do this later. Other tools ask the testers to insert verification methods after the script recording. However, the automated test scripts are not automatically generated by any tools. A tool user is still required to have in-depth knowledge of programming and be skillful at using the tools. Especially when a tool comes with a unique script language, it isolates the testers from the developers.

In order to address the automatic verification approach effectively, this section will guide you through developing a general test script for different GUI components and preparing the data objects for verification. Chapter 8 will elaborate on the prepared data and discuss how to automatically complete the verification in depth.

To conduct effective GUI testing, this tool will heavily reuse the functions of the GUI test library implemented. In order to catch up with new testing tasks, this GUI test library will be under continuous development. However, the general test script to be developed in this section will remain relatively stable. The users of this tool will not be required to see and edit this script.

Traditional testing methods and tools need a script for each single test case. As the number of test cases increases, the test scripts and testing data become difficult to track and maintain. This tool uses a general test script to address the following issues:

- *One test script is for all test cases.* The test execution is totally driven by XML testing data stores. Increased testing capabilities will be implemented in the GUI test library.

- *Users will not be required to learn programming.* But a good understanding of XML is the key to effectively creating and maintaining testing cases.

- *Each new method to expand the GUI test library has only one purpose.* As you have implemented the methods to handle the ListBox, TextBox and Button controls, each method has only a few lines of code. The test script becomes aware of and reuses the methods in the GUI test library by reading an XML document.

- *An XML data store is easy to create, read, and understand.* This will allow the users to edit the data store with ease. In addition, a well-formatted test plan can be translated into a testing data store automatically. The test is completely driven by the collected data thereafter.

For developing the AutomatedGUITest tool, you have added three Windows forms. Now you need to add one more for the `GUITestScript` class. As usual, after you choose Project ➢ Add Windows Form, type a class name such as `GUITestScript` in the Name field. Then click the Open button. The IDE automatically generates the form. On this form, you don't need to add any GUI controls because you don't want the testers to watch a form when the tool is conducting a fully automated GUI test. The only thing you need to do when the form is active is to add four Timer controls by dragging them from the Toolbox and dropping them on the form. Then use the values in the following list to modify the default values of the Timer properties:

Control	Property	Value
Timer	Name	tmrAutomatedTest
	Enabled	true
	Interval	100
	Modifier	private
Timer	Name	tmrRunScript
	Enabled	false
	Interval	100
	Modifier	private
Timer	Name	tmrStopScript
	Enabled	false
	Interval	100
	Modifier	private
Timer	Name	tmrVerifyTest
	Enabled	false
	Interval	100
	Modifier	private

The first Timer control is for starting the application under test. The second and third Timer controls are for running and stopping the script execution. The last Timer control starts to save the test results and terminates the test execution. The form of the GUI test script is empty.

Now, right-click the mouse button on the empty form and select View Code from the pop-up menu. When the cursor is in the code editor, move it to the beginning of the using statement section to add the following namespace beside the already generated using directives:

```
using System.Reflection;
using System.IO;
using GUITestLibrary;
using System.Text;
```

The purpose of the System.Reflection namespace is for loading the application to test. The System.IO namespace provides a method for the tool to find the correct path for the testing data. The GUITestLibrary and System.Text namespaces are for the purpose discussed earlier.

Next, add the private field declarations and overload the constructor immediately after the GUITestScript class declaration, as shown in Listing 7.10. (Microsoft Visual Studio .NET IDE–generated declarations are omitted here.)

Listing 7.10   **Code for the Field Declarations and the Overloaded Constructor of the** *GUITestDataScript* **Class**

```
...
private string guiTestDataStore;
private string progDir;


private Form AUT;
private GUITestUtility.GUIInfoSerializable seqGUIUT;

private string guiTestActionLib;
private int clickNum;
private ArrayList resultList;

public GUITestScript(string _testDataStore, string _progDir)
{
  InitializeComponent();
  GuiTestDataStore = _testDataStore;
  progDir = _progDir;
}
```

The first string field, GuiTestDataStore, is prepared to accept a pathname of the data store originated from the GUITestDataColloector class. The progDir field refers to the root directory of the GUI testing tool. The two fields are assigned with values by the overloaded constructor.

The next two fields work together. The AUT is an object of the System.Windows.Forms.Form class. At this point, we can assume the targets of GUI testing are all derived from Windows forms to simplify the discussion. Later, we will enhance this tool to test various GUI components, such as, for example, custom controls and ActiveX controls. The seqGUIUT object holds the collected data store after deserialization and then passes the startup information and test script information to execute the test.

The last three fields complete the real test and verifications. The string variable, GuiTest-ActionLib, refers to the GUITestActionLib.xml document prepared in Listing 5.2 of Chapter 5. Before you proceed with the code, I recommend that you copy this file from the C:\GUISource-Code\Chapter05\XMLCreator\bin\Debug folder to the C:\GUISourceCode\Chapter07\Automated-GUITest\bin\Debug folder to avoid overlooking it later. This document contains a list of different GUI types and their respective GUI handling methods from the GUI test library. The clickNum variable is for counting how many GUI test actions have been performed with regard to the count of the seqGUIUT.GUIList object. The resultList field collects the status of the application after each GUI test action.

After the field declaration, you need to overload the constructor of the GUITestScript class to accept where the testing data and the testing tool are located. The last three lines of code in Listing 7.10 initialize the test script first and then assign the data store and the program directory to the respective fields.

The major tasking of coding the GUITestScript class is for the Tick() events of the four Timer controls. Similar to the implementation of the button click events, you can double-click a Timer control from the GUITestScript form and auto-generate the respective Timer tick delegates and event handler. Then you can add the needed code. Now, let's double-click the tmrAutomatedTest on the form. The IDE brings the cursor between a pair of curly brackets of the tmrAutomatedTest_Tick() event. Since this event calls a StartAUT() helper method, the code for the event and the helper method are shown in Listing 7.11.

Listing 7.11   Code for the *tmrAutomatedTest_Tick()* Event and the *StartAUT()* Helper Method

```
private void tmrAutomatedTest_Tick(object sender, System.EventArgs e)
{
  StartAUT();

  tmrAutomatedTest.Enabled = false;
  resultList = new ArrayList();
  tmrRunScript.Enabled = true;

}

private void StartAUT()
```

```
{
  seqGUIUT = new GUITestUtility.GUIInfoSerializable();
  object obj = (object)seqGUIUT;
  GUITestUtility.DeSerializeInfo(guiTestDataStore, ref obj);
  seqGUIUT = (GUITestUtility.GUIInfoSerializable)obj;

  string AUTPath = seqGUIUT.AUTPath;
  string startupType = seqGUIUT.AUTStartupForm;

  if (AUT == null)
    AUT = (Form)GUITestUtility.StartAUT(AUTPath, startupType);

  int hwnd = (int)AUT.Handle;
  StringBuilder sbClsName = new StringBuilder(128);
  GUITestActions.GetClassName(hwnd, sbClsName, 128);
  string clsName = sbClsName.ToString();
  string winText = AUT.Text;
  string pText = "";
  GUITestActions.SynchronizeWindow(ref hwnd, ref winText,
  ➥ref clsName, ref pText);
}
```

The tmrAutomatedTest_Tick() event simply invokes the helper method, disables itself, initializes the resultList, and enables the second Timer control to execute the test script. Most of the actions happen in the StartAUT() helper method.

The StartAUT() method first initializes the GUIInfoSerializable object, seqGUIUT. Then it uses the boxing techniques to convert the seqGUIUT of an object, obj. This obj object is required by the DeSerializeInfo() method of the GUITestLibrary. After the invocation of the DeSerializeInfo() method, the obj is assigned with the data store of the testing information and is converted back to the seqGUIUT object by unboxing.

Next, it extracts the path and name of the startup form of the application under test from the seqGUIUT object. Using an if statement to check that the same application is not currently run by the script, it invokes the method from GUITestLibrary and returns the application under test as a Form object to AUT by another unboxing.

After a command is issued, a Windows application with GUI components usually doesn't appear on the display instantly. Under a normal operation condition, the user usually waits for a few milliseconds, even nanoseconds unnoticeable to a human. But to a high-speed computer system, this much time will be enough to execute many lines of the code that follows the command. In order to make sure the GUI application is visible for the following code, a synchronization method is needed for an automatic GUI testing tool. In Chapter 4, such a method was implemented in the GUITestLibrary. Thus, the last cluster of the code is to retrieve the needed information of the application under test. The SynchronizeWindow() method of the

GUITestLibrary uses the retrieved information and makes sure this application is visible on the screen.

The second Timer control event is the tmrRunScript_Tick() event. From the form design editor, double-click the tmrRunScript control and add code for it. This event also calls another helper method, RunScript(). The code for the event and the helper method is in Listing 7.12.

Listing 7.12   Code for the *tmrRunScript_Tick()* Event and the *RunScript()* Helper Method

```csharp
private void tmrRunScript_Tick(object sender, System.EventArgs e)
{
  RunsScript();
  tmrRunScript.Enabled = false;

}

private void RunsScript()
{
  guiTestActionLib = Path.Combine(progDir, "GUITestActionLib.xml");

  GUITestUtility.GUIInfo guiUnit =
➥(GUITestUtility.GUIInfo)seqGUIUT.GUIList[clickNum];

  string ctrlAction =
➥GUITestUtility.GetAGUIAction(guiTestActionLib, guiUnit.GUIControlType);

  StringBuilder sb = new StringBuilder(10000);

  Control ctrlTested =
➥(Control)GUITestUtility.VerifyField(AUT, guiUnit.GUIControlName);
  GUITestActions.GetWindowText((int)ctrlTested.Handle, sb, 10000);

  object[] paramArr = new object[4];
  paramArr[0] = 0;
  paramArr[1] = sb.ToString();
  paramArr[2] = guiUnit.GUIClassName;
  paramArr[3] = guiUnit.GUIParentText;

  Type guiTestLibType = new GUITestActions().GetType();
  object obj = Activator.CreateInstance(guiTestLibType);
  MethodInfo mi = guiTestLibType.GetMethod(ctrlAction);

  try
  {
    mi.Invoke(obj, paramArr);
  }
  catch (Exception ex)
  {
    MessageBox.Show(ex.Message);
```

```
      }

      if (clickNum < seqGUIUT.GUIList.Count)
      {
        clickNum++;
        tmrRunScript.Enabled = false;
        tmrStopScript.Enabled = true;
      }
    }
```

The code for the `tmrRunScript_Tick()` event simply invokes the `RunScript()` helper method and disables itself. The majority of the tasks of the testing actions are the burden of the `RunScript()` method.

The first action of the `RunScript()` method is to grab the `GUITestActionLib.xml` document from the tool program directory. Then, guided with the value of the `clickNum` variable, it locates the property values of the next GUI target from the `seqGUIUT.GUIList` object. Based on the data type of the targeted GUI control, the method looks for the handling method from the `GUITestActionLib.xml` document.

NOTE   You need to copy the `GUITestActionLib.xml` document from the `C:\GUISourceCode\Chapter05\XMLCreator\bin\Debug` folder to the `C:\GUISourceCode\Chapter07\AutomatedGUITest\bin\Debug` folder, if you have not done so. This will enable you to start the first fully automated GUI test at the end of this chapter without error.

The next cluster of the code is to prepare the values of parameters needed for execution of the respective handling method with late binding. Each GUI action by late binding indicates the moment when a method from the GUI test library performs a mouse or a keystroke action on the GUI object under test until all the desired actions are performed. The `Invoke()` method of the `MethodInfo` object to achieve the late binding is executed within a `try-catch` clause. A `try-catch` clause will allow the test script to proceed to the next step if exception occurs with one GUI action. Thus, it increases the robustness of the GUI script and the tool.

TIP   When I approached a group of software developers with the topic of late binding, some of them asked me to explain the differences between early binding and late binding. I tried to use the definitions I have learned from various books and articles to answer this question. However, some of developers were not convinced of the benefits of late binding. Then I compared early binding to the actions of a housekeeper who foresaw all needs in advance and spent the money necessary to purchase and store them. Another housekeeper uses late binding, but this one doesn't purchase materials to store. Instead, whenever he needs anything, he drives to the closest store to purchase it and uses it immediately. If the material is not consumable, he may take the advantage of the return policy.

After one GUI action is completed, an if statement inspects whether the late binding executions reach the last GUI action in the data store. If not, the RunScript() method increases the value of the clickNum by 1 in order to perform the next GUI action. Then it turns the tmrRunScript off by setting its Enabled property to false and enables the tmrStopScript object.

The third event is the tmrStopScript_Tick() event. After you double-click the tmrStopScript control from the form design editor, add code to make the tmrStopScript_Tick() event, as shown in Listing 7.13.

Listing 7.13   Code for the *tmrStopScript_Tick()* Event

```
private void tmrStopScript_Tick(object sender, System.EventArgs e)
{
  GUITestUtility.GUIInfo guiUnit =
➡(GUITestUtility.GUIInfo)seqGUIUT.GUIList[clickNum - 1];
  Control ctrlTested;
  ctrlTested = (Control)GUITestUtility.VerifyField(AUT, guiUnit.GUIControlName);
  resultList.Add(ctrlTested);

  if (clickNum >= seqGUIUT.GUIList.Count)
  {
    tmrRunScript.Enabled = false;
    tmrStopScript.Enabled = false;
        tmrVerifyTest.Enabled = true;
    try
    {
      AUT.Dispose();
    }
    catch{}
  }
  else
  {
    tmrRunScript.Enabled = true;
    tmrStopScript.Enabled = false;
  }

}
```

The code of the tmrStopScript_Tick() event is similar to the code in Listing 6.13 in Chapter 6. It first makes the effort to collect the current status of the application under test into the resultList object. Then it turns the tmrRunScript object on and itself off if the test doesn't reach the last GUI action in the data store. After all GUI actions are performed, it turns off the Timer controls for the test script and disposes of the application under test. The last action of this event turns on the tmrVerifyTest.

As usual, you can double-click the `tmrVerifyTest` control from the test script form and add between the curly brackets the code in Listing 7.14.

Listing 7.14   **Code for the *tmrVerifyTest_Tick()* Event**

```
private void tmrVerifyTest_Tick(object sender, System.EventArgs e)
{
  tmrVerifyTest.Enabled = false;


  string resultDataStore = guiTestDataStore.Replace(".xml", "_result.xml");
  GUITestUtility.SerilizeInfo(resultDataStore, resultList);

  this.Dispose();
}
```

The `tmrVerifyTest_Tick()` event first turns itself off. In order to achieve the automatic verification, the rest of the code saves the test outcome in an XML document. The process of saving the results assigns a filename first and then calls the `GUITestUtility.SerilizeInfo()`. Finally, it concludes this test by disposing the form of the test script itself.

At this point, the `resultList` only collects the status of the GUI component just tested. This limits the verification capability of an automatic testing tool. However, it shows the possibility of the fully automated GUI test process. The next chapter will be dedicated to broadening the scope of the test verification automation.

Now you can compile the project to check whether the new code has errors. Listing 7.15 has the full code for the `GUITestSctipt` class with the IDE-generated code omitted.

Listing 7.15   **Full Code Listing of the *GUITestSctipt* Class**

```
using System;
using System.Drawing;
using System.Collections;
using System.ComponentModel;
using System.Windows.Forms;
using System.Data;
using System.Reflection;
using System.IO;
using GUITestLibrary;
using System.Text;

namespace AutomatedGUITest
{

    public class GUITestScript : System.Windows.Forms.Form
```

```
{
  //generated by planting the GUI controls
  private System.ComponentModel.IContainer components;
  private System.Windows.Forms.Timer tmrStopScript;
  private System.Windows.Forms.Timer tmrAutomatedTest;
  private System.Windows.Forms.Timer tmrRunScript;
  private System.Windows.Forms.Timer tmrVerifyTest;

  //fields added
  private string guiTestDataStore;
  private string progDir;

  private Form AUT;
  private GUITestUtility.GUIInfoSerializable seqGUIUT;

  private string guiTestActionLib;
  private ArrayList resultList;
  private int clickNum;

  // default constructor
  public GUITestScript()
  {
    InitializeComponent();
  }

  //overloaded constructor
  public GUITestScript(string _testDataStore, string _progDir)
  {
    InitializeComponent();
    guiTestDataStore = _testDataStore;
    progDir = _progDir;
  }

  ...
  //Some Microsoft Visual Studio .NET IDE generated code
  ...


  private void tmrAutomatedTest_Tick(object sender, System.EventArgs e)
  {
    StartAUT();

    tmrAutomatedTest.Enabled = false;
    tmrRunScript.Enabled = true;
    resultList = new ArrayList();
  }

  private void StartAUT()
  {
```

```csharp
      seqGUIUT = new GUITestUtility.GUIInfoSerializable();
      object obj = (object)seqGUIUT;
      GUITestUtility.DeSerializeInfo(guiTestDataStore, ref obj);
      seqGUIUT = (GUITestUtility.GUIInfoSerializable)obj;

      string AUTPath = seqGUIUT.AUTPath;
      string startupType = seqGUIUT.AUTStartupForm;

      if (AUT == null)
        AUT = (Form)GUITestUtility.StartAUT(AUTPath, startupType);

      int hwnd = (int)AUT.Handle;
      StringBuilder sbClsName = new StringBuilder(128);
      GUITestActions.GetClassName(hwnd, sbClsName, 128);
      string clsName = sbClsName.ToString();
      string winText = AUT.Text;
      string pText = "";
      GUITestActions.SynchronizeWindow(ref hwnd, ref winText,
➥ref clsName, ref pText);
    }

    private void tmrRunScript_Tick(object sender, System.EventArgs e)
    {
      RunsScript();
      tmrRunScript.Enabled = false;

    }

    private void RunsScript()
    {
      guiTestActionLib = Path.Combine(progDir, "GUITestActionLib.xml");

      GUITestUtility.GUIInfo guiUnit =
➥(GUITestUtility.GUIInfo)seqGUIUT.GUIList[clickNum];

      string ctrlAction =
➥GUITestUtility.GetAGUIAction(guiTestActionLib, guiUnit.GUIControlType);

      StringBuilder sb = new StringBuilder(10000);

      Control ctrlTested =
➥(Control)GUITestUtility.VerifyField(AUT, guiUnit.GUIControlName);
      GUITestActions.GetWindowText((int)ctrlTested.Handle, sb, 10000);

      object[] paramArr = new object[4];
      paramArr[0] = 0;
      paramArr[1] = sb.ToString();
      paramArr[2] = guiUnit.GUIClassName;
      paramArr[3] = guiUnit.GUIParentText;

      Type guiTestLibType = new GUITestActions().GetType();
```

```
      object obj = Activator.CreateInstance(guiTestLibType);
      MethodInfo mi = guiTestLibType.GetMethod(ctrlAction);

      try
      {
        mi.Invoke(obj, paramArr);
      }
      catch (Exception ex)
      {
        MessageBox.Show(ex.Message);
      }

      if (clickNum < seqGUIUT.GUIList.Count)
      {
        clickNum++;
        tmrRunScript.Enabled = false;
        tmrStopScript.Enabled = true;
      }

    }

    private void tmrStopScript_Tick(object sender, System.EventArgs e)
    {
      GUITestUtility.GUIInfo guiUnit =
➥(GUITestUtility.GUIInfo)seqGUIUT.GUIList[clickNum - 1];
      Control ctrlTested;
      ctrlTested =
➥(Control)GUITestUtility.VerifyField(AUT, guiUnit.GUIControlName);;
      resultList.Add(ctrlTested);

      if (clickNum >= seqGUIUT.GUIList.Count)
      {
        tmrRunScript.Enabled = false;
        tmrStopScript.Enabled = false;

        tmrVerifyTest.Enabled = true;
        try
        {
          AUT.Dispose();
        }
        catch{}
      }
      else
      {
        tmrRunScript.Enabled = true;
        tmrStopScript.Enabled = false;
      }
    }

    private void tmrVerifyTest_Tick(object sender, System.EventArgs e)
    {
```

```
      tmrVerifyTest.Enabled = false;

            string resultDataStore = guiTestDataStore.Replace(".xml", "_
result.xml");
         GUITestUtility.SerilizeInfo(resultDataStore, resultList);

         this.Dispose();
      }
    }
  }
```

Putting Together the *AutomatedGUITest* Tool

Now all the help classes are completely coded. Code can be added to the AutomatedGUI-
Test startup form created in the beginning of the project. As you recall, you accepted all the
default values when the Windows form template was created; the class name of the startup
form is Form1 . You can rename it to frmMain by making three changes to the IDE generated template:

1. Right-click on the form and choose View Code from the pop-up menu. In the code editor,
    change the class declaration from

```
      public class Form1 : System.Windows.Forms.Form
```

to

```
      public class frmMain : System.Windows.Forms.Form
```

2. Change the default constructor from (comments are omitted in the code snippet)

```
      public Form1()
      {
        InitializeComponent();
      }
```

to

```
      public frmMain()
      {
        InitializeComponent();
      }
```

3. Change the entry point Main() method from

```
      static void Main()
      {
        Application.Run(new Form1());
      }
```

to

```
static void Main()
{
  Application.Run(new frmMain());
}
```

Hereafter, this book will refer to the AutomatedGUITest tool as frmMain for short, such as the frmMain code editor and the frmMain design editor.

To start coding, move the cursor to the beginning to the using directives and add the following additional using statement:

```
using System.Reflection;
using GUITestLibrary;
```

The frmMain class will use reflection to load the application under test and the GUITest-Library for its GUITestUtility.GUIInfoSerializable object.

The frmMain class requires a few private fields to help the integration of the other classes. The fields are declared, as shown in Listing 7.16, immediately below the frmMain class declaration and with the other IDE-generated fields.

Listing 7.16   Declaration of the Private Fields in the *frmMain* Class

```
private string currDir = Environment.CurrentDirectory;
private string applicationUT;
private string StartupForm;
private Form formUT;

private GUISurveyClass guiSurveyCls;
private GUITestDataCollector GUITDC;

private GUITestUtility.GUIInfoSerializable GUITestSeqList;

private ArrayList tempList;
private string GuiProperty;
private string TestCaseStore;
```

The first string field, currDir, is declared and assigned with a value of the program root directory, which is the folder where the AutomatedGUITest.exe resides. Then, the applicationUT, startup-Form, and formUT are related to the application under test. The formUT is prepared to hold an object of the application under test as a Form object. The fields of guiSurveyCls and GUITDC are the objects of the GUISurvey and the GUITestDataCollector classes. These objects are prepared to be referred within the frmMain class. The GUITestSeqList field of a GUITestUtility.GUIInfo-Serializable object is prepared to save and open the test data store. And last, the tempList will be used to store all child GUI components of the application under test, the GuiProperty field for looking for a GUI property value, and TestCaseStore for a filename to save the test data.

Starting the Application under Test

After the fields are added, the first coding task is the Start GUI Test button event. You need to go to the frmMain design editor and double-click the button labeled Start GUI Test. When you are on the frmMain code editor, you can add code to make the btnStartGUITest_Click() event look like it does in Listing 7.17.

Listing 7.17   Coding the *btnStartGUITest_Click()* Event

```
private void btnStartGUITest_Click(object sender, System.EventArgs e)
{
  GUITestSeqList = new GUITestUtility.GUIInfoSerializable();

  opnAUT.Title = "Specify an Application Under Test";
  opnAUT.Filter =
➥"GUI Applications(*.EXE; *.DLL)|*.EXE;*.DLL|All files (*.*)|*.*";

  if (opnAUT.ShowDialog() == DialogResult.OK)
  {
    applicationUT = opnAUT.FileName;
    GUITestSeqList.AUTPath = applicationUT;

    GetTypeToTestFromAUT();

    try
    {
      formUT = (Form) GUITestUtility.StartAUT(applicationUT, startupForm);
    }
    catch (InvalidCastException ex)
    {
        MessageBox.Show(ex.Message);
    }
  }
  else
  {
    return;
  }
}
```

After the user clicks the Start GUI Test button on frmMain, the tool first initialize a GUITestUtility.GUIInfoSerializable object, GUITestSeqList, using a default constructor. Then it assigns some modification values to the OpenFileDialog control and shows the open file dialog on the screen. The user selects an application (*.exe or *.dll) to test. After an application is selected by clicking the OK button in the open file dialog box, the application path and filename is assigned to the applicationUT field and a GetTypeToTestFromAUT() helper method is called. Invocation of the GetTypeToTestFromAUT() method assigns the startup form of the application under test to the startupForm field.

Finally, a `try-catch` clause is used to invoke the `GUITestUtility.StartAUT()` from the `GUITestLibrary`. Within the `try` statement, the invocation of the `GUITestUtility.StartAUT()` converts its returned object to a `System.Windows.Forms.Form` object. This is the case when the GUI application under test has a startup form. However, GUI components in need of testing could be a custom control or a traditional ActiveX control, which can't be converted to a Form object. When the latter is the case, the object conversion to a Form instance will generate a `System.InvalidCastException`. At this point, I have not discussed methods of testing such GUI components. The `catch` statement is left empty and will be coded later, and the test will be aborted.

Listing 7.18 has the implementation for the `GetTypeToTestFromAUT()` helper method to obtain the startup form of the application under test.

Listing 7.18   Code for the *GetTypeToTestFromAUT()* Helper Method

```
private void GetTypeToTestFromAUT()
{
  if (applicationUT.Length <= 0)
  {
    return;
  }

  TypeUnderTest typeDUT = new TypeUnderTest();

  try
  {
    Assembly asm = Assembly.LoadFrom(applicationUT);
    Type[] tys = asm.GetTypes();
    foreach (Type ty in tys)
    {
      typeDUT.chckListType.Items.Add(ty.Namespace + "." + ty.Name);
    }

  }
  catch(Exception ex)
  {
    MessageBox.Show(ex.Message);
    return;
  }

  if (typeDUT.ShowDialog() == DialogResult.OK)
  {
    GetSelectedTypesUT(typeDUT);
  }
  else
  {
    return;
  }
}
```

The `GetTypeToTestFromAUT()` helper method first inspects whether a filename is selected from the open file dialog. For example, when the Cancel button is clicked in the open file dialog, the tool aborts the execution at this point by returning to the program (without the `return` statements, the program will crash by proceeding to the code afterward when a application pathe is not appropriately assigned). Then it initializes a `TypeUnderTest` object, `typeDUT`. In the `try` statement, a reflection process is started to find all the types included in the application, looking for a startup form among the types. Using a `foreach` loop, it displays all the possible types in the `CheckedListBox` object, `chckListType`.

The `ShowDialog()` method is executed with an `if` statement to inspect which button is clicked from the `typeDUT` form. After the `ShowDialog()` method of the `typeDUT` object is invoked, the `typeDUT` appears as a modal window. The tool waits for a user interaction to close this form by clicking the OK or the Cancel button. Normally, the user is expected to select the name of the startup form from the check box list and click the OK button. Clicking the Cancel button often means that the user changes their mind and wants to do nothing. If the user clicks the OK button, the method continues to invoke a `GetSelectedTypesUT()` helper method. The code of the `GetSelectedTypesUT()` is in Listing 7.19.

Listing 7.19   **Code for the *GetSelectedTypesUT()* Helper Method**

```
private void GetSelectedTypesUT(TypeUnderTest typeDUT)
{
  startupForm = "";
  for (int i = 0; i<typeDUT.chckListType.Items.Count; i++)
  {
    if (typeDUT.chckListType.GetItemChecked(i))
      startupForm = typeDUT.chckListType.GetItemText(
➡typeDUT.chckListType.Items[i]);
  }
}
```

The `GetSelectedTypesUT()` method uses a `for` loop to look into the `chckListType` object the `typeDUT` form for a checked item. When the checked item is encountered, it assigns the checked item to the `startupForm` field. Thus, the startup form and the application path are given and the application under test is started.

However, the application is started at this point not for testing, but for conducting the GUI survey in the next step. Before running the automated test script, this application should be terminated. The test script will have an automatic mechanism to start the application in order to grab the handle of the startup form and inspect the status of the application at different testing stages.

Conducting a GUI Survey

You have implemented a GUISurveyClass, which is able to detect the existence of all the available GUI components by surveying every pixel of the application on the desktop. Such a search is designed to be systematic, active, and exhaustive. After this survey is completed, the available GUI components need to be displayed. The tool should provide a workbench on which the tester can interact with GUI components.

This section guides you in adding code and enabling the GUI Survey button. Double-click the GUI Survey button from the frmMain design editor. The IDE creates a template for a btnGUISurvey_Click() event. The code for this event looks like the code in Listing 7.20.

Listing 7.20   **Code for the *btnGUISurvey_Click()* Event**

```
private void btnGUISurvey_Click(object sender, System.EventArgs e)
{
   this.WindowState = FormWindowState.Minimized;

   try
   {
      guiSurveyCls = new GUISurveyClass((int)formUT.Handle);
   }
   catch (Exception ex)
   {
      MessageBox.Show(ex.Message);
   }
   guiSurveyCls.StartGUISurvey();

   SetGUIListToTest();

   this.WindowState = FormWindowState.Normal;
}
```

This event assumes that at this moment, there are only two applications running on the desktop: the application under test and the tool itself. When the btnGUISurvey_Click() event is triggered, it first minimizes the tool itself. Then it uses a try-catch clause to initialize a GUISurveyClass instance, guiSurveyCls, by passing the handle of the Form object under test. The statement in the try clause is for testing .NET Windows Form applications and the catch clause is prepared for testing applications that are not Windows Form objects (Chapters 13 and 14 will discuss such methods). At this point a message box is used to alert tester that the initialization of the GUI survey was unsuccessful. Once the guiSurveyCls is initialized successfully, the event invokes the StartGUISurvey() method from the guiSurveyCls instance. The completion of the StartGUISurvey() method collects the application GUI components into a

GUISortedList as GUITestUtility.GUIInfo objects. The next task is to call a SetGUIListToTest() helper method to set the GUI identifiers into the designed DataGrid control. After all the GUI information is visible on the tool, the last line of the event returns the tool interface to its normal size. Listing 7.21 has code for the SetGUIListToTest() helper method.

Listing 7.21   **Code for the *SetGUIListToTest()* Helper Method**

```
private void SetGUIListToTest()
{
  DataTable dtGUITable = new DataTable();

  MakeDataTableColumn(dtGUITable, "Handle", "System.Int32");
  MakeDataTableColumn(dtGUITable, "Window Text", "System.String");
  MakeDataTableColumn(dtGUITable, "Class Name", "System.String");
  MakeDataTableColumn(dtGUITable, "Parent Text", "System.String");

  for (int i = 0; i < guiSurveyCls.GUISortedList.Count; i++)
  {
    GUITestUtility.GUIInfo gui =
➥(GUITestUtility.GUIInfo)guiSurveyCls.GUISortedList.GetByIndex(i);
    DataRow dtRow;
    dtRow = dtGUITable.NewRow();
    dtRow["Handle"] = gui.GUIHandle;
    dtRow["Window Text"] = gui.GUIText;
    dtRow["Class Name"] = gui.GUIClassName;
    dtRow["Parent Text"] = gui.GUIParentText;
    dtGUITable.Rows.Add(dtRow);
  }

  dgAvailableGUIs.DataSource = dtGUITable;
}
```

The task of the SetGUIListToTest() helper method is divided into three portions by the code clusters. The first cluster has only one line to initialize a DataTable object, dtGUITable.

The second task calls a MakeDataTableColumn() helper method four times to create four columns for the dtGUITable object.

The third is composed of a for loop. This loop enumerates the guiSurveyCls.GUISorted-List for each GUI component found. Then it creates a table row for each GUI component and adds the GUI's handle, text, class name, and parent text into the respective columns of the row. Finally, the row is appended to the data table object.

And last, the dtGUITable object is connected to the DataSource property of the DataGrid. The GUI information is displayed on the tool form in text format. After the tester's specification, the tool saves this text information and conducts the designed GUI test. The last coding task for the GUI survey is for the MakeDataTableColumn() helper method (Listing 7.22).

Listing 7.22	Code for the *MakeDataTableColumn()* helper method

```
private void MakeDataTableColumn(
➥DataTable dtAvailableGUIs, string colName, string dataType)
{
  DataColumn guiColumn = new DataColumn(colName, Type.GetType(dataType));
  guiColumn.ReadOnly = true;
  guiColumn.AllowDBNull = true;
  guiColumn.Unique = false;
  dtAvailableGUIs.Columns.Add(guiColumn);
}
```

The MakeDataTableColumn() helper method simply creates a guiColumn object from the DataColumn class. Such a column is read-only and allows null values and identical entries in the rows. Then the created column is added to the designed data table.

After the GUI survey, the tool form displays the detected GUI components in the DataGrid. The tester can select a GUI description from the DataGrid in sequence. The tool knows how to test the selected GUI components sequentially. In the next section, you'll add code for the GUI testing data specification. The required user interaction occurs here.

Specifying Data for the GUI Test

If a software product is designed for full automation, a GUI is not needed, such as embedded software, the software to start a machine or a computer, and other stand-alone applications. A non-GUI test is enough for such applications and test cases are more predictable. However, most of the applications are designed for human users today. A human is intelligent and creative. The same software will be used in numerous ways by different people at different times and places. There will be no tool that can be intelligent enough in the near future to figure out by itself a correct sequence to use even a simple application. The traditional testing methods have used the recording mechanism to remember the operation sequence in a test script. But experts have reported some limitation of such a mechanism:

- *A recorded script has a lot of unneeded code.* It records every activity occurring in the computer during a recording session. If the user performed an operation by mistake, the mistake is not removed from the script. Manually removing such a mistake requires a skillful tool user and programmer. Otherwise, the script has to be abandoned and rerecorded.

- *A raw recorded script has no verification functions.* The recording mechanism records only the physical action. Verification is a mental process to analyze the consequence caused by the physical actions. The user is required to insert such processes into the recorded scripts during or after the recording session.

- *Some tools use their own unique script languages.* Tool users need to be trained to become good programmers in order to use the tool effectively. The code in some script languages differs from that in programming languages. This causes at least two side effects. First, it separates the testers from the developers. Second, the recorded test script can't be executed on a system without the same testing tool environment. Of course, some tools do use programming languages as their script language, such as Visual Basic and Java.

- *Using traditional tools to obtain an automated GUI test script takes 5 to 10 times longer than conducting the same test scenario manually.* These automated test scripts need to be run many times in order to pay off the efforts. However, such a script easily becomes obsolete when the application changes during the development life cycle. The test scripts are hard to manage for a quality project.

You may add other unresolved issues into this list. However, these are the obvious challenges of the current testing infrastructure. To address these pitfalls, the preceding section discussed developing the tool to discover the possible GUI components. The user is required to specify a sequence of GUI events to invoke the application. This is much easier and costs less time than physically performing the operation. Chapter 8 will discuss an automatic verification method to address the second point. Because this tool doesn't record any operations, it is totally data driven. The other difficulties will all be solved as you continuously improve this tool using the basic concepts this book discusses.

In order to provide an interface for the testers to instruct the tool for testing a specific GUI component, this section adds code to the dgAvailableGUIs_CurrentCellChanged() and the dgAvailableGUIs_DoubleClick() events. The dgAvailableGUIs_DoubleClick() event calls two helper methods, PopulateGUINameTypeLists() and GetMemberType(). Listing 7.23 presents the code for the two events of the dgAvailableGUIs control.

Listing 7.23   **Code for the *dgAvailableGUIs_CurrentCellChanged()* and *dgAvailableGUIs_ DoubleClick()* Events**

```
private void dgAvailableGUIs_CurrentCellChanged(
➥object sender, System.EventArgs e)
{
  GUITestActions.IndicateSelectedGUI(
➥(int)guiSurveyCls.GUISortedList.GetKey(dgAvailableGUIs.CurrentCell.RowNumber));
}


private void dgAvailableGUIs_DoubleClick(object sender, System.EventArgs e)
{
```

```
GUITDC = new GUITestDataCollector();

GUITDC.guiInfo = (GUITestUtility.GUIInfo)
➡guiSurveyCls.GUISortedList.GetByIndex(dgAvailableGUIs.CurrentCell.RowNumber);

TempList = new ArrayList();
GUITDC.guiInfo.GUIControlName = PopulateGUINameTypeLists(
➡(Control)formUT, GUITDC.guiInfo.GUIHandle, true);
TempList.Sort();
GUITDC.ControlNameList = TempList;

TempList = new ArrayList();
GUITDC.guiInfo.GUIControlType = PopulateGUINameTypeLists(
➡(Control)formUT, GUITDC.guiInfo.GUIHandle, false);
TempList.Sort();
GUITDC.controlTypeList =   TempList;

GUITDC.PopulateGUIInfo();

if (GUITDC.ShowDialog() == DialogResult.OK)
{
  GUITDC.guiInfo.GUIMemberType = GetMemberType(GUITDC.guiInfo.GUIControlName);
  GUITestSeqList.GUIList.Add(GUITDC.guiInfo);
}

}
```

The dgAvailableGUIs_CurrentCellChanged() event takes only one line of code to animate the corresponding GUI component when a cell containing the GUI description in the Data-Grid is selected. This confirms that the user has selected the GUI component they wants to manipulate at this moment. Otherwise, they can move to the next until the desired GUI component is chosen. Since the GUI presentation in the DataGrid is intuitive and descriptive, in most cases such a confirmation is for extra assurance.

The second event is for the dgAvailableGUIs_DoubleClick(). A double-click event of a Data-Grid in .NET is designed for the user to click two times continuously on the index column (indicated with gray color by default) beside the first column on the left or on the blue title bar on the top.

When this event is triggered, it first initializes a GUITestDataCollector object for the GUITDC field. The items in the dgAvailableGUIs data grid are arranged in the same order as the items in the guiSurveyCls.GUISortedList. Using the currently selected row number as the index, the next statement retrieves an item from the guiSurveyCls.GUISortedList by invoking its GetByIndex() method. This item is derived from a GUITestUtility.GUIInfo object when the

GUI survey is conducted. At this moment, this object is converted back and assigned to the public `GUITDC.guiInfo` field.

Next, the `TempList` field is initialized and a `PopulateGUINameTypeLists()` helper method is invoked. This helper method fills the `TempList` with the names of the GUI controls assigned at development time and also retrieves a particular name for the GUI component indicated by the current row in the DataGrid. Last, it sorts the name list and assigns the list to the `GUITDC.ControlNameList`.

The following section of the code just repeats the actions described in the preceding paragraph. The `TempList` is reset. The difference is that this time it fills the list with the GUI type names visible in the Microsoft Visual Studio .NET IDE by calling the method the second time. It also retrieves the GUI type name of the current row. The list containing the type names of GUI components is assigned to the `GUITDC.controlTypeList`.

After all of the information for the GUI component in the selected row of the DataGrid is located, the double-click event invokes the `GUITDC.PopulateGUIInfo()` method to assign values to the appropriate GUI controls. The code of this method is in Listing 7.5.

Finally, an `if` statement is used to inspect whether the OK or the Cancel button is clicked. If the OK button is clicked, the double-click event calls a `GetMemberType()` helper method. This method finds out a method from the `GUITestLibrary` for the GUI selected in the `GUITDC` object. Finally, the event adds the GUI information and its test method into the `GUITestSeqList.GUIList`.

The double-click event of the DataGrid calls two helper methods. The first is the `Populate-GUINameTypeLists()` helper method as coded in Listing 7.24.

Listing 7.24   Code for the *PopulateGUINameTypeLists()* Helper Method

```
private string PopulateGUINameTypeLists(
➥Control formUT, int hwnd, bool enforceName)
{
  if (formUT == null)
    return "";

  foreach( Control ctrl in formUT.Controls)
  {
    if (enforceName)
    {
      TempList.Add(ctrl.Name);
     if ((int)ctrl.Handle == hwnd)
        GuiProperty = ctrl.Name;
    }
    else
    {
      if (!TempList.Contains(ctrl.GetType().ToString()))
        TempList.Add(ctrl.GetType().ToString());
```

```
      if ((int)ctrl.Handle == hwnd)
        GuiProperty = ctrl.GetType().ToString();
    }
    PopulateGUINameTypeLists(ctrl, hwnd, enforceName);
  }
  return GuiProperty;
}
```

The first line in Listing 7.24 checks whether the testing tool has successfully initialized an object for GUI data collection. If not, the code stops the execution. The PopulateGUIName-TypeLists() is a recursive method. It performs two tasks each execution. If the enforceName parameter is set to true, it finds all the GUI control names given by developers at design time from the specified application as the first parameter. When a name is found, it is added into the TempList field. It also extracts the particular control name based on the GUI handle as the second parameter. The dgAvailableGUIs_DoubleClick() event assigns the content in the TempList to the ControlNameList field of the GUITestDataCollector form. Eventually the ControlNameList is connected with the Items property of the ComboBox control that has been prepared to hold a list of control names of the application under test. The particular name is set to be the value of the Control Name ComboBox. The recursive invocation of the PopulateGUINameTypeLists() ensures that all the child and grandchild GUI components of the application are enlisted.

When the enforceName parameter is set to false, the PopulateGUINameTypeLists() recursively looks for all the type names of the GUI components as defined by .NET developers instead of the control names given by the application programmers. The logic is the same as it looks for the control names of the GUI components given at development time.

As mentioned in the discussion of Listing 7.5, the reason for adding the control names and types into the ComboBox controls is in case the tool can't correctly assign the property values on the data collection interface, although this is rare. If it happens, the tester can easily pick up the correct value from the drop-down list.

The second method the dgAvailableGUIs_DoubleClick() event calls for help is the GetMemberType() helper method, as shown in Listing 7.25.

Listing 7.25   Code for the *GetMemberType()* Helper Method

```
private string GetMemberType(string ctrlName)
{
  if (formUT == null)
    return "";

  BindingFlags allFlags = BindingFlags.Public | BindingFlags.NonPublic |
    BindingFlags.Static | BindingFlags.Instance;

  Type StartupForm = formUT.GetType();
```

```
FieldInfo[] fis = StartupForm.GetFields(allFlags);
foreach (FieldInfo fi in fis)
{
  if (fi.Name == ctrlName)
  {
    return "VerifyField";
  }
}

PropertyInfo[] ppis = StartupForm.GetProperties(allFlags);
foreach (PropertyInfo ppi in ppis)
{
  if (ppi.Name == ctrlName)
  {
    return "VerifyProperty";
  }
}
return "";
}
```

The GetMemberType() method first inspects whether the application under test has been initialized as an object. If the application object exists, the following code initializes a BindingFlags variable with the assignment of the combination of the BindingFlags.Public | BindingFlags .NonPublic | BindingFlags.Static | BindingFlags.Instance values. When such an assignment is passed as a parameter to invoke the methods from the Reflection classes of the .NET environment, these methods will discover members regardless of their modifiers of public, private, or protected. Such a discovery is helpful for software test purposes.

Usually the testers are interested in verifying the status change of fields and properties of an application under GUI test. This method finds each member in need of verification by inspecting whether it is a field or a property. If it is a field, it requests that the tool invoke the VerifyField() method of the GUITestLibary namespace. If it is a property, then the tool should invoke the VerifyProperty() method.

Thus, you have coded the tool to collect a testing sequence for a particular testing case. The rest of the coding task is to enable the tool to execute the specified sequence.

Running the Test

During the design time for frmMain, you placed a Run Test button to complete the specified GUI test. You have coded for conducting a GUI survey, specifying a sequence to activate the GUI events and stored the sequence in a list; the rest of the testing task is to save the sequence, run the sequence, and verify the consequence of each GUI event.

At this point the GUI events in the saved sequence make up a GUI test scenario. In Chapter 8, you will enhance the tool to determine a verification method and conduct an automatic verification. Thus, the GUI event sequence collection and the verification determination are included for a complete GUI test data store. This data store is saved in an XML document that can be modified to derive more testing scenarios, such as changing the order of the sequence, adding more GUI events, and modifying the verification objects. Such a modification can be achieved by enhancing the capability of the tool or by the assistance of the existing XML applications. The tool can then re-execute the data stores in a batch mode to increase the efficiency of finding bugs.

In the frmMain design editor, double-click the Run Test button. After the IDE generates the respective btnRun button delegate, add code for the btnRunTest_Click() event as shown in Listing 7.26.

Listing 7.26   **Code for the *btnRunTest_Click()* Event**

```
private void btnRunTest_Click(object sender, System.EventArgs e)
{
  sveDataStore.Title = "Location to save GUI test data";
  sveDataStore.Filter = "XML Files (*.xml)|*.xml|All Files (*.*)|*.*";

  if (sveDataStore.ShowDialog() == DialogResult.OK)
  {
    TestCaseStore = sveDataStore.FileName;
  }
  else
  {
    return;
  }


  GUITestSeqList.AUTStartupForm = startupForm;

  GUITestUtility.SerilizeInfo(TestCaseStore, GUITestSeqList);

  GUITestScript guiTS = new GUITestScript(TestCaseStore, currDir);

  GUITestSeqList = null;
}
```

When the btnRunTest_Click() event is triggered, it completes the first test session of the newly specified sequence by doing the following:

1. The event initializes a SaveFileDialog box: The first line of the code assigning a title to the dialog box informs the user of what is happening. Using a filter value, the next line asks the dialog box to display files with XML extensions. Such a filter enables the user to easily locate the testing data.

2. After the dialog box is shown, the user types in a filename and clicks the OK button. The TestCaseStore variable grabs the filename.

3. Using this filename, the btnRunTest_Click() event invokes the SerilizeInfo() method of the GUITestLibary to save the specified GUI sequence as well as the path and the name of the startup form of the application under test. This data store will be executed immediately by the following code and can be reused throughout the development life cycle.

4. After saving the collected data, the code immediately initializes a GUITestScript object, guiTS. The initialization passes the filename as the first parameter. The second parameter is the root directory of the tool and is usded for finding the GUITestActionLib.xml file. Once the GUITestScript object is initialized, the execution of the testing has been implemented to be automatic.

5. The last statement resets the GUITestSeqList object to null and prepares a session for the next GUI survey and testing.

In order to rerun an existing test data store, a Rerun Test button is also designed on the frmMain class. To start coding such an event, double click the Rerun Test button in the frmMain design editor. The code for this event is in Listing 7.27.

Listing 7.27   Code for the *btnRerun_Click()* event

```
private void btnRerun_Click(object sender, System.EventArgs e)
{
  opnAUT.Title = "Select an existing data store";
  opnAUT.Filter = "XLM test cases (*.xml)|*.xml|All Files (*.*)|*.*";

  if (opnAUT.ShowDialog() == DialogResult.OK)
  {
    GUITestScript guiTS = new GUITestScript(opnAUT.FileName, currDir);
  }
}
```

The code for the btnRerun_Click() event is slightly different from that of the btnRunTest_Click() event. Instead of initializing a save file dialog box, it pops up an open file dialog box for opening an existing XML data store. Then it directly initializes a GUITestScript object using the selected data store and the root directory of the tool.

At this point, you have implemented all the fields, properties and methods, and events with their functions for completing a GUI test. Listing 7.28 has the code for a btnExit_Click() and a frmMain_Resize() event for the user to terminate the AutomatedGUITest tool and resize frmMain on the screen.

Listing 7.28 **Code for the *btnExit_Click()* and the *frmMain_Resize()* Events**

```
private void btnExit_Click(object sender,System.EventArgs e)
{
  Application.Exit();
}

private void frmMain_Resize(object sender, System.EventArgs e)
{
  dgAvailableGUIs.Width = this.Width - 48;
  dgAvailableGUIs.Height = this.Height - 144;
}
```

The btnExit_Click() event invokes an Exit() method with only one line of code. When the Exit button is clicked, your current testing task is completed.

The second part of the frmMain_Resize() event simply resizes the width and the height of the DataGrid when the size of frmMain is changed. This event allows the user to view the collected GUI information with ease.

Now you can press F5 to build and run your AutomatedGUITest tool. If there are compiling errors, you can use the full code in Listing 7.29 for comparison and correcting the errors.

Listing 7.29 **The Full List of the Code for the *frmMain* Class with IDE-Generated Code Omitted**

```
using System;
using System.Drawing;
using System.Collections;
using System.ComponentModel;
using System.Windows.Forms;
using System.Data;
using System.Reflection;
using GUITestLibrary;

namespace AutomatedGUITest
{

  public class frmMain : System.Windows.Forms.Form
  {
    //... IDE generated code omitted

    private string currDir = Environment.CurrentDirectory;
    private string applicationUT;
    private string startupForm;
```

```
private Form formUT;

private GUISurveyClass guiSurveyCls;

private GUITestDataCollector GUITDC;
private GUITestUtility.GUIInfoSerializable GUITestSeqList;
private ArrayList tempList;

private string GuiProperty;

private string TestCaseStore;

//Microsoft Visual Studio .NET IDE generated code
...

private void btnStartGUITest_Click(object sender, System.EventArgs e)
{
  GUITestSeqList = new GUITestUtility.GUIInfoSerializable();

  opnAUT.Title = "Specify an Application Under Test";
  opnAUT.Filter = "GUI Applications(*.EXE;
*.DLL)|*.EXE;*.DLL|All files (*.*)|*.*";
  if (opnAUT.ShowDialog() == DialogResult.OK)
  {
    applicationUT = opnAUT.FileName;
    GUITestSeqList.AUTPath = applicationUT;

    GetTypeToTestFromAUT();
    try
    {
      formUT = (Form)GUITestUtility.StartAUT(applicationUT, startupForm);
    }
    catch (InvalidCastException ex)
    {
      MessageBox.Show(ex.Message);
    }
  }
  else
  {
    return;
  }
}

private void GetTypeToTestFromAUT()
{
  if (applicationUT.Length <= 0)
  {
    return;
  }
  TypeUnderTest typeDUT = new TypeUnderTest();
  try
  {
```

```
        Assembly asm = Assembly.LoadFrom(applicationUT);
        Type[] tys = asm.GetTypes();
        foreach (Type ty in tys)
        {
          typeDUT.chckListType.Items.Add(ty.Namespace + "." + ty.Name);
        }

    }
    catch(Exception ex)
    {
      MessageBox.Show(ex.Message);
      return;
    }

    if (typeDUT.ShowDialog() == DialogResult.OK)
    {
      GetSelectedTypesUT(typeDUT);
    }
    else
    {
      return;
    }
  }

  private void GetSelectedTypesUT(TypeUnderTest typeDUT)
  {

    startupForm = "";
    for (int i = 0; i<typeDUT.chckListType.Items.Count; i++)
    {
      if (typeDUT.chckListType.GetItemChecked(i))
         startupForm =
➥typeDUT.chckListType.GetItemText(typeDUT.chckListType.Items[i]);
    }
  }


  private void btnGUISurvey_Click(object sender, System.EventArgs e)
  {

    this.WindowState = FormWindowState.Minimized;

    try
    {
      guiSurveyCls = new GUISurveyClass((int)formUT.Handle);
    }
    catch
    {

      MessageBox.Show(ex.Message);

    }
```

```
      guiSurveyCls.StartGUISurvey();

      SetGUIListToTest();

      this.WindowState = FormWindowState.Normal;
   }

   private void SetGUIListToTest()
   {
      DataTable dtGUITable = new DataTable();
      MakeDataTableColumn(dtGUITable, "Handle", "System.Int32");
      MakeDataTableColumn(dtGUITable, "Window Text", "System.String");
      MakeDataTableColumn(dtGUITable, "Class Name", "System.String");
      MakeDataTableColumn(dtGUITable, "Parent Text", "System.String");

      for (int i = 0; i < guiSurveyCls.GUISortedList.Count; i++)
      {
         GUITestUtility.GUIInfo gui =
➥(GUITestUtility.GUIInfo)guiSurveyCls.GUISortedList.GetByIndex(i);// obj;
         DataRow dtRow;
         dtRow = dtGUITable.NewRow();
         dtRow["Handle"] = gui.GUIHandle;
         dtRow["Window Text"] = gui.GUIText;
         dtRow["Class Name"] = gui.GUIClassName;
         dtRow["Parent Text"] = gui.GUIParentText;
         dtGUITable.Rows.Add(dtRow);

      }
      dgAvailableGUIs.DataSource = dtGUITable;


   }

   private void MakeDataTableColumn(DataTable dtAvailableGUIs,
➥string colName, string dataType)
   {
      DataColumn guiColumn = new DataColumn(colName, Type.GetType(dataType));
      guiColumn.ReadOnly = true;
      guiColumn.AllowDBNull = true;
      guiColumn.Unique = false;
      dtAvailableGUIs.Columns.Add(guiColumn);
   }

   private void dgAvailableGUIs_CurrentCellChanged(object sender,
➥System.EventArgs e)
   {
      GUITestActions.IndicateSelectedGUI((int)
➥guiSurveyCls.GUISortedList.GetKey(dgAvailableGUIs.CurrentCell.RowNumber));
   }

   private void dgAvailableGUIs_DoubleClick(object sender, System.EventArgs e)
```

```
        {


            GUITDC = new GUITestDataCollector();

            GUITDC.guiInfo = new GUITestUtility.GUIInfo();


               tempList = new ArrayList();
            GUITDC.guiInfo.GUIControlName =
➥PopulateGUINameTypeLists(formUTBoxed, GUITDC.guiInfo.GUIHandle, true);
               tempList.Sort();
            GUITDC.ControlNameList =   tempList;

               tempList = new ArrayList();
            GUITDC.guiInfo.GUIControlType =
➥PopulateGUINameTypeLists(formUTBoxed, GUITDC.guiInfo.GUIHandle, false);
               tempList.Sort();
            GUITDC.controlTypeList = tempList;

            GUITDC.PopulateGUIInfo();


            if (GUITDC.GUIInfoState == DialogResult.OK)
            {
               GUITDC.guiInfo.GUIMemberType =
➥GetMemberType(GUITDC.guiInfo.GUIControlName);
               GUITestSeqList.GUIList.Add(GUITDC.guiInfo);
            }

        }

        private string PopulateGUINameTypeLists(
➥Control formUT, int hwnd, bool enforceName)
        {
          if (formUT == null)
             return "";


          foreach( Control ctrl in formUT.Controls)
          {
            if (enforceName)
            {
              tempList.Add(ctrl.Name);
              if ((int)ctrl.Handle == hwnd)
                GuiProperty = ctrl.Name;
            }
            else
            {
              if (!tempList.Contains(ctrl.GetType().ToString()))
```

```
          tempList.Add(ctrl.GetType().ToString());
        if ((int)ctrl.Handle == hwnd)
          GuiProperty = ctrl.GetType().ToString();
      }
      PopulateGUINameTypeLists(ctrl, hwnd, enforceName);
    }
    return GuiProperty;
}


private string GetMemberType(string ctrlName)
{
  if (formUT == null)
    return "";
  BindingFlags allFlags = BindingFlags.Public | BindingFlags.NonPublic |
    BindingFlags.Static | BindingFlags.Instance;

  Type StartupForm = formUT.GetType();
  FieldInfo[] fis = StartupForm.GetFields(allFlags);
  foreach (FieldInfo fi in fis)
  {
    if (fi.Name == ctrlName)
    {
      return "VerifyField";
    }
  }

  PropertyInfo[] ppis = StartupForm.GetProperties(allFlags);
  foreach (PropertyInfo ppi in ppis)
  {
    if (ppi.Name == ctrlName)
    {
      return "VerifyProperty";
    }
  }
  return "";
}


private void btnRunTest_Click(object sender, System.EventArgs e)
{
  sveDataStore.Title = "Location to save GUI test data";
  sveDataStore.Filter = "XML Files (*.xml)|*.xml|All Files (*.*)|*.*";
  if (sveDataStore.ShowDialog() == DialogResult.OK)
  {
    TestCaseStore = sveDataStore.FileName;
  }
  else
  {
    return;
  }

  GUITestSeqList.AUTStartupForm = startupForm;
```

```
      GUITestUtility.SerilizeInfo(TestCaseStore, GUITestSeqList);

      GUITestScript guiTS = new GUITestScript(TestCaseStore, currDir);

      GUITestSeqList = null;
    }
    private void btnRerun_Click(object sender, System.EventArgs e)
    {
      opnAUT.Title = "Select an existing data store";
      opnAUT.Filter = "XLM test cases (*.xml)|*.xml|All Files (*.*)|*.*";

      if (opnAUT.ShowDialog() == DialogResult.OK)
      {
        GUITestScript guiTS = new GUITestScript(opnAUT.FileName, currDir);
      }
    }
    private void btnExit_Click(object sender, System.EventArgs e)
    {
      Application.Exit();
    }
    private void Form1_Resize(object sender, System.EventArgs e)
    {
      dgAvailableGUIs.Width = this.Width - 48;
      dgAvailableGUIs.Height = this.Height - 144;
    }
  }
}
```

After you successfully build this project, your tool is ready for software testing projects with the implemented capabilities. Although more testing functions are on the way, the Automated-GUITest tool has been enabled with a lot of automatic testing features for functions that require tedious, time-consuming, and manual interactions in other tools. The next section will walk you through the first automatic GUI test without writing and recording a test script.

Conducting the First Automatic GUI Testing

Now, you have pressed F5, the building is successful, and the AutomatedGUITest tool, which looks similar to Figure 7.5, debuts on your desktop. This tool separates a GUI test process into five big steps indicated by the five buttons implemented in the frmMain class:

1. Start the application under test, which makes the GUI components of the application visible to the tool.

2. Conduct a GUI survey, which enables a thorough test.

FIGURE 7.5
The GUI interface of
the AutomatedGUITest
for the first test run

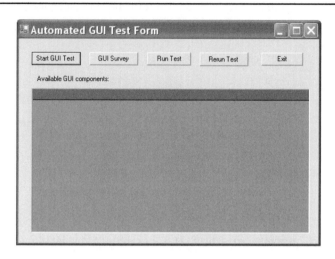

FIGURE 7.5
The GUI interface of
the AutomatedGUITest
for the first test run

3. Run the specified test from the GUI survey results.

4. Rerun the saved test scenario to accomplish an effective regression testing.

5. The test is completed. Click the Exit button to terminate the tool.

Based on the test script developed in Chapter 6 for testing the C# API Text Viewer, this section uses the same scenario for exemplary purposes. A normal scenario is reiterated here:

1. When the C# API Text Viewer is running on the desktop, click the ListBox control to advance the vertical scroll bar and select a name of a custom function.

2. Click the Add button to add the selected C# marshalling code into the RichTextBox control.

3. Click the Copy button set the selected function to the clipboard, from which it can be transferred to other word processors or code editors.

4. Click inside the RichTextBox control and it gets the focus.

5. Click the Remove button to remove the first line of code inside the RichTextBox.

6. Click the Clear button to empty the RichTextBox. Complete the test and close the application under test.

To complete this scenario with the AutomatedGUITest tool, you can follow these steps:

1. Click the Start GUI Test button. An open file dialog box pops up. From this dialog box, navigate to the C:\GUISourceCode\Chapter03\CSharpAPITextViewer\bin\Debug folder, select the CSharpAPITextViewer.exe file, and click the Open button. The Types under Test form shows up with the possible class names in the check box list. Among them, one is the startup form class, Form1 in this case. Figure 7.6 displays the Types under Test form of this running session.

FIGURE 7.6
Selecting the startup
form class from the
possible class names
of the C# API Text
Viewer

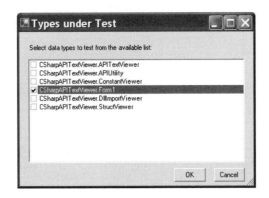

2. Check the check box beside `CSharpAPITextViewer.Form1` and click the OK button. The C#
   API Text Viewer starts on the desktop. If it covers the AutomatedGUITest application,
   you can rearrange the applications on your screen and make the AutomatedGUITest tool
   visible. But make sure there is only one copy of the C# API Text Viewer is running on your
   system.

3. Click the GUI Survey button on the AutomatedGUITest tool. The tool minimizes itself to
   expose the application under test. You can visualize the mouse movement from the top downward to the bottom, and from the left toward the right inside the application until every spot
   of this window is visited. Then, the AutomatedGUITest tool appears normally on the screen
   with DataGrid filled with the available GUI descriptions, as shown in Figure 7.7. The first
   column lists the values of the child GUI components, which is for reference purposes so that
   the tool can collect specific information, not for test data collection. The second, third, and
   fourth columns list the values of the associated GUI text, class name, and parent text.

4. You first collect the GUI information for the ListBox of the C# API Text Viewer. The value
   of the GUI text for this ListBox is empty at the initial stage when no item is selected from
   the ListBox. You can read its class name as its identifier, `WindowsForms10.LISTBOX.app3`, to
   locate the row index and double-click besides the row in the left edge. The GUI Test Data
   Collector form appears on the screen with the ComboBox and TextBox controls populated
   with correct values of the respective GUI properties (Figure 7.8). From the GUI Test Data
   Collector form, you simply click the OK button.

NOTE   To select a GUI object from the DataGrid, you first place the cursor on the row containing
the GUI object, then double-click the gray or blue area on the left edge or on the top to
popup the GUI Test Data Collector.

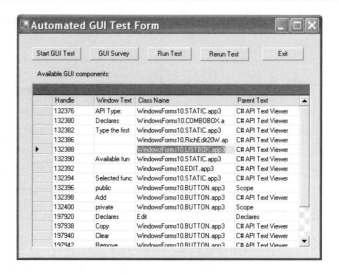

5. Repeat step 4 for the Add, Copy, RichTextBox, Remove, and Clear controls in the available GUI comploment list. These controls can be easily identified by reading their GUI texts. However, the text for the RichTextBox is still empty.

6. After the designated six GUI events are selected from the available GUI list and confirmed in the GUI Test Data Collector form, you need to terminate the C# API Text Viewer because, when you click the Run button to execute the test, the test script of the tool will start up another copy of the application under test. Two copies of the application running

on the same system will confuse the tool at this point. However, when you develop a tool for web page stress testing, you need to run multiple copies of the same application.

7. Simply click the Run Test button from the AutomatedGUITest tool. When the save file dialog box appears, type in a filename with an XML extension, such as C:\Temp\TestC#APIText-Viewer.xml. Then click the Save button. Sit and watch. The C# API Text Viewer shows up again, the GUI actions of the mouse clicking occur in sequence, and the application closes by itself after the execution. The first test is completed. At this point, you can view or edit the saved XML document in any text editor or XML editor; the document is shown in Listing 7.30. You can also use the XmlTreeViewer.exe developed in Chapter 5 to view this XML document by expanding the child XML elements one by one.

Listing 7.30   **The XML Data Store Containing the GUI Test Instruction to Drive the Execution of the Test Script by Late Binding**

```xml
<?xml version="1.0" encoding="utf-8"?>
<GUIInfoSerializable xmlns:xsd=
➥"http://www.w3.org/2001/XMLSchema" xmlns:xsi=
➥"http://www.w3.org/2001/XMLSchema-instance">
  <AUTPath>C:\GUISourceCode\Chapter03\
➥CSharpAPITextViewer\bin\Debug\CSharpAPITextViewer.exe</AUTPath>
  <AUTStartupForm>CSharpAPITextViewer.Form1</AUTStartupForm>
  <GUIInfoSerializable>
    <GUIInfo>
      <GUIHandle>1246684</GUIHandle>
      <GUIText />
      <GUIClassName>WindowsForms10.LISTBOX.app3</GUIClassName>
      <GUIParentText>C# API Text Viewer</GUIParentText>
      <GUIControlName>lstAvailableFuncs</GUIControlName>
      <GUIControlType>System.Windows.Forms.ListBox</GUIControlType>
      <GUIMemberType>VerifyField</GUIMemberType>
    </GUIInfo>
    <GUIInfo>
      <GUIHandle>2819536</GUIHandle>
      <GUIText>Add</GUIText>
      <GUIClassName>WindowsForms10.BUTTON.app3</GUIClassName>
      <GUIParentText>C# API Text Viewer</GUIParentText>
      <GUIControlName>btnAdd</GUIControlName>
      <GUIControlType>System.Windows.Forms.Button</GUIControlType>
      <GUIMemberType>VerifyField</GUIMemberType>
    </GUIInfo>
    <GUIInfo>
      <GUIHandle>1639876</GUIHandle>
      <GUIText>Copy</GUIText>
      <GUIClassName>WindowsForms10.BUTTON.app3</GUIClassName>
      <GUIParentText>C# API Text Viewer</GUIParentText>
      <GUIControlName>btnCopy</GUIControlName>
      <GUIControlType>System.Windows.Forms.Button</GUIControlType>
```

```
        <GUIMemberType>VerifyField</GUIMemberType>
      </GUIInfo>
      <GUIInfo>
        <GUIHandle>1377762</GUIHandle>
        <GUIText />
        <GUIClassName>WindowsForms10.RichEdit20W.app3</GUIClassName>
        <GUIParentText>C# API Text Viewer</GUIParentText>
        <GUIControlName>txtSelected</GUIControlName>
        <GUIControlType>System.Windows.Forms.RichTextBox</GUIControlType>
        <GUIMemberType>VerifyField</GUIMemberType>
      </GUIInfo>
      <GUIInfo>
        <GUIHandle>787840</GUIHandle>
        <GUIText>Remove</GUIText>
        <GUIClassName>WindowsForms10.BUTTON.app3</GUIClassName>
        <GUIParentText>C# API Text Viewer</GUIParentText>
        <GUIControlName>btnRemove</GUIControlName>
        <GUIControlType>System.Windows.Forms.Button</GUIControlType>
        <GUIMemberType>VerifyField</GUIMemberType>
      </GUIInfo>
      <GUIInfo>
        <GUIHandle>722368</GUIHandle>
        <GUIText>Clear</GUIText>
        <GUIClassName>WindowsForms10.BUTTON.app3</GUIClassName>
        <GUIParentText>C# API Text Viewer</GUIParentText>
        <GUIControlName>btnClear</GUIControlName>
        <GUIControlType>System.Windows.Forms.Button</GUIControlType>
        <GUIMemberType>VerifyField</GUIMemberType>
      </GUIInfo>
    </GUIInfoSerializable>
  </GUIInfoSerializable>
```

8. Click the Rerun Test button. When the open file dialog box pops up, navigate to the data store you just saved, `C:\Temp\TestC#APITextViewer.xml` in this case. Click the Open button. The test is run again and the first regression testing is completed.

After steps 7 and 8, the test results are saved in the same folder where the test data store is saved, but the filename is appended with `_result.xml`. You can open the `C:\Temp\TestC#APIText-Viewer_result.xml` in a text editor such as Notepad; the results are shown in Listing 7.31. The XML document saves the value of the Text property of a GUI control only at the moment it receives a test action in sequence.

Listing 7.31   **The Test Results at This Stage of the Tool Saved in an XML Document**

```
<?xml version="1.0" encoding="utf-8"?>
<ArrayOfAnyType xmlns:xsd="http://www.w3.org/2001/XMLSchema" xmlns:xsi=
➥"http://www.w3.org/2001/XMLSchema-instance">
  <anyType xsi:type="xsd:string">AddAccessAllowedAce</anyType>
  <anyType xsi:type="xsd:string">Add</anyType>
```

```
 <anyType xsi:type="xsd:string">Copy</anyType>
 <anyType xsi:type="xsd:string">[DllImport("advapi32.dll")]
public static extern int AddAccessAllowedAce([MarshalAs(UnmanagedType.Struct)]
 ➥ref  ACL pAcl, int dwAceRevision, int AccessMask, int pSid);

</anyType>
 <anyType xsi:type="xsd:string">Remove</anyType>
 <anyType xsi:type="xsd:string">Clear</anyType>
</ArrayOfAnyType>
```

Although this tool is still in an early stage at this point, you can use it to test a complex application. It will find bugs in a product at its earlier development stage, which the other tools can't do. The available GUI test tools require the user to successfully and manually operate the application under test in order to record a test script. If there is a bug, the recording has to be abandoned. The tool user reports this bug for the developers to fix. After the bug is fixed, the user is able to resume the recording process and, possibly, encounter the next bug. The whole process of recording a successful test script detects bugs one by one manually.

However, the AutomatedGUITest tool collects the descriptive properties of the GUI components and runs the test. Once the GUI components are visible in the application, the operation can be entered into the test data store. There is no physical operation needed until the test executes. Thus, it will automatically find the early stage bugs of a project under development by verifying the behavior of the desired GUI event. Chapter 8 will discuss how to conduct effective verifications and continue to develop the AutomatedGUITest tool with more functions.

Summary

This chapter discussed the requirements of a fully automated test tool. The improvements of the current testing infrastructures are based on such requirements. A brief introduction presented the fundamentals of the AutomatedGUITest architecture. The rest of this chapter completely implemented a workable GUI test tool and elaborated on its architecture in detail. You can follow the discussion to understand the principles and the techniques for developing such a tool with high degrees of automation.

The first time this tool was used, GUI test automation was easily achieved. Since defining a sequence of operating an application, even a simple application, is a highly intellectual and mental process, a machine can't figure out a suitable order by itself. The traditional test tools have used the capture/playback broadly to make this compensation. However, this tool completes a GUI survey and informs the user of all the GUI components in need of testing. The specification of a GUI event sequence has reduced the need for human user interaction to a minimum. The process is error proof, easy, and not time consuming.

Based on your testing requirements, you may not need to have a dedicated form for the GUI Test Data Collector if you are confident that the tool will assign all of the GUI property values correctly. Using such a form in this book is mainly for instructive purpose and to make the discussion clearer. For some software projects, if the sequential triggering is not important, the tool developers can enable this tool to make numerous combinations of the GUI events randomly, thus the tool becomes totally automatic.

Usually, it is easier to modify a document by cutting, copying, and pasting than to build a document by specification. Another effective approach for this tool, to avoid manipulating the application manually, is to include all the GUI events from the survey in the XML test data store. Then users scrutinize the GUI actions and make the following modifications:

- Remove the unneeded events
- Rearrange the order of events in a desired sequence
- Duplicate some events in a proper order if they are desired

In the next chapter, I will discuss some effective test verification and result presentation methods. Thereafter, the rest of the chapters will be dedicated to developing methods for specific testing requirements and presenting general ideas on how to extend these methods for the test requirements of your organization.

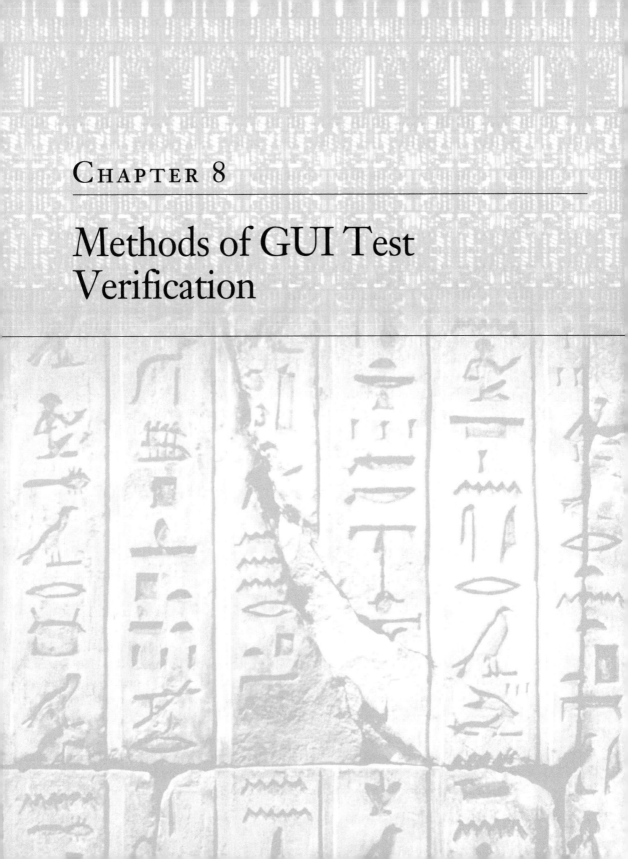

CHAPTER 8

Methods of GUI Test Verification

Using traditional capture/playback methods to record test scripts is often a tedious, time-consuming, and error-prone task. After all, the raw scripts recorded can only repeat the input, or actions, of the tester. The output comparison and verification require either editing the recorded scripts or visually observing the execution of the test scripts. Automation by such tools and methods is limited.

Chapter 7 introduced a different approach to collect GUI information and conduct an active GUI test. At this point, the AutomatedGUITest tool is developed and able to conduct a thorough survey of the GUI components contained in an application. Users can choose the GUI components to invoke actions from the survey list in a desired order. After the selected events are saved in an XML test data store, the tool executes mouse actions on the selected GUI components. Since an XML document is readable, users can easily edit the data store later by adding more actions or changing the execution order.

Most of the available testing tools provide scripting languages. A tester must be proficient in one of the scripting languages in order to use a tool to find bugs effectively. The AutomatedGUITest project is developed in a programming language (C#.NET). The test script is also a built-in facility within the tool in the same programming language. This test script is designed to accept the saved XML data stores and execute them dynamically. Users don't need to see and maintain the test script. Thus, the test automation becomes easier and quicker.

However, the verification capabilities of the tool at this point are still at the primitive stage. This chapter will first discuss the basic methods for verifying the output of the test. The rest of the chapter will guide you through the process of adding automatic verification to the AutomatedGUITest tool.

Verification Requirements

Software test verification is the process of inspecting whether the outcome of executing an application under test is correct. It can be accomplished either by manual checking or by automatic comparisons. Manual checking is performed by a human tester who compares the outcome on the screen with the result he expects. Sometimes, the result of the software execution is not displayed on the screen. For example, when the execution is expected to save a file on a disk drive, the tester needs to check the existence of the saved file and read its content. When the execution sends a message to another computer, the tester needs to have a way to intercept the message by exploring with a third-party tool or to confirm with the receiver. Thus, a manual verification is tedious, time consuming, boring, and error prone.

With a software testing tool, an automatic mechanism for test verification is expected. The method of automatic verification should be the same as the method for manual testing, which compares the actual results of executing the application against a predefined expected value. The difference is that a manual tester has the flexibility to choose an aspect to verify and configure an expected result instantly. But automated software testing requires that the details of the verification are carefully planned in advance so that the tool can pinpoint to the area and confirm the results. Many of these verifications can be done programmatically. For example, you can program to read a saved file into the computer memory and compare its content with a predefined baseline file. If the application sends a message to another computer via message queue, you can program to check the message queue. On the other hand, if the application sends the message via an e-mail server, you can program to access to the mail root folder on the server.

Once the verification methods are implemented, the tool can compare extensive lists of numbers, screen outputs, databases, and other kinds of results that a human tester couldn't easily compare. The automatic verification is faster and reliable.

Front-end Actions and Back-end Business Functions

Today, software users interact with an application through a GUI-rich interface. The business layer receives commands from the presentation layer, performs the tasks, and yields the result. Thus, for a GUI test script, the mouse and keyboard actions performed on the GUI interface are the testing inputs or testing cases. The tasks and results occur in the business layer, and the presentation layer is usually not aware of them.

The multitiered software architecture is used to create and preserve reusable software components. This architecture helps organize a project and allows construction and validation of each layer. Software testing can be conducted on each layer independently. The presentation layer consists of GUI components defined to receive user input and display some application output. In a Windows environment, these GUI components are arranged in a hierarchical manner for an application. Chapter 6 discussed the relative merits and proper uses of some of the GUI components. Chapter 7 implemented the AutomatedGUITest tool to trigger some of the GUI events in the presentation layer.

Test verification is used to confirm whether the output is consistent between the dynamic status of the presentation layer and the business layer. Some of the actual output can be captured from the screen and some has to be obtained via different means. The GUI testing tool should handle the business layer complexity independently from the presentation layer. In other words, the tool uses a portion of the test script to manipulate the GUI components in the front and another portion of the script to capture and compare the test results from the business layer. To understand this process, you need to understand that the business layer serves the following purposes:

- It rigorously and unambiguously comprehends and processes knowledge in the business layer of the application.

- It provides a common and shared basis to enhance communication about solving particular problems.

- It provides a solid foundation to implement and maintain the application's capability to perform its intended functions.

The business layer is often subject to many different types of change due to commands from the presentation layer. These changes affect the appearance of the presentation layer at a particular moment, how the data is accessed, and other nonfunctional characteristics. In order to test the application, the tool needs to check whether the changes are desirable for each action performed from the presentation layer. An automatic verification method will improve the GUI testing infrastructure by checking more aspects of the changes within different layers of the architecture.

Verifying Changes of an Application under Test

An application has a multitiered architecture. Each layer in the architecture could be nested with one or more data types to perform functions for presentation, business, and data manipulations. These functions are represented by fields, properties, and methods when the application is being developed. The simplest GUI testing verification is to check that the expected output is visible on the screen as each test case is performed. But this is not adequate enough for an effective GUI testing job and for finding bugs.

In addition to the changes the users see, the content of the fields and properties are added, deleted, and altered. One action can cause status changes of one or several fields or properties of the application under test. Verifying the change of one member at a time is simple. But verifying changes of multiple members adds complexity to the software test and increases the possibilities of finding more defects.

The fields and properties are different from application to application. That is the reason testers have created one test script to test against each testing case. Testing a single application may require several test scripts and testing data stores. However many test scripts there are, no testing method can ensure that an application can be thoroughly tested because manual test scripts created by humans can not cover all the aspects of an application under test.

On the other hand, it's required to know the names and the functionality of the fields and properties before manual test script and verification are implemented. A good understanding of the purpose of the application under test is essential for a manual test and a test using the available testing tools. However, the AutomatedGUITest tool developed in the preceding chapter has provided a better foundation to understand the the application under test through a thorough GUI component survey. It is possible for the tool to programmatically comprehend the fields and properties within the data types of the business layers and data layers. The test script inside the tool can be implemented to make a simple change of one member or to change all of the fields and properties. Verification of one member will result in many other aspects of the application execution being ignored. Checking the status of all the members produces overwhelming information for the testers, most of it unnecessary. The best practice is to focus on the critical areas and produce verification data to check whether the expected results are obtained.

Verifications Based on the Users' Interest

The final result of verification is usually indicated by a value that represents pass or fail. In a programming language, a Boolean variable usually has the value true or false. If one or more actual results of an execution match the expected results, the verification passes. Otherwise, it fails. The GUI testing tool is able to compare the actual outcomes with the expected results.

In contrast to the fields and properties of the application that are unknown at the time the tool is developed, there are some known aspects that require verification for each field or property after each step of the application execution. Based on manual testing experiences, the following types of verification are often conducted under certain circumstances:

Field and property verification   A data type within software architecture, such as a class, has members called fields, properties, and methods. The methods are invoked through the GUI events of the presentation layer and perform the business functions. The invocation of a method changes the status of the field or property members. Although the users are not supposed to access the contents of the fields and properties directly, a testing tool capable of retrieving the values of these fields and properties will find bugs with high efficiency.

Verification of text and numbers   Some fields and properties of the application are defined to hold string or numeric values. A testing tool can obtain the value of such an object and compare it with the expected value. Sometimes a value of the field or property is supposed to display on the GUI interface. The testing tool should be able to compare the value of the field obtained by directly accessing the object to the interface display.

Clipboard verification   When a function copies the contents of a field, property, or GUI control into the clipboard, a manual tester can run the `clipbrd.exe` utility to verify the result. However, it is not practical for an automated testing tool to run a third-party tool. You can implement the automated testing tool to look into the clipboard directly and complete the verification.

GUI component existence   The GUI components in the presentation layer are functional parts of the application. They are also designed for usability and cosmetic purposes. The GUI test verification should include the capabilities to check the existence of a GUI component and its proper location, size, text, font, color, and other properties. Sometimes, the verification of GUI components can be conducted by comparing the actual snapshot of the window with a presaved image file.

File verification   End users expect a software application to perform complex jobs upon execution. The results are usually saved into a physical file. These files could be plain-text files, image files, and a binary database. A plain-text file can be easily compared to a predefined baseline file by implementing a file comparator inside the tool. Image files are usually compared to a bitmap baseline. However, data saved in a binary file is hard to compare. It is common for testers to convert machine-readable binary files into text files and complete the verification.

Object data verification   Today, a software application takes every piece of data as an object. An object has fields, properties, and methods. The objects reside in different layers and enable the application to perform complex tasks. If the objects preserve their expected behaviors after each step of the execution, the software has no defects. To test whether the status of objects is correct, a tool can compare the actual status of an object with an expected status. For example, when the object under test is serializable, you can enable the tool to save a copy of the expected object. Later, the tool can compare the object with the saved object by deserialization and reconstruction.

Communication Applications   Software products produce outcomes for communication between applications or hardware devices and require testing tools to track the message. The actual trace can happen on the local system or on the destination device.

Web test verification   Although web page test is beyond the scope of the discussion of this book, you can turn this tool into a web testing tool. The web test verification can check the existence of the web page in memory, the access statistics of the website, and a snapshot of the web page and scan the web site.

As computer science has been advancing rapidly for the last decade, there are a lot of available technologies that enable a tool to verify testing data effectively. Based on the testing requirements of your organization, you may have other areas to be verified. However, not all data types or objects can be verified automatically. For example, multimedia applications produce sound and video, which are not readily comparable by a machine. A computer can replay the sound and video, but lacks the capability to appreciate a master piece.

This book discusses different aspects of verification and will implement the AutomatedGUITest tool with a few of them as examples. You can use these examples to enhance the testing and verifying capabilities of the tool later for your specific test projects.

Automated Verifications

Testing tools can easily achieve the automatic playback of the mouse and keyboard actions by recording a test script. The AutomatedGUITest tool even can read instructions from an XML document to perform the desired mouse clicks. However, that is only the first part of the GUI testing. Saving the testing output and automating the verification process are more important and beneficial to a fully automated GUI test. The other testing methods focus more on generating testing inputs than automatically generating code for outcome verification. The verification result is the only means useful to fix the bugs and increase the reliability of the application under test.

Test results are produced each time a test case is executed. A GUI testing case can be executed many times reusing the various testing inputs. The testing outcome varies from one execution to another. The discussion in the preceding section presented some possible aspects in need of verification. The number of fields and properties of any application is finite. A thorough verification can be conducted based on the GUI survey results. If each member of the application needs to be verified from all the aspects discussed in the previous section, the maximum times of verification for each testing step can be expressed by a linear equation:

$$y = k \cdot x$$

In this equation, y is the maximum number of verifications needed for each testing step, k is the number of the possible aspects in need of verification, and x is the total number of fields and properties within an application. If GUI test consists of n steps, the overall number of verifications is $n \cdot y$. The result might be a large number. But it is a finite number. The verification by automatic comparison is fast. Working with an effective test presentation method, a thorough test and verification will increase the testing sensitivity to find bugs. However, a maximum verification is not always desired. You can implement the AutomatedGUITest tool with the verification options discussed in the following sections.

Simple Object Verification

A GUI test often starts by triggering the action of a GUI component by either a mouse event or a keyboard event. The business layer knows which GUI component is triggered and performs the desired functions. Simple object verification takes this GUI component as the object to verify at this testing step. Such verification compares the status of the current GUI with an expected status and presents the test result. For example, in Chapter 7 the AutomatedGUITest tool was implemented with a primitive testing capability, which saved the text property of the immediate GUI component receiving a mouse click.

This verification method is the simplest and can be automated with ease. However, the triggered GUI is not always of interest to the tester. Its status may not change at all before and after the GUI event. This kind of verification can be meaningless to the business functions of the application.

Specific Object Verification

When we tested the C# API Text Viewer at the end of Chapter 6, we implemented six testing steps. Each step of the test script focuses on the text status of the rich text box because the rich text box is used to collect the desired C# code when the Add button is clicked. In this book, this type of verification is called specific object verification. A certain object is specified for verification at the beginning of the testing data collection and is verified after each step throughout the testing. The verified object can be a GUI component or a non-GUI data member. This kind of verification is more meaningful to find bugs.

But often a GUI event or a testing step changes the status of more than one member of the application. Specific object verification may be focused on the most important member, but it overlooks the other members and decreases the possibilities of finding more bugs.

Lump Sum Verification

The opposite of the simple and specific object verification is to collect all the members in an application, extract the status after each testing step, and compare them with the respective expected results. Lump sum verification is a very sensitive verification method. It produces the most complex testing cases and can find most of the defects. However, if any mismatch between the actual and expected results occurs, a testing failure will be reported and set off false alarms. Presenting the preconditions and postconditions beside the verification results, the testers can distinguish the false alarms from the real failures. This verification method takes the longest time. Using this verification method requires the testers and developers to spend time on recognizing the real bugs. If the test script and the thorough verification accounts for 80 to 90 percent of the testing efforts, 10 to 20 percent of the manual reviewing of the test report is worthwhile.

The lump sum verification not only completes the most complex testing cases, it is also a simple method to be automated when collecting testing data. The disadvantage of this method is that it catches a lot of undesirable information. Some of it is redundant and has the same cause. The useless information is sometimes annoying and contributes to a confusing testing report. Testers expect a more effective testing tool to verify only the members to find bugs.

Best Practice Verification

The simple and specific object verification methods are too simple; they waste testing resources and miss real bugs. The lump sum verification method generates too much output, which can be overwhelming to the tester and wastes time that could be used to find the real bugs. We can enable the testing tool to make the right choice by verifying the appropriate members and comparing sufficient outcomes. Then the amount of the redundant verification results will be reduced, and the efficiency of finding software errors will be increased. This is the best practice verification and is the most effective one. But the testers need to have knowledge of the application under test and know the critical areas in need of verification. Testers will be required to carefully develop a test plan. Because testers know where defects will and will not occur, they can specify the appropriate members to be verified with each testing step.

The information presented thus far will help you in adding automatic verification capabilities to the AutomatedGUITest project.

Enhancing the AutomatedGUITest Tool

You implemented the AutomatedGUITest tool in Chapter 7. This tool is fully capable of seeing and handling the GUI components by invoking methods from the GUI test library. But it conducts the minimum verification at this point. Test script execution is driven by a collected GUI data store in the format of an XML document. Each GUI component has a counterpart handling method in the GUI test library. When other GUI controls need to be handled, you will always be able to add new GUI handling methods into the library. In this chapter, you will add code to the AutomatedGUITest tool and enhance its capability for test verification.

To resume coding the AutomatedGUITest tool, you can create a project folder for this chapter, C:\GUISourceCode\Chapter08. Then, copy the AutomatedGUITest and the GUITestLibrary projects from the C:\GUISourceCode\Chapter07 folder to the new folder. After the projects are copied, start the Microsoft Visual Studio .NET IDE and open the AutomatedGUITest project from the new folder. At this point, you are ready to update the existing classes and add new classes and code to the project.

Updating the *GUITestDataCollector* Interface

Similar to the GUI information collection process in Chapter 7, verification information can also be collected from the GUITestDataCollector class, which has a GUI form. In order to add some more GUI controls to this Windows form, you can go to the form design editor of the GUITestDataCollector class by navigating the AutomatedGUITest solution explorer. When the GUITestDataCollector form appears, you need to increase its size by changing the values of its Size property to 552 and 408 as its width and height, respectively. Then, add the GUI controls and manipulate their property values as shown in the following list:

Control	Property	Value
GroupBox	Name	grpVerifyMethod
	Text	Verification Method
RadioButton	Name	rdSimple

Control	Property	Value
	Text	Simple
RadioButton	Name	btnSpecific
	Text	Specific
RadioButton	Name	rdLumpsum
	Text	Lump Sum
RadioButton	Name	rdJustEnough
	Text	Just Enough
CheckBox	Name	chckCustomDiglog
	Text	Custom Dialog Box
Label	Name	lblAvailableMembers
	Text	Select Fields and Properties to Verify:
Label	Name	lblExpectedResult
	Text	Expected Results:
CheckedListBox	Name	chckLstMembersToVerify
RichTextBox	Name	txtExpectedResult
Button	Name	btnResetSpecificVerify
	Text	Reset Specific Member
	Size	144, 23
Button	Name	btnOK
	Text	OK
Button	Name	btnCancel
	Text	Cancel

The preceding list adds a GroupBox, one CheckBox, two Label, one CheckedListBox, one RichTextBox, and three Button controls to the form. Then, the four RadioButton controls are added inside the GroupBox. After the control population, the GUITestDataCollector form should look like Figure 8.1.

The coding of this updated GUITestDataCollector class focuses on the verification methods discussed in the preceding sections. There are four radio buttons in the group box and each one corresponds to one of the verification methods the tester can choose from. First, double-click the Specific radio button and add the code in Listing 8.1.

FIGURE 8.1
The updated GUITest-
DataCollector form for
GUI testing and verifi-
cation data collection

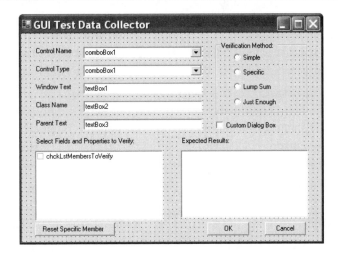

Listing 8.1   **Code for the Added Fields and the *rdSpecific_CheckedChanged()* Event of
                      the Updated *GUITestDataCollector* Class**

```csharp
private static string SpecificType;
private static string SpecificMember;

public string startupForm;

private void rdSpecific_CheckedChanged(object sender, System.EventArgs e)
{
  if (rdSpecific.Checked)
  {
    try
    {
      GetSpecificVerifyMember(chckLstMembersToVerify);
      AddExpectedContent();
    }
    catch (Exception ex)
    {
      Console.WriteLine(ex.Message);
    }
  }

}
```

Recall from the discussion of the specific verification method that at the beginning of the
session the user can specify a member to be verified throughout the GUI test data collection.
Before the event declaration, two static string fields are created to locate the specific member

inside the specific application. A static field will keep the value until the current testing session is terminated. However, a button is placed at the bottom of the form, which enables the users to change the specific verification member during the current testing session. The third field is a public string variable. When a new `GUITestDataCollector` instance is initialized, this field will receive a value for the name of the startup form .

The `rdSpecific_CheckedChanged()` declaration is generated by double-clicking the Specific radio button on the form design editor of the IDE. The code between the curly brackets uses an `if` statement to inspect whether the radio box is checked or not. If it is checked, it calls two helper methods, `GetSpecificVerifyMember()` and `AddExpectedContent()`, within a `try-catch` clause.

The code for the `GetSpecificVerifyMember()` method is in Listing 8.2.

Listing 8.2   Code for the *GetSpecificVerifyEvent()* Helper Method

```
private void GetSpecificVerifyMember(CheckedListBox chckLst)
{
  if (SpecificType == null)
  {
    ArrayList selectedMems = new ArrayList();
    for (int i = 0; i < chckLst.Items.Count; i ++)
    {
      if (chckLst.GetItemChecked(i))
      {
        selectedMems.Add(chckLst.GetItemText(chckLst.Items[i]));
      }
    }
    if (selectedMems.Count == 2)
    {
      SpecificType = (string)selectedMems[0];
      SpecificMember = (string)selectedMems[1];
      SpecificMember = SpecificMember.Trim();
    }
  }
  SetSimpleVerification(SpecificType, SpecificMember, chckLst);
}
```

The code uses an `if` statement to check whether the specific member for verification is already defined. If it is not, the value of the `SpecificType` field is `null`. At this point, the method initializes a new `ArrayList` object, `selectedMems`. Then, it uses a `for` loop to search through the CheckedListBox to add the selected items into the `selectedMems` object. After the `for` loop, the method expects that only two items are checked in the CheckedListBox by the tester. One is the name of the startup form and the other is the member in need of verification throughout the test script. The values of these two items are assigned to the `SpecificType` and the `SpecificMember` fields. A `Trim()` method of the `String` class is used to get rid of the escape character (\t). Finally, a `SetSimpleVerification()` helper method is called to recheck the items in the CheckedListBox.

The `SetSimpleVerification()` helper method is coded as shown in Listing 8.3. This method will also be invoked by the Simple verification radio button.

Listing 8.3   Code for the *SetSimpleVerification()* Helper Method

```
private void SetSimpleVerification(string typeName, string memName,
➥CheckedListBox chckLst)
{
  int index1 = 0;
  int index2 = 0;

  try
  {
    index1 = chckLst.FindString(typeName);
    index2 = chckLst.FindString("\t" + memName, index1);
  }
  catch (Exception ex)
  {
    Console.WriteLine(ex.Message);
  }
  if (index2 > index1)
  {
    chckLst.SetItemChecked(index1, true);
    chckLst.SetItemChecked(index2, true);
  }
}
```

The `SetSimpleVerification()` helper method takes the name of the startup form, the name of the verification member, and a `CheckedListBox` object as parameters. Then, it invokes a `FindString()` method of the `CheckedListBox` class to locate the indices by the names of the startup form and member. After the values of the indices are located, it sets the corresponding items to be checked in the CheckedListBox control.

Listing 8.4 implements the `AddExpectedContent()` helper method required by Listing 8.1.

Listing 8.4   Code for the *AddExpectedContent()* Helper Method

```
private void AddExpectedContent()
{
  string expectedStr = "";
  for (int i = 0; i<chckLstMembersToVerify.Items.Count; i++)
  {
    if (chckLstMembersToVerify.GetItemChecked(i))
    {
```

```
    string typeMember = chckLstMembersToVerify.GetItemText(
➥chckLstMembersToVerify.Items[i]);
    if (typeMember.StartsWith("\t"))
    {
      expectedStr += "<" + typeMember.Trim() + ">\n|";
    }
  }
}
  txtExpectedResult.Text = expectedStr;
}
```

The expected contents are expected to be entered in the rich text box by the tester. However, the AddExpectedContent() helper method walks through the CheckedListBox control and inspects the checked member with a for loop. If the member is checked for verification, it adds the name of the member between a pair of < and > brackets to the rich text box. Each member name occupies one line. This serves as a hint and a prompt for the users to know where to enter the expected results. Furthermore, the AddExpectedContent() helper method will be invoked by the rest of the verification radio buttons.

Now the specific verification can be conducted by the GUITestDataCollector class. You need to double-click the Simple radio button for implementation of the simple verification method. Listing 8.5 shows the code for the rdSimple_CheckedChanged() event.

Listing 8.5   Code for the *rdSimple_CheckedChanged()* Event

```
private void rdSimple_CheckedChanged(object sender, System.EventArgs e)
{
  MakeAllChecked(chckLstMembersToVerify, false);

  if (rdSimple.Checked)
  {
    SetSimpleVerification(startupForm,
➥cmbControlName.Text, chckLstMembersToVerify);
    AddExpectedContent();
  }
}
```

The rdSimple_CheckedChanged() event first calls a MakeAllChecked() helper method to clear all the checked items in the CheckedListBox control in order to reset the items. Then it reads the value of the Checked property of the simple radio button. If the value is true, the startup form and the current GUI item are checked inside the CheckedListBox control. It also adds the GUI control name to the rich text box by calling the AddExpectedContent() method.

The MakeAllChecked() helper method is coded as in Listing 8.6.

Listing 8.6   **Code for the *MakeAllChecked()* Helper Method**

```
private void MakeAllChecked(CheckedListBox chckLst, bool checkAll)
{
  for (int i = 0; i < chckLst.Items.Count; i++)
  {
    chckLst.SetItemChecked(i, checkAll);
  }
}
```

This method simply follows the for loop to check or uncheck all the items in the Checked-ListBox control based on the Boolean value of the second parameter.

The code for the lump sum and the best practice verification methods is in Listing 8.7. Before you add this code to the project, you should double-click the Lump Sum and finish coding, and then double click the Just Enough radio button and finish coding.

Listing 8.7   **Code for the *rdLumpsum_CheckedChanged()* and *rdJustEnough_*
                          ***CheckedChanged()* Events**

```
private void rdLumpsum_CheckedChanged(object sender, System.EventArgs e)
{
  MakeAllChecked(chckLstMembersToVerify, rdLumpsum.Checked);
  AddExpectedContent();
}

private void rdJustEnough_CheckedChanged(object sender, System.EventArgs e)
{
  if (rdJustEnough.Checked)
  {
    MakeAllChecked(chckLstMembersToVerify, false);
  }
}
```

The rdLumpsum_CheckedChanged() event enables the tool to verify all the available members of the application by checking all the items in the CheckedListBox control when the lump sum radio button is checked. It adds all the names of the members to the rich text box in order for the testers to enter expected results for each of the members.

The rdJustEnough_CheckedChanged() event is prepared for the best practice verification method. It calls the same MakeAllChecked() helper method the rdLumpsum_CheckedChanged() event calls. But the rdJustEnough_CheckedChanged() event simply unchecks all of the items in the CheckedListBox control. After the event completes, the tool is ready for the users to specify the desired members to verify. The issue of entering the expected content will be handled by an event of the CheckedListBox control.

After coding the radio button events, you can continue to implement a SelectedIndexChanged() event for the CheckedListBox control. To do this, you can go to the form design editor again and double-click on the CheckedListBox control. Listing 8.8 contains the code for this event.

Listing 8.8   **Code for the *chckLstMembersToVerify_SelectedIndexChanged()* Event**

```
private void chckLstMembersToVerify_SelectedIndexChanged (object sender,
➥System. EventArgs e)
{
  AddExpectedContent();
}
```

The code simply calls the AddExpectedContent() method. Whenever the user selects and checks an item from the CheckedListBox control, this event will be triggered and add hints for the user to enter expected results into the rich text box.

Finally, to make the tool flexible and handle the specific verification method, a Reset Specific Member button has been placed in the GUITestDataCollector form. Users can click this button and reset a member in need of verification at any time. You can double-click this button from the form design editor and add the code in Listing 8.9 between the curly brackets.

Listing 8.9   **Code for the *btnResetSpecificVerify_Click()* Event**

```
private void btnResetSpecificVerify_Click(object sender, System.EventArgs e)
{
  SpecificType = null;
  SpecificMember = null;
  MakeAllChecked(chckLstMembersToVerify, false);
}
```

After you update the GUITestDataCollector class with the GUI control addition and the code, you can build this project to check whether all the code is correct. A full list of the code for updating the GUITestDataCollector class is in Listing 8.10 (the code generated by the IDE and added in Chapter 7 is omitted). You can compare your project with the full list code and correct the errors.

Listing 8.10   **The Code Added to Update the *GUITestDataCollector* Class**

```
//omitted using directives
...
namespace AutomatedGUITest
{
  /// <summary>
  /// Summary description for GUITestDataCollector.
  /// </summary>
```

```
    public class GUITestDataCollector : System.Windows.Forms.Form
    {

//code generated by IDE and from Chapter 7 omitted
    ...

    //chapter 8
    private static string SpecificType;
    private static string SpecificMember;
    public string startupForm;

    private void rdSpecific_CheckedChanged(object sender, System.EventArgs e)
    {
      if (rdSpecific.Checked)
      {
        try
        {
          GetSpecificVerifyMember(chckLstMembersToVerify);
          AddExpectedContent();
        }
        catch (Exception ex)
        {
          Console.WriteLine(ex.Message);
        }
      }

    }

    private void GetSpecificVerifyMember(CheckedListBox chckLst)
    {
      if (SpecificType == null)
      {
        ArrayList selectedMems = new ArrayList();
        for (int i = 0; i < chckLst.Items.Count; i ++)
        {
          if (chckLst.GetItemChecked(i))
          {
            selectedMems.Add(chckLst.GetItemText(chckLst.Items[i]));
          }
        }
        if (selectedMems.Count == 2)
        {
          SpecificType = (string)selectedMems[0];
          SpecificMember = (string)selectedMems[1];
          SpecificMember = SpecificMember.Trim();
        }
      }
      SetSimpleVerification(SpecificType, SpecificMember, chckLst);

    }

    private void SetSimpleVerification(string typeName,
```

```
➥string memName, CheckedListBox chckLst)
    {
      int index1 = 0;
      int index2 = 0;

      try
      {
        index1 = chckLst.FindString(typeName);
        index2 = chckLst.FindString("\t" + memName, index1);
      }
      catch (Exception ex)
      {
        Console.WriteLine(ex.Message);
      }
      if (index2 > index1)
      {
        chckLst.SetItemChecked(index1, true);
        chckLst.SetItemChecked(index2, true);
      }
    }

    private void AddExpectedContent()
    {
      string expectedStr = "";
      for (int i = 0; i<chckLstMembersToVerify.Items.Count; i++)
      {
        if (chckLstMembersToVerify.GetItemChecked(i))
        {
          string typeMember = chckLstMembersToVerify.GetItemText(
➥chckLstMembersToVerify.Items[i]);
          if (typeMember.StartsWith("\t"))
          {
            expectedStr += "<" + typeMember.Trim() + ">\n|";
          }
        }
      }
      txtExpectedResult.Text = expectedStr;
    }

    private void rdSimple_CheckedChanged(object sender, System.EventArgs e)
    {
      MakeAllChecked(chckLstMembersToVerify, false);

      if (rdSimple.Checked)
      {
        SetSimpleVerification(startupForm,
➥cmbControlName.Text, chckLstMembersToVerify);
        AddExpectedContent();
      }
    }

    private void MakeAllChecked(CheckedListBox chckLst, bool checkAll)
```

```
    {
      for (int i = 0; i < chckLst.Items.Count; i++)
      {
        chckLst.SetItemChecked(i, checkAll);
      }
    }


    private void rdLumpsum_CheckedChanged(object sender, System.EventArgs e)
    {
      MakeAllChecked(chckLstMembersToVerify, rdLumpsum.Checked);
      AddExpectedContent();
    }

    private void rdJustEnough_CheckedChanged(object sender, System.EventArgs e)
    {
      if (rdJustEnough.Checked)
      {
        MakeAllChecked(chckLstMembersToVerify, false);
      }
    }

    private void chckLstMembersToVerify_SelectedIndexChanged(
➥object sender, System.EventArgs e)
    {
      AddExpectedContent();
    }

    private void btnResetSpecificVerify_Click(object sender, System.EventArgs e)
    {
      SpecificType = null;
      SpecificMember = null;
      MakeAllChecked(chckLstMembersToVerify, false);
    }
  }
}
```

After correcting the code and building the project with success, you can proceed to the next section.

Building a GUI Test Verification Class

To implement the AutomatedGUITest tool with verification functions, you need to create a new a GUITestVerification class to get information from the updated GUITestDataCollector class. When the Microsoft Visual Studio .NET IDE is open with the AutomatedGUITest project, choose Project ➢ Add Class . When the Add New Item dialog box appears, type **GUITest-Verification** in the Name field for the class name. Then click the Open button and the Microsoft Visual Studio .NET IDE brings up the code editor for the GUITestVerification class. You can keep the IDE-generated code intact and add the code in the code listings.

First, you need to add a few using directives below the using System statement at the beginning of the code. The addition looks similar to the following:

```
using System.Windows.Forms;
using System.Reflection;
using System.Collections;
using System.Xml.Serialization;
```

Using the System.Windows.Forms namespace enables the class to pass parameters as Windows form objects. This is always necessary for testing GUI components. The System.Reflection namespace provides classes and methods for the GUITestVerification class to find all the possible members in need of verification. The System.Collections namespace provides the ArrayList class for collecting information for test verification. Finally, the System.Xml.Serialization namespace allows you to implement some serializable helper classes. Listings 8.11 through 8.13 include the code for three of the helper classes. Each of these classes is created under the AutomatedGUITest namespace hierarchy at the same level as the GUITestVerification class.

Listing 8.11   **Code for the First Helper Class, the *TestExpectation* Class**

```
[Serializable]
public class TestExpectation
{
  // for general purpose
  public string EventMember;
  public string VerifyingMember;
  public int GUIActionSequence;

  // for existence verification
  public bool isGUI = false;
  public bool isField = false;
  public bool isProperty = false;

  // for alphanumeric verification
  public string ExpectingResult="";
  public string ActualResult="";
  public string ScreenSnapshot = "";
  public bool ExpectAlphaNumericEqual = true;
  public bool AlphanumericPass = true;

  // For clipboard verification
  public object ActualClpbrdObj;
  public object ExpectedClpbrdObj;
  public bool ExpectClipBrdEqual = true;
  public bool ClipboardPass = true;

  // For file existence and content verification
  public object ActualFileObj;
  public object ExpectedFileObj;
```

```
public bool FileTestPass = true;

// object verification
public object ActualObj;
public object ExpectedObj;
public bool OjectTestPass = true;

// Non-Business GUI verification
public object ActualCosmeticStr;
public object ExpectedCosmeticStr;
public object CosmeticTestPass = true;

public void AssertAlphanumericTest(bool expectedEqual)
{
  bool actual = true;
  if (ExpectingResult.Trim().Equals(""))
  {
    if (!ScreenSnapshot.Trim().Equals(""))
    {
      if (!ActualResult.Trim().Equals(ScreenSnapshot.Trim()))
      {
        actual = false;
      }
    }
  }
  else
  {
    if (ScreenSnapshot.Trim().Equals(""))
    {
      if (!ExpectingResult.Trim().Equals(ScreenSnapshot.Trim()))
      {
        actual = false;
      }
    }
    else if ((!ExpectingResult.Equals(ScreenSnapshot)) ||
        (!ExpectingResult.Equals(ActualResult)) ||
        (!ActualResult.Equals(ScreenSnapshot)))
    {
      actual = false;
    }
  }

  if (actual == expectedEqual)
    AlphanumericPass = true;
  else
    AlphanumericPass = false;
}

public void AssertClipboardTest(bool expectedEqual)
{
  bool actual = false;
```

```
   if (ActualClpbrdObj.ToString() == ExpectedClpbrdObj.ToString())
     actual = true;

   if (actual == expectedEqual)
     ClipboardPass = true;
   else
     ClipboardPass = false;
  }
 }
```

The first line of Listing 8.11 declares the TestExpectation class to be serializable. This class consists of a number of public fields and methods. These fields are used to hold the current status and expected results of a member with respect to different verification purposes. The first cluster uses three fields to retain the name to identify which GUI event is under immediate activation, which member is currently verified, and the order of the steps in the testing sequence, respectively. The second cluster determines whether the member under verification is a GUI component, a field, or a property. The third cluster has five public fields, which are for text verification. Text could be a string of alphanumeric characters. Thus, this class terms it as alphanumeric verification. The alphanumeric string can be set by the testers as an expected result, obtained from the live member, or captured from the screen if the member that is currently verified is a GUI component. For testing verification, in some cases, the tester considers the test to pass when the actual results match the expected results. In other cases, the test passes when the expected results are different from the actual results. A given true or false value of the ExpectAlphaNumericEqual field sets a value of the AlphanumericPass field to true or false when the value of the ActualResult matches that of the ExpectingResult.

The next four code clusters define the necessary fields to verify the clipboard, the existence of the file, the entire object, and some decorative properties. As we have discussed, these are the known verification aspects. The upcoming chapters will cover these in more detail.

After the public fields are declared, you need to implement a method to assert the verification with regard to each known aspect. However, the sample code implements only two methods in this chapter, one to verify whether the value of the ActualResult matches that of the ExpectingResult and one to verify whether the value of the ActualClpbrdObj matches that of the ExpectedClpbrdObj. The rest of the declared aspects in need of verification are not implemented with their needed methods, which offers some hints for your future tool development and leaves spacious room for you to meet your own testing requirements.

The first assertion method, AssertAlphanumericTest(), takes a Boolean parameter, expectedEqual, to check whether the actual result matches the expected results. A true value of the expectedEqual parameter means that the actual result must match the expected result to pass the test. Otherwise, an unmatched pair is needed to pass the test. The main body of the method simply uses a series of if statements to compare the actual result against the screen-captured result and the predefined expected results until the final result is reached.

The second assertion method, AssertClipboardTest(), is for clipboard verification. The parameter is similar to the first method. It also uses some if statements to reach the final result.

After this class implementation, add the code for the second helper class (shown in Listing 8.12).

Listing 8.12   Code for the *TypeVerification* Helper Class

```
[Serializable]public class TypeVerification
{
  public string AUTPath;
  public string TypeName;
  public string GUIEvent;

  [XmlArray("TestEvents")]
  [XmlArrayItem("TestAndVerify",typeof(TestExpectation))]
  public ArrayList MemberList = new ArrayList();
}
```

The TypeVerification helper class defines four public fields. The first three fields are string variables to present the pathname of the application under test, the name of the startup form of the application, and the triggered GUI event currently being verified. The last field is an ArrayList variable, MemberList. The MemberList is modified by the attributes of the System.Xml .Serialization.XmlArrayAttribute class. The purpose of these modifications is to add objects of the TestExpectation class into the field and keep these objects still serializable. These objects are serialized to store the verification data and the final test results.

The third helper class is similar to the second helper class. The purpose of this class is to add the objects initialized from the second class to an ArrayList field and makes the verification data store persistent. The code for this class is in Listing 8.13.

Listing 8.13   Code for the *TypeVerificationSerializable* Helper Class

```
[Serializable]public class TypeVerificationSerializable
{
  public string AUTPath;
  public string AUTStartupForm;

  [XmlArray("TypeVerificationSerializable")]
  [XmlArrayItem("FormUnderTest",typeof(TypeVerification))]
  public ArrayList TypeList = new ArrayList();
}
```

The TypeVerificationSerializable helper class also has a string field to hold the pathname of the application under test. The second field is for the name of the startup form of the application. The third ArrayList field, TypeList, is also modified by attributes of the System.Xml .Serialization.XmlArrayAttribute class to collect objects of the TypeVerification class and make the objects of the TypeVerification class serializable within this ArrayList field.

After the implementation of the helper classes, you are ready to code the designated GUITestVerification class with fields and methods. Listing 8.14 shows the needed fields for the GUITestVerification class.

Listing 8.14   **Field Declarations of the Code for the *GUITestVerification* Class**

```
private string AUT;
private string StartForm;
private string GUIEvent;
```

The first field continues to track the pathname of the application under test. The second and third fields are also similar to the helper classes and used to remember the names of the startup form and the GUI event under test. However, these fields are declared to be private.

Besides the IDE-generated default constructor, you need to code an overloaded constructor such as shown in Listing 8.15.

Listing 8.15   **The Overloaded Constructor for the *GUITestVerification* Class**

```
public GUITestVerification(string _aut, string _startForm, string _guiEvent)
{
  AUT = _aut;
  StartForm = _startForm;
  GUIEvent = _guiEvent;
}
```

The overloaded constructor simply passes three string parameters to initialize the three private fields, respectively. The main coding task of this class is the implementation of FindMembersToVerify() and BuildVerificationList() as public methods.

You have used a few methods to find the GUI components for data-driven software testing. First, in Chapter 7 you implemented a StartGUISurvey() method for the GUISurveyClass, which sets the mouse pointer on a journey for finding all the GUI members of the application under test. Visibly, this journey represents a tester moving the mouse pointer pixel by pixel across the window of interest vertically and horizontally. Then, you used a PopulateGUINameTypeLists() method in the AutomatedGUITest startup class to extrapolate the names of the GUI components given at coding time. This method also finds the corresponding names of the .NET classes from which the GUI components are derived. Note that the second method doesn't need to work physically as hard as the first method. It grabs the handle of the application under test and queries the .NET Framework. A for loop enumeration recursively gives away the privacy of the related GUI components to the automated GUI testing tool. This enumeration also confirms the consistency between the visible GUI components and the intended GUI components. With the help of these two methods, users can easily specify the steps of a GUI testing execution.

After the execution of the testing steps, the tool needs to conduct verification and check whether the execution produces desired outputs. The strategy is to visit all the affected members in the application and query their contents. These members include GUI and non-GUI components. Sometimes, these GUI and non-GUI components are fields and properties. Listing 8.16 is the code for the `FindMembersToVerify()` method.

Listing 8.16   The Code for the *FindMembersToVerify()* Method

```
public void FindMembersToVerify(string AUT, GUITestDataCollector guiTDC)
{
  Assembly asm = Assembly.LoadFrom(AUT);
  Type[] types = asm.GetTypes();

  BindingFlags allFlags = BindingFlags.Public | BindingFlags.NonPublic |
    BindingFlags.Static | BindingFlags.Instance;

  foreach(Type typ in types)
  {
    if (typ.Namespace + "." + typ.Name ==  StartForm)
    {
      guiTDC.chckLstFieldsToVerify.Items.Add(typ.Namespace + "." + typ.Name);
      foreach (FieldInfo fld in typ.GetFields(allFlags))
      {
        guiTDC.chckLstFieldsToVerify.Items.Add("\t" + fld.Name);
      }

      foreach (PropertyInfo prpty in typ.GetProperties(allFlags))
      {
        guiTDC.chckLstFieldsToVerify.Items.Add("\t" + prpty.Name);

      }
    }
  }
}
```

Instead of collecting GUI information by the methods used in Chapter 7, the `FindMembers-ToVerify()` method loads the application under test to create a new object of the application by using the `Assembly` class of the .NET Reflection namespace. Then it prepares a variable in order to access all the members of the application with modifications of `public`, `private`, or protected. Finally, it uses a `foreach` loop to extract all the fields and properties, respectively, and makes their names visible to a `GUITestDataCollector` object.

The second public method is a `BuildVerificationList()` method (Listing 8.17).

➲ **Listing 8.17**   **The Code for the *BuildVerificationList()* Method**

```
public void BuildVerificationList(GUITestDataCollector guiTDC, int guiSeq,
➥ref TypeVerificationSerializable typesToVerify)
{
  if (AUT == null)
    return;

  typesToVerify.AUTPath = AUT;
  typesToVerify.AUTStartupForm = StartForm;

  TypeVerification typeVerify = new TypeVerification();
  GetSelectedMembers(guiTDC, guiSeq, ref typeVerify);;

  typesToVerify.TypeList.Add(typeVerify);
}
```

The `FindMembersToVerify()` method accepts a `guiTDC` object, a `guiSeq` object, and a `typesToVerify` object as parameters. After the declaration, it first assigns the path and the startup form of the application under test (AUT) to the `typesToVerify` object. Then it initializes a new `TypeVerification` object and uses the information from the `guiTDC` object to set the current status of the new object. The information exchange between the new object and the `guiTDC` object is via a helper method, `GetSelectedMembers()`. Finally, the new object is queued in the `TypesToVerify.TypeList` waiting to be verified. The code for the `GetSelectedMembers()` helper method is in Listing 8.18.

➲ **Listing 8.18**   **The Code for the *GetSelectedMembers()* Helper Method**

```
private void GetSelectedMembers(GUITestDataCollector guiTDC, int guiSeq,
➥ref TypeVerification typeVerify)
{
  int itemCounter = 0;
  string typeMember = "";
  string[] expectedItems = GetExpectedOutcome(guiTDC.txtExpectedResult);

  for (int i = 0; i<guiTDC.chckLstMembersToVerify.Items.Count; i++)
  {
    if (guiTDC.chckLstMembersToVerify.GetItemChecked(i))
    {
      typeMember = guiTDC.chckLstMembersToVerify.GetItemText(
➥guiTDC.chckLstMembersToVerify.Items[i]);
      if (!typeMember.StartsWith("\t"))
```

```
    {
      typeVerify.TypeName = typeMember;
      typeVerify.GUIEvent = GUIEvent;
    }
    else
    {
      TestExpectation individualTest = new TestExpectation();
      individualTest.EventMember = GUIEvent;
      individualTest.VerifyingMember = typeMember.Trim();
      individualTest.ExpectingResult = expectedItems[itemCounter];
      individualTest.GUIActionSequence = guiSeq;
      itemCounter++;

      typeVerify.MemberList.Add(individualTest);

    }
  }
  }
  }
```

The goal of the GetSelectedMembers() helper method is to collect as much information as possible from the guiTDC object for verifying each specified member. It first initializes an integer and a string variable to track the number and name of a member specified for verification in the guiTDC object. The third variable is a string array that is initialized by invoking a GetExpectedOutcome() helper method (Listing 8.19). After the needed variables are prepared, a for loop walks the typeVerify object through the CheckedListBox of the guiTDC object. The check list box has a full list of the members (GUI components, fields, and properties) of the application. During the walk-through, the method inspects each of the members. If there is a check mark beside a member, it recognizes that this is a member in need of verification.

In the check list box of the guiTDC object, the name of a member starts with a Tab indent (an escape character, \t, in C# code) to be separated from the name of the startup form. Thus, a nested if statement is used to perform different functions based on whether the checked item is a member or is a startup form. When the visited item is the startup form, the method assigns the startup form name and the current GUI event to the typeVerify object. When the checked item is a member, it initializes a new TestExpectation object, individualTest, and assigns specific verification information to the object. The information includes the expected results. After all the available information is collected by the individualTest object, the object is added to typeVerify.MemberList, indicating that it's in need of verification when a GUI test is executed.

The last helper method is the GetExpectedOutcome() helper method for the GUITest-Verification class, as coded in Listing 8.19. In the preceding section, the GUITestData-Collector class was updated with controls and events for verification purposes. This method gets information from one of them about expected results. In fact, the previous methods have already received information from the other controls of the updated GUITestDataCollector class.

Listing 8.19   The Code for the *GetExpectedOutcome()* Helper Method

```
private string[] GetExpectedOutcome(RichTextBox rtfBox)
{
  string[] expectedItems = rtfBox.Text.Split('|');

  for (int i = 0; i< expectedItems.Length; i++)
  {
    string tempItem = expectedItems[i].Trim();
    if (tempItem.StartsWith("<"))
      expectedItems[i] = tempItem.Substring(tempItem.IndexOf(">") + 1).Trim();
  }

  return expectedItems;
}
```

The declaration of the GetExpectedOutcome() method searches through a rich text box and returns a string array containing expected outcomes to the preceding method. The code simply converts the text inside the box into an array by calling the Split() method of the String class using a '|' character as a separator between object names in need of verification. Because the raw text in the box contains the name of the member in need of verification between a pair of < and > brackets, a for loop walks through the array and removes the member name with the < and > brackets from each item. Thus, the returned items in the array are purely the text of the expected results. Since the expected results will be serialized in addition to the other verification data, the corresponding member names will appear in the same XML node of the saved data store.

After you completely code the GUITestVerification class, you can build this project by choosing Build ➢ Build Solution. If you observe compiling errors, Listing 8.20 is the full list of the GUITestVerification class.

Listing 8.20   The Full Code List for the *GUITestVerification* Class

```
using System;
using System.Windows.Forms;
using System.Reflection;
using System.Collections;
using System.Xml.Serialization;

namespace AutomatedGUITest
{
  public class GUITestVerification
  {
```

```csharp
    private string AUT;
    private string StartForm;
    private string GUIEvent;

  public GUITestVerification()
  {
  }

public GUITestVerification(string _aut, string _startForm, string _guiEvent)
{
  AUT = _aut;
  StartForm = _startForm;
  GUIEvent = _guiEvent;
}

public void FindMembersToVerify(string AUT, GUITestDataCollector guiTDC)
{
  Assembly asm = Assembly.LoadFrom(AUT);
  Type[] types = asm.GetTypes();

  BindingFlags allFlags = BindingFlags.Public | BindingFlags.NonPublic |
    BindingFlags.Static | BindingFlags.Instance;

  foreach(Type typ in types)
  {
    if (typ.Namespace + "." + typ.Name ==  StartForm)
    {
      guiTDC.chckLstMembersToVerify.Items.Add(typ.Namespace + "." + typ.Name);
      foreach (FieldInfo fld in typ.GetFields(allFlags))
      {
        guiTDC.chckLstMembersToVerify.Items.Add("\t" + fld.Name);
      }

      foreach (PropertyInfo prpty in typ.GetProperties(allFlags))
      {
        guiTDC.chckLstMembersToVerify.Items.Add("\t" + prpty.Name);
      }

    }
  }
}


public void BuildVerificationList(GUITestDataCollector guiTDC, int guiSeq,
➥ref TypeVerificationSerializable TypesToVerify)
{
  if (AUT == null)
    return;


  TypesToVerify.AUTPath = AUT;
```

```
    TypesToVerify.AUTStartupForm = StartForm;

    TypeVerification typeVerify = new TypeVerification();
    GetSelectedMembers(guiTDC, guiSeq, ref typeVerify);

    TypesToVerify.TypeList.Add(typeVerify);
}

private void GetSelectedMembers(GUITestDataCollector guiTDC, int guiSeq,
➡ref TypeVerification typeVerify)
{
  int itemCounter = 0;
  string typeMember = "";
  string[] expectedItems = GetExpectedOutcome(guiTDC.txtExpectedResult);

  for (int i = 0; i<guiTDC.chckLstMembersToVerify.Items.Count; i++)
  {
    if (guiTDC.chckLstMembersToVerify.GetItemChecked(i))
    {
      typeMember = guiTDC.chckLstMembersToVerify.GetItemText(
➡guiTDC.chckLstMembersToVerify.Items[i]);
      if (!typeMember.StartsWith("\t"))
      {
        typeVerify.TypeName = typeMember;
        typeVerify.GUIEvent = GUIEvent;
      }
      else
      {
        TestExpectation individualTest = new TestExpectation();
        individualTest.EventMember = GUIEvent;
        individualTest.VerifyingMember = typeMember.Trim();
        individualTest.ExpectingResult = expectedItems[itemCounter];
        individualTest.GUIActionSequence = guiSeq;
        itemCounter++;

        typeVerify.MemberList.Add(individualTest);

      }
    }
  }
}

private string[] GetExpectedOutcome(RichTextBox rtfBox)
{
  string[] expectedItems = rtfBox.Text.Split('|');

  for (int i = 0; i< expectedItems.Length; i++)
  {
    string tempItem = expectedItems[i].Trim();
    if (tempItem.StartsWith("<"))
      expectedItems[i] = tempItem.Substring(tempItem.IndexOf(">") + 1).Trim();
```

```
  }
  return expectedItems;
}

  }

  [Serializable]public class TestExpectation
  {
// for general purpose
public string EventMember;
public string VerifyingMember;
public int GUIActionSequence;

// for existence verification
public bool isGUI = false;
public bool isField = false;
public bool isProperty = false;

// for alphanumeric verification
public string ExpectingResult="";
public string ActualResult="";
public string ScreenSnapshot = "";
public bool ExpectAlphaNumericEqual = true;
public bool AlphanumericPass = true;

// For clipboard verification
public object ActualClpbrdObj;
public object ExpectedClpbrdObj;
public bool ExpectClipBrdEqual = true;
public bool ClipboardPass = true;

// For file existence and content verification
public object ActualFileObj;
public object ExpectedFileObj;
public bool FileTestPass = true;

// object verification
public object ActualObj;
public object ExpectedObj;
public bool OjectTestPass = true;

// Non-Business GUI verification
public object ActualCosmeticStr;
public object ExpectedCosmeticStr;
public object CosmeticTestPass = true;


public void AssertAlphanumericTest(bool expectedEqual)
{
  bool actual = true;
  if (ExpectingResult.Trim().Equals(""))
```

```
    {
      if (!ScreenSnapshot.Trim().Equals(""))
      {
        if (!ActualResult.Trim().Equals(ScreenSnapshot.Trim()))
        {
          actual = false;
        }
      }
    }
    else
    {
      if (ScreenSnapshot.Trim().Equals(""))
      {
        if (!ExpectingResult.Trim().Equals(ScreenSnapshot.Trim()))
        {
          actual = false;
        }
      }
      else if ((!ExpectingResult.Equals(ScreenSnapshot)) ||
        (!ExpectingResult.Equals(ActualResult)) ||
        (!ActualResult.Equals(ScreenSnapshot)))
      {
        actual = false;
      }
    }
    if (actual == expectedEqual)
      AlphanumericPass = true;
    else
      AlphanumericPass = false;
}

public void AssertClipboardTest(bool expectedEqual)
{
  bool actual = false;
  if (ActualClpbrdObj.ToString() == ExpectedClpbrdObj.ToString())
    actual = true;

  if (actual == expectedEqual)
    ClipboardPass = true;
  else
    ClipboardPass = false;
}

  }

  [Serializable]public class TypeVerification
  {
public string AUTPath;
public string TypeName;
public string GUIEvent;

[XmlArray("TestEvents")]
```

```
[XmlArrayItem("TestAndVerify",typeof(TestExpectation))]
public ArrayList MemberList = new ArrayList();
    }

    [Serializable]public class TypeVerificationSerializable
    {
public string AUTPath;
public string AUTStartupForm;

[XmlArray("TypeVerificationSerializable")]
[XmlArrayItem("FormUnderTest",typeof(TypeVerification))]
public ArrayList TypeList = new ArrayList();
    }
}
```

After this implementation, the GUITestVerification class affects the other two existing classes, which are AutomatedGUITest and GUITestScript. In order to incorporate the new testing capabilities into the tool, you need to update these two classes, as shown in the following sections.

Updating the AutomatedGUITest Startup Form

Compared with the coding task for updating the GUITestDataCollector class, updating the AutomatedGUITest class doesn't involve creating new methods or events. Besides the need for three new fields, there are only some minor modifications of three events in order to integrate the GUITestVerification class. The three fields are added as follows:

```
private GUITestVerification guiTestVrfy;
private int GUISequence;
TypeVerificationSerializable TypesToVerify;
```

The first field, guiTestVrfy, is defined as a GUITestVerification object. The second field uses a GUISequence integer variable to track the step of the current testing sequence. Finally, a TypeVerificationSerializable object is declared.

The first modification is the dgAvailableGUIs_DoubleClick() event. Listing 8.21 shows the code of the updated event with the newly added code in bold.

Listing 8.21   The Modified Code for the *dgAvailableGUIs_DoubleClick()* Event with the Newly Added Code in Bold

```
private void dgAvailableGUIs_DoubleClick(object sender, System.EventArgs e)
{

    GUITDC = new GUITestDataCollector();

    GUITDC.guiInfo = (GUITestUtility.GUIInfo)
```

```
➥guiSurveyCls.GUISortedList.GetByIndex(dgAvailableGUIs.CurrentCell.RowNumber);

    TempList = new ArrayList();
    GUITDC.guiInfo.GUIControlName = PopulateGUINameTypeLists(
➥(Control)formUT, GUITDC.guiInfo.GUIHandle, true);
    TempList.Sort();
    GUITDC.ControlNameList = TempList;

    TempList = new ArrayList();
    GUITDC.guiInfo.GUIControlType = PopulateGUINameTypeLists(
➥(Control)formUT, GUITDC.guiInfo.GUIHandle, false);
    TempList.Sort();
    GUITDC.controlTypeList = TempList;

    GUITDC.PopulateGUIInfo();

    //chapter 8
    GUITDC.startupForm = startupForm; //for simple verification
    guiTestVrfy = new GUITestVerification(applicationUT,
➥startupForm, GUITDC.guiInfo.GUIControlName);
    guiTestVrfy.FindMembersToVerify(applicationUT, GUITDC);

    //chapter 7
    if (GUITDC.ShowDialog() == DialogResult.OK)
    {
      GUITDC.guiInfo.GUIMemberType = GetMemberType(GUITDC.guiInfo.GUIControlName);
      GUITestSeqList.GUIList.Add(GUITDC.guiInfo);

      //chapter 8
      GUISequence++;
      guiTestVrfy.BuildVerificationList(GUITDC, GUISequence, ref TypesToVerify);
    }
}
```

The first cluster of the newly added code passes the name of the startup form of the application under test to the GUITDC object. Thus, the specific verification option will always know where to locate a member to verify from the specified application. Then, it initializes the GUITestVerification object, guiTestVrfy, by invoking the overloaded constructor. After the guiTestVrfy object is ready, it simply calls the FindMembersToVerify() method to add all the available members to the CheckedListBox of the GUITDC object. Thus, users can see and pick up the members for verification.

The second cluster of the newly added code continues from the first cluster. Within an if statement waiting for a click of the OK button, the code in bold first increments the GUISequence variable by one for each step of the GUI manipulation, which is similar to how a human tester would behave. Then it collects the selected items and the expected results from the GUITDC object to store the verification information by invoking the BuildVerificationList() method of the guiTestVrfy object.

Another modification is the btnRunTest_Click() event. You can locate this event and add two lines of code:

```
string verifyStore = TestCaseStore.Replace(".xml", "_verify.xml");
GUITestUtility.SerilizeInfo(verifyStore, TypesToVerify);
```

When the Run Test button is clicked, a save file dialog pops up and lets the user assign a name to the file in which to save the testing input data store. After the testing data store is saved, the initialization of a new string variable adds a _veryfy.xml suffix to the data store. The second line invokes the SerializeInfo() method from the GUI test library to save the verification information.

This tool has already separated testing data store from test scripts. At this point, it wants to separate the verification data store from the testing data store. Such a separation will enable the tester to focus on one job at a time and modify the testing data and the verification data with ease. These two data sets are saved as XML documents, behave independently at editing time, and collaborate seamlessly when the test is executing.

The code for the modified btnRunTest_Click() event is in Listing 8.22.

Listing 8.22 **The Modified Code for the *btnRunTest_Click()* Event with the Newly Added Lines in Bold**

```
private void btnRunTest_Click(object sender, System.EventArgs e)
{
    sveDataStore.Title = "Location to save GUI test data";
    sveDataStore.Filter = "XML Files (*.xml)|*.xml|All Files (*.*)|*.*";
    if (sveDataStore.ShowDialog() == DialogResult.OK)
    {
        TestCaseStore = sveDataStore.FileName;
    }
    else
    {
      return;
    }

    GUITestSeqList.AUTPath = applicationUT;
    GUITestSeqList.AUTStartupForm = startupForm;

    GUITestUtility.SerilizeInfo(TestCaseStore, GUITestSeqList);

    //chapter 8
    string verifyStore = TestCaseStore.Replace(".xml", "_verify.xml");
    GUITestUtility.SerilizeInfo(verifyStore, TypesToVerify);


    GUITestScript guiTS = new GUITestScript(TestCaseStore, currDir);
}
```

The last update happens for the event of the Start GUI Test button. You can navigate to the code section of the btnStartGUITest_Click() event. Then add the following two lines of code at the beginning of this event body:

```
TypesToVerify = new TypeVerificationSerializable();
GUISequence = 0; //added for chapter 8
```

These two lines of code are for starting a new testing session when the AutomatedGUITest tool is run. The first refreshes the TypesToVerify object, and the second one resets the GUISequence step counter to 0.

The final update is for the btnStartGUITest_Click() event, shown in Listing 8.23 with the new lines in bold.

Listing 8.23   **The Modified Code for the *btnStartGUITest_Click()* Event with the Newly Added Lines in Bold**

```
private void btnStartGUITest_Click(object sender, System.EventArgs e)
{
  TypesToVerify = new TypeVerificationSerializable();
  GUISequence = 0;//added for chapter 8

  GUITestSeqList = new GUITestUtility.GUIInfoSerializable();

  opnAUT.Title = "Specify an Application Under Test";
  opnAUT.Filter = "GUI Applications(
➥*.EXE; *.DLL)|*.EXE;*.DLL|All files (*.*)|*.*";
  if (opnAUT.ShowDialog() == DialogResult.OK)
  {
    applicationUT = opnAUT.FileName;
    GetTypeToTestFromAUT();
    try
    {
      formUT = (Form)GUITestUtility.StartAUT(applicationUT, startupForm);
    }
    catch (InvalidCastException ex)
    {
      MessageBox.Show(ex.Message);
    }
  }
  else
  {
    return;
  }
}
```

After you insert the new lines of code into these three events, the updating of the Automated-GUITest class is completed. You can build the project and correct the errors. Since only a few lines of code were changed in this chapter, the full code listing is not reposted here for the

AutomatedGUITest class. You can refer to the full listing by downloading the sample source code from this book's web pages at www.sybex.com.

The next section will guide you through entering the last batch of code into the GUITestScript class.

Updating the *GUITestScript* Class

Since verifications happen after the execution of the test, the modification of the AutomateGUITest class and the GUITestDataCollector class prepares basic information for verification. The final verification occurs within the GUITestScript class. In this section, you will add code to obtain a fully functional test script and complete the project with many of the advanced testing functions.

The modifications in this chapter often involve the addition of some new fields. The GUITestScript class also needs new fields, as shown here:

```
private TypeVerification testResult;
private int MaxLen = 10000;
```

The first field is in the place of the private ArrayList resultList as coded in Chapter 7. Thus, after the addition of the new field, you can remove the declaration of the resultList object. The second field initializes an integer variable as the definition of the maximum length of a string this test script can extract from a GUI control. The value 10,000 is an arbitrary number that represents the maximum length of a text string the tool can hold.

Next, you need to modify the four Timer tick events. The tmrAutomatedTest_Tick() event code after the modification should be similar to the code in Listing 8.24 (the newly added lines are in bold and an obsolete line is commented and in bold).

Listing 8.24   **The Modified Code for the *tmrAutomatedTest_Tick()* Event**

```
private void tmrAutomatedTest_Tick(object sender, System.EventArgs e)
{
  StartAUT();

  tmrAutomatedTest.Enabled = false;
  tmrRunScript.Enabled = true;

  //resultList = new ArrayList();
  testResult = new TypeVerification();
  testResult.AUTPath = seqGUIUT.AUTPath;
  testResult.TypeName = seqGUIUT.AUTStartupForm;
}
```

The new lines of code simply initialize the newly added field, a `testResult` object of the `TypeVerification` class. The initialization includes tagging this object with the pathname of the AUT and its startup form. It will be used to store the verification results step-by-step during the test execution and make the result persistent.

The `tmrStopScript_Tick()` event is another easy update, as shown in Listing 8.25 (the newly added line is in bold and the obsolete line is commented and in bold).

Listing 8.25   **One-Line Addition to the *tmrStopScript_Tick()* Event**

```
private void tmrStopScript_Tick(object sender, System.EventArgs e)
{
  AddTestVerification();

  //GUITestUtility.GUIInfo guiUnit =
➥(GUITestUtility.GUIInfo)seqGUIUT.GUIList[clickNum - 1];
  //Control ctrlTested;
  //ctrlTested = (Control)GUITestUtility.VerifyField(AUT, "txtSelected");
  //resultList.Add(ctrlTested.Text);

  if (clickNum >= seqGUIUT.GUIList.Count)
  {
    tmrRunScript.Enabled = false;
    tmrStopScript.Enabled = false;
    tmrVerifyTest.Enabled = true;
    AUT.Dispose();

  }
  else
  {
    tmrRunScript.Enabled = true;
    tmrStopScript.Enabled = false;
  }

}
```

The addition simply invokes an `AddTestVerification()` helper method. The code for this method is in Listing 8.26.

Listing 8.26   **A new *AddTestVerification()* Helper Method to Update the *GUITestScript* Class**

```
private void AddTestVerification()
{
  if (AUT == null)
    return;

  string VerifyDataStore = guiTestDataStore.Replace(".xml", "_verify.xml");

  TypeVerificationSerializable verifyTypes = new TypeVerificationSerializable();
```

```
    object obj = (object)verifyTypes;
    GUITestUtility.DeSerializeInfo(VerifyDataStore, ref obj);
    verifyTypes = (TypeVerificationSerializable)obj;

    TypeVerification oneType =
➡ (TypeVerification)verifyTypes.TypeList[clickNum - 1];
    object resulted = null;

    foreach (TestExpectation fieldName in oneType.MemberList)
    {
      TestExpectation tested = fieldName;
      try
      {
        resulted =  GUITestUtility.VerifyField(AUT, tested.VerifyingMember);
        tested.isField = true;


      }
      catch(Exception ex4)
      {
        resulted =  GUITestUtility.VerifyProperty(AUT, tested.VerifyingMember);
        tested.isProperty = true;
      }
      VerifyAlphanumericResult(ref tested, resulted);
      VerifyClipboard(ref tested, resulted);

    }
}
```

The first line of the AddTestVerification() helper method obtains the filename of the verification data store by recognizing the suffix, _verify.xml. This suffix was introduced to the testing tool when you modified the AutomatedGUITest class.

Then it initializes a new TypeVerificationSerializable instance, verifyTypes. The boxing method converts the verifyTypes instance into an object instance in order to call the DeSerializeInfo() method from the GUI test library. After the deserialization reconstructs the object, an unboxing method converts this object back to a verifyTypes instance that includes all the members in need of verification.

This tool regards each GUI action as a step in the execution of the GUI test. The step is counted by the clickNum variable. Using the value of the clickNum, each step of the test initializes a TypeVerification object, oneType, by retrieving the content from the verifyTypes.TypeList. Then a foreach loop is used to find how many members are specified for verification. Since this helper method needs to assign verification results into the oneType.MemberList, it assigns each fieldName object to a new TestExpectation object, tested. A try-catch clause is used to get the current status of the member in need of verification. Because the member is either a field or a property, the try statement invokes the VerifyField() from the GUI test library. If the try invocation fails, the catch statement invokes the VerifyProperty() method to complete the task. The try-catch clause easily tells the verification whether the current member is a field or a property.

Finally, it invokes the other two helper methods, VerifyAlphanumericResult() and VerifyClipboard(), to determine whether this verification matches the expected alphanumeric and the clipboard results at this step of the test.

The code for the VerifyAlphanumericResult() method is in Listing 8.27.

Listing 8.27   Code for the *VerifyAlphanumericResult()* Method

```
private void VerifyAlphanumericResult(ref TestExpectation fieldName,
➡object resulted)
{
  try
  {
    Control cntl = (Control)resulted;
    fieldName.isGUI = true;
    fieldName.ActualResult = cntl.Text;
    StringBuilder sb = new StringBuilder(MaxLen);
    GUITestActions.GetWindowText((int)cntl.Handle, sb, MaxLen);
    fieldName.ScreenSnapshot = sb.ToString();
  }
  catch (InvalidCastException ex1)
  {
    fieldName.ActualResult = resulted.ToString()+ "\n" + ex1.Message;
  }
  catch (Exception ex2)
  {
    fieldName.ActualResult =
➡fieldName.VerifyingMember + " is not found as a member.\n" + ex2.Message;
  }

  fieldName.AssertAlphanumericTest(fieldName.ExpectAlphaNumericEqual);
  testResult.MemberList.Add(fieldName);
}
```

This method takes two parameters. The first parameter holds the verification information and the second holds the object of field or a property. Then it uses a compound try-catch clause. A majority of the verification activities occur inside the try statement. If the member currently being verified is a GUI component, it retrieves the values of the GUI properties and assigns it to the related fields of the first parameter, which is passed by reference. The catch statements are used to report the reason when one line of the code in the try statement encounters an error. After the invocation of the try-catch clause, the AssertAlphanumericTest() method of the GUITestVerification class is called and determines whether to let this test step pass or fail. The verification result is added to the testResult.MemberList and will be serialized at the end of the test.

Listing 8.28 shows the code for the `VerifyClipboard()` method.

Listing 8.28   Code for the *VerifyClipboard()* Method

```
private void VerifyClipboard(ref TestExpectation fieldName, object resulted)
{
  fieldName.ActualClpbrdObj =
➥Clipboard.GetDataObject().GetData(DataFormats.Text);
  try
  {
    Control cntl = (Control)resulted;
    fieldName.ExpectedClpbrdObj = cntl.Text;
    fieldName.AssertClipboardTest(fieldName.ExpectClipBrdEqual);

  }
  catch (Exception ex)
  {
    Console.WriteLine(ex.Message);
  }
}
```

The `VerifyClipboard()` method takes the same set of parameters as the `VerifyAlphanumeric-Result()` method does. It goes directly to the clipboard and gets the actual clipboard content. Then, inside the `try` statement it retrieves the value of the Text property of the current member if this is a GUI control. The last line of code inside the `try` statement invokes the `AssertClipboardTest()` method and determines whether the clipboard content is consistent with the expected result of the GUI control.

We discussed a few types of verification at the beginning of this chapter. However, this test script class implements only two examples to verify the alphanumeric results and clipboard results. In order to meet the specific testing requirements of your organization, this kind of implementation leaves enough room for you to enhance the testing capabilities of the tool in the future. In Chapters 9 and 11, for example, you will learn how to add methods to verify the test of Label, CheckBox and RadionButton controls.

Now, you have only one more modification for the `tmrVerifyTest_Tick()` event. Listing 8.29 displays the new code of this event in bold with the obsolete code commented and in bold.

Listing 8.29   Code for the *tmrVerifyTest_Tick()* Event

```
private void tmrVerifyTest_Tick(object sender, System.EventArgs e)
{
  tmrVerifyTest.Enabled = false;

  string resultDataStore = guiTestDataStore.Replace(".xml", "_result.xml");
  //GUITestUtility.SerilizeInfo(resultDataStore, resultList);
```

```
GUITestUtility.SerilizeInfo(resultDataStore, testResult);

//Display the test result
try
{
  XmlTreeViewer.Form1 xmlTV = new XmlTreeViewer.Form1();
  xmlTV.OpenXmlDoc(resultDataStore);
  xmlTV.Show();
}
catch{}

//Test completed
this.Dispose();
}
```

When the `tmrVerifyTest_Tick()` event is ready to be triggered, the test and verification activities have already completed. But the verification result is still not saved and can not be viewed. Without confirmation from a human tester reading the saved test results, the verification can never be completed. The `tmrVerifyTest_Tick()` event invokes methods to save the results and displays the results.

The test results are saved to a file with a name with a `_result.xml` suffix, which was introduced since Chapter 7. The invocation of the `SerilizeInfo()` of the GUI test library saves the test and verification results immediately at the end of the test. In fact, this invocation occurred in Chapter 7 for the obsolete `resultList` object. Then the rest of the new code initializes an XML document viewer object, `XmlTreeViewer.Form1`, to open the saved XML result document. At this point, the tester can scrutinize the results and reports the defects found by the testing tool. The developers can view this report to fix the defects.

The coding task for the `GUITestScript` class is completed. If you build the project, you will observe compiling errors. The reason is that there is no implementation of an `XmlTreeViewer.Form1` class in the AutomatedGUITest project. In the next section, you will enable this class with a few configuration steps by reusing the XmlTreeViewer project developed in Chapter 5.

NOTE   For a full code listing of the updated `GUITestScript` class, you can download the source code from www.sybex.com.

Adding the XML Document Viewer for Result Presentation

Up to now, there is no implementation of any XML document viewer for the AutomatedGUITest tool. But, you may remember that you developed an XmlTreeViewer project earlier in the book. The XmlTreeViewer project displays XML documents, but editing the XML document is not allowed, which fits the purpose of displaying test results perfectly. You don't need to add any code to the XmlTreeViewer project to reuse it. You can follow these steps to incorporate it into the AutomatedGUITest project and perform some configuration steps:

1. Copy the XmlTreeViewer project folder with all the files from `C:\GUISourceCode\Chapter05\` to the `C:\GUISourceCode\Chapter08\` folder. This enables you to organize all the needed project files in the same folder for the AutomatedGUITest project.

2. When the AutomatedGUITest is still open, choose File ➢ Add Project ➢ Existing Project from the main window of the IDE.

3. When the Add Existing Project dialog box appears, navigate to the `C:\GUISourceCode\Chapter08\XmlTreeViewer` folder and select the `XmlTreeViewer.csproj` project. Click the Open button to finish the addition.

4. In the Solution Explorer of the IDE, select the XmlTreeViewer project and right-click on it. A pop-up menu appears.

5. Choose Properties from the pop-up menu. The XmlTreeViewer Property Pages dialog box appears.

6. In the right pane of the dialog box, use your mouse to locate the Output Type field under the Application category. If the Application category is collapsed, showing a + sign, click the + sign to expand it. The XmlTreeViewer project was originally created as a Windows Application as shown in the Output Type field. In order for it to be used by the AutomatedGUITest tool as a class library, on the right edge of the Output Type field, click the arrow (similar to the arrow on a combo box) and select Class Library. Finally, click the OK button to close the Property Pages dialog box.

7. From the main window of the IDE, choose Project ➢ Add Reference to bring the Add Reference dialog box up.

8. Activate the Projects tab by clicking it. At this point, you have added two projects, GUITestLibrary and XmlTreeViewer, into the AutomatedGUITest solution. The GUITestLibrary project has already been referenced in Chapter 7. Select the XmlTreeViewer project and click the OK button to add the reference and close the dialog box.

Now, you can build and run the AutomatedGUITest tool by pressing F5 and start to feed it with an application in need of testing. If compiling errors are observed, you can correct the errors by comparing your code with source code downloadable from `www.sybex.com`. After the AutomatedGUITest project is successfully built, you can go on to the next section, which will demonstrate the new capabilities of the updated GUI testing tool by testing the C# API Text Viewer again.

Conducting a Fully Automated GUI Test

After you press F5 in the Microsoft Visual Studio .NET IDE, the AutomatedGUITest tool is successfully built and runs on your desktop. The use of this tool has been illustrated in the previous chapters. The steps of testing the C# API Text Viewer in this section will be similar to those in Chapter 7:

1. Click the Start GUI Test button. An open file dialog box appears. From this dialog box, navigate to the C:\GUISourceCode\Chapter03\CSharpAPITextViewer\bin\Debug folder, select the CSharpAPITextViewer.exe file, and click the Open button. The Types under Test form shows up with names of the classes implemented for the CSharpAPITextViewer project. One of them is the Form1 class. Select it and click the OK button.

2. The C# API Text Viewer starts on the desktop. If it covers the AutomatedGUITest application, you can rearrange the applications on your screen and make the AutomatedGUITest tool visible. But make sure there is only one copy of the C# API Text Viewer running on your system.

3. Click the GUI Survey button on the AutomatedGUITest tool. The tool minimizes itself to expose the application under test. It takes a few seconds for the tool to complete the survey and reappear on the screen. The survey results are shown in the DataGrid control of the GUI interface. Now you can double-click the gray or blue area on the left edge or on the top to specify the selected GUI component for an invocation by the GUITesctScript class.

4. Your first GUI action is to manipulate the ListBox. As explained, the value of the GUI text for this ListBox is empty in the first column. You recognize it by reading its class name, WindowsForms10.LISTBOX.app3, in the third column to locate the row index. Double-click beside the row on the left edge. The GUI Test Data Collector form appears on the screen with the GUI controls populated with possible GUI testing and verification information (Figure 8.2).

5. At this point, you can decide which verification method to use for this testing step. For the purpose of simplicity and setting up a testing example, this test will use the specific verification method. First, make sure the Specific radio button is not checked. In the CheckedList-Box control at the lower-left, check the box beside CSharpAPITextViewer.Form1. Then click the vertical scroll bar downward to locate the txtSelected member and check the box beside it. Now select the Specific radio button. You may see that the selected txtSelected member is entered into the rich text box in the left. The GUI Test Data Collector at this point looks like Figure 8.2. Click the OK button.

6. After the GUI Test Data Collector closes, you are ready to specify the second GUI invocation. From the DataGrid of the Automated GUI Test form, locate the Add button control. Double-click on the left edge of the Add button. The GUI Test Data Collector appears again. All the radio buttons are unchecked. Because the first step specified to verify the txtSelected field, select the Specific radio button again and click the OK button.

FIGURE 8.2
The GUI testing and
verification data shown
on the GUI Test Data
Collector

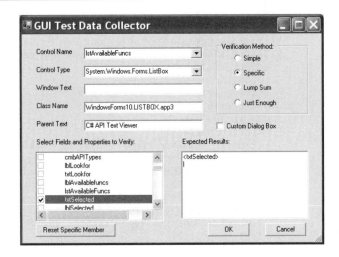

7. Repeat step 6 four more times by selecting the Copy, RichTextBox, Remove, and Clear controls from the DataGrid. You have specified a total of six steps for this testing case.

8. Next, you need to terminate the C# API Text Viewer. When you click the Run Test button to execute the test, the test script will start up another copy of the application under test, and two copies of the application running on the same system will confuse the tool.

9. Click the Run Test button from the AutomatedGUITest tool. When the save file dialog box appears, type in a filename with an XML extension, such as `C:\Temp \TestC#APITextViewer.xml`. Then click the Save button. A copy of the verification data is saved as `C:\Temp\TestC#APITextViewer_verify.xml` at the same time (Listing 8.30). The designated testing starts and the C# API Text Viewer shows up again. The GUI actions of the mouse clicking occur in sequence, and the application closes by itself after the automatic testing and verification.

Listing 8.30   Members in Need of Verifiation Saved with the _C:\Temp_
_\TestC#APITextViewer_verify.xml_ in Step 9

```
<?xml version="1.0" encoding="utf-8"?>
<TypeVerificationSerializable xmlns:xsd="http://www.w3.org/2001/XMLSchema"
➥xmlns:xsi="http://www.w3.org/2001/XMLSchema-instance">
  <AUTPath>C:\GUISourceCode\Chapter03\CSharpAPITextViewer\
➥bin\Debug\CSharpAPITextViewer.exe</AUTPath>
  <AUTStartupForm>CSharpAPITextViewer.Form1</AUTStartupForm>
  <TypeVerificationSerializable>
    <FormUnderTest>
      <TypeName>CSharpAPITextViewer.Form1</TypeName>
      <GUIEvent>lstAvailableFuncs</GUIEvent>
```

```xml
<TestEvents>
  <TestAndVerify>
    <EventMember>lstAvailableFuncs</EventMember>
    <VerifyingMember>txtSelected</VerifyingMember>
    <GUIActionSequence>1</GUIActionSequence>
    <isGUI>false</isGUI>
    <isField>false</isField>
    <isProperty>false</isProperty>
    <ExpectingResult />
    <ActualResult />
    <ScreenSnapshot />
    <ExpectAlphaNumericEqual>true</ExpectAlphaNumericEqual>
    <AlphanumericPass>true</AlphanumericPass>
    <ExpectClipBrdEqual>true</ExpectClipBrdEqual>
    <ClipboardPass>true</ClipboardPass>
    <FileTestPass>true</FileTestPass>
    <OjectTestPass>true</OjectTestPass>
    <ImageTestPass xsi:type="xsd:boolean">true</ImageTestPass>
  </TestAndVerify>
</TestEvents>
</FormUnderTest>
<FormUnderTest>
  <TypeName>CSharpAPITextViewer.Form1</TypeName>
  <GUIEvent>btnAdd</GUIEvent>
  <TestEvents>
    <TestAndVerify>
      <EventMember>btnAdd</EventMember>
      <VerifyingMember>txtSelected</VerifyingMember>
      <GUIActionSequence>2</GUIActionSequence>
      <isGUI>false</isGUI>
      <isField>false</isField>
      <isProperty>false</isProperty>
      <ExpectingResult />
      <ActualResult />
      <ScreenSnapshot />
      <ExpectAlphaNumericEqual>true</ExpectAlphaNumericEqual>
      <AlphanumericPass>true</AlphanumericPass>
      <ExpectClipBrdEqual>true</ExpectClipBrdEqual>
      <ClipboardPass>true</ClipboardPass>
      <FileTestPass>true</FileTestPass>
      <OjectTestPass>true</OjectTestPass>
      <ImageTestPass xsi:type="xsd:boolean">true</ImageTestPass>
    </TestAndVerify>
  </TestEvents>
</FormUnderTest>
<FormUnderTest>
  <TypeName>CSharpAPITextViewer.Form1</TypeName>
  <GUIEvent>btnCopy</GUIEvent>
  <TestEvents>
    <TestAndVerify>
      <EventMember>btnCopy</EventMember>
      <VerifyingMember>txtSelected</VerifyingMember>
```

```
            <GUIActionSequence>3</GUIActionSequence>
            <isGUI>false</isGUI>
            <isField>false</isField>
            <isProperty>false</isProperty>
            <ExpectingResult />
            <ActualResult />
            <ScreenSnapshot />
            <ExpectAlphaNumericEqual>true</ExpectAlphaNumericEqual>
            <AlphanumericPass>true</AlphanumericPass>
            <ExpectClipBrdEqual>true</ExpectClipBrdEqual>
            <ClipboardPass>true</ClipboardPass>
            <FileTestPass>true</FileTestPass>
            <OjectTestPass>true</OjectTestPass>
            <ImageTestPass xsi:type="xsd:boolean">true</ImageTestPass>
          </TestAndVerify>
        </TestEvents>
    </FormUnderTest>
    <FormUnderTest>
      <TypeName>CSharpAPITextViewer.Form1</TypeName>
      <GUIEvent>txtSelected</GUIEvent>
      <TestEvents>
        <TestAndVerify>
            <EventMember>txtSelected</EventMember>
            <VerifyingMember>txtSelected</VerifyingMember>
            <GUIActionSequence>4</GUIActionSequence>
            <isGUI>false</isGUI>
            <isField>false</isField>
            <isProperty>false</isProperty>
            <ExpectingResult />
            <ActualResult />
            <ScreenSnapshot />
            <ExpectAlphaNumericEqual>true</ExpectAlphaNumericEqual>
            <AlphanumericPass>true</AlphanumericPass>
            <ExpectClipBrdEqual>true</ExpectClipBrdEqual>
            <ClipboardPass>true</ClipboardPass>
            <FileTestPass>true</FileTestPass>
            <OjectTestPass>true</OjectTestPass>
            <ImageTestPass xsi:type="xsd:boolean">true</ImageTestPass>
          </TestAndVerify>
        </TestEvents>
    </FormUnderTest>
    <FormUnderTest>
      <TypeName>CSharpAPITextViewer.Form1</TypeName>
      <GUIEvent>btnRemove</GUIEvent>
      <TestEvents>
        <TestAndVerify>
            <EventMember>btnRemove</EventMember>
            <VerifyingMember>txtSelected</VerifyingMember>
            <GUIActionSequence>5</GUIActionSequence>
            <isGUI>false</isGUI>
            <isField>false</isField>
            <isProperty>false</isProperty>
```

```
            <ExpectingResult />
            <ActualResult />
            <ScreenSnapshot />
            <ExpectAlphaNumericEqual>true</ExpectAlphaNumericEqual>
            <AlphanumericPass>true</AlphanumericPass>
            <ExpectClipBrdEqual>true</ExpectClipBrdEqual>
            <ClipboardPass>true</ClipboardPass>
            <FileTestPass>true</FileTestPass>
            <OjectTestPass>true</OjectTestPass>
            <ImageTestPass xsi:type="xsd:boolean">true</ImageTestPass>
          </TestAndVerify>
        </TestEvents>
      </FormUnderTest>
      <FormUnderTest>
        <TypeName>CSharpAPITextViewer.Form1</TypeName>
        <GUIEvent>btnClear</GUIEvent>
        <TestEvents>
          <TestAndVerify>
            <EventMember>btnClear</EventMember>
            <VerifyingMember>txtSelected</VerifyingMember>
            <GUIActionSequence>6</GUIActionSequence>
            <isGUI>false</isGUI>
            <isField>false</isField>
            <isProperty>false</isProperty>
            <ExpectingResult />
            <ActualResult />
            <ScreenSnapshot />
            <ExpectAlphaNumericEqual>true</ExpectAlphaNumericEqual>
            <AlphanumericPass>true</AlphanumericPass>
            <ExpectClipBrdEqual>true</ExpectClipBrdEqual>
            <ClipboardPass>true</ClipboardPass>
            <FileTestPass>true</FileTestPass>
            <OjectTestPass>true</OjectTestPass>
            <ImageTestPass xsi:type="xsd:boolean">true</ImageTestPass>
          </TestAndVerify>
        </TestEvents>
      </FormUnderTest>
    </TypeVerificationSerializable>
  </TypeVerificationSerializable>
```

10. The XmlTreeViewer appears on the screen with the verification results as shown in Figure 8.3. This document is saved with a name C:\Temp\TestC#APITextViewer_result.xml. You see some nodes highlighted with red characters. If you are testing a project with bugs, you can report the bugs found by this tool and ask the developers to fix them. Thus, a tester has only three XML documents to be concerned about: the testing data, verification data, and result data stores. The test can duplicate and edit the testing data and verification data store at any time. The result data store need not be modified and tells the causes of the software defects.

FIGURE 8.3
The final test report
in the XMLTreeViever
application

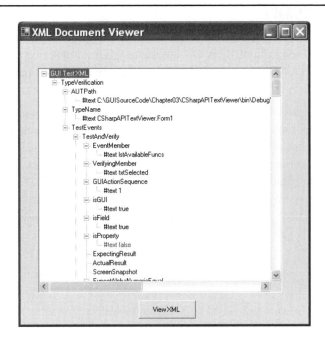

If you scroll the XML tree viewer for this testing case, you'll spot at steps 2 and 3 that the alpha-numeric test reports a false value by matching the text read from the object and the text cap-tured from the screen. This is because the C# API Text Viewer adds escape characters, such as \n, when marshalling the custom functions. When a set of \n escape characters is added to the rich text box, it becomes a set of \r\n escape characters. \r and \n represent carriage return and new line, respectively. However, the clipboard test yields a true value because the texts read from the field object of the application and the clipboard match. There are other false alarms in the report, which need to be clarified by updating the tool in the future.

11. After the bugs are fixed you don't need to repeat the previous steps to recollect the testing and verification data. You simply start this testing tool, click the Rerun Test button, and navigate to the saved testing data store. A regression testing can be completed with the minimum efforts.

12. If you want to modify the testing steps and the verification scope, you can modify the test-ing data store and the verification data store instead of rerunning the testing tool. For this demonstration, the testing data store is the TestC#APITextViewer.xml document and the verification data store is the TestC#APITextViewer_verify.xml document. Remember, adding more testing steps and more verification members into the data stores will increase the efficiency of finding bugs.

Summary

Throughout the course of this book, you have turned a soulless test monkey into an automatic GUI testing tool. This tool has the capabilities of seeing and manipulating the GUI components. GUI testing can be conducted by reusing these capabilities in a desired order with simple to complex verifications.

At this point, the GUI test library has accumulated a few GUI handling methods for command buttons, text boxes, and list boxes. The available software development environments usually have a lot more types of GUI controls than these. Although we will not add code for an exhaustive testing of all the prefabricated GUI controls, in the rest of the book we will implement some typical GUI handling methods, such as those for labels, menus, and check boxes. The testing capability of your tool is not limited to the GUI controls covered next. They are designed to set up examples so that you can meet all of your future testing requirements.

CHAPTER 9

Testing Label and Cosmetic GUI Controls

In Chapters 7 and 8, we implemented the AutomatedGUITest tool with a test script, a GUI testing data collector, and methods for GUI test verification. The data is collected into XML documents. GUI testing input data and verification data are stored separately. Such a separation makes it easy for the testers to create more testing cases or scenarios later by copying, pasting, and editing. This data drives the execution of the test script. Thus, the AutomatedGUITest tool forms the backbone for a high degree of GUI test automation. Based on this backbone, other testing functions can be added when there are new testing tasks.

Modern software development platforms are rich in prefabricated GUI controls. The GUI controls are in the front end of an application. They don't perform any business tasks themselves but provide an interface for end users. Some controls undertake different tasks by collaborating with components in the business and data layers of the architecture. In general, GUI components have the following responsibilities:

- Dispatching modules of other layers to accomplish business functions

- Performing decorative or cosmetic, and nonbusiness functions

- Providing feedback and intuitive instructions for end users to complete jobs

- Making applications easy and friendly to end users with respect to usability

So far, the AutomatedGUITest tool has been enabled to test rich text boxes, list boxes, and command buttons, which invoke functions in business and data layers. This chapter uses the Label control as an example and shows how to add code to the tool project for testing GUI controls for cosmetic or nonbusiness functions.

How to Test Label and Other Cosmetic Controls

GUI components need to be labeled so that the end users understand what they are. Some GUI components, such as radio buttons and checkboxes, use the values of their Text properties to label themselves. The others have to be labeled by some cosmetic controls. Among the cosmetic controls, the Label control is the most widely used to label the others, such as text boxes, combo boxes, and list boxes.

Normally, Label controls only put labels onto the other controls and perform no business tasks. When a Label control is tested, the focus is more on its decoration purpose than the other functionality. The decorative effects of a label for another control and the entire application are affected by the values of the following properties:

Size   The Size property has values for two dimensions, width and height. The values of the width and height must be less than the parent control but must be big enough to show the full caption text and not to overlap with other controls. The testers also take into consideration that the size and caption of a Label control may change as the status of the application changes.

Text   The value of the Text property is usually fixed at coding time. It is directly visible as the caption of the Label control. One function of a testing tool will be spell-checking the text.

Font   The Font property usually involves in the style, the size, and the color of the characters. These values require different sizes of a Label control to display the full length of the text.

Color   For a usable and pleasing interface, Label controls have different foreground and background colors.

Location   The Location property affects the usability of most of the GUI controls. For example, the location and the size of GUI controls should be tested to verify that they don't overlap one another. The location of a Label control should also be checked to ensure that the control labels a designated GUI object without ambiguity.

Enabled   The value of the Enabled property could change as the application status changes. Conventionally, a label appears gray when it isn't enabled.

Visible   Some functionality of an application may not be available at certain stages, and a label may not be visible to the end users. However, it will appear when the functionality is available.

There are other GUI controls that perform more decorative tasks for an application than invoking business functions, such as PictureBox, GroupBox, and Panel. These controls can be self-labeled. A Panel control usually contains other GUI components. A GroupBox control also serves as a container for other controls, especially for a group of radio buttons. Thus, only one of the radio buttons can be checked within a GroupBox control.

The values of the properties affecting the appearance of a Label control affect its decorative effects. In general, each control has a `hasChildren` property. The value of the `hasChildren` property of a Label usually is false. But, GroupBox and Panel controls usually have a true value for the `hasChildren` property and will have children. A PictureBox control has an image property, which is usually a picture filename, such as files with extensions of `.bmp`, `.jpg`, and `.ico`.

To test these nonbusiness functional controls, testers first are interested in inspecting their existences. Then they will check the values of the properties affecting their appearance. Eventually, the appearances of these controls affects usability and attracts end users.

Upgrading the AutomatedGUITest Tool

The AutomatedGUITest tool uses one test script to test different applications. To increase the efficiency of finding more bugs, such a tool allows testers to input a lot of testing data and save time by avoiding recording, handwriting, editing, and debugging test scripts. The execution of this test script is driven by different GUI controls in an application. Figure 9.1 shows the data-driven GUI testing process, which involves five components of the Automated-GUITest tool and four major interactions:

1. After the GUI testing inputs are loaded, the test script starts the application under test.

2. The test script looks for a GUI handling method from the GUI test library and invokes the business functions dynamically.

3. Upon the invocation of the business functions, the test script determines the status of each of the members in need of verification.

4. Finally, the test script saves and displays the test results.

Among the involved five components, the GUI testing and verification information needs to be collected at the time when an application is specified for testing. Updating this tool for testing more GUI controls requires adding code to the GUITestVerification, GUITestScript, and GUITestActions classes.

FIGURE 9.1
Dynamic data-driven execution and interactions between the test script and the data stores

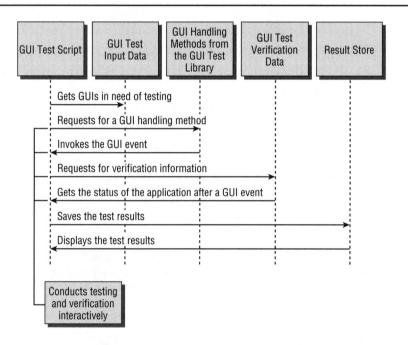

Adding a Method to the *GUITestVerification* Class

By the end of Chapter 8, the development of the AutomatedGUITest tool included three projects, all of which reused the code from Chapters 4, 5 and 7, respectively. We have made a new directory at the beginning of each chapter for these projects. Now you need to make a `C:\GUISourceCode\Chapter09\` folder, and copy the folders of the three projects, Automated-GUITest, GUITestLibrary, and XmlTreeViewer, from `C:\GUISourceCode\Chapter08\` to `C:\GUISourceCode\Chapter09\`.

Start the Microsoft Visual Studio .NET IDE and open the AutomatedGUITest solution from the new folder. Locate the `GUITestVerification` class. You coded this class with an `ActualCosmeticStr` and an `ExpectedCosmeticStr` field in Chapter 8. These two fields are prepared to test the nonbusiness functional controls. In this chapter, only one method, `AssertCosmeticGUITest()`, is needed for the `GUITestVerification` class to assert that the values of these two fields match for testing a specified GUI control. The code of the `AssertCosmeticGUITest()` method is in Listing 9.1.

Listing 9.1   **Adding Code for the *AssertCosmeticGUITest()* Method to the *GUITestVerification* Class**

```
public void AssertCosmeticGUITest()
{
  if (ActualCosmeticStr.Equals(ExpectedCosmeticStr))
  {
    CosmeticTestPass = true;
  }else
  {
    CosmeticTestPass = false;
  }
}
```

The `AssertCosmeticGUITest()` method simply checks the actual and the expected values of the properties of a GUI component, which affects the appearance of the application. After coding, choose Build ➤ Build Solution to build the project. Thus, the `GUITestVerification` class is updated.

Expanding the Testing Capability of the *GUITestScript* Class

Software development IDEs have been manufactured with various kinds of GUI controls. The nonbusiness functional controls are responsible for decorating the application and providing feedback and instruction to the users. Testers are more interested in testing their appearance than their business functions. For the development of the AutomatedGUITest tool, testing the Label and other cosmetic GUI controls shares a `VerifyCosmeticGUIs()` method. This method is coded in Listing 9.2.

Listing 9.2   **Code for the *VerifyCosmeticGUIs()* Method of the *GUITestScript* Class**

```
private void VerifyCosmeticGUIs(ref TestExpectation fieldName, object resulted)
{
  try
  {
    Control cntl = (Control)resulted;
    fieldName.ActualCosmeticStr =
"Caption: " + cntl.Text + "\n Size: " + cntl.Size +
"\n Child GUIs: " + cntl.Controls.Count + "\n Font: " + cntl.Font +
"\n Location: " + cntl.Location + "\n Back Color: " + cntl.BackColor +
"\n Fore Color: " + cntl.ForeColor + "\n Enabled: " + cntl.Enabled +
"\n Visible: " + cntl.Visible + "\n hasChildren: " + cntl.HasChildren;
    PictureBox pb;

    fieldName. AssertCosmeticGUITest();
  }
  catch (Exception ex)
  {
    fieldName.ActualCosmeticStr = ex.Message;
  }
}
```

The verification method for the cosmetic controls requires the same kinds of parameters the business functional controls require. Within a `try-catch` clause, this method first converts the GUI object under test into a Control object by unboxing. Then it assigns the values of the cosmetic properties of this GUI control to the `ActualCosmeticStr` field. The availability of the GUI properties in Listing 9.2 is based on the Microsoft Visual Studio .NET IDE 2003. If your testing projects involves GUI controls from other development environments, the names of the properties may need to be adjusted.

Finally, it invokes the `AssertCosmeticGUITest()` to check whether the actual cosmetic values meet the expected values for verification. If any error occurs within the `try` statement, the `catch` statement will assign the error message to the `ActualCosmeticStr` field to report the reason for the error.

After you add this code segment into the `GUITestScript` class, the `VerifyCosmeticGUIs()` method can be reused to verify any cosmetic GUI testing. Listings 9.3 and 9.4 use a similar code pattern to verify the Label and GroupBox controls, respectively.

Listing 9.3　　　**Code for the *VerifyLabel()* Method**

```
private void VerifyLabel(ref TestExpectation fieldName, object resulted)
{
  try
  {
    Label lbl = (Label)resulted;
    VerifyCosmeticGUIs(ref fieldName, lbl);
  }
  catch(Exception ex)
  {
    Console.WriteLine(ex.Message);
  }
}
```

To verify a Label control, the VerifyLabel() method tries to convert the GUI object under test into a Label object. If the conversion succeeds, the VerifyCosmeticGUIs() will be invoked and the verification results will be collected. Otherwise, the GUI object under test is not a Label and the execution proceeds to the next step.

Listing 9.4 is the code to verify a GroupBox control.

Listing 9.4　　　**Code for the *VerifyGroupBox()* Method**

```
private void VerifyGroupBox(ref TestExpectation fieldName, object resulted)
{
  try
  {
    GroupBox grp = (GroupBox)resulted;
    VerifyCosmeticGUIs(ref fieldName, grp);
  }
  catch(Exception ex)
  {
    Console.WriteLine(ex.Message);
  }
}
```

Inspecting the code in Listings 9.3 and 9.4, you find that the VerifyGroupBox() method also uses a try statement to ensure that the GUI object under test is GroupBox object. The rest of the code in these two methods is identical.

The last step is to add code to the AddTestVerification() method of the GUITestScript class to call the VerifyLabel() and VerifyGroupBox() methods. After the addition of the new code, the code for the AddTestVerification() method becomes similar to Listing 9.5 (some of the existing code is omitted and the new code is in bold).

```
private void AddTestVerification()
{
  ...

  foreach (TestExpectation fieldName in oneType.MemberList)
  {
    ...
    try
    {
      ...
    }
    catch(Exception ex4)
    {
      ...
    }

    VerifyAlphanumericResult(ref tested, resulted);
    VerifyClipboard(ref tested, resulted);

    //chapter 9
    VerifyLabel(ref tested, resulted);
    VerifyGroupBox(ref tested, resulted);
  }
}
```

At this point, you should have added three methods and updated the AddTestVerification() method for the GUITestScript class. You can now choose Build ➢ Build Solution to compile the new code. If there are compiling errors, you can inspect and correct the errors by comparing your code with the preceding code listings.

In this chapter, I coded the verification methods for the Label and GroupBox controls for example purposes. You can add more methods for testing other cosmetic GUI components using the same coding pattern.

Updating the *GUITestActions* class

In the previous chapters, you developed two classes for the GUI test library. The GUITestUtility contains methods to check the application status resulting from the business function invocations. The methods in the GUITestActions class directly trigger the GUI events from the presentation layer of the application. A GUI control is usually triggered by turning the mouse wheel, clicking or double-clicking a mouse button or hovering the pointer over the control. However, a cosmetic GUI control usually doesn't need to be triggered as a business functional GUI control does. In order for the automated testing tool to bring the cosmetic control under test, the mouse pointer needs to hover over the GUI object. To conduct such a mouse movement, the GUITest-Actions class in the GUITestLibrary project needs to be updated with a HandleCosmeticGUIs() method. The code of the HandleCosmeticGUIs() method is in Listing 9.6. This method simply moves the mouse pointer to the center of the GUI control under verification so testers can visualize the testing steps of the execution.

Listing 9.6   **Code for the *HandleCosmeticGUIs()* Method for the *GUITestActions* Class of the GUITestLibrary Project**

```
public static void HandleCosmeticGUIs(ref int hwnd, ref string winText,
➥ref string clsName, ref string pText)
{

  int r = FindGUILike(ref hwnd, 0, ref winText, ref clsName, ref pText);

  CenterMouseOn(hwnd);
}
```

After you add the code segment of Listing 9.5 to the GUITestActions class, you can press F5 to build and run the AutomatedGUITest tool. But in order for the tool to know the cosmetic GUI handling method, you need to add the new GUI handling method to the GUITestActionLib.xml document, which is currently saved in the C:\GUISourceCode\Chapter09\AutomatedGUITest\bin\Debug folder based on the discussion in this book. You can use any text editor (such as Notepad, for example) for this modification. The modified GUITestActionLib.xml document is shown in Listing 9.7 with the new lines in bold.

Listing 9.7   **The Modified *GUITestActionLib.xml* Document with the New GUI Handling Methods in Bold**

```
<GUIActions>
 <System.Windows.Forms.Label>HandleCosmeticGUIs</System.Windows.Forms.Label>
  <System.Windows.Forms.GroupBox>HandleCosmeticGUIs
➥</System.Windows.Forms.GroupBox>
  <System.Windows.Forms.ListBox>HandleListBox</System.Windows.Forms.ListBox>
  <System.Windows.Forms.RichTextBox>HandleTextBox
➥</System.Windows.Forms.RichTextBox>
  <System.Windows.Forms.TextBox>HandleTextBox
➥</System.Windows.Forms.TextBox>
 <System.Windows.Forms.Button>HandleCommandButton</System.Windows.Forms.Button>
  <Field>VerifyField</Field>
  <Property>VerifyProperty</Property>
  <Synchronization>SynchronizeWindow</Synchronization>
</GUIActions>
```

Now, the testing capabilities of the AutomatedGUITest project are expanded to test Label and GroupBox controls. The next section conducts a demonstration of these testing tasks.

Testing Cosmetic GUI Properties

In order to validate the newly added methods, we use the AutomatedGUITest tool to test the C# API Text Viewer at the end of each chapter. Now, press F5 to build and run the tool. Complete the following sections with the new GUI testing data collection and execution.

Collecting Testing Data

While the AutomatedGUITest tool is running, proceed to the following steps:

1. Click the Start GUI Test button.

2. When the file dialog box appears, navigate to the `C:\GUISourceCode\Chapter03\CSharp-APITextViewer\bin\Debug` folder and select `CSharpAPITextViewer.exe`.

3. After you click the Open button, the form with all the available classes of the C# API Text Viewer appears. Among them, the `CSharpAPITextViewer.Form1` is the startup class. Select the check box beside this class and click the OK button.

4. The C# API Text Viewer application is running. Make sure it is visible on the screen and only one copy of it is running. Then click the GUI Survey button on the AutomatedGUI-Test application. You can see that the AutomatedGUITest user interface becomes minimized and the mouse pointer traverses all over the GUI controls inside the C# API Text Viewer. After the entire area of the application is visited, the AutomatedGUITest tool reappears with the collected GUI information of the application under test, including GUI handles, window text, class names, and parent window text.

5. From the available GUIs, double-click on the left edge beside the Label control with the caption text *API Type:*. (This section focuses on testing the cosmetic GUI controls; only the Label and GroupBox controls will be specified for testing.)

6. When the GUI Test Data Collector appears, select the Simple radio button under Verification Method. Then click OK.

7. Repeat steps 5 and 6 for the Label controls and a GroupBox control with caption text *Type the first few letters of the function name you look for:*, *Available functions:*, *Selected functions:*, and *Scope*, respectively.

8. Close the C# API Text Viewer application.

9. From the AutomatedGUITest user interface, click the Run Test button. A save file dialog box appears. Type in a filename such as `C:\Temp\TestCosmeticGUIs.xml` and click the

Save button. The GUI testing data is saved and the test execution is completed within one second or two.

10. The verification results are displayed by the XML Document Viewer. When you specified GUI controls for testing, you also specified the simple verification method. But no expected cosmetic values were defined. The test execution fails the verification at this point. In order to make the test more effective, you can edit the data store and re-execute the test.

Editing and Rerunning the Data Store

The first execution against the data store completed a test without the tester entering any expected results. But it yielded the actual caption text for each of the GUI controls tested. Testers can check these results against the specifications and use them as the expected baselines for regression testing.

As it has been mentioned, any text editor or XML utility can be used to edit the saved XML data store. In this section, the Microsoft Visual Studio .NET IDE is used to open and edit the C:\Temp\TestCosmeticGUIs_verify.xml document, which is saved separately from the C:\Temp\ TestCosmeticGUIs.xml file specified in step 9 of the preceding section.

You can open an XML document from an active Microsoft Visual Studio .NET IDE session by choosing File ➢ Open. From the open file dialog box, navigate to the C:\Temp\TestCosmetic-GUIs_verify.xml document. When the file is open, you can select to view the raw XML document or a tabulated data format from the lower-bottom portion of the IDE. The default view is the raw XML text, and you can locate the five <FormUnderTest> child nodes. The first child node is an event to test the Label control with a name of lblAPITypes. You can now open the C:\Temp\ TestCosmeticGUIs_result.xml document and locate the respective test event and copy the text value of the <ActualCosmeticStr> node. Then insert into the TestCosmeticGUIs_verify.xml document an <ExpectedCosmeticStr> child element to the <TestAndVerify> node and paste the content as the text value of the new child. After the modification, the first <FormUnderTest> child node looks similar to Listing 9.8 with the added node in bold.

Listing 9.8   **Value of the *<ExpectedCosmeticStr>* Element Inserted into the**
                    C:\ *Temp \TestCosmeticGUIs_verify.xml*

```
...
<FormUnderTest>
      <TypeName>CSharpAPITextViewer.Form1</TypeName>
      <GUIEvent>lblAPITypes</GUIEvent>
      <TestEvents>
        <TestAndVerify>
          <EventMember>lblAPITypes</EventMember>
          <VerifyingMember>lblAPITypes</VerifyingMember>
          <GUIActionSequence>1</GUIActionSequence>
```

```
          <isGUI>false</isGUI>
          <isField>false</isField>
          <isProperty>false</isProperty>
          <ExpectingResult />
          <ActualResult />
          <ScreenSnapshot />
          <ExpectAlphaNumericEqual>true</ExpectAlphaNumericEqual>
          <AlphanumericPass>true</AlphanumericPass>
          <ExpectClipBrdEqual>true</ExpectClipBrdEqual>
          <ClipboardPass>true</ClipboardPass>
          <FileTestPass>true</FileTestPass>
          <OjectTestPass>true</OjectTestPass>
          <ExpectedCosmeticStr xsi:type="xsd:string">Caption: API Type:
  Size: {Width=100, Height=23}
  Child GUIs: 0
  Font: [Font: Name=Microsoft Sans Serif, Size=8.25,
 ➥Units=3, GdiCharSet=0, GdiVerticalFont=False]
  Location: {X=16,Y=8}
  Back Color: Color [Control]
  Fore Color: Color [ControlText]
  Enabled: True
  Visible: True
  hasChildren: False</ExpectedCosmeticStr>
        </TestAndVerify>
      </TestEvents>
    </FormUnderTest>
  ...
```

After the first test verification event is modified, you can use this approach for the other four test events. After the modifications are saved, you can re-execute the test by clicking the Rerun Test button from the AutomatedGUITest user interface. When the open file dialog box appears, navigate to the C:\Temp\TestCosmeticGUIs.xml document and click the Open button. After the execution is accomplished, inspect the results.

NOTE   For your convenience, a copy of the TestCosmeticGUIs.xml and the TestCosmeticGUIs_ verify.xml documents are included with the sample code downloadable in the ..\Chapter09\TestCosmeticGUIs folder.

Among the improved testing features, the AutomatedGUITest tool saves testers time from recording, writing, editing, and debugging test scripts. It is reported that test scripts need to be re-executed against multiple copies of data stores in order to find the most bugs. Using this tool, testers are able to devote their time to creating many effective testing data cases.

Summary

Although the cosmetic controls don't invoke business functions, they affect the appearance and the usability of an application. It happens often that some software projects become successful because their appearance is more attractive to end users than the appearance of others. Thus, it is important to have the nonbusiness functional GUI components tested.

In the past, we have been pleased by the GUI handling methods of the commercial testing tools. This chapter showed how to add more testing methods and demonstrated how to test the Label and GroupBox controls. The rest of the book will use a few more examples to add methods handling other specific tasks and make the AutomatedGUITest tool flexible.

Testing a TextBox Control with Input from a Keyboard

A keyboard contains alphanumeric keys and special keys such as navigational and function keys. Some GUI components can be triggered by a set of keystrokes. A TextBox control is designed to accept alphanumeric keys and function as a word processor. Once you know how to operate a keyboard programmatically, you can manipulate the content of a TextBox control within a test script.

This chapter shows you how to enable the AutomatedGUITest tool for GUI testing using a keyboard.

The *SendKeys* Class of the .NET Framework

Software developers have used *dynamic data exchange (DDE)* to enable communication of data between different programs. DDE is a mechanism supported by the Microsoft Windows operating system that enables two applications to exchange data continuously and automatically (for example, it can be used to automate the manual copying and pasting processes).

When two applications start a DDE to exchange data, the process is similar to a conversation between two people. One of the applications initiates the conversation and the other responds. Although you can implement a testing tool using the DDE mechanism to exchange data between a test script and an application under test, some applications don't support DDE. However, there are new technologies that have created data communication between applications. In order to make the AutomatedGUITest tool useful for testing different applications, this section introduces a way to exchange data between the testing tool and the application under test by direct keystrokes.

There is a `SendKeys` class in the `System.Windows.Forms` namespace defined by Microsoft developers. This class has methods to send keystrokes to an active application. Compared with the DDE mechanism, these methods are more similar to a person operating the keyboard.

When the `Sendkyes` class is used, each key on the keyboard is represented by a code consisting of one or more characters. For example, to specify a single alphanumeric keystroke, you can use the character itself in the program. If you want to enter a letter *A* into a text editor, you can pass a character *A* into a `SendKey` method. Coding a string of letters for the `SendKeys` class, you can enter a sentence into a text editor. However, the special keys are coded differently. The next sections will show you step-by-step how to accomplish such tasks.

Code for Special Keys Using the *SendKeys* Class

Alphanumeric characters are visible and easy to code in a program. But, the plus sign (+), caret (^), percent sign (%), tilde (~), and parentheses have special meanings to the methods of the `SendKeys` class. To specify one of these characters, you enclose it within a pair of braces (curly brackets, {}). For example, to specify the plus sign, you use {+}. On the other hand, the square brackets, [ ], have no special meaning to the SendKeys class, but you must enclose them in a pair of curly brackets, such as {[}. You can also enter a curly bracket { by enclosing it between a pair of curly brackets.

There are some keys on the keyboard that are not visible after they are pressed. These characters need to be specifically coded when using the SendKeys class. Table 10.1 lists these special keys and their corresponding code.

TABLE 10.1 The Code for Special Keys When Used with the *SendKeys* Class

Key	Code in SendKeys
Shift	+
Ctrl	^
Alt	%
Backspace	{BACKSPACE}, {BS}, or {BKSP}
Break	{BREAK}
Caps Lock	{CAPSLOCK}
Del or Delete	{DEL} or {DELETE}
Down arrow	{DOWN}
End	{END}
Enter	{ENTER} or ~
Esc	{ESC}
Help	{HELP}
Home	{HOME}
INS or INSERT	{INSERT} or {INS}
Left arrow	{LEFT}
Num Lock	{NUMLOCK}
Page Down	{PGDN}
Page Up	{PGUP}
Print Screen	{PRTSC} (reserved for future use)
Right arrow	{RIGHT}
Scroll Lock	{SCROLLLOCK}
Tab	{TAB}
Up arrow	{UP}
F1	{F1}
F2	{F2}
F3	{F3}
F4	{F4}
F5	{F5}

Continued on next page

TABLE 10.1 CONTINUED The Code for Special Keys When Used with the *SendKeys* Class

Key	Code in SendKeys
F6	{F6}
F7	{F7}
F8	{F8}
F9	{F9}
F10	{F10}
F11	{F11}
F12	{F12}
F13	{F13}
F14	{F14}
F15	{F15}
F16	{F16}
Keypad Add	{ADD}
Keypad Subtract	{SUBTRACT}
Keypad Multiply	{MULTIPLY}
Keypad Divide	{DIVIDE}

For example, to cause the Enter key to be pressed, you can code {ENTER} as the parameter in a method of the SendKeys class. A code of ^C in the SendKeys class represents the key combination of holding down the Ctrl key and pressing the C key. You can also ask the SendKeys class to press a key repeatedly by appending a space and a number inside the curly brackets. For example, the code {DOWN 168} will cause the down arrow key to be pressed 168 times continuously.

Methods of the *SendKeys* Class

Compared to the other data types defined in the .NET Framework, the SendKeys class of the System.Windows.Forms namespace is relatively light. It inherits four methods, including Equals(), GetHashCode(), GetType(), and ToString(), and implements three public static methods of its own. In programs, often only the three public static methods are used:

Flush()   Invoke this method to process all the Windows messages currently in the message queue.

Send()   Use this method to send keystrokes to an active application.

SendWait()   Call this method to send keystrokes to an active application and wait for the processing of the keystrokes to be completed.

Because all these are static methods, the SendKeys class doesn't need to be instantiated. In a program, you can immediately continue with the flow of your code to send a keystroke by using the Send() or the SendWait() method. Now, an example will be the best way to demonstrate how to use these methods programmatically.

An Example to Connect to Your FTP Server

The Send() and SendWait() methods of the SendKeys class activate keystrokes for the active application. Developers can use these methods to build demo or tutorial programs that show audiences what happens when a sequence of keystrokes is pressed.

In this section, you will develop a C# console application to simulate a user logging onto an FTP server and uploading a C:\Temp\readme.txt file. You can complete the following steps for this example:

1. Start your Microsoft Visual Studio .NET IDE.

2. Choose File ➤ New ➤ Project. The New Project dialog box appears.

3. From the left pane, select Visual C# Project.

4. From the right pane, select Console Application.

5. In the Name field, type **SimulateFTPConn**. In the Location field, type **C:\GUISourceCode\Chapter10**.

6. Click the OK button to bring up the default Class1.cs code editor. The filename Class1.cs is given by the Microsoft Visual Studio .NET IDE.

7. Choose Project ➤ Add Reference in the main window of the Microsoft Visual Studio .NET IDE. The Add Reference dialog box pops up.

8. In the .NET tab, navigate to and select the System.Windows.Forms.dll. Click the OK button to return to the code editor. Now, you are ready to code the SimulateFTPConn program.

As usual, this program needs three using directives at the beginning of the code file. They are coded as follows:

```
using System;
using System.Diagnostics;
using System.Windows.Forms;
```

The first using System statement is added by the Microsoft Visual Studio .NET IDE when the SimulateFTPConn project is created. The System.Diagnostics namespace has a Process class that can start external applications. In this example, we want it to start a DOS command prompt window. Finally, the System.Windows.Forms namespace provides the SendKeys class.

The rest of the coding task is for the entry point method, the Main() method. The Main() method has been declared by the Microsoft Visual Studio .NET IDE. The code needs to initialize a Process object to start a DOS command prompt and invoke a series of the SendWait() method of the SendKeys class. Listing 10.1 shows the complete code for the Class1.cs code file of the SimulateFTPConn project.

Listing 10.1   **The Code for the SimulateFTPConn Project to Transfer a File to Your FTP Server**

```
using System;
using System.Diagnostics;
using System.Windows.Forms;

namespace SimulateFTPConn
{

  class Class1
  {

    [STAThread]
    static void Main(string[] args)
    {

      //Start a DOS command prompt
      Process p = new Process();
      p.StartInfo.FileName = "cmd";
      p.Start();

      //Enter DOS command
      SendKeys.Flush();
      SendKeys.SendWait("CD C:\\Temp{ENTER}");
      SendKeys.SendWait("dir{ENTER}");

      //Simulate a FTP connection
      SendKeys.SendWait("ftp ftp.your_ftp_site.com{ENTER}");
      SendKeys.SendWait("your_user_id{ENTER}");
      SendKeys.SendWait("your_password{ENTER}");
      SendKeys.SendWait("cd your_folder{ENTER}");
      SendKeys.SendWait("put readme.txt{ENTER}");
      SendKeys.SendWait("bye{ENTER}");

      //p.Kill();
    }
  }
}
```

After the needed using directives are added to Listing 10.1, the namespace and class name are declared by the Microsoft Visual Studio .NET IDE. The coding all happens in the Main() method. It first initializes a Process object to start a DOS command prompt window. After the command prompt window is open, the static SendKeys.Flush() method is executed to clear the

Windows message queue. Then a series of `SendKeys.SendWait()` methods is invoked to issue different line commands on the command prompt window in sequence. I assume you have an FTP account with a provider. You need to replace the corresponding values in the quotation marks with your real FTP address, , user ID, and password. You also need an active connection to the Internet via a modem or a digital subscriber line (DSL). Finally, make sure you have a `readme.txt` file in the `C:\Temp` folder of your system. This file will be uploaded to your FTP server. The last line, `p.Kill()`, is commented out. Thus, the DOS prompt window will remain on the screen after the program finishes running. If you remove the `//` to activate this line of code, the program will close the command prompt window after running the SimulateFTP-Conn project.

> **NOTE**   The discussion in this book doesn't require a modem or a DSL connection. You don't have to successfully execute this program to understand the syntax of the `SendWait()` method. The sole purpose of this example is to show you how to code when using the `SendKeys` class.

After you add the code and press F5 to build and run the SimulateFTPConn project from the Microsoft Visual Studio .NET IDE, the `reademe.txt` file is uploaded. The purpose of the SimulateFTPConn project is to simulate a user logging on to an FTP server using the `SendKeys` class. Such a situation happens when you test a line command application. In the rest of this chapter, you will enable the AutomatedGUITest tool to manipulate the content of TextBox controls.

Updating the Tool for Testing TextBox Controls

In the .NET Framework, a text box can be a `System.Windows.Forms.RichTextBox` or a `System.Windows.Forms.TextBox` object. These are versatile controls that are used to get input from users and display text. Because they allow users to modify their content, testers are interested in testing them in an application to see whether they treat the text as expected.

A TextBox control represents a basic text editor you can use for creating any plain-text documents. A RichTextBox control can be used to create and edit text files that contain formatting or graphics. The user can change the foreground color, background color, and the font of the text.

In the previous chapters, you developed a `HandleTextBox()` method for the `GUITestLibrary.GUITestActions` class. The `HandleTextBox()` method simply gets a TextBox control in focus and performs a mouse click. Because the tool has not been implemented with any mechanism to operate the keyboard, the testing tool is not capable of testing the text content of a text box. To update the AutomatedGUITest tool so it can test the text properties, you will add one more public string field into the `GUITestLibrary.GUITestUtility.GUIInfo` structure originally developed in Chapter 6 and then make corresponding additions to the other classes.

Adding a Field to the *GUIInfo* Structure

You have implemented the tool to conduct a GUI survey and collect GUI information with regard to a GUI object's name, class name, window text, parent text, and corresponding .NET control type. Note that the class name and the .NET control type are supposed to point at the same piece of information about a GUI object. However, within the AutomatedGUITest tool, the class name is found by a Win32 API function, GetClassName(), and the .NET control type is named by the .NET developers and located by using methods of the System.Reflection namespace. The literal text of the two are different as recorded by the GUI survey result of the AutomatedGUITest tool.

Such GUI information found by the AutomatedGUITest tool is not allowed to be altered by users and is currently mapped as a serializable GUIInfo structure inside the GUITestLibrary .GUITestUtility class. In order to inform the test script of the content modification for a text box, you need to add a string field in the GUIInfo structure.

You created a C:\GUISourceCode\Chapter10 folder when implementing the example to connect to an FTP server. You can copy the GUITestLibrary, the XmlTreeViewer, and the AutomatedGUITest projects from the C:\GUISourceCode\Chapter09 folder to the C:\GUISourceCode\Chapter10 folder and open the AutomatedGUITest project from the new folder. Then, from the Solution Explorer of the Microsoft Visual Studio .NET IDE, locate the GUITestLibrary project and double-click the GUITestUtility.cs code file. Near the end of the GUITestUtility.cs code file, you can add a line of code as a public field into the GUIInfo structure as shown here:

```
public string TextEntry;
```

Listing 10.2 shows the code of the GUIInfo structure after a new line addition in bold.

Listing 10.2   **The Code for the Updated *GUITestLibrary.GUITestUtility.GUIInfo* Structure with the New Line in Bold**

```
[Serializable]public struct GUIInfo
{
  public int GUIHandle;
  public string GUIText;
  public string GUIClassName;
  public string GUIParentText;
  public string GUIControlName;
  public string GUIControlType;
  public string GUIMemberType;
  public string TextEntry; //chapter 10

}
```

The new field, TextEntry, will be used to hold text for modifying a TextBox or a RichText-Box control. In fact, it can be used to modify other controls if modification is allowed. For example, if you want to press a Tab key on one control in order to navigate to the next GUI control, the content of the TextEntry field should be {TAB} (as you saw in Table 10.1). Or, if you want to test the key combination of Ctrl+C as a shortcut to the Copy menu of a word processor, the value of the TextEntry field is ^C.

Modifying the Control Handling Methods in the *GUITestActions* Class

As we have discussed, the GUITestLibrary.GUITestActions class has been used to hold different GUI control handling methods. All the control handling methods have the same parameter signatures so the test script will invoke them by one late binding method. The late binding method can be programmed to use the same set of parameters as an array object, although some of these methods may not require all the parameters.

Currently, each of these GUI control handling methods passes four parameters to represent values of the GUI handler, the window text, the GUI class name, and the parent text, which are the identifiers to enable the testing tool and the test script to locate a GUI component to test. The values of these GUI properties were decided at development time and, except for the window text, are not to be modified by users. They are also represented by the corresponding fields of the GUITestLibrary.GUITestUtility.GUIInfo class.

After the new addition of the TextEntry field to the GUIInfo structure, each of the control handling methods needs a parameter to pass the TextEntry value. Thus, the control handling methods in the GUITestLibrary.GUITestActions class should all have five parameters:

```
(ref int hwnd, ref string winText, ref string clsName, ref string pText, string
textEntry)
```

In this example, the new parameter is in bold at the end. The affected declarations of the control handling methods include the following:

```
public static void HandleListBox(ref int hwnd, ref string winText,
➥ref string clsName, ref string pText, string textEntry)
public static void HandleTextBox(ref int hwnd, ref string winText,
➥ref string clsName, ref string pText, string textEntry)
public static void HandleCommandButton(ref int hwnd, ref string winText,
➥ref string clsName, ref string pText, string textEntry)
public static void HandleCosmeticGUIs(ref int hwnd, ref string winText,
➥ref string clsName, ref string pText, string textEntry)
```

At this point, you can double-click the GUITestActions.cs filename from the Solution Explorer. Then locate the affected lines of code and add the new parameter signatures. After an extra parameter is added to each method, the code must not be modified. Such parameter name additions are extra for the previously coded GUI handling methods but needed to match the GUI handling methods to be coded in this section. When new control handling methods are needed in the future, the new methods need to include the five parameters.

Now, you need to implement a HandleTextBoxWithTextEntry() method. The code for this method is in Listing 10.3.

Listing 10.3 **The Code for the *HandleTextBoxWithTextEntry()* Method in the Updated *GUITestLibrary.GUITestActions* Class with the New Parameter Signatures**

```
//Chapter 10
public static void HandleTextBoxWithTextEntry(ref int hwnd,
➡ref string winText, ref string clsName, ref string pText, string textEntry)
{
  SendKeys.Flush();
  SendKeys.SendWait(textEntry);

  return;
}
```

You may have noticed that the HandleTextBoxWithTextEntry() method consumes only the value of the last parameter. The other four parameters are extra and are required as a standard to invoke the HandleTextBoxWithTextEntry() method by late binding in the test scripts. This method simply invokes the SendKeys.Flush() and SendKeys.SendWait() methods. You might want to use the SendKeys.Send() method if the purpose of sending the keystrokes is to alter the content of the text property of a GUI object.

The HandleTextBoxWithTextEntry() method doesn't move the mouse to activate a designated GUI object. When this method is called in the test script, it needs to be called in conjunction to one of the other GUI handling methods so the SendKeys class can send keystrokes to the designated GUI component. Now you can compile the project to see if the syntax is correctly coded.

Revising the Late Binding Method in the *AutomatedGUITest.GUITestScript* Class

In the preceding sections, you updated the two classes of the GUI test library for new testing tasks. Now you need to make corresponding changes within the other related code files of the AutomatedGUITest project. The first change is to make the late binding invocation of the control handling methods in the GUITestScript class consistent with the modification of the parameter signatures in the GUI test library.

From the Solution Explorer of the Microsoft Visual Studio .NET IDE, double-click the GUITestScript.cs and bring the GUITestScript code editor to the front of the screen. Within the code editor, locate the RunsScript() method definition. Change the length of the paramArr variable initialization from 4 to 5:

```
//object[] paramArr = new object[4];
object[] paramArr = new object[5];
```

Then add a line of code to assign a value to the last item of the paramArr variable:

```
paramArr[4] = guiUnit.TextEntry;
```

After the modification, the code for the RunsScript() method looks like Listing 10.4.

Listing 10.4 **The Updated code for the *RunsScript()* Method in the *AutomatedGUITest* .*GUITestScript* Class with the New and Obsolete Code in Bold**

```
private void RunsScript()
{
  guiTestActionLib = Path.Combine(progDir, "GUITestActionLib.xml");

  GUITestUtility.GUIInfo guiUnit =
➥(GUITestUtility.GUIInfo)seqGUIUT.GUIList[clickNum];

  string ctrlAction =
➥GUITestUtility.GetAGUIAction(guiTestActionLib, guiUnit.GUIControlType);

  Control ctrlTested =
➥(Control)GUITestUtility.VerifyField(AUT, guiUnit.GUIControlName);
  StringBuilder sb = new StringBuilder(10000);
  GUITestActions.GetWindowText((int)ctrlTested.Handle, sb, 10000);


  //object[] paramArr = new object[4];
  object[] paramArr = new object[5]; //chapter 10
  paramArr[0] = 0;
  paramArr[1] = sb.ToString();
  paramArr[2] = guiUnit.GUIClassName;
  paramArr[3] = guiUnit.GUIParentText;
  paramArr[4] = guiUnit.TextEntry; //chapter 10

  Type guiTestLibType = new GUITestActions().GetType();
  object obj = Activator.CreateInstance(guiTestLibType);
  MethodInfo mi = guiTestLibType.GetMethod(ctrlAction);

  try
  {
    mi.Invoke(obj, paramArr);
  }
  catch (Exception ex)
  {
    MessageBox.Show(ex.Message);
```

```
    }

    if (clickNum < seqGUIUT.GUIList.Count)
    {
      clickNum++;
      tmrRunScript.Enabled = false;
      tmrStopScript.Enabled = true;
    }
  }
}
```

The modification of the method is slight. If you build a new solution of the Automated-GUITest project by pressing Ctrl+Shift+B, the project can be compiled successfully.

Adding a TextBox to the GUITestDataCollector Form

The values of the fields of the GUIInfo structure are initialized from reading the text boxes of the GUITestDataCollector form at the time the testing data is collected. In order to specify a value for the newly added TextEntry field of the GUIInfo structure, you can add a Label and a TextBox control to the existing GUITestDataCollector form in the AutomatedGUITest project by double-clicking the code file from the Solution Explorer.

When the form appears, you can follow these steps to finish the updating:

1. Assuming you have followed along in the previous chapters to develop the Automated-GUITest project, you need to expand the GUITestDataCollector form in order to add more GUI controls to it. Select the GUITestDataCollector form and when the form is in focus and selected, choosing View ➢ Properties Window from the main menu. The properties of the GUITestDataCollector form appear (usually at the left side pane). Locate the Size property inside the Properties window and reset a pair of new values of the Size property to **552** and **448**, representing its width and height, respectively.

2. Select the seven GUI controls near the bottom of the form at the same time by holding down the Shift key and clicking them one by one. Then move the selected GUI controls downwards by pressing the down arrow key a few times to make space below the existing Label and TextBox controls. Drag and drop a Label and a TextBox from the tool box to the form. Assign a name such as lblTextEntry to the Label control and txtTextEntry to the TextBox control. Keep other property values intact. The new appearance of the GUITest-DataCollector form should look similar to Figure 10.1.

3. Double-click the OK button on the modified form to bring the GUITestDataCollector.cs code editor to the front. The cursor is currently at the first line of the btnOK_Click() event definition. Before the closing curly bracket, add a line of code to assign the text value of the added TextBox control to the newly coded TextEntry field of the GUIInfo structure as follows:

    ```
    guiInfo.TextEntry = txtTextEntry.Text;
    ```

FIGURE 10.1
The updated GUITest-
DataCollector form
with a new field for
entering text to a GUI
object under test

Listing 10.5 shows the modified code for the btnOK_Click() event with the new addition
in bold.

Listing 10.5   **The Modified Code for the *btnOK_Click()* Event in the
AutomatedGUITest.GUITestDataCollector Class with the New Line in Bold**

```
private void btnOK_Click(object sender, System.EventArgs e)
{
  guiInfo.GUIControlName = cmbControlName.Text;
  guiInfo.GUIControlType = cmbControlType.Text;
  guiInfo.GUIText = txtWindowText.Text;
  guiInfo.GUIClassName = txtClassName.Text;
  guiInfo.GUIParentText = txtParentText.Text;
  guiInfo.TextEntry = txtTextEntry.Text;//chapter 10
}
```

4. With the GUITestDataCollector.cs code editor still active, locate the PopulateGUIInfo()
method (immediately above the btnOK_Click() event definition if your code is identical to
the code in the book). Add a new line of code immediately before its closing curly bracket:

```
txtTextEntry.Text = guiInfo.TextEntry;
```

This line of code is exactly the reverse of the code added for the btnOK_Click() event in
step 3. Step 3 sets a value to the TextEntry field and step 4 sets a value to the text box added
in step 2. The modified code for the PopulateGUIInfo() method is in Listing 10.6.

Listing 10.6   **The Modified *PopulateGUIInfo()* Method in the *AutomatedGUITest* .*GUITestDataCollector* Class with the New Line in Bold**

```
public void PopulateGUIInfo()
{
  cmbControlName.DataSource = ControlNameList;
  cmbControlType.DataSource = controlTypeList;

  cmbControlName.Text = guiInfo.GUIControlName;
  cmbControlType.Text = guiInfo.GUIControlType;
  txtWindowText.Text = guiInfo.GUIText.ToString();
  txtClassName.Text = guiInfo.GUIClassName.ToString();
  txtParentText.Text = guiInfo.GUIParentText.ToString();
  txtTextEntry.Text = guiInfo.TextEntry;//chapter 10
}
```

You have prepared the helper classes for the tool to automatically manipulate text values of a GUI control.

The remaining job is to add a method into the `AutomatedGUITest.cs` file to save and pass the desired text for the GUI control manipulation.

Adding a Step to Send Keystrokes to a GUI Component

To automatically manipulate a GUI component, the AutomatedGUITest tool must hold the GUI object and prevent other programs from accessing it. For example, when a TextBox control is under test by the AutomatedGUITest tool, the testing actions occur within a tick cycle of a Timer control. Within the tick cycle, the testing tool first invokes the `HandleTextBox()` method to move the mouse to the TextBox control and click to activate it. When the TextBox control is activated, the testing tool holds the TextBox control before it can be altered. Then the `HandleTextBoxWithTextEntry()` method must be invoked within the next tick cycle of the Timer control. To enable this sequence in the `GUITestScript` class, you need to add an `AddTextEntryStep()` method into the `AutomatedGUITest.cs` code file.

From the Solution Explorer of the Microsoft Visual Studio .NET IDE, right-click the `AutomatedGUITest.cs` filename. When the pop-up menu appears, select View Code to bring the code editor to the screen. Locate a proper spot near the closing curly bracket within the frmMain class and code the `AddTextEntryStep()` method as shown in Listing 10.7.

Listing 10.7   **The Code for the *AddTextEntryStep()* Method in the *AutomatedGUITest* .frmMain Class**

```
//Chapter 10
private void AddTextEntryStep(GUITestUtility.GUIInfo guiInfo,
➡GUITestDataCollector GUITDC, ref int GUISeq,
➡TypeVerificationSerializable TypesToVerify)
{
  if (guiInfo.TextEntry.Length <= 0 )
  {
    return;
  }

  GUITestUtility.GUIInfo tempGuiInfo = guiInfo;

  tempGuiInfo.GUIControlType = "HandleTextBoxWithTextEntry";
  GUITestSeqList.GUIList.Add(tempGuiInfo);

  //GUISequence++;
  guiTestVrfy.BuildVerificationList(GUITDC, GUISequence, ref TypesToVerify);
}
```

The AddTextEntryStep() is implemented as a helper method for the dgAvailableGUIs_ DoubleClick() event. After GUI information is collected from the GUITestDataCollector form, this method first inspects the value of the TextEntry field in the GUIInfo object. If the tester has specified that the GUI component under test needs to be manipulated with text, the method continues to the rest of the code. Otherwise, the execution exits this method by the naked return statement within the if statement.

You may recall that the GUITestUtility.GUIInfo was implemented as a structure in Chapter 6. The AddTextEntryStep() method passes a parameter as a GUITestUtility .GUIInfo object, guiInfo. It can be assigned using an equivalent operator to initialize a new GUIInfo object, tempGuiInfo. Because a structure object is value based with regard to memory allocation, modification of the tempGuiInfo object will not affect the original guiInfo object. Therefore, the value of the GUIControlType field in the tempGuiInfo object field is set to HandleTextBoxWithTextEntry. This setup is to instruct the test script to look for the HandleTextBoxWithTextEntry() method when a GUI component under test needs manipulation with key strokes. After the tempGuiInfo object is ready, it is added to the GUITest-SeqList.GUIList object. The last line of the code simply adds the defined text alteration actions into the same verification step and concludes the method.

After the `AddTextEntryStep()` method is coded, you can locate the `dgAvailableGUIs_DoubleClick()` event and add a line of code near the end of this event definition. This line of code looks like the following line:

```
AddTextEntryStep(GUITDC.guiInfo, GUITDC, ref GUISequence, TypesToVerify);
```

Listing 10.8 shows the modified `dgAvailableGUIs_DoubleClick()` event with the new line of code in bold.

Listing 10.8   The Slightly Modified *dgAvailableGUIs_DoubleClick()* Event in the *AutomatedGUITest.frmMain* Class with the New Code in Bold

```
private void dgAvailableGUIs_DoubleClick(object sender, System.EventArgs e)
{

  GUITDC = new GUITestDataCollector();

  GUITDC.guiInfo = (GUITestUtility.GUIInfo)
➥guiSurveyCls.GUISortedList.GetByIndex(dgAvailableGUIs.CurrentCell.RowNumber);

  TempList = new ArrayList();
  GUITDC.guiInfo.GUIControlName = PopulateGUINameTypeLists(
➥(Control)formUT, GUITDC.guiInfo.GUIHandle, true);
  TempList.Sort();
  GUITDC.ControlNameList = TempList;

  TempList = new ArrayList();
  GUITDC.guiInfo.GUIControlType = PopulateGUINameTypeLists(
➥(Control)formUT, GUITDC.guiInfo.GUIHandle, false);
  TempList.Sort();
  GUITDC.controlTypeList = TempList;

  GUITDC.PopulateGUIInfo();

  //chapter 8
  GUITDC.startupForm = startupForm; //for simple verification
  guiTestVrfy = new GUITestVerification(applicationUT, startupForm,
➥GUITDC.guiInfo.GUIControlName);
  guiTestVrfy.FindMembersToVerify(applicationUT, GUITDC);

  //chapter 7
  if (GUITDC.ShowDialog() == DialogResult.OK)
  {
    GUITDC.guiInfo.GUIMemberType = GetMemberType(GUITDC.guiInfo.GUIControlName);
    GUITestSeqList.GUIList.Add(GUITDC.guiInfo);

    //chapter 8
    GUISequence++;
    guiTestVrfy.BuildVerificationList(GUITDC, GUISequence, ref TypesToVerify);
```

```
    //chapter 10
    AddTextEntryStep(GUITDC.guiInfo, GUITDC, ref GUISequence, TypesToVerify);
  }
}
```

At this point, you have completed the code for manipulating the content of a text box. The new code can also be used to trigger keystrokes for other GUI controls. You can press F5 when the Microsoft Visual Studio .NET IDE is still active to build and run the AutomatedGUITest tool. If there are compiling errors, inspect your code by comparing it with the modified code listed in this chapter.

Finally, you can add the HandleTextBoxWithTextEntry() method into the GUITestAction-Lib.xml document. Thus, the GUI test script can find the HandleTextBoxWithTextEntry() method when it is needed. To do this, open the GUITestActionLib.xml document from the C:\GUISourceCode\Chapter10\AutomatedGUITest\bin\Debug folder with a text editor (e.g., Notepad). Then add an XML node as follows:

```
<HandleTextBoxWithTextEntry>
➥HandleTextBoxWithTextEntry</HandleTextBoxWithTextEntry>
```

After the addition, the GUITestActionLib.xml document has the content shown in Listing 10.9.

Listing 10.9   **The *GUITestActionLib.xml* Document with the Node for the New Handling Method in Bold**

```
<GUIActions>
  <HandleTextBoxWithTextEntry>
➥HandleTextBoxWithTextEntry</HandleTextBoxWithTextEntry>
  <System.Windows.Forms.Label>HandleCosmeticGUIs</System.Windows.Forms.Label>
  <System.Windows.Forms.GroupBox>
➥HandleCosmeticGUIs</System.Windows.Forms.GroupBox>
  <System.Windows.Forms.ListBox>HandleListBox</System.Windows.Forms.ListBox>
  <System.Windows.Forms.RichTextBox>
➥HandleTextBox</System.Windows.Forms.RichTextBox>
  <System.Windows.Forms.TextBox>HandleTextBox</System.Windows.Forms.TextBox>
  <System.Windows.Forms.Button>HandleCommandButton</System.Windows.Forms.Button>
  <Field>VerifyField</Field>
  <Property>VerifyProperty</Property>
  <Synchronization>SynchronizeWindow</Synchronization>
</GUIActions>
```

Now, you have completely updated the AutomatedGUITest tool and are ready to test the enhanced capabilities.

Testing the C# API Text Viewer with the Updated Capabilities

When you developed the C# API Text Viewer, you implemented a method to let users type in a name of a function, constant, or data type in a TextBox control, txtLookfor, and highlight the respective item in the ListBox control. Thus, users don't have to navigate the long list in the ListBox for a particular item. Now, let's use the AutomatedGUITest to test whether this function works for the C# API Text Viewer.

This testing case will simulate a manual tester doing the following:

1. Starting the C# API Text Viewer

2. Activating the txtLookfor text box and entering a function name such as AccessCheckAndAuditAlarm

3. Clicking the Add button

4. Clicking the Copy button

5. Concluding the test

I assume the AutomatedGUITest project is still open in the Microsoft Visual Studio .NET IDE and you have pressed F5 to compile and run the testing tool. Follow these steps to operate the testing tool:

1. Click the Start GUI Test button to bring up an open file dialog box. Navigate to the C:\GUISourceCode\Chapter03\CSharpAPITextViewer\bin\Debug folder, select the CSharpAPITextViewer.exe executable, and click the Open button.

2. The Types Under Test dialog box of the testing tool appears. Select the check box beside the CSharpAPITextViewer.Form1. Click the OK button. The C# API Text Viewer application runs.

3. Make sure the C# API Text Viewer is visible on the screen. Go back to the Automated GUI testing tool (it is okay if the tool is the only application on top of the C# API Text Viewer). Click the GUI Survey button. The testing tool minimizes itself. The GUI survey starts and finishes in a few seconds. The Automated GUI testing tool reappears with the information for all the GUI objects listed in a data grid.

4. In the column holding the class names of the GUI controls inside the data grid, locate the WindowsForms10.EDIT.app3 item. Then double-click on the left edge of this item. The GUITestDataCollector form pops up. The text boxes of the form are populated with the values of the GUI properties of the selected TextBox control. For example, the selected TextBox control in this case is named txtLookfor and its window text is empty. You need to type **AccessCheckAndAuditAlarm** in the Text Entry field. Specify the Simple verification method and click the OK button. Figure 10.2 shows the GUITestDataCollector form at this moment.

FIGURE 10.2
The appearance of the GUITestDataCollector form when collecting data to test a TextBox control

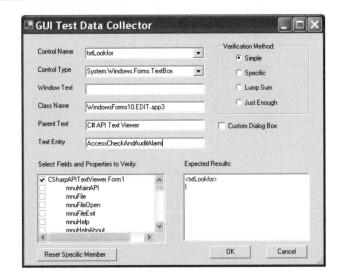

5. Go back to the testing tool interface. Repeat step 4 to locate and add the Add and Copy button clicks into the testing data store, but leave the Text Entry field empty. Click the OK button.

6. Close the C# API Text Viewer application. Click the Run Test button from the testing tool. When the save file dialog box appears, navigate to a folder and type a filename for the data store, such as C:\Temp\TestTextEntry.xml. Click the Save button. The first execution of this testing case will be completed in a few seconds and the test result appears.

From the result, you can see that the C# marshaling code for the Win32 AccessCheckAndAuditAlarm() function is copied into the clipboard. The testing tool performed the testing task as expected and the test passes.

Summary

In the previous chapters, the AutomatedGUITest tool was enabled to generate inputs from mouse actions. This chapter used the SendKeys class of the System.Windows.Forms namespace of the .NET Framework to generate keystrokes for GUI testing. The chapter included an example that showed how to store text input and enable the tool to test a TextBox control. You can also use the AutomatedGUITest tool to test a shortcut for triggering a GUI event with a set of keystrokes.

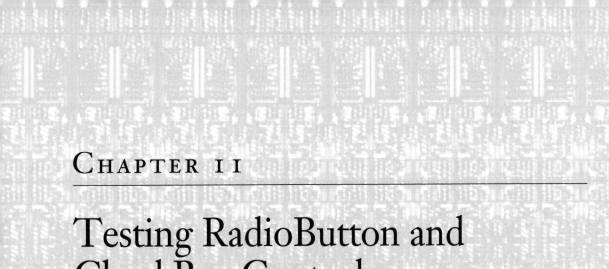

Chapter 11

Testing RadioButton and CheckBox Controls

T he C# API Text Viewer has been implemented with various kinds of GUI controls to help with our Win32 API programming as well as to serve as a sample application to be tested automatically. The previous chapters have demonstrated how to build the AutomatedGUITest tool to test Command Button, ListBox, TextBox, and Label controls. This chapter introduces methods to upgrade the tool for testing RadioButton and CheckBox controls.

Characteristics of RadioButton and CheckBox Controls

When the values of a property are expressed with a Boolean type, the software developer usually places a RadioButton or a CheckBox control on the front-end GUI interface. Users can check or uncheck such a control to change its value between true and false (or 1 and 0). Thus, the RadioButton or CheckBox control of the .NET Framework has a property with a name of Checked. A checked RadioButton object has a solid black dot inside an empty circle, and a checked CheckBox object has a check mark inside a square box. Otherwise the circle or the square is empty. In order to test whether a RadioButton or CheckBox control acts as desired, the value of the Checked property is in need of inspection.

However, the RadioButton and the CheckBox controls are used under different circumstances. With regard to increasing automation of software testing, here I list some differences in the usage of these two controls:

- *When an application needs to provide several options for the users to choose from, the RadioButton controls are used.* RadioButton controls are presented in groups; that is, a group has more than one RadioButton control. No more than one control in a group can be checked. To test a RadioButton control, the tester should be aware of the behaviors of the other RadioButton controls in the same group. A CheckBox control can be presented alone.

- *A group of RadioButton controls are usually contained within a GroupBox control.* An application can have more than one group of RadioButton controls to represent different option categories. The RadioButton controls within the same GroupBox control are related to one another and only one control's Checked property can have a true value. The others must have false values. But when an application has a group of CheckBox controls, an individual CheckBox control behaves independently from the others. More than one or all of the CheckBox controls can be checked.

- *The Checked property of a RadioButton control becomes true whenever the RadioButton control is clicked.* For example, when an unchecked RadioButton control is clicked, the value of its Checked property changes from false to true. But if the RadioButton control is already true and is clicked, the value of its Checked property remains true. However, the Checked property of a CheckBox control changes from true to false or from false to true whenever the control is clicked. A testing tool should be able to read the Checked value before and after a click is performed and assign an expected result for the automated testing.

Based on the discussion in this section, the rest of this chapter will show how to update the AutomatedGUITest tool to test RadioButton and CheckBox controls of an application.

Updating the AutomatedGUITest Project

To complete this chapter, the GUITestActionLib.xml document and three classes, GUITest-Utility, GUITestVerification, and GUITestScrip, are in need of updating. After the updating, the AutomatedGUITest tool will be able to test whether a click turns on/off a CheckBox control and whether only the desired option is selected from a group of RadioButton controls.

Overloading a Method in the *GUITestUtility* Class

The AutomatedGUITest project has implemented methods in the GUITestUtility class to start applications under test, serialize and deserialize testing data and results, and find the appropriate handling method for testing a specified GUI object. It also provides methods to determine whether the member under verification is a field or a property of the application under test. Among them is the VerifyField() method to ensure that the member in need of verification is a field. The VerifyField() method takes an object of the application being tested and the name of the GUI control of interest as parameters.

The first coding task in updating the AutomatedGUITest tool is to overload the VerifyField() method so that it can pass the application object and the handle of the GUI control as parameters. Such a method is necessary when a RadioButton control is under test. The overloaded method will be used to find the GroupBox control as a parent window containing a group of RadioButton controls.

As you have for the previous chapters, make a C:\GUISourceCode\Chapter11 folder and copy the AutomatedGUITest, GUITestLibrary, and XmlTreeViewer project folders from the C:\GUISourceCode\Chapter10 folder to the C:\GUISourceCode\Chapter11 folder.

When a RadioButton or CheckBox control is tested, the mouse action on the control is the same as clicking a command Button control. Thus, this chapter will use the existing HandleCommandButton() method for testing a RadioButton or CheckBox control. Before start the coding tasks, let's add this GUI handling method into the C:\GUISourceCode\ Chapter11\AutomatedGUITest\bin\Debug\GUITestActionLib.xml document as shown in bold in Listing 11.1.

Listing 11.1   The Modified *GUITestActionLib.xml* Document

```
<GUIActions>
   <System.Windows.Forms.CheckBox>HandleCommandButton
➡</System.Windows.Forms.CheckBox>
   <System.Windows.Forms.RadioButton>HandleCommandButton
```

```
➥</System.Windows.Forms.RadioButton>
  <HandleTextBoxWithTextEntry>HandleTextBoxWithTextEntry
➥</HandleTextBoxWithTextEntry>
  <System.Windows.Forms.Label>HandleCosmeticGUIs
➥</System.Windows.Forms.Label>
  <System.Windows.Forms.GroupBox>HandleCosmeticGUIs
➥</System.Windows.Forms.GroupBox>
  <System.Windows.Forms.ListBox>HandleListBox
➥</System.Windows.Forms.ListBox>
  <System.Windows.Forms.RichTextBox>HandleTextBox
➥</System.Windows.Forms.RichTextBox>
  <System.Windows.Forms.TextBox>HandleTextBox
➥</System.Windows.Forms.TextBox>
  <System.Windows.Forms.Button>HandleCommandButton
➥</System.Windows.Forms.Button>
  <Field>VerifyField</Field>
  <Property>VerifyProperty</Property>
  <Synchronization>SynchronizeWindow</Synchronization>
</GUIActions>
```

Then open the AutomatedGUITest project from the new C:\GUISourceCode\Chapter11 folder. When the AutomatedGUITest project is open, the GUITestLibrary and the XmlTreeViewer projects are also open in the Solution Explorer. From the Solution Explorer, navigate to the GUITestLibrary project and the GUITestUtility.cs file. Double-click the GUITestUtility.cs filename. The cursor is now in the code editor for the GUITestUtility class.

Next, start a new VerifyField() method. The code for overloading the method is in Listing 11.2.

Listing 11.2   The Code for the Overloaded *VerifyField()* Method

```
//chapter 11 overload for finding Parent window
public static object VerifyField(object typeUnderTest, int fieldHandle)
{
  System.Windows.Forms.Form frm = (System.Windows.Forms.Form)typeUnderTest;
  string fieldName = "";
  foreach (Control ctrl in frm.Controls)
  {
    if ((int)ctrl.Handle == fieldHandle)
      fieldName = ctrl.Name;
  }

  return VerifyField(typeUnderTest, fieldName);
}
```

As discussed, the new VerifyField() method takes an object of the application under test and the handle of the GUI control of interest as parameters. Since the application is passed as an object, the first line of the code uses an unboxing method to explicitly convert the object to a Form object. A Form object is a parent window to house the other child GUI controls. These child GUI controls are declared as the fields of the application. After a `fieldName` variable is initialized as a string object, a `foreach` loop enumerates the child controls until the handle value of the passed parameter matches the enumerated child GUI control. Then it assigns the name of this GUI control to the `fieldName` variable. After the `foreach` iteration, the name of the GUI control is found and the original `VerifyField()` method can be invoked to return an object of this GUI control.

Now you can build the GUITestLibrary project to make sure the code is correctly added. If there are compiling errors, you can correct them by comparing your code with that in Listing 11.2.

Adding Code to the *TestExpectation* Class

The `TestExpectation` class is included in the `GUITestVerification.cs` file beside the `GUITestVerification` class. You have implemented quite a few public fields for the `TestExpectation` class to hold data of the expected results and actual results for testing different aspects of a GUI control. Since a RadioButton or a CheckBox control has a `Checked` property, you need to add public fields to the `TestExpectation` class as shown in Listing 11.3.

Listing 11.3   **The Public Fields for Testing RadioButton and CheckBox Controls in the** *TestExpectation* **Class**

```
// Chapter 11
// Properties of RadioButton and CheckBox controls
public bool ExpectedCheckVal;
public bool ActualCheckVal;
public bool RadioCheckboxPass;
public string RadioBtnErrMsg;
```

The first and the second Boolean fields get the checked status of the expected and the actual value, respectively. The third Boolean field determines whether the testing passes or fails. If the test fails, the `RadioBtnErrMsg` field reports the cause of the failure.

After preparing these fields, you can code an `AssertRadioButtonCheckBox()` method to read and assign values to these fields. Listing 11.4 shows the code for the `AssertRadioButton-CheckBox()` method.

Listing 11.4   **The Added Code for the** *AssertRadioButtonCheckBox()* **of the** *TestExpectation* **Class**

```
// Chapter 11
public void AssertRadioButtonCheckBox(bool oneRdChecked, string errMsg)
{
  if (!oneRdChecked)
  {
```

```
      RadioCheckboxPass = false;
      RadioBtnErrMsg = errMsg;
      return;
   }
   if (ActualCheckVal.Equals(ExpectedCheckVal))
   {
      RadioCheckboxPass = true;
   }
   else
   {
      RadioCheckboxPass = false;
   }
}
```

The AssertRadioButtonCheckBox() method uses two if statements. The first if statement takes the values of the passed parameters and determines that only one RadioButton control is checked in the group. Otherwise, the test fails and the RadioBtnErrMsg field is assigned.

The second if statement executes when only one of the RadioButton controls in a group has a true Checked value. It compares the ActualCheckVal against the ExpectedCheckVal to determine whether the test passes or fails and then completes the verification.

After you finish typing the code, you can compile the project and correct the compiling errors if there are any. The full code list for the updated TestExpectation class is also included in the downloadable sample code from www.sybex.com.

Enhancing the Testing Scope of the *GUITestScript* Class

The fields and methods in the GUITestUtility and TestExpectation classes are implemented to help the GUITestScript class conduct the testing. In this section, you will add the needed helper methods to the GUITestScript class and enable the AutomatedGUITest to test RadioButton and CheckBox controls. Listing 11.5 shows the code for a GetCheckedButtonInGroup() method to count the number of true Checked values in a group of RadioButton controls.

Listing 11.5 **The Code for the *GetCheckedButtonInGroup()* Method of the GUITestScript Class**

```
private bool GetCheckedButtonInGroup(RadioButton rdBtn, ref string ErrorMsg)
{
   int parentHandle = GUITestActions.GetParent((int)rdBtn.Handle);
   Control parentGrp = (Control)GUITestUtility.VerifyField(AUT, parentHandle);
   foreach (Control ctrl in parentGrp.Controls)
   {
      try
      {
         RadioButton rdCtrl = (RadioButton)ctrl;
```

```
           if (rdCtrl.Name == rdBtn.Name)
           {
             if (!rdBtn.Checked)
             {
               ErrorMsg = rdBtn.Name + " is not checked!";
               return false;
             }
           }
           else
           {
             if (rdCtrl.Checked)
             {
               ErrorMsg = "Other than or beside the " + rdBtn.Name +
                 " is checked, the " + rdCtrl.Name + " is also checked!";
               return false;
             }
           }

         }
       catch{}
     }
   return true;
 }
```

The `GetCheckedButtonInGroup()` method takes two parameters, the RadioButton control under inspection and the `ErrorMsg` string as a reference parameter, which will be reassigned if an error occurs. The first line of the `GetCheckedButtonInGroup()` method calls the `GetParent()` method from the `GUITestActions` class to obtain the handle value of the GroupBox control that hosts the group of the RadioButton controls. Then it calls the overloaded `VerifyField()` method to find the GroupBox control as a Control object. A Control object can be a child of another window or it can have child GUI objects. In the case of testing a RadioButton control, a `foreach` loop enumerates the group of RadioButtons and determines if the clicked RadionButton control has a true `Checked` value or whether any of the not-clicked RadioButton controls have true `Checked` values. If the clicked RadioButton control is the only control that has a true `Checked` value, the method returns a true value to conclude the enumeration.

After the `GetCheckedButtonInGroup()` method is coded, you can code a `VerifyCheckedValue()` helper method, as shown in Listing 11.6.

Listing 11.6   The Code for the *VerifyCheckedValue()* Method

```
private void VerifyCheckedValue(ref TestExpectation fieldName,
➥RadioButton resulted)
{
  try
  {
```

```
      fieldName.ActualCheckVal = resulted.Checked;
      string errMsg = "";
      bool oneIsChecked = GetCheckedButtonInGroup(resulted, ref errMsg);
      fieldName.AssertRadioButtonCheckBox(oneIsChecked, errMsg);
   }
   catch (Exception ex)
   {
      fieldName.RadioBtnErrMsg = ex.Message;
   }
}
```

A TestExpectation object, fieldName, and the actual object of the RadioButton control under verification are passed into the VerifyCheckedValue() method. Within a try-catch clause, the VerifyCheckedValue() method obtains the actual value of the Checked property. Then it invokes the GetCheckedButtonInGroup() in Listing 11.5 and the AssertRadioButtonCheckBox() method of the fieldName object. If the executions in the try clause encounter difficulties, the catch clause assigns an error message to the fieldName.RadioBtnErrMsg field.

Listings 11.5 and 11.6 are the code of the helper methods for RadioButton control testing. Now you need to add another field and two helper methods in the GUITestScript class for testing a CheckBox control. Listing 11.7 is the code for a preChecked field and a DeterminePreCheckedStatus() method in the GUITestScrip class.

Listing 11.7   **Code for Creating a *preChecked* Field and a *DeterminePreCheckedStatus()* Method in the *GUITestScript* Class**

```
//Determine prechecked conditions for assigning expected check value

private bool preChecked;

private bool DeterminePreCheckedStatus(GUITestUtility.GUIInfo guiUnit)
{
   bool isChecked = false;
   if (guiUnit.GUIControlType == "System.Windows.Form.CheckBox")
   {
      CheckBox chckBx =
➥(CheckBox)GUITestUtility.VerifyField(AUT, guiUnit.GUIControlName);
      isChecked = chckBx.Checked;
   }
   return isChecked;
}
```

After the declaration for the preChecked field, the DeterminePreCheckedStatus() method uses an if statement to inspect whether a CheckBox object is already checked or not before the click occurs. The value of the preChecked field will be assigned by calling the DeterminePreCheckedStatus() method in the RunsScript() method of the GUITestScript class.

Corresponding to the `VerifyCheckedValue()` method for testing a RadioButton control coded in Listing 11.6, the code in Listing 11.8 overloads the `VerifyCheckedValue()` method to test a CheckBox control.

Listing 11.8   The Code Overloading the *VerifyCheckedValue()* Method to Test a CheckBox Control

```
private void VerifyCheckedValue(ref TestExpectation fieldName,
➥CheckBox resulted)
{
  try
  {
    fieldName.ActualCheckVal = resulted.Checked;
    fieldName.AssertRadioButtonCheckBox(true, null);
  }
  catch (Exception ex)
  {
    fieldName.RadioBtnErrMsg = ex.Message;
  }
}
```

Instead of taking a RadioButton object as its parameter, the overloaded `VerifyCheckedValue()` method takes a CheckBox object as its parameter. The code within the `try` clause ignores the `GetCheckedButtonInGroup()` for testing a CheckBox control and the rest of the code remains identical to the code for testing a RadioButton control.

Finally, the last helper method we need for updating the `GUITestScript` class is a `VerifyRadioButtonCheckBox()` method, shown in Listing 11.9.

Listing 11.9   The Code for the *VerifyRadioButtonCheckBox()* Helper Method

```
//chapter 11
private void VerifyRadioButtonCheckBox(ref TestExpectation fieldName,
➥object resulted)
{
  try
  {
    try
    {
      RadioButton rdBtn = (RadioButton)resulted;
      fieldName.ExpectedCheckVal = true;
      VerifyCheckedValue(ref fieldName, rdBtn);
    }
    catch
    {
      CheckBox chckBx  = (CheckBox)resulted;
      fieldName.ExpectedCheckVal= preChecked ? false : true;
```

```
      VerifyCheckedValue(ref fieldName, chckBx);
    }
  }
  catch(Exception ex)
  {
    Console.WriteLine(ex.Message);
  }
}
```

The VerifyRadioButtonCheckBox() method nests a try-catch clause within another try-catch clause. The nested try clause invokes the helper methods and tests a RadioButton control, and the nested catch clause waits for the nested try clause to fail when the GUI control under test is a CheckBox control.

Inside the nested catch clause, the statements prepare and invoke the helper methods to test a CheckBox control. The second line assigns the reverse value of the preChecked field to the ExpectedCheckVal field of the fieldName object using a conditional operator (? :) in the catch clause. A conditional operator is a ternary operator; that is, it takes three operands. The first operand is implicitly converted to a Boolean value. If the first operand evaluates to true, the second operand is evaluated. Otherwise, the third operand is evaluated.

After the VerifyRadioButtonCheckBox() method is executed within a try-catch clause, the AutomatedGUITest tool completes the tasks for testing a RadioButton or CheckBox control.

Now, the helper fields and methods are coded. But the GUITestScript class has not been implemented to use these fields and methods. To do this, only two more lines of code are in need. The first line assigns a value to the preChecked field in the RunsScript() method, such as in the following example:

```
    preChecked = DeterminePreCheckedStatus(guiUnit);
```

The code for the RunsScript() method after the addition is in Listing 11.10; some lines of the old code are omitted and the newly added code is in bold.

Listing 11.10   A New Line in the *RunsScript()* Method to Inspect the Prechecked Condition of a CheckBox Control

```
private void RunsScript()
{
  ...
  paramArr[4] = guiUnit.TextEntry; //chapter 10

  Type guiTestLibType = new GUITestActions().GetType();
  object obj = Activator.CreateInstance(guiTestLibType);
  MethodInfo mi = guiTestLibType.GetMethod(ctrlAction);
```

```
//chapter 11
preChecked = DeterminePreCheckedStatus(guiUnit);

try
{
  mi.Invoke(obj, paramArr);
}
...

}
```

The new assignment of the preChecked field by calling the DeterminePreCheckedStatus() method occurs before the GUI object under test is clicked.

Finally, you need to add a line of code into the AddTestVerification() method of the GUITestScript class:

```
VerifyRadioButtonCheckBox(ref tested, resulted);
```

The modified AddTestVerification() method is in Listing 11.11; some code is omitted and the new code is in bold.

Listing 11.11   **The Modified Code for the *AddTestVerification()* Method**

```
private void AddTestVerification()
{
    ...
    //chapter 9
    VerifyLabel(ref tested, resulted);
    VerifyGroupBox(ref tested, resulted);

    //Chapter 11
    VerifyRadioButtonCheckBox(ref tested, resulted);

  }
}
```

The new code is appended to the end of the existing code of the AddTestVerification() method. The execution of the new code is the last step to completely testing and verifying a GUI control at this point.

Now, if there is no error in the code, you can press F5 to build and run the AutomatedGUI-Test tool. As I've done in the previous chapters, in the next section I will use an example to demonstrate the new capabilities of the AutomatedGUITest tool.

Testing RadionButton Controls

When developing the C# API Text Viewer, you implemented two RadioButton controls inside a GroupBox control. The RadionButton controls are labeled with captions of public and private, respectively. When the public RadioButton is checked, the C# API Text Viewer generates C# code for calling the Win32 functions as public methods or structures. The checked private RadioButton control makes the C# API Text Viewer produce private C# members.

With the AutomatedGUITest tool running on your system, you can follow these steps to test whether the C# API Text Viewer makes a public and a private method for marshaling two Win32 API functions:

1. Click the Start GUI Test button on the tool. When the file open dialog box appears, navigate to the `C:\GUISourceCode\Chapter03\CSharpAPITextViewer\bin\Debug\` `CSharpAPITextViewer.exe` file and click the Open button.

2. From the pop-up dialog box, select the check box beside the `CSharpAPITextViewer.Form1`. Click the OK button. The C# API Text Viewer application runs.

3. After the tool starts the C# API Text Viewer, make sure the C# API Text Viewer is visible on the screen and click the GUI Survey button on the tool. The GUI information is collected in a few seconds.

4. From the second column (labeled Window Text) of the DataGrid control in the tool interface, look for the text *public* and double-click on the left edge of the first column. The GUI Test Data Collector appears.

5. On the GUI Test Data Collector, the verification methods are presented by a group of RadioButton controls. Click the Simple radio button to choose the simple verification method for this test. Then click the OK button to add the public radio button into the test data store. Now the tool is ready for the next testing action.

6. Repeat steps 4 and 5 six more times, but instead of choosing the public radio button control on the AutomatedGUITest tool, add the following GUI controls in this order into the testing data store:

   WindowsForms10.LISTBOX.app3   (shown as Class Name in column 3)

   Add   (shown as Window Text in column 2)

   private   (shown as Window Text in column 2)

   WindowsForms10.LISTBOX.app3   (again)

   Add   (again)

   Copy   (shown as Window Text in column 2)

7. After the GUI controls are added for testing, close the C# API Text Viewer and click the Run Test button in the testing tool. When the save file dialog box appears, type in a filename, such as C:\Temp\TestRadioButtons.xml, and click the Save button to save the testing input data. After the testing data is saved, the tool automatically completes the test driven by the saved data. You can see the testing actions and view the test results displayed on the screen in a few seconds.

Summary

Developers use CheckBox controls to present a piece of data that has two states, such as true /false, on/off, or 1/0. They use RadioButton controls in a group to attain more than two states, one of which must be checked as true under any circumstances. However, when there are many possible states for a piece of data, developers will use a ListBox or ComboBox control instead of a group of RadioButton controls for good appearance and usability purposes.

This book has introduced methods to test various GUI controls in the C# API Text Viewer. You can use these methods to enhance your testing tool for testing other GUI objects with similar behaviors. If the project under test and the tool to be developed are .NET applications, you can directly apply the methods and the sample code. Otherwise, you can only use the introduced methods and translate the sample code into your selected language in order to develop a similar tool.

In the last three chapters, I will show you the methods for testing pop-up menus, some user-defined GUI controls, and applications other than .NET applications.

CHAPTER 12

Menu Clicking for GUI Test Automation

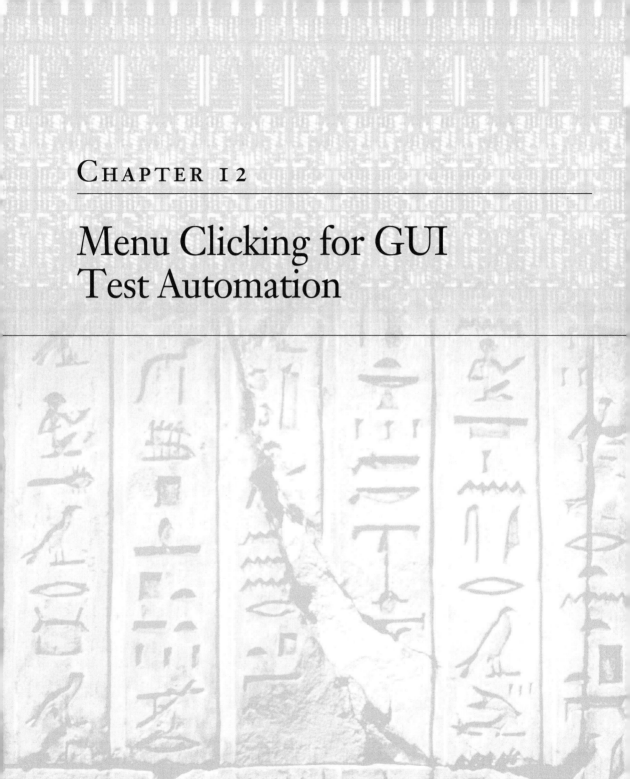

V ery often, Windows applications that allow the user to select actions use menus. A menu is a list of options from which the user chooses to perform a task. Some applications present menus as words in a list or as a collection of icons. The user can press an arrow key, enter a number or a letter with a keystroke, or move a mouse pointer to make choices.

The most common structure for menu items has a hierarchical organization. In the Microsoft Visual Studio .NET Framework, the top-level menu is called a *main menu*. The options of the main menu are visible from the front-end interface. The next level of menus are revealed only by the user clicking items on the top-level menu and are known as *submenus*. Very often, submenus have their own submenus. When a menu is revealed, it belongs to a newly created window with a unique handle. Each revealed menu item has a unique menu handle from session to session. These features of menu items make automatic menu manipulation different from manipulation of other GUI objects.

Fortunately, the Win32 API includes functions with regard to menu identification. I will use this chapter to discuss these functions and show you how to enhance the AutomatedGUITest tool. At the end of this chapter, the tool will be able to conduct a complete menu survey and the test script will be able to find the path to a desired item and automatically perform the menu selection.

Characteristics of Menu Testing

A menu with a list of words or icons is like the menu hanging on the wall of a McDonald's restaurant. The items are easily visible. You can order a meal by selecting the items from the limited options. For example, it is usually not possible for you to order a taco from the options on a McDonald's menu. A taco is more likely to be on the menu in a Taco Bell restaurant.

Using a hierarchically organized menu in a computer application reminds me of how we used to order in a restaurant in my hometown, where there were no printed menus. After we were seated, we ordered our meals by starting a dialogue with the hostess. We always initiated the conversation with a query about the items on the day's menu. The hostess would respond that there were meats, vegetables, soups, and appetizers. We continued with the next part of the query by asking about the meats and then the vegetables and so on until we completed our order with a perfect set of choices. If we didn't hear what we wanted from the hostess, we could suggest a particular item, such as French dips because we were treating a guest from France.

This discussion of testing menus will focus on the hierarchically organized menu system. Only the items of the top-level menus (main menus), analogous to the restaurant hostess, are visible. The submenu items of the hierarchical menu system are contained in the main menu. The top-level items categorize the tasks into groups. When an item from the top level is clicked, the menu items in the sub-levels will pop up, as in a dialog box. A user can select the desired tasks via the dialog box.

A dialog box containing a list of menu options is also a window that has a handle. Because the pop-up dialog boxes are not created before they are clicked, the GUI survey methods of the previous chapters are not able to detect the existence of the menu. In order to proceed to the next automation level for the AutomatedGUITest tool, I would like to clarify a few concepts with regard to menu testing.

NOTE   Software and text engineers often regard menus and wizard-like question/answer forms as pop-up dialog boxes. This chapter uses only the menu test as a demonstration to update the AutomatedGUITest project. You can use the method introduced in this chapter to develop a tool for other types of pop-up dialog boxes.

Window Handle and Menu Handle

By testing different GUI controls for the C# API Text Viewer, you should now be familiar with the concept that every GUI component is a window. Each window has a window handle that is created at the time the GUI object is created and visible on the screen. It is easy to understand that the AutomatedGUITest tool doesn't have the capability to see the invisible GUI objects of an application. But the menu items on the top level are visible from the menu bar of every Windows application. The GUI survey of the AutomatedGUITest tool has inspected the GUI interface of the C# API Text Viewer pixel by pixel several times, so why is there no trace of the top-level menus?

The answer is that the menu items are indeed contained within a window. If a window contains a set of menu options, it contains a menu handle. Only via the menu handle can the Automated-GUITest tool find the menu items. A menu handle can be obtained by a Win32 API function, `GetMenu()`. The `GetMenu()` function takes the handle of a window to query for a menu handle. If the queried window contains a main menu, the `GetMenu()` function returns the menu handle. Otherwise, the `GetMenu()` function returns a null value. A menu item always belongs to a menu handle. A menu handle can have more than one menu item. At this point, the AutomatedGUITest tool has not been implemented with such a function for the GUI survey.

Menu and Submenu

In the discussion and the code of this chapter, the items on the top level are referred to as menus. The top-level items are visible when the application starts. For example, the top-level usually has a File, an Edit, and a Help item.

The items of the submenus are contained inside a top-level menu. But the submenu items are not visible on the screen until an item of the top-level menu is clicked. Whenever a menu item is clicked, the application first creates a window to host the submenu items. The handle value of such a window varies for each creation and contains menu handles for the submenus. The submenu handles can be obtained by another Win32 API function, `GetSubMenu()`, with parameters of its menu handle and submenu position. Each submenu can have the submenus at the next. Similar to the values of the window handles, the values of the menu and submenu handles are also different from session to session. Thus, menu handles can not be hard-coded for the automated GUI test scripts.

Other properties of a menu will also be used to identify a particular menu item, such as the following:

Position index   A menu or submenu window can have several menu items differentiated by a position index based on zero. For example, Figure 12.1 is a snapshot for the menu items of the C# API Text Viewer after the File menu is clicked. The position index of the File menu as an item on the top level is 0, and that of the Help item is 1. The Open item under the File menu has a position index of 0. The separator, indicated as a horizontal line, has index value of 1, and the Exit item has an index of 2. The operating system always uses this method to position the menu items of applications and values are predictable.

Menu ID   The Windows operating system also assigns a unique number as a menu ID to each menu item as it is created on the screen. The values of the menu IDs are incremented consecutively. For example, the first time the GetMenu() function is called, the menu item with a position index 0 on the top-level menu is assigned a menu ID of 256. In the case of Figure 12.1, the File item will have a menu ID of 256, the Open item under the File menu will have a menu ID of 257, and the Help item on the top level will have a menu ID of 260. However, when you click the File menu, the values for the menu IDs of an application will not always start from number 256.

WARNING   In order to concentrate on the methods of developing a general GUI testing tool, the discussion about the order and the assignment of the menu item ID numbers applies mainly to the applications developed with Microsoft Visual Studio .NET. Applications originated from other environments or platforms may be different. For example, Notepad, which comes with the Windows operating system, assigns menu IDs based on zero. For a testing tool developer, what's important is to find out how menu IDs are assigned and implement a menu survey method accordingly. The sample code of this chapter will continue to focus on the menu exploration for testing .NET applications.

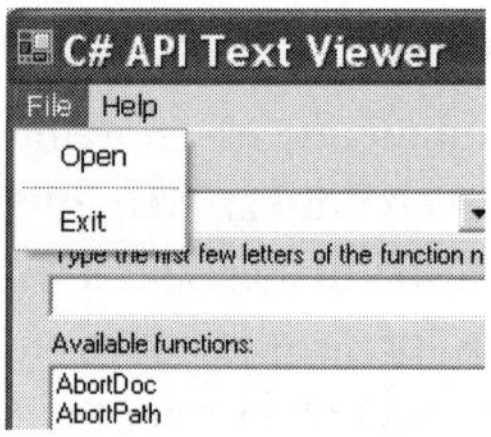

FIGURE 12.1
The top menu and the
File menu items of the
C# API Text Viewer

Menu caption   Similar to the position index, the caption of a menu item is stable because it is assigned at the time of development, such as File, Help, Open, and Exit, which are common labels for menu items (see Figure 12.1).

Class Name of Menu Windows

Class names have been used to help the AutomatedGUITest tool find the correct GUI object to test. A menu window is also derived from a class. When the application under test is developed within the Microsoft Visual Studio .NET Framework, the class name of the menu windows are all called #32768.

There are exceptions. For example, when you investigate the menu items of Microsoft Internet Explorer, you find the submenu windows are mostly inherited from the #32768 class. But the sublevel of the Favorites menu window has a class name of ToolbarWindow32. In another situation, when you inspect the menu items of Microsoft Word or Excel, the class name of their submenu windows is MsoCommandBarPopup. The AutomatedGUITest tool in this chapter will only cope with the most general class name, #32768.

In addition to the class name, the menu window has values for its window text and its parent window text. The parent window text is usually the text appearing on the application title bar on the top. But the menu window text is often empty. In the previous chapters, the AutomatedGUITest tool has implemented a FindGUILike() method to locate the window handle of a GUI object by using the window text, the class name, and the parent window text. To use the FindGUILike() method to find the handle value of a menu window, you will find that the values for the class name, the window text, and the parent window text will often be identical for all the submenu windows. Such a situation creates difficulties for programmatically finding the correct submenu item to click. One suggestion is to use the SetWindowText() Win32 function to set a value to the window text for each item click. An alternative is to use the submenu handle to obtain its parent window handle.

Now that you have an understanding of the menu handles and window handles, the rest of this chapter will add methods for the AutomatedGUITest tool to automatically conduct a menu survey and a specific menu clicking sequence.

Updating the *GUITestAction* Class with API Programming

Menu testing is a new topic in this book for the AutomatedGUITest tool. The implementation must start from the GUITestActions class of the GUITestLibrary project. In fact, most of the new code in this chapter happens in this class.

Marshaling a Few More Win32 Functions

In the previous chapters, when you added new methods to the GUITestActions class, you were required to use the C# API Text Viewer to add the related Win32 API functions. You can recall that the GUITestActions class was added with the following menu-related functions in Chapter 4:

```
GetMenuItemCount()
GetMenuItemInfo()
GetMenuItemID()
GetMenu()
GetMenuItemRect()
```

A MENUITEMINFO structure was also added then and will be used in this chapter to help the GetMenuItemInfo() function to identify a menu item of interest. You can refer to Chapter 4 for a detailed discussion of the MENUITEMINFO structure.

At this point, you only need seven additional Win32 API constants and two more functions, GetSubMenu() and GetMenuString(). Listing 12.1 shows the newly added Win32 API constants and functions.

Listing 12.1   **The Newly Added Win32 API Constants and Functions for the**
GUITestActions class

```
public const int MF_BYPOSITION = 0x400;
public const int MIIM_DATA  = 0x20;
public const int MIIM_ID  = 0x2;
public const int MIIM_STATE  = 0x1;
public const int MIIM_SUBMENU  = 0x4;
public const int MIIM_TYPE  = 0x10;
public const int MIIM_CHECKMARKS  = 0x8;

[DllImport("user32.dll")]
public static extern int GetMenuString(int hMenu, int wIDItem,
➡StringBuilder lpString, int nMaxCount, int wFlag);

[DllImport("user32.dll")]
public static extern int GetSubMenu(int hMenu, int nPos);
```

Move the cursor to the beginning of the GUITestActions.cs file and add another using directive:

```
using System.Collections;
```

This new using statement helps the new code with the ArrayList class of the System.Collections namespace to collect menu items.

Adding Methods to Identify Menu Items

The first implementation is a FindMenuTextAndID() method after the addition of the Win32 API functions and the using directive. The code is shown in Listing 12.2.

Listing 12.2   **The Code for the *FindMenuTextAndID()* Method for a Menu Item Collection**

```
public static void FindMenuTextAndID(int menuHnd,
➥string prntTxt, ref int absPosID, ref SortedList menuList)
{
  MENUITEMINFO menuinfo = new MENUITEMINFO();
  menuinfo.cbSize = 44;
  StringBuilder menuStr = new StringBuilder(128);
  int menuLen = GetMenuItemCount(menuHnd);

  for (int thisMenu = 0; thisMenu < menuLen; thisMenu++)
  {
    menuinfo.fMask = MIIM_DATA | MIIM_ID | MIIM_STATE |
➥MIIM_SUBMENU | MIIM_TYPE | MIIM_CHECKMARKS;
    int di = GetMenuItemInfo(menuHnd, thisMenu, 1, ref menuinfo);
    int db = GetMenuString(menuHnd, thisMenu, menuStr, 127, MF_BYPOSITION);

    GUITestUtility.GUIInfo mItem = new GUITestUtility.GUIInfo();
    mItem.GUIText = menuStr.ToString();
    mItem.GUIParentText = prntTxt;
    mItem.GUIHandle = menuinfo.wID;
    mItem.GUIClassName = absPosID.ToString();
    absPosID++;
    try
    {
      menuList.Add(menuinfo.wID, mItem);
    }
    catch{}
    int menuID = thisMenu;
    FindMenuTextAndID(GetSubMenu(menuHnd, menuID), prntTxt,
➥ref absPosID, ref menuList);

  }//for
  return;
}
```

We continue to define the methods in the GUITestActions class as static methods. The FindMenuTextAndID() method takes four parameters and is recursive. The first parameter takes the value of the menu handle. The second is the parent window text, which is usually the text on the title bar of the application. The absPosID parameter is used to track the absolute position of the entire menu system based on 0. It is passed by reference and incremented by one when a menu item is encountered. At the end of the execution of the `FindMenuTextAndID()` method, the value of the `absPosID` parameter will be equal to the count of the menu and sub-menu items of an application. The value will also equal the difference between the maximum and minimum values of the menu IDs for applications developed with the Microsoft Visual Studio .NET IDE. Thus, the test script can use a value of the `absPosID` parameter to find a relative menu ID. Finally, a `SortedList` object, `menuList`, is passed to collect all the menu items found. The items are presented as `GUITestUtility.GUIInfo` objects.

After the method declaration, the first two lines of the code instantiate a new `MenuItemInfo` object, `menuinfo`. Then it initializes a `StringBuilder` object, `menuStr`, to retrieve the menu caption. The `menuLen` variable receives a value return by calling the `GetMenuItemCount()` method. The value of the `menuLen` variable indicates the count of menu items within a menu or a sub-menu window (not the count of all menu items of the entire application).

After the count of the menu items within a menu window is obtained, a `for` loop is used to find out the information of each menu item one by one. The `menuinfo.fMask` is assigned to include all types of menus. The `GetMenuItemInfo()` function is then called to assign the menu item to the `menuinfo` object and the `GetMenuString()` method is called to obtain the menu caption. The rest of the code considers the item as a regular GUI object and initializes a `GUITestUtility.GUIInfo` object. Note that one of the assignments sets the value of the menu ID as a GUI handle value and another sets the absolute `absPosID` value as the GUI class name. These assignments enable us to reuse the `GUITestUtility.GUIInfo` structure instead of declaring a new structure specifically for menu information. Next, the information of the menu item is added to the `menuList` within a `try-catch` clause. The last line of the code within the `for` loop recursively calls the `FindMenuTextAndID()` to inspect whether the menu item has the next sub-level menus. Thus, all the menu items are collected.

For the survey purpose, The `FindMenuTextAndID()` method is implemented for finding all the menu items of an application and collected in a `SortedList` object. But testers are interested in the menu items one by one. Therefore, the `FindMenuTextAndID()` method is overloaded to find a particular menu item with a given menu ID. You can code the overloaded method as shown in Listing 12.3.

Listing 12.3   **The Overloaded *FindMenuTextAndID()* Method to Find a Menu Item with a Given Menu ID**

```
public static void FindMenuTextAndID(int menuHnd,
➥int wID, ref int posFound, ref int handleFound)
{
  MENUITEMINFO menuinfo = new MENUITEMINFO();
  menuinfo.cbSize = 44;
  int menuLen = GetMenuItemCount(menuHnd);

  for (int thisMenu = 0; thisMenu < menuLen; thisMenu++)
```

```
    {
      menuinfo.fMask = MIIM_DATA | MIIM_ID | MIIM_STATE |
➥MIIM_SUBMENU | MIIM_TYPE | MIIM_CHECKMARKS;
      int di = GetMenuItemInfo(menuHnd, thisMenu, 1, ref menuinfo);

      if (menuinfo.wID == wID)
      {
        posFound = thisMenu;
        handleFound = menuHnd;
      }
      int menuID = thisMenu;

      FindMenuTextAndID(GetSubMenu(menuHnd,
➥menuID), wID, ref posFound, ref handleFound);

    }
    return;
  }
```

The overloaded FindMenuTextAndID() method doesn't use a SortedList object to collect the items found but finds a particular menu item with a given ID. Its first parameter is identical to its original version. The rest of the three parameters are related to the menu item of interest. The method holds up the given menu ID, wID, and checks whether the value of the wID variable matches the current menu ID by recursive execution of the FindMenuTextAndID() method. When there is a match, the posFound and handleFound variables yank the position index and the handle of the menu. The recursion continues until menu items of all levels are visited.

Navigating a Menu Click Pathway

The FindMenuClickPathByID() method uses the overloaded method to find the path of an item deep in the sub-levels. Position indexes are collected in an ArrayList object. The ArrayList uses its own index to represent the level of a menu item and guides the path to reach a menu item to perform a click. Listing 12.4 is the code for the FindMenuClickPathByID() method.

Listing 12.4   **The Code for the *FindMenuClickPathByID()* Method**

```
public static ArrayList FindMenuClickPathByID(int parentWinHandle, int menuID)
{
  int wHnd = GetMenu(parentWinHandle);
  int thisPath = int.MaxValue;
  int handleFound = 0;

  ArrayList menuPath = new ArrayList();
  ArrayList handleLst = new ArrayList();

  for (int i = menuID; i >= 0; i--)
  {
```

```
        FindMenuTextAndID(wHnd, i, ref thisPath, ref handleFound);
        if (!handleLst.Contains(handleFound))
        {
          handleLst.Add(handleFound);
          menuPath.Insert(0, thisPath);
        }
        if (handleFound == wHnd)
        {
          break;
        }
      }
    return menuPath;
  }
```

The `FindMenuClickPathByID()` method takes the handle of the parent window of the menu as its first parameter value. The second parameter value is the menu ID under the parent window, which may also be the grandparent of the ID of interest. After the handle of the parent window and the menu ID of interest are given in the method declaration, the first three lines of code initialize variables to retrieve the menu handle from the parent window, set a big value to a path position, and set a small value to the handle to be found. An initialization of a big value (`int.MaxValue = 2,147,483,647` in the .NET Framework) for the `thisPath` variable ensures that the position index of any menu item will be found and be a smaller number. An initialization of a small value for the `handleFound` variable makes sure the handle of a menu item is usually a bigger number.

Next, two `ArrayList` objects are initialized. The `menuPath` list is used to collect the position index to indicate a path to a menu item. The `handleLst` list collects the menu handles starting from the level where the menu item is upward to the top level. Because multiple items can belong to the same menu handle, only unique handles are collected in the `handleLst` list. The `FindMenuClickPathByID()` method uses the unique handle collection to tell when the menu level changes.

The actual work for finding the path is done within a `for` loop. The `for` loop starts from a value of the menu ID of interest. The minimum value for a menu ID is a number greater than or equal to 0 (in applications developed with the .NET Framework, the minimum value of a menu ID is 256). A descending iteration makes the `for` loop visit each of the menu item with a menu ID smaller than the menu ID of interest until the top-level menu is reached. Then, each iteration invokes the `FindMenuTextAndID()` method to grab the menu handle under investigation. If the handle is not collected in the `handleLst` object yet, the method adds the handle to the `handleLst` collection and piles the position index at the top of the `menuPath` listing using an `Insert()` method. You may suggest using a `Stack` object in place of the `menuPath` list. The second `if` statement inside the `for` loop checks whether the top-level menu is reached. If the current level is the top level, the loop is broken. Finally, the `FindMenuClickPathByID()` method returns the `menuPath` list to the caller.

Performing a Click on a Menu Item

Now the testing tool can use one of the two FindMenuClickPathByID() methods to find all menu items of an application or a specific one. After a desired menu item is identified, a mouse click method is needed to make the menu pop up. However, accomplishing the menu handling method requires two additional helper methods. Listing 12.5 shows the code for a FindMenuWindow() method.

Listing 12.5   **The Code for the *FindMenuWindow()* Method**

```
private static void FindMenuWindow(ref int menuWin,
➥ref string winText, ref string parentText)
{
  string clsName = "#32768";
  FindGUILike(ref menuWin, 0, ref winText, ref clsName, ref parentText);
}
```

Menu items have their menu handles and window handles. A mouse click on a correct menu item requires knowing the window handle and the menu handle. To find the window handle, the GUI test library has had a FindGUILike() method, which uses the class name, the window text, and the parent window text to find the handle of a GUI object. The FindMenuWindow() method uses the existing FindGUILike() method to discover the handle of a menu window by looking for the class name, #32768, and the parent window text (usually the title caption of the application under test).

You need to keep in mind that all the submenu items belong to menu windows having the same class name and the same parent window text. It becomes confusing for the recursive methods to find a deep submenu window. To reduce the length of the code, the effort in this chapter will not handle all the specific menu architectures. But I make two suggestions for you to develop your testing tool after reading this book:

- One is to make another FindGUILike() method that collects all the window handles with the same class name (e.g., #32768) and parent window text. The most recently created window handle is the one that contains the menu item of interest.

- Another option is to modify the FindMenuWindow() method by setting up window text for the visited menu window. Then the FindMenuWindow() method has unique window text in addition to the class name and the parent window text to find the correct handle of the menu window in different levels.

The second helper method is needed to find the location of a menu item and perform a left click on it. Listing 12.6 shows the code for a ClickMenuItem() method.

Listing 12.6   The *ClickMenuItem()* Helper Method to Complete a Menu Item Click

```
private static void ClickMenuItem(int mWnd, int hMenu, int Pos)
{
  RECT rct = new RECT();
  POINTAPI pnt;

  int ret = GetMenuItemRect(mWnd, hMenu, Pos, ref rct);

  if (ret == 0)
  {
    return;
  }
  pnt.x = (rct.Left + rct.Right) / 2;
  pnt.y = (rct.Top + rct.Bottom) / 2;
  PixelXYToMickeyXY(ref pnt.x, ref pnt.y);

  mouse_event(MOUSEEVENTF_ABSOLUTE | MOUSEEVENTF_MOVE,
➥pnt.x, pnt.y, 0, GetMessageExtraInfo());
  ClickMouse(MonkeyButtons.btcLeft, pnt.x, pnt.y, 0, 0);
}
```

The ClickMenuItem() method is similar to the ClickMouse() method conducting clicks on GUI objects. But it needs to find the rectangle of a menu item first. The rectangle of a menu item can only be found using a GetMenuItemRect() Win32 API function. The GetMenuItemRect() function requires knowing the menu window handle, the menu handle, and the position index of the menu item. The code in Listing 12.6 finds the location of the menu item as a rectangle on the screen and converts the rectangle's position from pixels to mickey steps. Then it moves the mouse pointer to the center of the rectangle and clicks the left button to conclude the method.

Finally, you can complete the implementation of a HandleMenuItems() method as shown in Listing 12.7.

Listing 12.7   The *HandleMenuItems()* Method to Be Used by the *GUITestScript* Class

```
public static void HandleMenuItems(int mWnd, string winText,
➥string clsName, ref string pText, string textEntry)
{
  int hMenu = GetMenu(mWnd);
  StringBuilder prntText = new StringBuilder(255);
  GetWindowText(mWnd, prntText, 255);

  SortedList IDLst = new SortedList();
  int absPosID = 0;
  FindMenuTextAndID(hMenu, prntText.ToString(), ref absPosID, ref IDLst);

  GUITestUtility.GUIInfo menuItem =
➥(GUITestUtility.GUIInfo)IDLst.GetByIndex(int.Parse(clsName));
```

```
int menuID = menuItem.GUIHandle;

ArrayList menuPath = FindMenuClickPathByID(mWnd, menuID);

if ((menuPath.Count - 1) == 0)
{
   ClickMenuItem(mWnd, hMenu, (int)menuPath[0]);
System.Threading.Thread.Sleep(500);
}

for (int subItem = 1; subItem < menuPath.Count; subItem++)
{
   int intA = (int)menuPath[subItem-1];
   int subMenu = GetSubMenu(hMenu, intA);
   intA = (int)menuPath[subItem];

   int subMenuWin = 0;
   FindMenuWindow(ref subMenuWin, ref winText, ref pText);
   if (subItem == (menuPath.Count - 1))
   {
      ClickMenuItem(subMenuWin, subMenu, intA);
      System.Threading.Thread.Sleep(500);
   }
}
}
}
```

In order to be integrated with the GUI test script, the declaration of the HandleMenuItems() method carries the same five parameter signatures as the other GUI object handling methods. The first parameter carries the value of the window handle. The second is for the window text. Parameter clsName actually passes the ID value of the menu item. The value of pText is defined as a reference and prepared to change the value of the parent text for window handle identification in the future. The textEntry parameter has been declared for text manipulation of GUI objects. You can specify a textEntry value to test the shortcut to a submenu item.

The first cluster of code in the HandleMenuItems() method uses the application window handle to find the top-level menu handle and the parent text of the menus. The second cluster of code defines two variables to be used by the FindMenuTextAndID() method to find all the menu items via the top-level menu handle. One of the variables is a SortedList object, IDLst, which holds the menu items as GUIInfo objects after the execution of the FindMenuTextAndID() method. The following code simply uses the GetByIndex() method of the SortedList object and the menu ID as a parameter value to find the specified menu item. After the specified menu item is found, the overloaded FindMenuClickPathByID() method finds the path from the top level to the specified item. The item position in each level is stored in the menuPath object.

The first if statement checks whether the menuPath object collects only one menu item, which indicates a click on a top-level menu item. In such a case, the ClickMenuItem() method is immediately invoked and the rest of the code is skipped. If the item of interest is situated in a sub-level, the for loop steps through the sub-levels guided by the path information collected in the menuPath list object. In each level, the FindMenuWindow() method is called to discover the menu window handle. When the loop is at the last item of the menuPath list, the second if statement invokes the ClickMenuItem() method to complete the clicking on the specified sub-menu item. Note that after each click on the menu item, the code requests the testing tool to sleep for 500 milliseconds to wait for the menu dialog box to pop up and then proceeds to the next action.

Updating the *GUITestActionLib.xml* Document

As was done for the other GUI handling method, the name of the menu handling method must be entered into the GUITestActionLib.xml document. To do this, open a Windows Explorer from the Start menu and navigate to the C:\GUISourceCode\Chapter12\AutomatedGUITest\bin\Debug folder. You can use a text editor or any other XML utility to load the GUITestActionLib.xml file. Add a new node to the XML document like this:

```
<Menu>HandleMenuItems</Menu>
```

Listing 12.8 shows the modified GUITestActionLib.xml document with the new addition in bold.

Listing 12.8   **The *GUITestActionLib.xml* Document with the Menu Handling Method Line in Bold**

```
<GUIActions>
  <Menu>HandleMenuItems</Menu>
  <System.Windows.Forms.CheckBox>HandleCommandButton
➥</System.Windows.Forms.CheckBox>
  <System.Windows.Forms.RadioButton>HandleCommandButton
➥</System.Windows.Forms.RadioButton>
  <HandleTextBoxWithTextEntry>HandleTextBoxWithTextEntry
➥</HandleTextBoxWithTextEntry>
  <System.Windows.Forms.Label>HandleCosmeticGUIs</System.Windows.Forms.Label>
  <System.Windows.Forms.GroupBox>HandleCosmeticGUIs
➥</System.Windows.Forms.GroupBox>
  <System.Windows.Forms.ListBox>HandleListBox</System.Windows.Forms.ListBox>
  <System.Windows.Forms.RichTextBox>HandleTextBox
➥</System.Windows.Forms.RichTextBox>
  <System.Windows.Forms.TextBox>HandleTextBox</System.Windows.Forms.TextBox>
  <System.Windows.Forms.Button>HandleCommandButton</System.Windows.Forms.Button>
  <Field>VerifyField</Field>
  <Property>VerifyProperty</Property>
  <Synchronization>SynchronizeWindow</Synchronization>
</GUIActions>
```

After adding the methods of this section into the `GUITestAction` class of the GUI test library, you can build the solution and correct the errors if there are any.

Enabling Menu Survey Capability

The preceding section showed you how to implement the needed methods to take care of the detail of testing menus automatically. The rest of the coding task is to add code to update some classes of the AutomatedGUITest project.

The AutomatedGUITest has used a `StartGUISurvey()` method to collect all the GUI components visible from the user interface into a DataGrid. Testers are able to use the survey to specify a test with ease. In this section, you will create a `StartMenuSurvey()` method, utilize the `FindMenuTextAndID()` method, and complete a menu survey with the `GUISurveyClass` class (Listing 12.9).

Listing 12.9   The *StartMenuSurvey()* Method Added to the *GUISurveyClass* Class

```
public void StartMenuSurvey()
{
   int wHnd = GUITestActions.GetMenu(HandleUnderSurvey);
   StringBuilder ParentText = new StringBuilder(1000);
   GUITestActions.GetWindowText(HandleUnderSurvey, ParentText, 1000);

   int absPosID = 0;
   GUITestActions.FindMenuTextAndID(wHnd,
➥ParentText.ToString(), ref absPosID, ref GUISortedList);
}
```

The `StartMenuSurvey()` method requires no parameters. The first line of the code initializes a `wHnd` variable and accepts the top-level menu handle of an application by calling the Win32 API `GetMenu()` function, which has been marshaled in the `GUITestActions` class. The parameter required by the `GetMenu()` function is the application handle passed by the `HandleUnderSurvey` variable from the AutomatedGUITest main form. The value of the `HandleUnderSurvey` variable has also been used by the `StartGUISurvey()` method.

Because the C# API Text Viewer has marshaled the `GetWindowText()` method by taking a parameter of `StringBuilder` object, the second line of code initializes a `ParentText` object to hold the title of the application with a maximum length of 1,000 characters. The `GetWindowText()` method is called from the GUI test library to find the title as the parent text of the menu windows. This parent window text is needed to discover all the top and submenu handles.

As discussed in the preceding section, the position indexes and IDs of the menu items vary from session to session, but they are in sequence. The GUI test library uses an absolute value, absPosID, to track and mark the menu items. The absPosID variable is initialized to be zero and will be incremented by the FindMenuTextAndID() method. After the execution of the FindMenuTextAndID() method, the value of the absPosID variable will be incremented to correspond to the number of menu items in the application. The menu items are collected into the public GUISortedList property beside the other GUI objects as GUITestUtility.GUIInfo objects.

The StartMenuSurvey() method is all the code needed to update the GUISurveyClass class for this chapter. After the addition, the project can be built without compiling errors. For the frmMain class (the AutomatedGUITest main form) and the GUITestScript class, only a little modification is needed, as discussed in the next section.

Enabling the AutomatedGUITest Tool for Menu Survey

The methods coded in the GUITestActions class are useful for performing desired actions on various GUI objects and menu items. The methods in the GUISurveyClass class, which use methods from the GUI test library, are for discovering and collecting all the GUI objects and menu items into a list. Testers specify GUI testing cases by making choices from the list. Specifying GUI objects for testing doesn't really start the application. Testing cases can be composed anytime after the user interface is developed. In contrast, the capture/playback strategy requires the user to use the application. An error will stop the capture/playback process. Thus, a testing case can not be completed until there are no bugs when the GUI interface is operated.

The frmMain class (the main form) of the AutomatedGUITest tool has a private GUISurveyClass field, guiSurveyCls. This private field has methods to start a GUI survey for a fully automated GUI test. But the menu survey method is not implemented in the frmMain class at this point. The next section will guide you in adding a few lines of code to the main form with regard to calling the StartMenuSurvey() method.

Invoking the Menu Survey Method

You implemented a GUI Survey button when the AutomatedGUITest project was started. Up to now, testers click on the GUI Survey button to start and complete a full GUI survey. The button click is represented by the code as a button click event, btnGUISurvey_Click(). Listing 12.10 shows in bold that only one line of code needs to be added to the btnGUISurvey_Click() event.

Listing 12.10   Adding One Line of Code to Call the *StartMenuSurvey()* Method to the *btnGUISurvey_Click()* Event

```
private void btnGUISurvey_Click(object sender, System.EventArgs e)
{

  this.WindowState = FormWindowState.Minimized;

  try
  {
    guiSurveyCls = new GUISurveyClass((int)formUT.Handle);
  }
  catch (Exception ex)
  {
    MessageBox.Show(ex.Message);
  }

  guiSurveyCls.StartGUISurvey();
  guiSurveyCls.StartMenuSurvey(); //Chapter 12
  SetGUIListToTest();

  this.WindowState = FormWindowState.Normal;
}
```

The added code simply invokes the StartMenuSurvey() method after the StartGUISurvey() method. The rest of the code is kept intact.

Handling a Possible Error

After you add the StartMenuSurvey() method, you may want to build and run the Automated-GUITest tool and complete a GUI survey that includes the menu items. It should work. When you tested the tool in the previous chapters, you could place the mouse pointer on a GUI object listed in the DataGrid. A blue rectangle blinked near the respective GUI object. This blinking blue bar told you which GUI object you selected from the survey result. But this time, when you place the mouse pointer on a menu item, an exception occurs. The debugging process stops the application. This exception is caused by the GUITestActions.IndicateSelectedGUI() method invoked by the dgAvailableGUIs_CurrentCellChanged() event because the menu window doesn't exist when you are making a selection from the survey list. A quick fix is to enclose the invocation of the IndicateSelectedGUI() method within a try-catch clause such as the one in Listing 12.11 (in bold).

> **Listing 12.11**   **Adding a *try-catch* Clause to Handle the Nonexisting Menu Window Error**

```
private void dgAvailableGUIs_CurrentCellChanged(
➥object sender, System.EventArgs e)
{
  try //chapter 12
  {
    GUITestActions.IndicateSelectedGUI((int)
➥guiSurveyCls.GUISortedList.GetKey(dgAvailableGUIs.CurrentCell.RowNumber));
  }
  catch{}
}
```

After you locate the code segment for the dgAvailableGUIs_CurrentCellChanged() event, the updating is simple. Now you can build and test-run the GUI survey functions. No error will occur to stop the application.

Updating the *GUITestScript* Class

The last coding task for this chapter is for the RunsScript() method of the GUITestScript class. Listing 12.12 shows the full code list of the RunsScript() method with the added lines in bold.

> **Listing 12.12**   **Adding a *try-catch* Clause to Handle the Nonexisting GUI Controls**

```
private void RunsScript()
{
  guiTestActionLib = Path.Combine(progDir, "GUITestActionLib.xml");

  GUITestUtility.GUIInfo guiUnit =
➥(GUITestUtility.GUIInfo)seqGUIUT.GUIList[clickNum];

  string ctrlAction =
➥GUITestUtility.GetAGUIAction(guiTestActionLib, guiUnit.GUIControlType);

  StringBuilder sb = new StringBuilder(10000);

  try //chapter 12
  {
    Control ctrlTested =
➥(Control)GUITestUtility.VerifyField(AUT, guiUnit.GUIControlName);
    GUITestActions.GetWindowText((int)ctrlTested.Handle, sb, 10000);
  }
  catch{}
  //object[] paramArr = new object[4];
```

```
object[] paramArr = new object[5]; //chapter 10

if (ctrlAction == "HandleMenuItems") //chapter 12
  paramArr[0] = AUT.Handle.ToInt32();
else
  paramArr[0] = 0;

paramArr[1] = sb.ToString();
paramArr[2] = guiUnit.GUIClassName;
paramArr[3] = guiUnit.GUIParentText;
paramArr[4] = guiUnit.TextEntry; //chapter 10

Type guiTestLibType = new GUITestActions().GetType();
object obj = Activator.CreateInstance(guiTestLibType);
MethodInfo mi = guiTestLibType.GetMethod(ctrlAction);

//chapter 11
preChecked = DeterminePreCheckedStatus(guiUnit);

try
{
  mi.Invoke(obj, paramArr);
}
catch (Exception ex)
{
  MessageBox.Show(ex.Message);
}

if (clickNum < seqGUIUT.GUIList.Count)
{
  clickNum++;
  tmrRunScript.Enabled = false;
  tmrStopScript.Enabled = true;
}

}
```

A try-catch clause was needed to handle the nonexisting menu window, and it is needed by the RunsScript() method of the GUITestScript class for a similar reason. The try-catch clause handles an error rising from converting a menu item object to a Control object. The invocation of the GetWindowText() method is not needed when a menu item is under test.

The second updating for the RunsScript() method handles the first item of the parameter array assignment. When a non-menu GUI object is tested, the first item of the array is initialized to be 0. The late binding invocation of the GUI handling method locates the correct value for the item as a window handle of the GUI under test. But when a menu item is under test, the handle of the top-level menu window is always the handle of the application's main form.

Therefore, an if-else clause is used after a name of the GUI handling method is enumerated from the GUITestActionsLib.xml document.

At this point, you have completely updated the AutomatedGUITest project for discovering and testing menu items of an application. You can build and run the AutomatedGUITest tool and conduct the following example for a trial of the new features.

A Menu Testing Example

The C# API Text Viewer happens to be developed to have a hierarchical menu system. This testing example will collect testing data to simulate a human clicking File ➢ Open menus and entering a file path and filename in the pop-up open file dialog box. After the file is open, the tool will continue to add and copy a Win32 API function into the clipboard and complete the test.

With the AutomatedGUITest tool running, click the Start GUI Test button to bring up the open file dialog box. Navigate to the C:\GUISourceCode\Chapter03\CSharpAPITextViewer\bin\Debug folder and select the CSharpAPITextViewer.exe executable. After you click the Open button, the Types under Test dialog box pops up. Check the CSharpAPITextViewer.Form1 in the check box list and click the OK button. The C# API Text Viewer application starts running. Make sure the application under test is visible on the screen. But it is okay if the application under test is immediately beneath the AutomatedGUITest tool.

Click the GUI Survey button. The user interface of the tool minimizes. You see the mouse pointer traverses up and down and left to right to visit every spot of the application. After the survey is accomplished, the tool becomes normal and visible on the screen with the survey result. This time, the six menu items of the application are added to the top of the survey list. You can select the menu and the GUI objects to form a normal operation of the C# API Text Viewer following these steps:

NOTE   A few users and testers have noted that the AutomatedGUITest tool doesn't seem to capture the Button controls for the first GUI Survey button click, but it does after clicking the GUI Survey button a second time. However, I've never run into this situation. If you find out the cause, please let me know via this book's web page on www.sybex.com. Thanks in advance.

1. Find the File menu item at the first row of the DataGrid. The File menu is marked as *File* under the Window Text column. For the menu items, the Handle column holds the menu ID and the Class Name column holds the absolute position number. The Parent Text is *C# API Text Viewer* for all the menu items. Double-click the row with the File menu item

(similar to when testing other GUI objects). When the GUI Test Data Collector appears, you need to modify the contents of the two combo boxes at the top of the form. Into the topmost combo box, replace the text with `mnuFile`, which can be found in the check box list in the bottom left and is the name of the File menu item given at development time. In the second combo box, type **Menu** to replace the old content. You also choose the simple verification method and click the OK button to complete this step.

2. Find the Open menu item (possibly in the second row) and double-click on the left edge. Always remember to type **Menu** in the second combo box when testing a menu item. The test script looks for the menu handling method by reading the case sensitive word *Menu*. But in the first combo box, type `mnuFileOpen` and choose the simple verification method.

3. Before you click the OK button to test the Open menu, type `C:\GUISourceCode\Chapter03\Win32API.txt{ENTER}` in the Text Entry field. This entry is used to handle the open file dialog box after the Open menu is clicked. The result will be that the specified file will open in the C# API Text Viewer. The `win32Api.txt` file comes with the sample code of this book, downloadable from `www.sybex.com`. The `{ENTER}` is the code for invoking the Enter keystroke by the `SendKeys` class, as discussed in Chapter 10. Now click the OK button. The GUI Test Data Collector disappears.

4. Double-click at the left edge of the DataGrid by the row that includes `WindowsForms10.LISTBOX.app3` as a class name to bring up the GUI Test Data Collector. Choose the simple verification method and click the OK button.

5. Double-click the DataGrid to specify the Add button (similar to specifying the `WindowsForms10.LISTBOX.app3` in step 4).

6. Double-click the DataGrid to add the Copy button into the testing data store.

At this point, the testing steps are added to a list. You need to close the C# API Text Viewer and click the Run Test button in the AutomatedGUITest tool. The tool pops up a save file dialog box. You can type in `C:\Temp\MenuTest.xml` to name the file in which to save the testing data store. After you click the Save button, the test script is invoked. The mouse clicks on the specified menu items and GUI objects. The test is finished.

WARNING For your convenience, the code of the AutomatedGUITest project is enabled to handle some errors, but not all possible errors. For example, if you collect data to test the File ➢ Exit clicking sequence at this point, the tool will be terminated and the test result will not be saved.

Summary

This chapter discussed menu-related Win32 API functions and used the functions in the AutomatedGUITest project. Following the sample code, you updated the tool and achieved the goal of conducting automated menu tests. The example also demonstrated a way to handle the open file dialog box by a method discussed in Chapter 10.

At development time, the pop-up dialog boxes are GUI components categorized in the same group as the pop-up submenu items. The contents of this chapter revealed that submenu windows are often derived from the #32768 class name. But a pop-up dialog box in an application is derived from a class with the name of #32770. This chapter used the SendKey class to operate an open file dialog box in the example. An approach such as the one introduced for menu testing in this chapter can be used to upgrade the AutomatedGUITest tool to test pop-up dialog boxes with mouse operations. However, I have tried in this book to cover different testing approaches in the discussions. Repetitive coding for testing dialog boxes will not be discussed. The remaining two chapters will introduce ideas for testing user-defined GUI controls and applications other than .NET applications.

User-Defined and COM-Based Controls

T he previous chapters mainly introduced methods to develop a GUI testing tool with the capability to start an active GUI survey and conduct a test based on the survey. The survey searches the entire area of the application on the screen. When a GUI component is encountered, the survey method grabs the GUI handle and stores the GUI object in a list with text descriptions, both machine and human readable.

When the test starts, the test script reads the GUI description stored in an XML document. To locate a GUI object under test, the GUI test uses a process that is exactly the reverse of the survey process. The test script has the GUI description first. Then the GUI handle is located based on the GUI description. The last step for the test script is to apply testing actions on the GUI objects and verify the consequences.

Chapters 9 through 12 discussed methods for testing some specific GUI objects. But the capability of an automatic testing tool is not limited to the methods discussed. The purpose of the discussion was to encourage you to incorporate these methods for testing other GUI controls. I will use this chapter to extend such methods once more for testing user-defined controls and ActiveX controls.

ActiveX controls are COM components that implement a number of interfaces. They are discrete software elements similar to discrete hardware components. Each ActiveX control provides functionality with a cooperating container and behaves like the other GUI controls. Developers tie together various ActiveX controls into more complex applications. ActiveX controls are used extensively in client-side and server-side technologies. This chapter will demonstrate how to build a simple ActiveX control and test the control.

Basics of User-Defined GUI Controls

User-defined GUI controls are *custom GUI components*. I will use these two terms interchangeably in this chapter. Developers can combine the functionality of several standard GUI components into a custom GUI control to accomplish complicated tasks. Custom GUI controls greatly enhance a program's usability by providing quick, one-step command actions. Within an application, a custom GUI control is usually a child window of a parent window and has the standard GUI controls for its own children. Custom GUI objects use information about their parent window's rectangle to position themselves. For software development, user-defined GUI controls have many advantages:

- *Fast development life cycle*: Instead of spending time on designing features that are already available, developers can use custom GUI controls, which allow the direct use of features by combining the standard GUI controls available in an IDE.

- *Reliability*: The standard GUI controls have been used and tested in many applications. The testing tool only needs to test whether the combination of the GUI components functions as it is expected to function.

- *Reusability*: The development of user-defined controls allows the reuse of existing standard GUI controls. After the user-defined controls are developed, they can be reused across an organization.

- *Minimizing testing time*: No matter what the purpose of the user-defined controls are, they can be tested in similar ways. Once the testing data is created and stored for testing a user-defined control, the data can later be reused for integration testing. If the user interface of an application consists of several user-defined GUI controls, a full testing of the application can be conducted by combining the existing data stores for testing the user-defined controls.

Since a user-defined control doesn't implement an entry point method, the AutomatedGUI-Test tool needs a different method to start a custom GUI control on the screen so the tool can test it. For illustration purposes, the following sections introduce two kinds of custom GUI controls: ActiveX controls based on Microsoft Visual Studio 6 and controls based on the .NET Framework.

Custom .NET GUI Controls

In Microsoft Visual Studio .NET IDE, the `System.Windows.Forms` namespace offers a number of types that represent the standard GUI components. Using these types, software developers have made the Windows Forms application to respond to user input. Because .NET is a system of types built on standard principles of object-oriented programming, the GUI controls are arranged in a hierarchy of related types. A Windows Forms application can include custom GUI controls.

Similar to the principles of object-oriented programming for software development, testers also prefer to divide a GUI-rich application into custom GUI objects, test the custom GUI controls individually, and reuse the individual test data stores and results for integration testing and system testing.

You have developed a C# API Text Viewer in Chapter 3 for testing the AutomatedGUITest project throughout this book. In this section, you'll develop a user-defined login control by combining some Label, TextBox, and Button controls. The purpose of developing this control is for you as a tester to have a good understanding of the .NET user-defined GUI controls and to conduct a testing example at the end of this chapter.

Start the Microsoft Visual Studio .NET IDE on your system. Follow these steps to build a simplified custom login control:

1. From the main window, choose File ➢ New ➢ Projects. The New Project dialog box pops up.

2. In the Project Types pane (on the left), select Visual C# Projects. In the Templates pane (on the right), select Windows Control Library. In the Name field, type **LoginCtrl**. In the Location field, type `C:\GUISourceCode\Chapter13`. Finally, click the OK button. A

LoginCtrl project is created and the design editor appears in the Microsoft Visual Studio .NET IDE.

3. Use the following list to drag and drop two Label, two TextBox, and two Button controls onto the design editor and modify the values of some properties accordingly:

Control	Property	Value
Label	Name	lblUserID
	Text	User ID
Label	Name	lblPwd
	Text	Password
TextBox	Name	txtUserID
TextBox	Name	txtPwd
Button	Name	btnOK
	Text	OK
Button	Name	btnCancel
	Text	Cancel

You only need to change the listed property values and leave the others intact. After the modification, the LoginCtrl control looks like Figure 13.1 in the design editor.

If this is a real login control, you may need to add a little code with some functions. For example, you can add code for the OK and Cancel buttons to receive clicking events. For testing purposes, you don't have to add any code manually for the LoginCtrl control. You simply, from the main window, choose Build ➤ Build Solution. A LoginCtrl.dll assembly is created in a C:\GUISource-Code\Chapter13\LoginCtrl\bin\Debug folder. The LoginCtrl control is ready to be tested and used in other applications. However, it will not be tested in this chapter until the AutomatedGUI-Test is updated with new functions.

You now have a basic understanding of the creation of a user-defined control. In the next section, you'll learn about the COM-based ActiveX GUI control.

FIGURE 13.1

The customized GUI control, LoginCtrl, in the design editor for a user ID and password entries

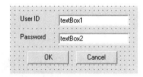

ActiveX Component from Microsoft Visual Studio 6

Before .NET, ActiveX controls played a major role in Microsoft's component-based applications. The development process of such controls is similar to the development process for the .NET user-defined GUI controls. However, the .NET GUI controls are managed assemblies. The ActiveX controls are COM-based components that implement a number of standard GUI interfaces in the Microsoft Visual Studio 6 IDE.

Developers can use several techniques in the Microsoft Visual Studio 6 IDE to develop user-defined GUI controls. One of them is to use the active template library (ATL), which generates a set of template-based C++ classes with which developers can easily create small, fast Component Object Model (COM) objects. Microsoft Visual C++ Microsoft Foundation Classes (MFCs) also supports the creation of ActiveX controls. To make use of the unmanaged MFC- and ATL-based GUI components, a computer system needs to know the correct Registry entries for the COM objects. This usually requires issuing a `RegSvr32` command from the DOS command prompt. However, in this chapter we will not use the ATL and MFC to develop COM components for testing.

> **NOTE** If you need details about ATL and MFC for developing COM components, you can refer to the sources in the bibliography at the end of this book.

There is another way to develop ActiveX controls: by using Visual Basic 6 in the Microsoft Visual Studio 6 IDE. Because Visual Basic 6 takes care of the templates and the Registry tasks for COM-based ActiveX development, this is an easy way to show how an ActiveX control is created, used, and tested by the .NET-based AutomatedGUITest tool. If you have the Microsoft Visual Studio 6 IDE installed on your system, you can choose Start ➤ Programs➤ Microsoft Visual Studio 6.0 ➤ Microsoft Visual Basic 6.0 to open a new session of the Microsoft Visual Basic 6 IDE. Then you can follow these steps to build an ActiveX control:

1. When the Microsoft Visual Basic 6 IDE starts, it brings up a New Project dialog box. Inside the dialog box, look for and select the ActiveX Control in the New tab. Then click the Open button to show the Visual Basic 6 design editor.

2. From the project property page, you can change the project name from Project1 (a default name given by the IDE) to VBLogin.

3. Use the following list to drag and drop the standard GUI controls from the toolbox to make a Visual Basic 6–based VBLogin control:

Control	Property	Value
Label	Name	lblUserID
	Caption	User ID

Control	Property	Value
Label	Name	lblPwd
	Caption	Password
TextBox	Name	txtUserID
TextBox	Name	txtPwd
CommandButton	Name	btnOK
	Caption	OK
CommandButton	Name	btnCancel
	Caption	Cancel

After you place these standard GUI controls for the VBLogin control according to the list, the VBLogin looks similar to the .NET-developed LoginCtrl control, as you can see in Figure 13.2.

There is also no need to add code manually for the VBLogin ActiveX control for the testing example in this chapter. You can save the project by making a VBLogin subfolder under C:\GUISourceCode\Chapter13 and choosing File ➢ Save Project. When the IDE prompts for the project and the source code filenames, you can type in **VBLogin.vbp** and **VBLogin.ctl**, respectively. Last, you can choose File ➢ Make VBLogin.ocx to build a VBLogin.ocx file in the C:\GUISourceCode\Chapter13\VBLogin folder.

NOTE   If you don't have Microsoft Visual Studio 6 IDE installed on your system, you can skip the VBLogin ActiveX sample project. Skipping this project will not affect your work in the rest of the chapter.

Now you have made a .NET user-defined control and a Visual Basic 6–based ActiveX control. The next job is to update the AutomatedGUITest tool to test these components.

FIGURE 13.2
The appearance of the VB 6–based VBLogin ActiveX control, which looks similar to the .NET LoginCtrl

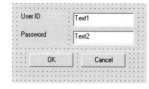

Needed Components for Testing User-Defined Controls

As we have discussed, an application under test asks the AutomatedGUITest tool to start the executable file. The .NET user-defined and ActiveX controls are not executable until they are implemented in an application. When you test these GUI controls, you need to add them into an application. Adding GUI controls into a .NET application is usually accomplished by following steps such as these:

1. Reference them in the component pane of the tool box.

2. Drag and drop the GUI control as you have the standard GUI controls.

3. Write code to use the controls.

   In the following sections, you will first add a test bench into the AutomatedGUITest tool to automatically accomplish these three steps and then you can add code to some existing classes.

Preparing a Testing Bench for Customized GUI Controls

In order for the AutomatedGUITest tool to start a user-defined control for a GUI survey and test, in this section you'll prepare a testing bench. To resume the development, you can follow the same pattern you used in previous chapters by copying the AutomatedGUITest, GUI-TestLibrary, and XmlTreeViewer projects from the C:\GUISourceCode\Chapter12 folder to the C:\GUISourceCode\Chapter13 folder. After the projects are copied, run the Microsoft Visual Studio .NET IDE to load the AutomatedGUITest project from the new folder. The following steps help you to add a Windows Form as a container for the custom GUI controls under test:

1. With the AutomatedGUITest project open in the Microsoft Visual Studio .NET IDE, from the Solution Explorer, select the GUITestLibrary project.

2. From the main window, choose Project ➤ Add Windows Form. An Add New Item dialog box appears.

3. In the Name field, type **ControlTestBench** and click the Open button. The Control-TestBench is created by the Microsoft Visual Studio .NET IDE as a Windows Form.

4. Right-click on the empty form to select the Properties menu. Locate the Text property and type in **Control Test Bench** as the new property value. This value appears on the title bar of the newly created Windows Form. Then locate the Size property to assign 300 and 300 as values for the width and the height of this Windows Form.

   Save the addition. That is all that is needed to build the custom GUI control testing bench.

A New Method for the *GUITestUtility* Class

Locate and double-click the GUITestUtility.cs file from the Solution Explorer. The GUITest-Utility code editor is brought into the Microsoft Visual Studio .NET IDE. Toward the end of the code section for the GUITestUtility class, place the cursor below the last method definition. You can code a StartControlUT() method for the GUITestUtility class for the new tasks to test custom GUI controls. The StartControlUT() method is the counterpart to the StartAUT() for testing .NET applications. Listing 13.1 shows the code for the StartControlUT() method.

Listing 13.1   **A New *StartControlUT()* Method to Start a Custom GUI Control for Survey and Testing**

```
public static ControlTestBench StartControlUT(string applicationPath,
➥string typeName)
{
  Control ctrlUT = (Control)StartAUT(applicationPath, typeName);
  ControlTestBench CTB = new ControlTestBench();
   CTB.Controls.Add(ctrlUT);
   return CTB;
}
```

The StartControlUT() method takes the same parameter signatures as the StartAUT() method does in the GUITestUtility class. It actually calls the StartAUT() method to create a Control object for the custom GUI control in the first line.

Next, a ControlTestBench object, CTB, is initialized. The CTB object inherits all the members from the System.Windows.Forms.Form class. Serving as a parent Windows Form, the CTB object has a Controls property, which is a collection of the child GUI controls. A child control can be added and removed from the collection. In this case, the code calls the Add() method to add the custom GUI Control object under test into the collection.

The last line of the code returns a test bench to the caller of the StartControlUT() method. The caller could be the AutomatedGUITest tool for starting a GUI survey or the GUITestScript class for completing a GUI testing.

After adding the code for the StartControlUT() method in the GUITestUtility class, you may build the project and make sure there are no syntax errors in the new code.

Invoking the Test Bench from the AutomatedGUITest Tool

In order to start a GUI survey for the custom GUI controls, a few lines of code are needed for the AutomatedGUITest.cs file. You can locate and right-click the AutomatedGUITest.cs file from the Solution Explorer and select the View Code item from the pop-up menu. When the code editor appears, navigate to the btnStartGUITest_Click() event. Inside the definition of this event, find the `try-catch` clause. You need to comment out the `Messege.Show()` line in the curly brackets of the `catch` statement and add two lines of code like this:

```
formUT = GUITestUtility.StartControlUT(applicationUT, startupForm);
formUT.Show();
```

The first line calls the `StartControlUT()` method coded in the preceding section and assigns the test bench to the `formUT` object as the application under test. The `formUT` object has a `Show()` method that makes the application under test visible and surveyable on the screen. Listing 13.2 shows the new code and the commented-out code in bold for the `btnStartGUITest_Click()` event.

Listing 13.2   **New and Commented Code in Bold for the *btnStartGUITest_Click()* Event**

```
private void btnStartGUITest_Click(object sender, System.EventArgs e)
{
  TypesToVerify = new TypeVerificationSerializable();
  GUISequence = 0;//added for chapter 8

  GUITestSeqList = new GUITestUtility.GUIInfoSerializable();

  opnAUT.Title = "Specify an Application Under Test";
  opnAUT.Filter = "GUI Applications(*.EXE;
*.DLL)|*.EXE;*.DLL|All files (*.*)|*.*";
  if (opnAUT.ShowDialog() == DialogResult.OK)
  {
    applicationUT = opnAUT.FileName;
    GUITestSeqList.AUTPath = applicationUT;

    GetTypeToTestFromAUT();

    try
    {
      formUT = (Form)GUITestUtility.StartAUT(applicationUT, startupForm);
    }
    catch (InvalidCastException ex)
    {
      //Chapter 13
      //MessageBox.Show(ex.Message);
      formUT = GUITestUtility.StartControlUT(applicationUT, startupForm);
      formUT.Show();
    }
  }
  else
  {
    return;
  }
}
```

As discussed, the `try-catch` clause in the `btnStartGUITest_Click()` event starts the application to test. When the object under test is a custom GUI control, the execution of the statement in the `try` curly brackets throws an error. The error will be caught and the statements in the `catch` curly brackets will work smoothly to start the custom GUI control on the screen. Thus, the updating of the `AutomatedGUITest.cs` file is completed. You can compile the project and correct errors.

The coding task in the next section for modifying the `GUITestScript` class seems a little clumsy. But it has been refactored and works pleasantly for testing the new GUI components.

Handling Exceptions in the *GUITestScript* Class

If you run the existing `GUITestScript` class at this moment and start to test a custom GUI control, several code fragments throw exceptions when they accept custom GUI controls as parameters. The code addition in this section will add a handful of `try-catch` statements to catch these exceptions. The existing code in the `try` clause has taken care of the regular .NET applications. New code will be added to process the custom control inside the `catch` statements.

A `StartAUT()` method has also been implemented for the `GUITestScript` class since Chapter 7, and it becomes the first target for code modification. You can locate the `StartAUT()` method in the `GUITestScript.cs` file and add some lines of code. Listing 13.3 shows the code that should be after the modification.

Listing 13.3   **The Modified *StartAUT()* Method for the *GUITestScript* Class with the New Code and the Commented Code in Bold**

```
private void StartAUT()
{
  seqGUIUT = new GUITestUtility.GUIInfoSerializable();
  object obj = (object)seqGUIUT;
  GUITestUtility.DeSerializeInfo(guiTestDataStore, ref obj);
  seqGUIUT = (GUITestUtility.GUIInfoSerializable)obj;

  string AUTPath = seqGUIUT.AUTPath;
  string startupType = seqGUIUT.AUTStartupForm;

  int hwnd = 0;

  if (AUT == null)
  {
    try //chapter 13
    {
      AUT = (Form)GUITestUtility.StartAUT(AUTPath, startupType);
      hwnd = (int)AUT.Handle;
    }
    catch (InvalidCastException ex) //chapter 13
```

```
    {
      AUT = GUITestUtility.StartControlUT(AUTPath, startupType);
      AUT.Show();
      Control ctrlAUT = AUT.Controls[0];
      hwnd = (int)ctrlAUT.Handle;
    }
  }
  //int hwnd = (int)AUT.Handle;

  StringBuilder sbClsName = new StringBuilder(128);
  GUITestActions.GetClassName(hwnd, sbClsName, 128);
  string clsName = sbClsName.ToString();
  string winText = AUT.Text;
  string pText = "";
  GUITestActions.SynchronizeWindow(ref hwnd,
➥ref winText, ref clsName, ref pText);
}
```

The first added line prepares a hwnd variable as an integer object to hold the handle of the application under test (note that the commented-out line at the end of the new code section has served this purpose). The statements inside the try clause were implemented for testing the regular .NET applications and have been discussed in previous chapters. Inside the catch clause, the first two lines of code are copied from the btnStartGUITest_Click() event of the AutomatedGUITest.cs file.

As it has been explained, the custom control is contained in the control test bench. The test bench serves as the parent window of the custom control. The custom control contains child controls, which will receive the testing actions. Thus, the test script needs to use the custom control window to retrieve the parent window handle. The third and fourth lines of code inside the catch clause simply get the window handle of the custom control, indexed to be zero inside the Controls property of the test bench. Thus, the custom control is invoked as a window application on the screen smoothly.

The second modification for the GUITestScript class happens to be the RunsScript() method, which has been modified a few times since its inception. The modified code is in Listing 13.4.

Listing 13.4 **The Code for the *RunsScript()* Method with the New and Commented Lines in Bold and the Second Part Omitted**

```
private void RunsScript()
{
  guiTestActionLib = Path.Combine(progDir, "GUITestActionLib.xml");

  GUITestUtility.GUIInfo guiUnit =
➥(GUITestUtility.GUIInfo)seqGUIUT.GUIList[clickNum];
```

```
    string ctrlAction =
➡GUITestUtility.GetAGUIAction(guiTestActionLib, guiUnit.GUIControlType);
    StringBuilder sb = new StringBuilder(10000);

    try //chapter 12
    {
      //Control ctrlTested =
➡(Control)GUITestUtility.VerifyField(AUT, guiUnit.GUIControlName);
      Control ctrlTested; //chapter 13
      try
      {
        ctrlTested =
➡(Control)GUITestUtility.VerifyField(AUT, guiUnit.GUIControlName);
      }
      catch(Exception ex)
      {
        ctrlTested =
➡(Control)GUITestUtility.VerifyField(AUT.Controls[0], guiUnit.GUIControlName);
      }
      GUITestActions.GetWindowText((int)ctrlTested.Handle, sb, 10000);
    }
    //catch{}
    catch
    {
      sb = new StringBuilder(guiUnit.GUIText);
    }

    //object[] paramArr = new object[4];
    ...
    ...
}
```

Within an existing try clause, a new try-catch clause is inserted. The first existing assignment for the Control object, ctrlTested, is commented out. But a new addition declares ctrlTested as a Control variable without assignment. Then the try statement starts to initialize the declared ctrlTested variable for a regular .NET application under test. If the try statement throws an exception, the catch statement locates the custom control inside the test bench by a zero index value of the Controls collection. Last, the window handle is found and the GetWindowText() method is invoked to find the current window text of the GUI object under test.

Finally, the existing catch clause, which has been empty, is modified for testing the ActiveX controls. At this point, the window text for a GUI object in an ActiveX control can not be found by calling the GetWindowText() method. When the GetWindowText() method fails, the existing catch statement catches the error and initializes the StringBuilder object with the value the window text of that GUI object had when the testing data was collected.

NOTE   To avoid repeating discussions in previous chapters, the AutomatedGUITest tool will not be
implemented for verification of testing the ActiveX controls.

Third, you need to locate the AddTestVerification() method within the GUITestScript
class and add a couple more try-catch clauses within the existing try-catch clause. The modified AddTestVerification() method is in Listing 13.5.

Listing 13.5   **The Modified *AddTestVerification()* Method with the Newly Added *try-catch***
Clause in Bold.

```
private void AddTestVerification()
{
  if (AUT == null)
    return;

  string VerifyDataStore = guiTestDataStore.Replace(".xml", "_verify.xml");

  TypeVerificationSerializable verifyTypes = new TypeVerificationSerializable();
  object obj = (object)verifyTypes;
  GUITestUtility.DeSerializeInfo(VerifyDataStore, ref obj);
  verifyTypes = (TypeVerificationSerializable)obj;

  TypeVerification oneType =
➥(TypeVerification)verifyTypes.TypeList[clickNum - 1];
  object resulted = null;

  foreach (TestExpectation fieldName in oneType.MemberList)
  {
    TestExpectation tested = fieldName;
    try
    {
      try
      {
        resulted =  GUITestUtility.VerifyField(AUT, tested.VerifyingMember);
      }
      catch //chapter 13
      {
        resulted =
➥GUITestUtility.VerifyField(AUT.Controls[0], tested.VerifyingMember);
      }
      tested.isField = true;


    }
    catch(Exception ex4)
    {
```

```
        try
        {
           resulted =  GUITestUtility.VerifyProperty(AUT, tested.VerifyingMember);
        }
        catch
        {
           resulted =
➡GUITestUtility.VerifyProperty(AUT.Controls[0], tested.VerifyingMember);
        }
        tested.isProperty = true;
     }

     VerifyAlphanumericResult(ref tested, resulted);
     VerifyClipboard(ref tested, resulted);
     //chapter 9
     VerifyLabel(ref tested, resulted);
     VerifyGroupBox(ref tested, resulted);

     //Chapter 11
     VerifyRadioButtonCheckBox(ref tested, resulted);

  }
}
```

You may have discovered that the added code inside the try clause is for testing the regular .NET applications. The code added into the catch clause is for testing the custom GUI control. The test script always locates the GUI object under test within the Control collection of the test bench by looking for a zero index value. We can use this deduction to complete the modification for two more methods, the GetCheckedButtonInGroup() method and the DeterminePreCheckedStatus() method. The new code for these two methods are in Listing 13.6 and Listing 13.7, respectively.

Listing 13.6   **The Added *try-catch* Clause for the *GetCheckedButtonInGroup()* Method with the New Code in Bold**

```
private bool GetCheckedButtonInGroup(RadioButton rdBtn, ref string ErrorMsg)
{

   int parentHandle = GUITestActions.GetParent((int)rdBtn.Handle);
   //Control parentGrp = (Control)GUITestUtility.VerifyField(AUT, parentHandle);
   Control parentGrp;
   try
   {
     parentGrp = (Control)GUITestUtility.VerifyField(AUT, parentHandle);
   }
   catch
   {
     parentGrp =
➡(Control)GUITestUtility.VerifyField(AUT.Controls[0], parentHandle);
   }
```

```
    foreach (Control ctrl in parentGrp.Controls)
    {
      try
      {
        RadioButton rdCtrl = (RadioButton)ctrl;
        if (rdCtrl.Name == rdBtn.Name)
        {
          if (!rdBtn.Checked)
          {
            ErrorMsg = rdBtn.Name + " is not checked!";
            return false;
          }
        }
        else
        {
          if (rdCtrl.Checked)
          {
            ErrorMsg = "Other than or beside the " + rdBtn.Name +
              " is checked, the " + rdCtrl.Name + " is also checked!";
            return false;
          }
        }

      }
      catch{}
    }
    return true;
}
```

The modification of Listing 13.6 simply comments and rewrites the existing statement:

```
Control parentGrp = (Control)GUITestUtility.VerifyField(AUT, parentHandle);
```

The rewritten code includes the commented-out statement inside a newly added `try-catch` statement in order to verify a check box or a radio button within a group box.

Listing 13.7   The Added *try-catch* Clause for the *DeterminePreCheckedStatus()* Method with the New Code in Bold

```
private bool DeterminePreCheckedStatus(GUITestUtility.GUIInfo guiUnit)
{

  bool isChecked = false;
  if (guiUnit.GUIControlType == "System.Windows.Form.CheckBox")
  {
    //CheckBox chckBx =
➥(CheckBox)GUITestUtility.VerifyField(AUT, guiUnit.GUIControlName);
    CheckBox chckBx;
    try
    {
      chckBx =
```

```
➥(CheckBox)GUITestUtility.VerifyField(AUT, guiUnit.GUIControlName);
    }
    catch
    {
      chckBx =
➥(CheckBox)GUITestUtility.VerifyField(AUT.Controls[0], guiUnit.GUIControlName);
    }

    isChecked = chckBx.Checked;
  }
  return isChecked;
}
```

Similar to the modification in Listing 13.6, Listing 13.7 commented out the existing statement:

```
CheckBox chckBx =
➥(CheckBox)GUITestUtility.VerifyField(AUT, guiUnit.GUIControlName);
```

The statement was rewritten in an added try-catch clause. The try statement helps to find out whether a CheckBox control under test in a regular .NET application is checked or not. The catch statement helps to find out whether a CheckBox control under test in a custom GUI control is checked or not.

Now the code is complete and you can press F5 to build and run the AutomatedGUITest tool. If there are any compiling errors, you can correct the code by comparing your code with the sample code downloaded from www.sybex.com. Thus, the AutomatedGUITest project is prepared for testing custom GUI controls, such as the developed user-defined .NET and the COM-based ActiveX controls. We will conclude this chapter with two testing examples.

Two More Examples

After the AutomatedGUITest project has been updated, testing a custom .NET GUI control is identical to testing a regular .NET application. It is well known that .NET programs produce managed assemblies and COM-based components are not managed code. Therefore, we still need a little trick to convert COM-based ActiveX controls into managed assemblies. The next sections will start with the .NET user-defined control and then solve the conversion dilemma.

Testing a Customized .NET GUI Control

After you build and run the AutomatedGUITest tool with the new enhancement, you can click the Start GUI Test button to test the customized LoginCtrl control developed with the Microsoft Visual Studio .NET IDE. The steps are as follows:

1. When the open file dialog box appears, navigate to the C:\GUISourceCode\Chapter13\ LoginCtrl\bin\Debug folder to select the LoginCtrl.dll assembly. Click the Open button.

2. The Types under Test form appears with the control class `LoginCtrl.UserControl1`. The class name, `UserControl1`, is assigned by the Microsoft Visual Studio .NET IDE by default. (You can change the default value, but for simplification, we didn't change it when we developed it.) Select the check box and click the OK button.

3. The LoginCtrl control appears within the test bench (Figure 13.3). From the Automated-GUITest tool, click the GUI Survey button. The testing tool completes the GUI survey in a few seconds (depending on the computer system).

4. When the AutomatedGUITest tool reappears, locate and double-click the left edge of textBox1 under the Window Text column in the DataGrid. When the GUI Test Data Collector pops up, in the Text Entry field, type {BS} and {DEL} key code to let the test script press the Backspace key and the Delete key nine times in order to clear the text box for a new entry and append a user ID to the key code. The complete entry looks similar to **{BS 9}{DEL 9}my user ID**. (If it is needed, you can refer to Table 10.1 for code of the special keys.) Select the simple verification method. At this moment, the GUI Test Data Collector looks like Figure 13.4. Click the OK button.

5. Locate and double-click the left edge of textBox2 in the DataGrid under the Window Text column. This time, type a password after the Backspace and Delete key code in the Text Entry field of the GUI Test Data Collector, such as **{BS 9}{DEL 9}my password**. Select the simple verification method and click the OK button.

6. Last, locate and double-click the left edge of the OK button in the DataGrid. Select the simple verification method and click the OK button.

7. Close the test bench and click the Run Test button from the AutomatedGUITest tool. When the save file dialog box appears, type in a filename such as `C:\Temp\TestLoginCtrl.xml`. After you click the Save button, the testing data is saved and the test completes in a few seconds.

FIGURE 13.3
The test bench
with the LoginCtrl
control started by
the testing tool

FIGURE 13.4
Collecting data to test
the txtUserID object

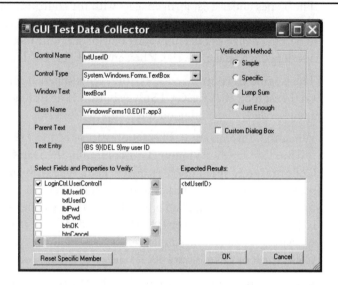

Note that the LoginCtrl control has only the standard GUI controls, but it has no custom code. The purpose of developing such a control is purely for testing the updated Automated-GUITest tool in this chapter. This statement also applies to the ActiveX example.

Testing an ActiveX GUI Control

The developed tool is now able to test .NET Windows Forms applications and custom controls. Although code has been added to the tool to handle the ActiveX control testing, a special treatment is in need before you submit the ActiveX control to testing.

The ActiveX controls are COM-based applications. The testing tool developed in C# doesn't consider the COM-based controls as .NET Windows forms. In order to adapt the Automated-GUITest tool to test the ActiveX controls, you must generate a wrapper control that derives from the System.Windows.Forms.AxHost class. This wrapper control contains an instance of the underlying ActiveX control. It knows how to communicate with the ActiveX control, but it appears as a Windows Forms control. The testing tool uses the wrapper control to access the properties, methods, and events of the ActiveX control.

To make things easy, the Microsoft Visual Studio .NET IDE comes with a tool, aximp.exe, which can be found in the C:\Program Files\Microsoft Visual Studio .NET 2003\SDK\v1.1\Bin folder. The tool is also called ActiveX Control Importer. It can convert ActiveX control type definitions in a COM type library into a Windows Forms control. When a line command is issued from the Visual Studio .NET 2003 command prompt, the aximp.exe generates a wrapper class for an ActiveX control that can be hosted on a Windows form. This allows the AutomatedGUITest project to use the same design-time support and programming methodology applicable for other Windows Forms controls.

You can start a session of a command prompt by choosing Start ➤ Visual Studio .NET 2003 Command Prompt. When the command prompt appears, change the directory to C:\GUISource-Code\Chapter13\VBLogin, which stores the VBLogin.ocx ActiveX control. Then issue the following command:

```
aximp VBLogin.ocx /out:DotNetVBLogin.dll
```

The first argument is the filename of the ActiveX control. An option, /out:, is used as the second parameter to specify a output name for the .NET wrapper. After the execution of the aximp command, you can issue another line command to see the resulting .NET assemblies:

```
dir *.dll
```

For your convenience, Figure 13.5 shows the prompt window after three of the line commands.

You find out that the aximp.exe generates two .NET assemblies (with .dll extensions). The DotNetVBLogin.dll filename is given at the prompt and is the Windows Forms proxy for the ActiveX control. The other assembly has the name VBLogin.dll, which contains the common language runtime proxy for COM types of the ActiveX control. The converted ActiveX control is now ready for the AutomatedGUITest tool to conduct a test.

NOTE   If you haven't had the chance to develop the VBLogin ActiveX control, you can use a system ActiveX control to continue this example. The system ActiveX controls are installed in the system root directory, C:\WINDOWS\System32 on my computer. For example, you may try mscomctl.ocx, which contains the Microsoft common controls.

FIGURE 13.5
The results of the
three line commands

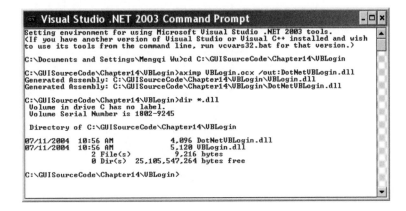

With the AutomatedGUITest tool running on your system, click the Start GUI Test button as usual to bring up the open file dialog box. Then navigate to select the C:\GUISourceCode\ Chapter13\VBLogin\DotNetVBLogin.dll assembly and click the Open button. When the Types under Test form appears, follow these steps to complete the example:

1. The DotNetVBLogin.dll assembly hosts two data types, AxVBLogin.AxUserControl1 and AxVBLogin.AxUserControl1EventMulticaster. Select the check box beside AxVBLogin .AxUserControl1. Click the OK button to bring up the test bench with the ActiveX control under test.

2. Make sure the test bench is visible on the screen. Click the GUI Survey button from the testing tool. The survey completes in a few seconds and the result is similar to Figure 13.6.

3. Similar to testing the .NET LoginCtrl control, double-click the left edge of the GUI object with Text1 as the value of its Window Text. Text1 is for the entry of a user ID. When the GUI Test Data Collector appears, you'll find that the tool is not enabled to find the control name and the control type for the individual GUI object. You can type in the control name as **txtUserID** and control type as **System.Windows.Forms.TextBox**. In the Text Entry field, type **{BS 6}{DEL 6}my user ID** (see Figure 13.7). For this test, the {BS} and {DEL} key presses repeat six times each to clear the text box. Then click the OK button.

4. Double-click the Text2 window text. Use Figure 13.8 as a sample to enter the values for this test step. After the values are entered, click the OK button.

FIGURE 13.6
The survey result of testing the ActiveX control

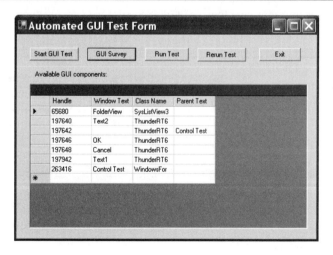

FIGURE 13.7
The entries for testing
the txtUserID field

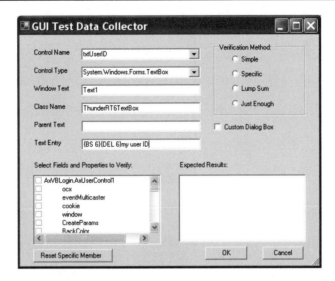

FIGURE 13.7
The entries for testing
the `txtUserID` field

5. The last step is to double-click the OK window text and enter the correct values for testing the OK command button as shown in Figure 13.9. Click the OK button from the GUI Test Data Collector.

6. Close the test bench and click the Run Test button from the testing tool. When the save file dialog box appears, type in **C:\Temp\TestActiveX.xml** as the filename to save the testing data store. The testing data is saved and the testing completes in a few second.

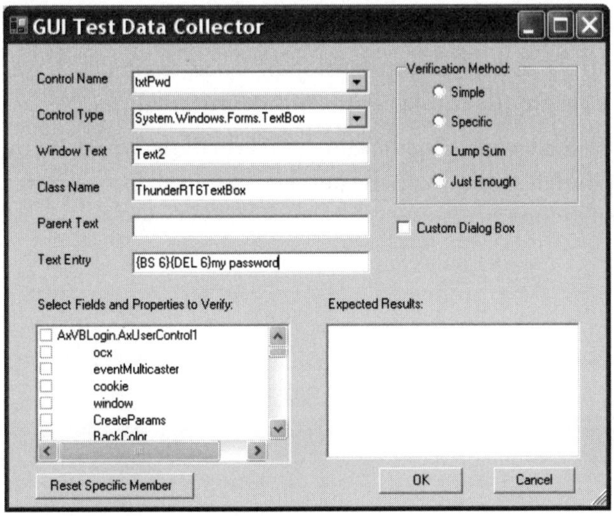

FIGURE 13.8
The entries for testing
the `txtPwd` field

FIGURE 13.9
The entries for
testing the cmdOK
command button

When the XML Document Viewer appears, the result doesn't show the test verification the tool hasn't been implemented with verification functions for testing applications other than .NET applications to avoid overwhelming and distracting you with too much code and redundancy. But you have learned the basic methods to enable such functionalities and you can reference to the previous chapters to develop a new tool.

Summary

You now have a basic idea of how to test user-defined GUI controls and COM-based ActiveX controls. When you are developing a new testing tool, you can use the methods introduced in this chapter to enable other testing functionalities.

I will keep updating the sample code in the web page for this book. You can visit www.sybex.com for the latest update. In the next chapter, I will discuss how to test applications other than .NET applications.

CHAPTER 14

Testing Issues for
Non .NET Applications

If you have been involved in testing software not developed with Microsoft Visual Studio .NET, you may have tried to test them using the AutomatedGUITest tool. The tool is able to test COM-based applications after the COM applications are converted to managed assemblies. Unfortunately, other non .NET applications define sole entry point methods, such as `WinMain()`, to access the executables, which are specific to platform and CPU. Although the .NET EXE binaries provide a `WinMain()` or `Main()` method as the entry point, the behind-the-scenes logic is different. The .NET binaries contain code constructed using Microsoft Intermediate Language (MSIL or IL), which is platform and CPU agnostic. At run time, the internal IL is compiled on-the-fly (using a just-in-time compiler) to platform- and CPU-specific instructions. The AutomatedGUITest tool can not start a survey for the traditional applications by using the code developed in the previous chapters.

This chapter will add some code to the AutomatedGUITest project so that the .NET developed tool can be used to find GUI objects for testing in traditional applications. At the end of this chapter, an example will be performed using the `Notepad.exe` application.

Intermediate Language

When compiling to managed code, the compiler translates the source code into Microsoft Intermediate language (MSIL), which is a CPU-independent set of instructions that can be efficiently converted to native code. MSIL includes instructions for loading, storing, initializing, and calling methods on objects as well as instructions for arithmetic and logical operations, control flow, direct memory access, exception handling, and other operations. Before code can be executed, MSIL must be converted to CPU-specific code by a just-in-time (JIT) compiler. Because the common language runtime supplies one or more JIT compilers for a computer architecture it supports, the same set of MSIL can be JIT-compiled and executed on any supported architecture.

When a compiler produces MSIL, it also produces metadata. Metadata describes the types in the code, including the definition of each type, the signatures of each type's members, the members that the code references, and other data that the runtime uses at execution time. The MSIL and metadata are contained in a portable executable (PE) file that is based on and extends the published Microsoft PE and Common Object File Format (COFF) used historically for executable content. This file format, which accommodates MSIL or native code as well as metadata, enables the operating system to recognize common language runtime images. The presence of metadata in the file along with the MSIL enables the code to describe itself, which means that there is no need for type libraries or Interface Definition Language (IDL). The runtime locates and extracts the metadata from the file as needed during execution.

Adding a Method to Start Traditional Applications

In the previous chapters, the AutomatedGUITest tool uses the late binding method to load .NET-aware applications and their specified startup forms for GUI survey and testing. After the application starts, the tool holds a copy of it as an object. Therefore, the GUI survey result list has two sources of data to specify testing steps and verification. Later, when testing starts, the GUITestScript class follows the testing steps in the testing data store and compares the consequences of the selected GUI components, the status changes of the object copy of the application held by the tool, and the expected results given by the testers.

The late binding method cannot be used to invoke a non .NET application for testing. An object of the application under test can not be held as they are when .NET aware applications are tested. However, the .NET platform provides classes in the System.Diagnostics namespace to start applications and keep track the status of the application. Using a Process class from the System .Diagnostics namespace, the following sections introduce the Process class and implement a method in the GUITestUtility class to expand the testing horizon of the AutomatedGUITest tool.

An Overview of the *System.Diagnostics* Namespace

The Microsoft Visual Studio .NET platform has a System.Diagnostics namespace. The System.Diagnostics namespace provides classes that allow you to interact with system processes, event logs, performance counters and a Debug class.

The Debug class provides a set of methods and properties that help debug the application under test. Methods in the Debug class can print debugging information and check code logic with assertions.

The EventLog component provides functionality to write to event logs, read event log entries, and create and delete event logs and event sources on the network.

The PerformanceCounter class enables a tester to monitor system performance, while the PerformanceCounterCategory class provides a way to create new custom counters and categories.

The Process class provides functionality to monitor system processes across the network and to start and stop local system processes. In addition to retrieving lists of running processes (by specifying the computer, the process name, or the process ID) or viewing information about the process that currently has access to the processor, you can get detailed knowledge of process threads and modules both through the Process class itself and by interacting with the ProcessThread and ProcessModule classes. In addition to the various methods, including Start() and Kill(), the Process class has numerous properties. Here are a few examples:

BasePriority   Gets the base priority of the associated process

Handle   Returns the associated process's native handle

HandleCount   Gets the number of handles opened by the process

`MachineName`   Gets the name of the computer the associated process is running on

`StandardError`   Gets a `StreamReader` through which to read error output from the application

`StartInfo`   Gets or sets the properties to pass to the `Start()` method of the `Process` class

The `ProcessStartInfo` class enables a program to specify a variety of elements with which to start a new process, such as input, output, and error streams; working directories; and command-line verbs and arguments. These give you fine control over the behavior of the processes. The following is a list of properties of the `ProcessStartInfo` class:

`Arguments`   Gets or sets the set of command line arguments to use when starting the application

`ErrorDialog`   Gets or sets a value indicating whether an error dialog is displayed to the user if the process cannot be started

`FileName`   Gets or sets the application or document to start

`RedirectStandardError`   Gets or sets a value indicating whether the process's error output is written to the `Process` instance's `StandardError` member

`UseShellExecute`   Gets or sets a value indicating whether to use the operating system shell to start the process

Although the `Debug`, `EventLog`, `PerformanceCounter`, `Process`, and `ProcessStartInfo` classes from the `System.Diagnostic` namespace can be explored and implemented in the Automated-GUITest tool to accomplish the GUI testing and verification tasks, to avoid repeating information presented in Chapters 7 through 12, this chapter will focus on only the `Process` class to start a non .NET application for a GUI survey. You can implement your tool based on the discussion in this chapter and the previous chapters for a fully functional tool with a high degree of testing automation.

Updating the *GUITestUtility* Class

You implemented a `StartAUT()` method for the `GUITestUtility` class of the GUI test library in Chapter 6. The `StartAUT()` method uses the late binding method to start the application under test. But this late binding method invokes .NET-aware components only. As a counterpart, this chapter adds a `StartAUTAsProcess()` method to the same `GUITestUtility` class.

As usual, you need to make a `C:\GUISourceCode\Chapter14` folder, and copy the three projects—AutomatedGUITest, GUITestLibrary and XmlTreeViewer—from the `C:\GUISourceCode\Chapter13` folder to the new folder. Then start the AutomatedGUITest project with the Microsoft Visual Studio .NET IDE. From the GUITestLibrary project, locate the GUITestUtility class and code a new method. The StartAUTAsProcess() method uses properties of the Process class to bring up non .NET applications under test. The code of the new method is in Listing 14.1.

Listing 14.1   **The Code for the *StartAUTAsProcess()* Method in the *GUITestUtility* Class**

```
public static object StartAUTAsProcess(string applicationPath, string arguments)
{
  System.Diagnostics.Process appProc = new System.Diagnostics.Process();
  appProc.StartInfo.FileName = applicationPath;
  appProc.StartInfo.Arguments = arguments;
  appProc.Start();

  return appProc;

}
```

The StartAUTAsProcess() method needs to know the path of the application as its parameter. The first line of the code uses the full qualifier of the System.Diagnostics namespace to initialize a Process object, appProc. Then the method dispatches the StartInfo property and assigns the given path of the application in need of testing to the Filename and the Arguments properties. The appProc object obtains enough information and starts the application under test by invoking the Start() method. The process for returning an object by the StartAUTAsProcess() method is similar to what is used by its counterpart, the StartAUT() method. You can explore the returned object to enable the AutomatedGUITest tool for more verification functions.

The StartInfo property can be used to accept background knowledge of the application under test. For example, some applications start with a command line of the program name appended with one or more arguments. The program name is assigned to the Filename property and the arguments to the Arguments property of the StartInfo property. For example, if you develop a GUI testing tool for Java projects, you can start a Java application by assigning word *Java* as the value of the Filename property and the name of the application under test as the value of the Arguments property. You can also manipulate the WindowStyle property to start a window program in minimized, maximized, or normal size.

After you copy the code in Listing 14.1 to the GUITestUtility class, you can save and build the project. But the newly added method is still not used in the AutomatedGUITest tool at this point. You need complete the rest of the updating before a test can be done.

Making the AutomatedGUITest Tool Probe the GUI Interface

When the AutomatedGUITest tool starts the application with the late binding method, the tool holds a complete object of the application. All the needed information can be queried instantly and be used for GUI survey and verification purposes. For example, the object first provides the window handle of the application to start the GUI survey. Using the Process class, you can code the method in Listing 14.1 to obtain other information about the application under test. However, to make the AutomatedGUITest tool more flexible, in the following sections, you'll add a GUI control and some methods into the AutomatedGUITest user interface to probe the GUI front end of an application.

Adding a PictureBox Control as a GUI Probe

Locate the AutomatedGUITest.cs code file in the Solution Explorer of the Microsoft Visual Studio .NET IDE. Double-click the AutomatedGUITest.cs file and the user interface designer appears. From the toolbox, drag and drop a PictureBox control to an area between the already coded buttons. Change the properties of the PictureBox as follows:

Name: **pbProbe**

BorderStyle: **Fixed3D**

Image: `C:\GUISourceCode\Chapter03\TestMonkey\Monkey.ico`

Leave the values of the other properties intact. The Monkey.ico was provided when you programmed a test monkey in Chapter 3 (downloadable from www.sybex.com). If you don't have this icon, you can use any picture you prefer. Figure 14.1 shows the AutomatedGUITest interface with the picture box under the GUI survey button.

FIGURE 14.1
The added picture box for a GUI survey probe on the AutomatedGUITest tool interface

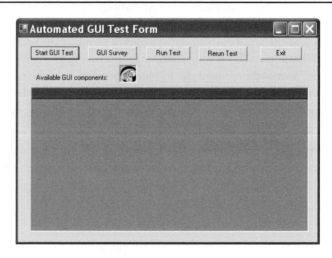

Story of the Monkey King

The image of the Monkey.ico is the head of the monkey king, Sun Wukong, who was the hero of the *Journey to the West* (Wu Chengen, 1500–1582). Sun Wukong was born from a rock and learned his stuff from Patriarch Subodhi. He was able to see through, hear from, and travel in the outer space with one somersault covering 54,000 kilometers. His golden and laser eyes could tell the good from the evil. He also had the ability to change himself into 72 different forms. Then, from the crystal palace in the sea, he acquired a golden ringed probe belonging to the dragon king. The probe weighed 6750 kilograms, measured longer than 6 meters, and was able to shrink to the size of a sewing needle and be carried behind his ear. Using the probe, he conquered immortals in heaven and demons in hell. Finally, he was captured and imprisoned under five mountains by Gautama Buddha (563–483 b.c.). After he was released in 500 years, he helped Tang Monk (602–664) through 81 (9 × 9) sufferings and helped him to get 5048 volumes of scriptures from India to China. You can read more about this legend at www.china-on-site.com/monkey.php.

In order to make the pbProbe picture box capable of being dragged across the screen and finding a GUI object of interest, you need to add three delegates for the pbProbe in the Initialize-Component() method of the AutomatedGUITest.cs file. You can right-click on the interface designer of the AutomatedGUITest tool and select the View Code item from the pop-up menu. When the code editor appears, use your mouse or arrow keys to move the cursor to the InitializeComponent() method. Most of the code inside the InitializeComponent() method is generated by the Microsoft Visual Studio .NET IDE and is concealed between a #region Windows Form Designer generated code and #endregion directive. If the region is concealed, you can reveal it by holding the Ctrl key and pressing M and L, or using the mouse to click the plus sign to expand it.

Inside the InitializeComponent() method, navigate to the code fragment indicated by the // pbProbe comment and append the three delegates to this code section:

```
this.pbProbe.MouseUp += new
➡System.Windows.Forms.MouseEventHandler(this.pbProbe_MouseUp);
this.pbProbe.MouseMove += new
➡System.Windows.Forms.MouseEventHandler(this.pbProbe_MouseMove);
this.pbProbe.MouseDown += new
➡System.Windows.Forms.MouseEventHandler(this.pbProbe_MouseDown);
```

The new code for the InitializeComponent() method is shown in Listing 14.2 in bold with the other IDE-generated code omitted.

Listing 14.2   The Code Fragment of the *pbProbe* in the *InitializeComponent()* Method

```
#region Windows Form Designer generated code
/// <summary>
/// Required method for Designer support - do not modify
/// the contents of this method with the code editor.
/// </summary>
private void InitializeComponent()
{
...
  this.lblAvailabelGUI.Text = "Available GUI components:";
  //
  // pbProbe
  //
  this.pbProbe.BorderStyle = System.Windows.Forms.BorderStyle.Fixed3D;
  this.pbProbe.Image = ((System.Drawing.Image)
➥(resources.GetObject("pbProbe.Image")));
  this.pbProbe.Location = new System.Drawing.Point(184, 56);
  this.pbProbe.Name = "pbProbe";
  this.pbProbe.Size = new System.Drawing.Size(32, 32);
  this.pbProbe.TabIndex = 9;
  this.pbProbe.TabStop = false;
  this.pbProbe.MouseUp += new
➥System.Windows.Forms.MouseEventHandler(this.pbProbe_MouseUp);
  this.pbProbe.MouseMove += new
➥System.Windows.Forms.MouseEventHandler(this.pbProbe_MouseMove);
  this.pbProbe.MouseDown += new
➥System.Windows.Forms.MouseEventHandler(this.pbProbe_MouseDown);
  //
  // frmMain
  //
  this.AutoScaleBaseSize = new System.Drawing.Size(5, 13);
...
}
```

Coding the Three Events for the GUI Probe

After the addition of the three delegates in Listing 14.2, the other code to tune the appearance and location of the picture box has been taken care of by the Microsoft Visual Studio .NET IDE. The added delegates invoke the MouseUp, MouseDown, and MouseMove events. The remaining task is to code these events. Listing 14.3 shows the definition of the needed fields and the code for the pbProbe_MouseDown() event.

Listing 14.3   Definition of the Needed Fields and the *pbProbe_MouseDown()* Event

```
private bool isDown;
private int dlgHandle;
private System.Text.StringBuilder dlgText;
```

```
private System.Text.StringBuilder dlgClsName;
private System.Text.StringBuilder dlgPText;

private void pbProbe_MouseDown(object sender,
➡System.Windows.Forms.MouseEventArgs e)
{
    isDown = true;
}
```

The first part of Listing 14.3 defines five private fields. When users drag a GUI object from one place to another, they needs to hold the left mouse button down. The isDown variable will be set to true when the mouse pointer is over the pbProbe object. The other four definitions are needed for holding the values of the handle, the text, the class name, and the parent text for a GUI object.

The second part is the code for the pbProbe_MouseDown() event. When the left mouse button is pressed, only one line of code is needed to set the isDown to true.

When you use a computer application, you move the mouse frequently. The purpose of programming a MouseMove event for the pbProb control is to enable a visual effect. Such an effect allows the user to distinguish the probe movement from the regular mouse movement. Listing 14.4 is the code for the pbProbe_MouseMove() event.

Listing 14.4   **The Code for the Tasks of the *pbProbe_MouseMove()* Event**

```
private void pbProbe_MouseMove(object sender,
➡System.Windows.Forms.MouseEventArgs e)
{

    Cursor csr = new Cursor(@"C:\GUISourceCode\Chapter03\TestMonkey\Monkey.ico");

    if (isDown)
    {
      pbProbe.Image = null;
      this.Cursor = csr;

      dlgText = new System.Text.StringBuilder();
      dlgClsName = new System.Text.StringBuilder();
      dlgPText = new System.Text.StringBuilder();

      GUITestActions.GetWindowFromPoint(ref
➡dlgHandle, ref dlgText, ref dlgClsName, ref dlgPText);

    }

}
```

The pbProbe_MouseMove() event first starts a Cursor object, csr. The picture, Monkey.ico, is used for the initialization of a Cursor object. Thereafter, the code in the if statement changes the mouse pointer to a monkey head when the user clicks the left button over the pbProbe object. Then the code renews the GUI text, class name, and parent window text by using the three new System.Text.StringBuilder() class constructors. The last line of the code invokes the GetWindowFromPoint() method from the GUITestActions class at each point the mouse is moved to with the left button still down. The handle, text, class name, and parent window text of the GUI object over which the mouse hovers are reported instantly by the GetWindowFromPoint() method.

In the sequence of pressing the left button on the pbProbe object and moving the mouse, the last action is the pbProbe_MouseUp() event. The code for this event is in Listing 14.5.

Listing 14.5   The Code for the _pbProbe_MouseUp()_ Event

```
private void pbProbe_MouseUp(object sender, System.Windows.Forms.MouseEventArgs e)
{
  this.Cursor = Cursors.Default;

  pbProbe.Image =
Image.FromFile(@"C:\GUISourceCode\Chapter03\TestMonkey\Monkey.ico");
  isDown = false;

  StartNonDotNetSurvey();

}
```

When the mouse button is released, the code of the pbProbe_MouseUp() event first reassigns the cursor to a default cursor value (the mouse down event has changed the default cursor to a monkey head). The mouse movement event has dragged the monkey head away from the pbProbe object. The pbProbe.Image assignment places the picture back into the object. This action uses the same picture, Monkey.ico. It also reevaluates the isDown variable to false. Last, a StartNonDotNetSurvey() helper method is invoked. The code for the StartNonDotNetSurvey() method is in Listing 14.6.

Listing 14.6   Code to Start a Non .NET GUI Survey

```
private void StartNonDotNetSurvey()
{
  this.WindowState = FormWindowState.Minimized;

  guiSurveyCls = new GUISurveyClass(dlgHandle);
  guiSurveyCls.StartGUISurvey();
  guiSurveyCls.StartMenuSurvey();
```

```
  SetGUIListToTest();

  this.WindowState = FormWindowState.Normal;
}
```

The first line of code in the `StartNonDotNetSurvey()` method minimizes the tool itself before the actual survey starts. Minimizing the tool ensures that the user interface of the application under survey is completely visible from the screen. Then the method initializes a new `GUISurveyClass` object, `guiSurveyCls`. The `guiSurveyCls` is used to invoke the `StartGUISurvey()` and the `StartMenuSurvey()` method, respectively.

Finally, the survey is accomplished and the user interface of the tool becomes normal and visible to the user. Thus, a non .NET GUI survey probe is prepared.

Invoking a Non .NET Application for GUI Survey

If you want to test the probe at this point, you can build and run the project. When the `AutomatedGUITest` tool starts on the screen, you can drag the monkey head to a running GUI interface. After you release the mouse button, a GUI survey will be conducted. At this point, the application under survey needs to be started manually. In this section you'll modify the `GetTypeToTestFromAUT()` method of the `AutomatedGUITest.cs` file. Then the non .NET application under test can also be started by the tool. To make this happen, locate the definition of the `GetTypeToTestFromAUT()` method and add into the method the bold lines of code shown in Listing 14.7.

Listing 14.7   **The Modified *GetTypeToTestFromAUT()* Method with the New Lines of Code in Bold**

```
private void GetTypeToTestFromAUT()
{
  if (applicationUT.Length <= 0)
  {
    return;
  }
  TypeUnderTest typeDUT = new TypeUnderTest();
  try
  {
    Assembly asm = Assembly.LoadFrom(applicationUT);
    Type[] tys = asm.GetTypes();
    foreach (Type ty in tys)
    {
      typeDUT.chckListType.Items.Add(ty.Namespace + "." + ty.Name);
    }

  }
    //Chapter 14
  catch(BadImageFormatException badImgEx)
```

```
  {
    GUITestUtility.StartAUTAsProcess(applicationUT, "");

    applicationUT = null;
    return;
  }
  catch(Exception ex)
  {
    MessageBox.Show(ex.Message);
    return;
  }

  if (typeDUT.ShowDialog() == DialogResult.OK)
  {
    GetSelectedTypesUT(typeDUT);
  }
  else
  {
    return;
  }

}
```

The existing code of the GetTypeToTestFromAUT() method is for starting the .NET applications for testing. When the method tries to start a non .NET application, the existing code throws a BadImageFormatException error. The added code catches the BadImageFormatException error and invokes the StartAUTAsProcess() method from the GUITestUtility class within a pair of curly brackets. It also assigns a null value to the applicationUT variable. This assignment lets the tool know that the application under test is not a .NET application. Last, a return statement exits the StartAUTAsProcess() method by skipping the rest of the code.

Now you can build the project. After the project is built successfully, the tool is able to conduct a GUI survey for testing .NET and non .NET applications. But in order for the GUITestScript class to start a non .NET application for testing, the StartAUTAsProcess() method also needs to be called. Therefore, the last update before finishing this chapter is to add such a method into the GUITestScript class.

Updating the *GUITestScript* Class

The code to update the GUITestScript class happens in the tmrAutomatedTest_Tick() event. When the tmrAutomatedTest object is enabled, it invokes the first line of code to start the application under test. The existing code calls the StartAUT() method only for testing .NET applications. To work with non .NET applications, the StartAUTAsProcess() method needs to be called by the GUITestScript class. Listing 14.8 makes a StartNonDotNetAUT() helper method for this purpose.

Listing 14.8   **The Code for the *StartNonDotNetAUT()* Helper Method in the**
                    ***GUITestScript* Class**

```
private void StartNonDotNetAUT()
{
   seqGUIUT = new GUITestUtility.GUIInfoSerializable();
   object obj = (object)seqGUIUT;
   GUITestUtility.DeSerializeInfo(guiTestDataStore, ref obj);
   seqGUIUT = (GUITestUtility.GUIInfoSerializable)obj;

   GUITestUtility.StartAUTAsProcess( seqGUIUT.AUTPath, "");
}
```

The first three lines of the StartNonDotNetAUT() method prepare and deserialize a given XML document stored by the variable guiTestDataStore to a GUIInfoSerializable object, obj. Then, the obj object is converted to a GUIInfoSerializable object, seqGUIUT. At last, by reading the value of the seqGUIUT.AUTPath, the StartAUTAsProcess() method invokes a non .NET application and the value of its arguments parameter is an empty string.

A .NET application under test has been started by the tmrAutomatedTest_Tick() event in the GUITestScript class by calling the StartAUT() method. A try-catch clause is going to be needed to catch a NullReferenceException error when a non .NET application is under test and invoke the newly coded StartNonDotNetAUT() method. Listing 14.9 shows the place where a try-catch clause with the method calling is added.

Listing 14.9   **New Code to Update the *tmrAutomatedTest_Tick()* Event for the**
                    ***GUITestScript* Class**

```
private void tmrAutomatedTest_Tick(object sender, System.EventArgs e)
{
   try
   {
      StartAUT();
   }
   catch(NullReferenceException nullEx)
   {
      StartNonDotNetAUT();
   }
   tmrAutomatedTest.Enabled = false;
   tmrRunScript.Enabled = true;

   //resultList = new ArrayList();
   testResult = new TypeVerification();
   testResult.AUTPath = seqGUIUT.AUTPath;
   testResult.TypeName = seqGUIUT.AUTStartupForm;
}
```

The tmrAutomatedTest_Tick() event first tries the StartAUT() method of the GUITest-Script class. But the StartAUT() method works only for .NET applications. When the application is not a .NET application, the invocation of the StartAUT() method throws a NullReferenceException error.

The error is caught by the catch statement code. Within the curly brackets of the catch statement, the StartNonDotNetAUT() method is invoked to start the non .NET application for testing.

To avoid repeating the discussions covered by the previous chapters, verification methods of non .NET GUI testing will not be implemented in this book. But you can reuse the ideas throughout this book to develop the tool with the new testing capabilities.

After you have copied the code, you can build and run the AutomatedGUITest project. The next section includes a demonstration of the tool invoking the NotePad.exe application as the last example in this book.

Putting the New Methods into Action

Notepad is a text editor that comes with the Windows operating system. In normal situation, you can start a new session of Notepad from the Start menu. To use the tool to start the Notepad, you need to know the file path in advance. You can right-click Notepad in the Start menu and select the Properties menu item. In the Target field in the Notepad Properties window, you can see that the executable path of the Notepad application is %SystemRoot%\system32\notepad.exe. The %SystemRoot% part is the name of an environmental variable, the value of which can be explored from the DOS prompt window by issuing the line command Set SystemRoot. From my system, the result of such a command is C:\Windows. Thus, the actual path for the executable Notepad.exe is C:\Windows\System32\Notepad.exe.

With the AutomatedGUITest running on your computer, click the Start GUI Test button as usual to bring up the open file dialog box. Navigate to C:\Windows\System32\Notepad.exe and click the Open button. The Notepad application starts. To conduct a GUI survey for the Notepad interface, drag the newly implemented probe to the title bar of the Notepad application. The AutomatedGUITest minimizes and the GUI survey starts for the Notepad GUI interface.

WARNING   Since the AutomatedGUITest tool has not been implemented with an error handling method, clicking the GUI Survey button will throw a NullReferenceException error to halt the testing tool when a non .NET application is started by the tool. In the real testing world, you can drag and drop the monkey head inside the front-end interface of any application. If you drag and release the newly implemented GUI probe to a point outside of the AutomatedGUITest tool, a GUI survey starts. However, if you drag and release the probe inside the AutomatedGUITest tool interface, the MoveMouseInsideHwnd() method of the GUITestActions class will encounter a math operation of dividing a number by zero (the tool itself is minimized) and throw the exception.

After the survey completes, the AutomatedGUITest tool reappears with the survey result. Notepad is not a GUI-rich application, but it has a lot of menu items. The GUI survey list collects the menu items and a handful of the other GUI objects, including the text editor. The editor has an empty value for its window text, *Edit* for its class name, and *Untitled - Notepad* for it parent window text. For demonstration purposes, this section enters the editor to the testing data store only as a test step.

NOTE   In this chapter, the GUI testing tool was able to conduct a menu survey for non .NET applications as it has for .NET applications, but we will not continue to add extra code to the GUI test script to test the menu items of a non .NET application. When you have the need, you can use the methods you learned in this book to enable the tool for non .NET menu item testing tasks.

Double-click on the left edge of the data grid by the side of the `Edit` class name. The GUI Test Data Collector appears. Only the class name and the parent text fields on the GUI Test Data Collector are populated with values. The other fields are empty. At this point, you need to enter the text `System.Windows.Forms.TextBox` in the Control Type field. This entry enables the testing tool to find the correct GUI handling method for this testing step. Also, you need to type some text in the Text Entry field, such as **Effective GUI Test Automation**. This entry will be typed in Notepad when it is under test by the AutomatedGUITest tool. The GUI Test Data Collector now appears as it does in Figure 14.2. Click the OK button. This is the only testing step for now.

FIGURE 14.2
The appearance of the GUI Test Data Collector after the entries for testing the Notepad application

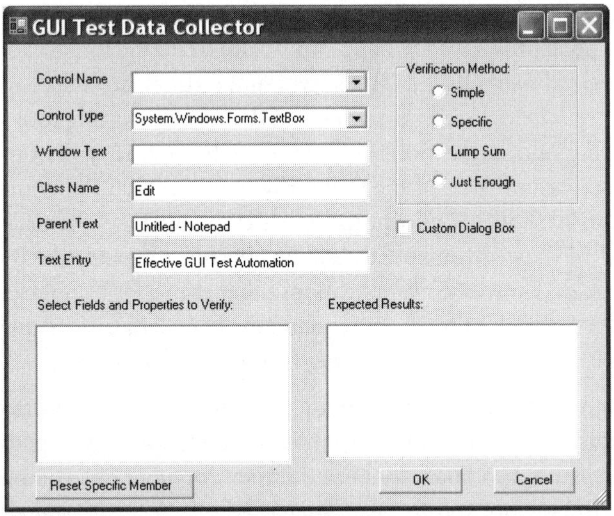

You can close the Notepad application, which was open for the GUI survey. Click the Run Test button from the AutomatedGUITest tool. The save file dialog box appears. Give a name to save the testing data, such as `TestNotepad.xml`, and click the Save button. The GUITest-Script starts to execute. First it starts the Notepad application, and then you'll see that text is entered into the Notepad editing area. After the test is completed, the test results are shown in the XML Document Viewer. However, in order not to repeat the coding tasks and discussions of the previous chapters, there is no code in the `GUITestScript` class to compare the test results for non .NET applications in this book.

Summary

Previous chapters have focused enabling the testing tool to test .NET applications. This chapter updated the AutomatedGUITest tool with a few methods for a GUI survey of applications other than .NET applications. Although the sample code in the book has not been updated to carry out a fully automated verification for testing these applications, you can incorporate the methods you learned in the book and make a tool for your testing purposes. In this way, there will be no repetitive discussions to overwhelm you.

The main idea of this book was to develop a fully automated GUI testing tool for different testing purposes. C# was used in the sample code, but developers can use the basic ideas presented to build a testing tool in other languages and on other platforms.

Chapters 1 and 2 elaborated on the necessity for improvement of the current testing infrastructure. A C# API Text Viewer was developed in Chapter 3 for two purposes: for manufacturing C# marshaling code of the Win32 API functions and for testing the AutomatedGUITest project as the book progressed. Chapters 4, 5, and 6 laid the foundation for a GUI test library. This library provided methods for GUI survey and testing. In Chapters 7 and 8, you used the foundation of the AutomatedGUITest project to develop the testing tool with basic functions for GUI survey, testing, and verification. In Chapters 9 through 12, you extended the methods from the previous chapters and enabled the tool for testing specific GUI components, such as ListBox, Button, TextBox, Label, RadioButton, CheckBox, and menu items. Finally, the discussion in Chapters 13 and 14 showed you how to use the C# code to enable the tool for testing-user defined controls, ActiveX controls, and applications other than .NET applications. The basics of GUI testing have been covered. You are ready to use the knowledge you gained from this book to develop testing tools for the special requirements of your organization.

In the end, I want to reiterate that this book is about effective ideas for the software testing infrastructure and not really about a testing tool developed in C#, even though I didn't go into detail about coding a tool in other development environments. Also, if you have had a chance to read my previous book, *Effective Software Test Automation: Developing an Automated Software*

Testing Tool (Sybex, 2004) for non-GUI testing, you might find that the narrative methods in my books are similar. In that book and this one, I mentioned some available tools for the purpose of locating areas of software testing that are currently inadequate. Although not mentioned, there are other tools that bear similar limitations. These books are not meant to be software testing dictionaries or bibles. Except for the fundamentals needed to develop the sample code, for the most part, the topics involve my testing experiences, which can not be found in other books and web pages. As I have stated, the sample code in C# has evolved from my previous VB 6 projects. I have also tested the methods discussed in these books in Java code. If you need to write a fully automated testing tool in Java, VB 6, or C++, the ideas from this book can be used directly. But if you need more knowledge about other testing topics or other programming techniques, please refer to the numerous other sources on the subject, some of which are listed in the bibliography at the end of this book.

I hope this book has guided you to achieve your goal of developing a fully automated GUI testing tool. Again, I want to wish you good luck.

Selected Bibliography

Armstrong, Tom. *ATL Developer's Guide*. 2nd Edition. Foster, Calif.: M&T Books, 2000.

Astels, David. *Test Driven Development: A Practical Guide, 1st Edition*. Upper Saddle River, New Jersey: Prentice Hall PTR, 2003.

Beuzer, B. *Software Testing Techniques*. Boston: International Thompson Computer Press, 1990.

Davis, Harold. *Visual C# .NET Programming*. Alameda, Calif.: Sybex, 2002.

Dustin, Elfriede, Jeff Rashka, and John Paul. *Automated Software Testing: Introduction, Management, and Performance*. Boston: Addison-Wesley, 1999.

Dustin, Elfriede. *Effective Software Testing: 50 Specific Ways to Improve Your Testing*. Boston: Addison-Wesley, 2002.

Graham, Dorothy, and Mark Fewster. *Software Test Automation: Effective Use of Test Execution Tools*. Boston: Addison-Wesley, 2000.

Koomen, Time, and Martin Pol. *Test Process Improvement: A practical step-by-step guide to structured testing*. Boston: Addison-Wesley, 1999.

Li, Kanglin, and Mengqi Wu. *Effective Software Test Automation: Developing an Automated Software Testing Tool*. Alameda, Calif.: Sybex, 2004.

Marick, Brian. *When Should a Test Be Automated?* [Cited Dec. 22, 2003]. Available from World Wide Web `www.testing.com/writings/automate.pdf`, 1998.

Messerschmidt, Thomas, and Mark Harbin. *WinRunner 7 in a Hurry! Software Test Automation With WinRunner*. Riverside, Calif.: Riverside Press International, 2001.

Mueller, John Paul. *Visual C#™ .NET Developer's Handbook™*. Alameda, Calif.: Sybex, 2003.

Mueller, John Paul. *.NET Framework Solutions: In Search of the Lost Win32 API*. Alameda, Calif.: Sybex, 2002.

Nyman, Noel. 2000. Using Monkey Test Tools: How to find bugs cost-effectively through random testing. *Software Testing & Quality Engineering* Jan./Feb. 2000 issue.

Petroutsos, Evangelos, and M. Ridgeway. *Visual Basic .NET Developer's Handbook*. Alameda, Calif.: Sybex, 2003.

Petroutsos, Evangelos, and Richard Mansfield. *Visual Basic .NET Power Tools*. Alameda, Calif.: Sybex, 2004.

Price, Jason, and Mike Gunderloy. *Mastering™ Visual C#™ .NET*. Alameda, Calif.: Sybex, 2002.

Shea, Billie. 2000. Software Testing Gets New Respect. *InformationWeek* [Cited Dec. 23, 2003]. Available from World Wild Web `www.informationweek.com/793/testing.htm`.

Tassey, Gregory, ed. *The Economic Impacts of Inadequate Infrastructure for Software Testing*. Collingdale, Penn.: DIANE Publishing Co., 2003.

Thomas, Arnold R. *Visual Test 6 Bible*. New York City: Hungry Minds, Inc., 1998.

Troelson, Andrew. *COM and .NET Interoperability*. Berkeley, Calif.: Apress, 2002.

Index

Note to the Reader: Throughout this index **boldfaced** page numbers indicate primary discussions of a topic. *Italicized* page numbers indicate illustrations.

A

H

U

Tools, Skills, & Strategies

for Software Engineer

Designing Highly Useable Software
By Jeff Cogswell • ISBN: 0-7821-4301-6 • US $39.99

"Highly useable" software is easy to use. It does what you expect it to. And it does it well. It's not easy to build but as this book demonstrates, it's well worth the effort. Highly useable software is highly successful software—and everyone wins.

Inside, an accomplished programmer who has made usability his business systematically explores the world of programming, showing you how every aspect of the work is implicated in the usability of the final product.

Effective Software Test Automation:
Developing an Automated Software Testing Tool
By Kanglin Li; Mengqi Wu • ISBN: 0-7821-4320-2 • US $44.99

Whatever its claims, commercially available testing software is not automatic. Configuring it to test your product is almost as time-consuming and error-prone as purely manual testing.

There is an alternative that makes both engineering and economic sense: building your own, truly automatic tool. Inside, you'll learn a repeatable, step-by-step approach, suitable for virtually any development environment. Code-intensive examples support the book's instruction.

Effective GUI Test Automation:
Developing an Automated GUI Testing Tool
By Kanglin Li; Mengqi Wu • 0-7821-4351-2 • US $44.99

Have you tried using an "automated" GUI testing tool, only to find that you spent most of your time configuring, adjusting, and directing it? This book presents a sensible and highly effective alternative: it teaches you to build and use your own truly automated tool. The procedure you'll learn is suitable for virtually any development environment, and the tool allows you to store your test data and verification standard separately, so you can build it once and use it for other GUIs.

Coder to Developer:
Tools and Strategies for Delivering Your Software
By Mike Gunderloy • ISBN: 0-7821-4327-X • US $29.99

Are you ready to take the leap from programmer to proficient developer? Based on the assumption that programmers need to grasp a broad set of core skills in order to develop high-quality software, this book teaches you these critical ground rules. Topics covered include project planning, source code control, error handling strategies, working with and managing teams, documenting the application, developing a build process, and delivering the product. All of the techniques taught in this unique book are language and platform neutral, and were selected to help you effectively design and develop complex applications.

SYB
www.syb